I0625731

www.ingramcontent.com/pod-product-compliance
Lightning Source LLC
Chambersburg PA
CBHW061602120626
46550CB00004B/1588

* 9 7 9 8 9 8 7 2 6 9 8 4 8 *

The Haggadah
of Wisdom

Published by:

Gerber's Miracle Publishers LLC
FORT LAUDERDALE, FL
HaggadahofWisdom.com

ISBN-13
979-8-9872698-4-8 (softcover)
979-8-9872698-5-5 (hardcover)

Copyediting by Carol Killman Rosenberg

Cover & Interior production by Gary A. Rosenberg

Cover image used by permission of
"Sinai" Publishing, Tel Aviv, Israel

**A portion of the sales of this book
will be donated to Colel Chabad**

In memory of
all Jewish victims of terrorism,
their families, and their loved ones
from the beginning of history to the present time.

May Hashem bless their souls,
and may we always stand up against hatred of Jews.

In memory of all the victims of
the October 7, 2023, massacre in Israel—
all those who were brutalized, who lost their lives,
who were injured, who were taken hostage,
and their families and their loved ones.

May Hashem protect all of Yiddishkeit.

—Julie & Richie Gerber

Other Books in the
RABBI YEHONATAN EYBESHITZ WISDOM SERIES

Pearls of Wisdom from Rabbi Yehonatan Eybeshitz:
Torah Giant, Preacher & Kabbalist

Thoughts on the weekly Torah readings, the festivals,
and the final redemeption

Sparks of Wisdom: From Rabbi Yehonatan Eybeshitz

Topic based with modern-day application

Gates of Wisdom:
How Rabbi Yehonatan Eybeshitz Created "AM YISRAEL CHAI"

Stories that display Reb Yehonatan's brilliant mind from a very
young age, including how he created "Am Yisrael Chai"

The Haggadah of Wisdom

RABBI YEHONATAN EYBESHITZ

RABBI YACOV BARBER, TRANSLATOR

Gerber's Miracle Publishers

Contents

Publisher's Note

Each and every year, Jews around the world share the bond of the Exodus from slavery to freedom. Passover and the Seder are some of our people's fondest childhood memories.

Although all Passover Seders seemed alike, it's also true that each one was different and unique—from the matzo balls that were too light or too heavy and the comparison of homemade versus store-bought gefilte fish to the charoset with too much wine or not enough apples. Like all things Jewish, when you get two Jews together in a room, you have three opinions. All kidding aside, we are G-ds chosen people and our opinions are extremely important.

Although we are one people, we come in all sizes, shapes, languages, and cultures. This gives us a mishmash identity, which makes for an interesting topic of conversation upon first meeting a fellow Jew. Variations among us include ethnic groups, denominations, and religious movements, among other niche characteristics. A telling question between newly acquainted Yidden might include "Where did your ancestors settle after the diaspora?" Lo and behold, when two Jews discover their ancestors settled in the *same* country and sometimes even the *same part* of the country, they become like long-lost siblings. Yes, we are a global people with infinite differences, but we all share the same odyssey of the Exodus and the giving of the Torah at Mount Sinai.

We (Julie and Richie Gerber) each recall our unique Passovers as children with fondness, and we feel honored to publish *The Haggadah of Wisdom* and bring Reb Yehonatan's teachings and thoughts on the Passover Seder to the Jewish world.

Born and raised in Havana, Cuba, Julie has the distinct distinction of being a descendent of Reb Yehonatan's. Her Pesach in Cuba was quite different from Richie's Pesach in Brooklyn, New York, where he lived behind a grocery store. As the publisher of this book, it is our pleasure to share our fondest childhood memories of Passover with you.

"Pesach in Cuba"
Julie Gerber

When I tell people I am a Jewban, they usually have no idea what I am talking about—unless, of course, they live in Miami. A Jewban is a Cuban Jew—and there are lots of us in South Florida.

Our family fled from Fidel Castro's Communist Cuba in 1961. I had just turned twelve years old at a time when Fidel was about to snatch children twelve years and older to indoctrinate them in the ABCs of Communism and send them into the countryside to teach the campesinos to read and write.

In their infinite wisdom, my parents did not want me taken from home and brainwashed. With a lot of difficulty, they were able to send me to the United States to live with my aunt Bertha and uncle Carlos in Brooklyn, New York. I was the first in my family to escape a life in a totalitarian state. Shortly after, my parents, younger sister, grandparents, aunts, uncles, and cousins followed my steps and left Cuba for the United States. We are all proud American citizens now.

I've never been back, but I have wonderful memories of growing up Jewish in Cuba. At that time, we did not experience any antisemitism. Cuba welcomed Polish Jews with open arms. My grandparents on both sides arrived in the 1920s, becoming part of a thriving Jewish community.

While the Jewish population was mostly Ashkenazi Polish Jews with several synagogues in Havana, this tropical oasis also hosted Sephardic Jews from Turkey. Our Shul, El Patronato, was a modern, beautiful building. Attending Sunday school was always fun for me. I had plenty of Jewish friends, and my mother was always busy volunteering for Jewish causes.

Abuelito José Ejbszyc (my grandfather) was an active member of the community. Because he was an Ejbszyc (our spelling of Eybeshitz), he was always honored and highly respected. I can still hear people calling out to him, *"Ejbszyc, ¿Cómo está?"* It's like people wanted to say the name of our great ancestor aloud, so they always called him by his last name.

My most favorite time of the year was Pesach. And the Seder at the home of my grandparents, José and Josefina Ejbszyc, was unforgettable.

Abuelito and Abuelita lived in a spacious apartment in La Habana Vieja (Old Havana), a well-known, historic neighborhood in Cuba's capital, Havana. With balconies at virtually every opening, the building exemplified classic Spanish architecture. The classy antique image continued inside the apartment, which was decorated with magnificent old-world Spanish furnishings. (My grandparents owned a furniture store; perhaps that is how they furnished their living quarters so richly.)

But on Pesach, all that Spanish style gave way to the aromas of traditional Jewish food. Abuelita Josefina was in the kitchen! My grandmother made everything from scratch. She was known for her delicious Jewish cuisine. And my favorite at Pesach was the gefilte fish. As you can imagine, she started with huge live fish, probably carp, which she kept in the bathtub—really!

Abuelita Josefina was a sweet woman who was quite short with short gray hair. She always wore sunglasses (even indoors) and an apron. Her helper, Nana, was a young, tall, slim Black Cuban woman with very few teeth. But that didn't stop her from always smiling! They made a great pair, always working side by side when the occasion called for it. It was clear they enjoyed cooking away together.

If only we had taken pictures during those times. Fortunately, I can close my eyes and picture the Seder table. As a little girl, the table seemed endless, with a crisp white tablecloth and so many plates of various sizes, silverware, drinking glasses, wine glasses, and more. (I inherited Abuelita Josefina's China and use it for special occasions.)

My grandparents held a traditional Seder. Although we were totally surrounded by the Caribbean Sea, we were not isolated. My grandparents had Haggadahs (Hebrew/Spanish) and plenty of matzoh and Kosher wine—everything needed for a Seder. Abuelito José Ejbszyc's Seder was in Hebrew, Spanish, some Polish, and of course, Yiddish!

Passover was one of the few times of the year the whole family would get together. My grandparents had four children, my *tios* and *tias* (aunts and uncles), who in turn had their own children, my *primos* (cousins). I had so much fun with my primos during the Seder, with me being the oldest of the lot. We would run around the apartment and get kind of wild and then we would ultimately get in trouble . . . but just a little bit. Some of us "secretly" drank some wine (they let us think it was in secret). On more than one occasion, I hid out in the library (a small room with a couch and shelves full of books in Hebrew, Yiddish, and Spanish). I would grab a copy of *El Tesoro de la Juventud*, a kind of kid's encyclopedia, and just sit and read until they found me.

We would all then trek to the Seder table and sit. That's when the real fun started. We always made "mushy pushey" (our name for a mixture of everything on the table). While everyone dipped for the plagues, we cousins dipped and mixed everything up on our plates (which always ended up the color of homemade beet horseradish!).

The big moment was always the search for the Afikomen. It was the same every year, and yet we looked forward to it with just as much anticipation as the years prior. Abuelito José would sit on a pillow so that he could recline and would always hide the wrapped Afikomen under the pillow. Our dilemma was getting him to stand up and walk away so we could grab that magical piece of matzoh, which was surprisingly *not* in crumbles. Now that was a miracle!

That's where my mother, Ana, came in. She would make arrangements with our Christian neighbor, Teresita, to make a call at an agreed-upon time. My grandfather would be told that something had happened and that he had to take the call. And, of course, he would get up and walk away. One of us would run and take the delicately wrapped Afikomen and run fast before he returned to the table. It was SO much fun!

Finally, I remember waiting for Elijah, the cup full of wine becoming the center of attention and the table shaking as the Prophet walked into our family's seder. Of course we all knew my father was shaking the table, but it did not matter. Everyone happily pretended.

Although these Ejbszyc Passover Seders took place in Havana, Cuba, more than sixty years ago, they could have taken place anywhere at any time in any Jewish home.

The Jewish People are eternal. *Am Yisrael Chai L'Olam Vaed.*

"Pesach in Brooklyn"
Richie Gerber

The four Gerber brothers (me being the youngest, then Eddie, Steve, and Artie, the oldest) lived with our parents in a one-bedroom, one-bathroom apartment behind my father's grocery store in the East New York section of Brooklyn. My parents slept in the bedroom, and the parlor was converted into a bedroom for us Gerber boys.

Most Jews' fondest memories of Pesach is sharing the Seder with family. Although I have wonderful memories of the Seders, my strongest and sweetest Pesach memories are of the week and a half leading up to the holiday.

Gerber's Miracle Grocery & Appetizing Store sat on a busy corner of Sutter Avenue with the local Orthodox shul just halfway down the block. Gerber's Miracle Grocery was the go-to store for all the neighborhood's Passover needs. The challenge for my father, Sam, was how to separate the

Kosher for Passover from the non-Passover items. My father and mother, Sam and Pearl, had been doing this for many years before I came along, so they had the whole system perfected.

Remember the one-bedroom, one-bathroom apartment behind my father's grocery store? Well, there was a door separating the store from the apartment, which came in handy. The non-Passover store would be the usual store upfront and our apartment would become the Kosher for Passover warehouse! Since this was done under the supervision and approval of our Orthodox rabbi from the shul down the block, everyone in the neighborhood knew all was Kosher!

Let me explain how this feat was accomplished.

About a week and a half before Passover, my mother began a meticulous cleaning of the apartment; she even hired cleaning ladies to help with her fastidious nook-and-cranny purge for schmutz and non-Passover items— scrubbing, scouring, washing, waxing, sanitizing, and anything else the ladies could think of. They stripped the linoleum and put on several new coats of wax. Then they placed a path of newspaper over the newly waxed linoleum. They also washed the windows and sheets and packed away the non-Pesach dishes.

Once finished, the rabbi came over to inspect the job and make sure the apartment was a Kosher-for-Passover warehouse to store the very special goods. My mother left a few pieces of chametz in several strategic spots so that, when the rabbi did his final run-through, he would find some prohibited items and dispose of them. He recited some blessings and declared the apartment acceptable to receive Kosher for Passover (KoP) products.

With my mother watching the store, the rabbi and my father would go outside, speaking Yiddish. The rabbi would take out a one-dollar bill and a handkerchief. He would give my father the dollar, and he would hold one end of the handkerchief and my father would hold the other. They spoke in Hebrew and Yiddish and then the deal was sealed. Sam Gerber had just sold all his chametz to the rabbi. The next day the KoP merchandise would start to arrive.

Everything for Pesach entered the apartment through the kitchen window. Nothing came through the store or was stored in the cellar. In the kitchen, wooden milk crates were placed upside down so that nothing touched the floor directly. Newspapers covered every surface.

My mother watched the store while my father took charge of receiving products through the kitchen window. He had developed and perfected his system many years before my birth.

Cases of matzos were stacked almost to the ceiling. Manischewitz and Streit's Matzos were the two largest inventory items in our makeshift Passover kitchen warehouse. There were also cases of delicacies such as dried apple slices, pear slices, and prunes—*lots and lots of prunes* (by far the king of dried fruit!). We had Rokeach, Gold's, and Manischewitz borscht and schav. And walnuts, almonds, and filberts (aka hazelnuts), which the kids used for an outdoor game.

And Passover would not be Passover without Gold's horseradish (classic or beet) and gefilte fish. We also had Fox's U-bet syrup for chocolate milk and the premier ingredient Brooklyn's famous Egg Cream (no egg or cream! Just milk, seltzer, and Fox's U-bet). Rokeach bar soap and cases of gelfilte fish and macaroons, plain or chocolate covered, were stacked to the sky, along with bottles of Manischewitz Concord grape wine and grape juice. The bags in which all this would ultimately be packed were also delivered through the kitchen window. There were so many products, but I can never forget the ubiquitous Manischewitz Passover Haggadah, which we gave out free to our customers.

Orders were taken on the kitchen phone, which sat on the sideboard with a pad and pencil next to it. Rules: 1) Write down the customer's name and phone number, 2) Make an itemized list of the requested products, 3) Read back the list, and 4) Get the best time for delivery. For years, I was too young to be placed on phone duty simply because I did not read or write.

While I played among the stacks of matzo and delicacies, one of my parents watched the store while the other bagged or boxed up each order, one at a time, and placed the finished order next to the kitchen window to be loaded into the red metal-wheeled delivery wagon. No order was too big or too small, but some orders were so large they took up the whole cart!

Steve and Eddie were too young to bag or deliver orders on their own, but Artie, the eldest, helped out by watching the store, bagging the orders, or making the deliveries. My father hired some extra hands to help with the Passover volume. Too young to help, I loved walking beside the cart when it was out for delivery.

Orders and deliveries went on both before Passover and even during the holiday itself. My father always said, "People got to eat!"

I will always remember my unique Passover experience.

This Year in Jerusalem!

Introduction

This is the fourth book in the Rabbi Yehonatan Eybeshitz *Wisdom* Series. The first is *Pearls of Wisdom,* which shares with the English-speaking world a glimpse of Reb Yehonatan's thoughts on the weekly Torah readings, the festivals, and the final redemption. I tried to be as true to his written word as possible while ensuring that English readers could understand his teachings.

The second in the series, *Sparks of Wisdom,* intends to impress upon the English-speaking audience how the teachings of a man born in 1696 are as relevant today as they were then. Hopefully, I accomplished this by not confining myself to a definitive translation of the texts cited. I also took the liberty of supplementing each thought with modern-day application.

The third book, *Gates of Wisdom,* retells the many stories that display Reb Yehonatan's brilliant mind from a very young age—how he was a true defender of the Jewish people against the rabid anti-Semites of the time and how he was a true father figure to so many. These stories have enthralled both young and old for generations.

This fourth book in the series is *The Haggadah of Wisdom.* Reb Yehonatan wrote a commentary on the first half of the Haggadah titled *Biur Al Haggadah Shel Pesach.* It was first printed in London in 1877 and subsequently in Yerushalayim in 1891. Unfortunately, the Haggadah is no longer available. There are also lengthy insights on the Haggadah transcribed by an unknown student. However, it remains as a manuscript. As such, undertaking this project demanded researching many of Reb Yehonatan's seforim. I can say that it was a labor of love researching and collating his interpretations and insights on the Haggadah. By no means does this Haggadah include everything written by Reb Yehonatan on the Haggadah. I have attempted to present to the reader a broad selection of his writings to offer a taste of Reb Yehonatan's incredible scholarship and breadth of knowledge.

As mentioned in the previous books, any errors rest squarely on my shoulders and are due to my inability to fathom and comprehend what Reb Yehonatan was attempting to impart.

The oldest surviving Haggadah, known as the Birds' Head Haggadah, was produced in Germany in the early 1300s and was designed for Ashkenazi Jews. (The birds' head depiction remains a curiosity to this day.) Since that time, more than 3,000 different Haggadot have been published, making it one of the most—if not *the* most—popular Jewish books printed. Some 700 years and more than 3,000 different Haggadot later, *The Haggadah of Wisdom* introduces the English-speaking audience to insights never before shared.

I hope that *The Haggadah of Wisdom* will allow us to feel as if we are sitting at Reb Yehonatan's Seder and being mesmerized and inspired by his teachings and that it will enrich our Seder experience.

What is the Seder experience?

It can be summed up in one word—*Tradition.*

More than any other Jewish experience, sitting at the Seder reinforces the understanding that we are a link in the golden chain of *Am Yisroel.*

I had the tremendous zechus of sitting at the seder of my two zaida's Reb Berish Barber and Reb Motel New. Reb Berish, together with my father and uncle, survived the war years in Siberia and ultimately arrived and settled in Sydney, Australia. His seder took us back to Pshevorsk in Galicia to the great tzaddik Reb Itzikel. My other Zaida, Reb Motel New, miraculously managed to escape Warsaw, Poland, in 1939 just prior to the Nazi's yemach shemom v'zichrom invasion of Poland. He came to Melbourne, Australia, together with his wife, Bubba Sima Leah, my aunt and mother. He was a Ger Chosid, and as a child, he saw the Sfas Emes. At his Seder, we heard Divrei Torah, and we sang the songs he had heard sitting at his own grandfather's Seder in Warsaw.

The same is true about my late wife Rivkie's Seder experience. Her grandparents Reb Leibish and Shprintza Perel Heber miraculously escaped Paris in 1940 after it had been invaded by the Nazis yemach shemom v'zichrom. Reb Leibish was a Lubavitcher Chosid and was very close with the Rebbe Rashab the Frierdike Rebbe and the Rebbe Reb Menachem Mendel Schneerson. His family roots were tied to the Alexander

Chasidic dynasty. What Rivkie experienced, she conveyed to her children and grandchildren.

Many years later, I have been blessed to have my einikleich sitting at my Seder. And we sing the same songs and I retell the same words of Torah I had heard more than fifty years ago. In a sense, when they sit at the Seder in New York, Atlanta, and Florida, they travel back six generations. They travel back in time via Sydney and Melbourne until they arrive in Pshevorsk, Warsaw, and Lodz. I am not sure what other places my ancestors called home. However, I do know they experienced Krias Yam Suf, and they stood at Har Sinai and received the Torah. I know this to be true as they had fulfilled the Torah obligation of *Vehigadata L'Bincha*, retelling the story of the Exodus from Egypt. That generation told their children, who in turn told theirs, until my grandchildren's generation. And with the help of Hashem, they will share with their grandchildren what they experienced when they were young—of course, including thoughts from *The Haggadah of Wisdom!*

As I write this introduction, I feel compelled to share the following: In the Haggadah, we read the section *The Story of Reb Eliezer,* how some of the greatest Rabbis of that generation traveled to Reb Akiva in Bnei Brak and participated in his Seder. There is a fascinating insight of this section. The question is posed, why couldn't they conduct their own Seder in their respective cities? Why did they need to travel to Reb Akiva?

This story takes place in the times of the Roman persecution of the Jewish people. It was a time of great hardship and suffering, and the Rabbis were at a loss as to how could they celebrate the Yom Tov of Freedom in such dire circumstances. In numerous places, the Talmud shares how Reb Akiva was the ultimate optimist. When he saw the ruins of the Beis Hamikdosh, he was joyous while his colleagues cried.

In the story, we read how the students of these great Rabbis were participating in the Seder. It is interesting that we are not told who these students were. Perhaps this was deliberate as the Haggadah wishes to impart that you and I need to be those students. Since the Exodus from Egypt, we as a nation have faced expulsions, pogroms, crusades, blood libels, indiscriminate persecution, and only some eighty years ago the Holocaust. On Simchat Torah, October 7, 2023, the Jewish people faced their worst day since the Holocaust when more than 1,200 men, women, and children were massacred and more than 200 taken hostage. Over a year later, the war continues on seven fronts, and we continue to lose our precious soldiers and many of the hostages remain in captivity. We are also witnessing an unprecedented rise in anti-Semitism throughout the Western world, especially on college campuses.

What is our response?

Whatever actions we take, remember this: We are the students of Reb Akiva, and we are sitting at his Seder and he is sharing with us the eternal message of optimism and hope, and we need to inculcate that into our hearts and minds.

May we truly be blessed with *L'shanah Haba'ah B'Yerushalayim*. May we merit the coming of Moshiach and be transported on the wings of eagles to the Holyland.

With blessings and gratitude to Hashem,

Rabbi Yacov Barber
19 Kislev 5785 – December 2024

מָרָן הַגָּאוֹן הַקָּדוֹשׁ רַבִּי יְהוֹנָתָן אַיְבְּשִׁיץ זי״ע
(ת״ן – תקכ״ד)

Our master the holy genius Rabbi Yehonatan Eybeshitz—
His memory should be a blessing (1696–1764)

Month of Nissan

The month of Nissan is significant as it relates to the Yidden and to Eretz Yisroel. It is seen in the following examples:

In the month of Nissan, the Yidden left Egypt as they began their journey to Eretz Yisroel.

The Mishna writes (Rosh Hashonoh 2b), "The first of Nissan is the New Year for kings [of Israel]." Rashi explains that even if a king ascended to the throne in Shevat or Adar, his [first] year ends at Nissan and then the second year of his reign commences.

Likewise, the grain for the Korban Omer, which is brought during the month of Nissan, must come from Eretz Yisroel.

During Nissan, Hashem passes judgment on the grains of Eretz Yisroel.

When Moshiach comes, Rosh Hashonoh will no longer be on the first day of Tishrei; rather, it will occur on the first day of Nissan, and Yom Kippur will be the tenth of Nissan.

(Ahavat Yehonatan Parshat Hachodesh)

Erev Pesach—Avrohom Avinu

Lomdus

On Erev Pesach, Avrohom was recovering from his bris milah. Hashem and the three angels dressed as Arabs came to visit.

The posuk says, "*Hashem appeared to him in the plains of Mamre and he was sitting in the entrance of the tent when the day was hot*" (Bereishis 18:1). The Talmud (Bava Metzia 86a) writes that Hashem had come to visit Avrohom as he was ill due to his bris milah.

How does the Talmud know that this was the reason for Hashem's visit?

When Hashem appeared to Avrohom in the plains of Mamre, this was Hashem's second visit. Hashem had previously visited him as the posuk says, "*And He finished speaking with him and Hashem went up from above Avrohom*" (Bereishis 17:22).

When Hashem left Avrohom the first time, the Torah describes Hashem's departure as "Hashem went up from above Avrohom." If Hashem left by ascending when Hashem visits Avrohom for the second time, the posuk should describe Hashem's appearance as "Hashem *descending*."

We find a similar expression by Kabolas Hatorah, "*And Hashem descended in the cloud*" (Shemos 34:5).

Why does our posuk say, "*Hashem appeared to him in the plains of Mamre*"?

The Talmud (Shabbos 12b) writes that the Shechinah hovers over the head of the ill. As Avrohom was unwell, Hashem was already in Avrohom's presence. As such,

Hashem did not need to descend. Therefore, the posuk says, *"Hashem appeared to him [Avrohom]."*

Since the Torah says Hashem *appeared* and did not say Hashem *descended*, the Talmud understands that Hashem's purpose of visiting Avrohom was because he was ill.

(Tiferet Yehonatan Lech Lecha)

Lomdus

The posuk says, *"Hashem appeared to him."* What is the significance of the Torah expressly saying that Hashem appeared to him [Avrohom]?

The Talmud (Bava Basra 15b) writes, "A precious stone hung around the neck of Avrohom, our forefather, and any sick person who looked at it would immediately be healed." As such, why did Hashem need to heal Avrohom? Avrohom could have healed himself by looking at the stone around his neck.

The Talmud (Brochos 5b) says, "A prisoner cannot free himself from prison, and depends on others to release him from his shackles." While Avrohom could heal others, he was unable to heal himself.

Therefore, the Torah specifically says that Hashem came to heal him, as normally Avrohom would be the one to heal others.

(Tiferet Yehonatan Lech Lecha)

☙

Avrohom was in pain during the first two days. Why did Hashem wait until day three?

In Pirkei Avos (Chapter 5), we are taught that the reward we will receive for fulfilling Hashem's mitzvos will be commensurate with our effort and suffering that we experience. As such, Hashem wanted to reward Avrohom and his descendants.

Why then did Hashem come on day three, as the longer Avrohom would be in pain, the greater would be his reward?

Hashem does not allow a tzaddik to be in pain for three consecutive days.

(Tiferet Yehonatan Lech Lecha)

Lomdus

The posuk says, *"And he [Avrohom] was sitting by the entrance of his tent"* (Bereishis 18:1)

The Midrash writes that Hashem appeared to Avrohom on the third day after his bris, and He inquired about his welfare. Why does the Midrash need to explain the purpose of Hashem's visit?

The Talmud (Shabbos 134b) writes, "When the day of a bris falls on Shabbos, one may wash the baby, both before and after the bris. However, if the second day after the bris is on Shabbos, one can only sprinkle water on the baby using one's hand, not using a vessel." Clearly, we are more lenient on the first day because it is the most painful.

The Maharsho asks, "According to the Talmud, the first day of the bris is the most severe, then why did Hashem visit Avrohom only on the third day?"

He answers that there is a distinction between a child having a bris and an adult having a bris. For a child who has a bris, the first day is the most painful, while the third day is the most difficult for an adult.

The halocho is to not visit someone who is deathly ill. We are, however, allowed to stand at the entrance of their home without entering and ask about their welfare.

Hashem appeared to Avrohom. Rashi explains that Hashem came to visit Avrohom, who was sick after his bris.

The Talmud asks, "Hashem visited Avrohom on the third day. The third day is the most painful and the most dangerous. How then could Hashem visit him on the third day?"

Therefore, the Midrash explains that Hashem came to inquire about his welfare. And one can inquire about a patient's welfare even when they are extremely ill.

While one may inquire, one is not permitted to enter the home of the patient. Therefore, the posuk says, "*Avrohom was sitting at the entrance to the tent.*" As such, Hashem did not need to enter Avrohom's home.

(Midrash Yehonatan Vayera)

❦

The posuk says, וְסַעֲדוּ לִבְּכֶם "*You may refresh yourselves*" (Bereishis 18:5).
Avrohom told the three angels, "*You may refresh yourselves.*"
The word לִבְּכֶם can also mean "your heart."

Rashi writes, "The posuk does not say לְבַבְכֶם [with two ב], but לִבְּכֶם [with one ב]. The word לְבַבְכֶם with two ב refer to the two inclinations, the yetzer tov and the yetzer hara. Since the posuk says לִבְּכֶם, it teaches that an angel does not have a yetzer hara."

❦

When a person eats, they are accomplishing two things: They are removing the spiritual essence found in the food. As the posuk says, "*In order to teach you that a human being does not live on bread alone, but that one may live on anything that Hashem decrees*" (Devorim 8:3). It isn't the actual bread itself that nourishes a person; rather, it is the spirituality that is imbued in the food that does.

The second is for the health and well-being of the person.

The angels do not eat to sustain themselves. Rather, it is to elevate the spiritual sparks contained within the food; therefore, the word לָבֶכֶם is written with one בּ.

(Tiferet Yehonatan Vayera)

Lomdus

The posuk says, *"Avrohom rushed to Sarah's tent, and he said, 'Quickly, get three se'ah of sifted flour, knead them and make loaves'"* (Bereishis 18:6).

The Midrash (Bereishis Rabbah 48:12) writes, פְּרוֹס הַפֶּסַח הֲוָה *"It was Erev Pesach when the three messengers came."*

The word פְּרוֹס translates to "a half." Why does the Midrash use this word to inform us that the angels came Erev Pesach?

In what way is Erev Pesach considered a half?

After visiting Avrohom in the afternoon, they immediately went to Lot. They arrived that night, and the posuk tells us they baked matzah together. As such, when they visited Avrohom, it was Erev Pesach.

The Torah says, אַךְ בַּיּוֹם הָרִאשׁוֹן *"On the first day you shall remove leaven from your houses"* (Shemos 12:15). The Talmud (Pesochim 5a) queries, "When does the obligation of removing the chametz commence?" The question stems from how we are to understand the posuk *"On the first day."* For if we interpret the posuk literally, then the obligation of removing one's chametz would be on the first day of Pesach.

The Talmud responds that the posuk says, אַךְ , which translates to "yet."—*"Yet the first day"*—meaning that the first day is divided into two time frames: the first part of the day when chametz may be eaten and the second part of the day when it is prohibited.

As such, when the posuk says, *"On the first day,"* it should not be understood literally.

When it wanted to inform us that it was Erev Pesach, the Midrash used the word פְּרוֹס, which also means "a half," acknowledging the fact that the angels came on a day that has two halves: half the day when we can eat chometz and half the day when we cannot.

(Tiferet Yehonatan Vayera)

Lomdus

The posuk says, *"And he took cream and milk and the calf he had prepared"* (Bereishis 18:8).

The Talmud (Bava Metzia 87a) writes that Avrohom did not serve bread because Sarah became a niddah and the dough became ritually unclean.

The Midrash, however, is of the opinion that Sarah did serve bread, as it seems unlikely that a meal of cream and meat would not be served with bread. The Midrash writes that she used coarse flour to bake the bread.

If Sarah had become a niddah, why does the grade of flour impact whether the bread would become tamei?

The angels came Erev Pesach when it is prohibited to eat chametz. As such, Avrohom could not serve them chametz. It is also prohibited to eat the type of matzah that would be eaten at the Seder. We are, however, allowed to eat *matzah ashira*, matzah that is made with fruit juice rather than with water. Therefore, Avrohom instructed Sarah to bake matzah with juice.

The laws of tumah is that impurity can be conveyed via water but not via fruit juice. Since this matzoh was kneaded with fruit juice, it could not become tamei.

Why then did Sarah use coarse flour?

Fine flour can convey tomei, as fine flour has been previously soaked in water. Therefore, the Midrash explains that the flour used was coarse.

(Tiferet Yehonatan Vayera)

Fast of the Firstborn

Lomdus

On Erev Pesach, a firstborn male, whether of the father or of the mother, needs to fast, as the firstborn of an Egyptian father also died during the plague of the firstborn.

Why then are we not obligated in redeeming the firstborn male of the father just as we are obligated in redeeming the firstborn male of the mother?

The reason a firstborn needs to fast and why we redeem a firstborn is not the same. As such, the firstborn of the father needs to fast but does not need to be redeemed.

The Midrash (Shemos Rabbah 18:2) writes that on the night of the plague of the slaying of the firstborn, the Egyptians placed their firstborn in the homes of the Yidden. They were hoping that Hashem would not be able to discern between the Jewish firstborn and the Egyptian firstborn.

However, this did not save the Egyptian firstborn. As the posuk says, "*I am Hashem.*" Hashem is able to tell which is the Jewish child and which is the Egyptian child. Hashem killed the firstborn Egyptian child and spared the firstborn Jewish child.

As such, the miracle of sparing the Jewish child was most evident in the Jewish home. As even though there were Jewish and non-Jewish firstborn in the home, Hashem distinguished between the two.

Which firstborn child did the Egyptians hide in the Jewish homes?

The firstborn of the mother, as everyone knew who her firstborn was. To mark this miracle, a firstborn needs to be redeemed. As only the firstborn of an Egyptian mother was placed in the home of the Yidden; likewise, the firstborn of a Jewish mother needs to be redeemed.

Concerning fasting, all firstborn Egyptian males died; therefore, all firstborn Jewish males need to fast.

(Pardes Reb Yehonatan)

Korban Pesach

The posuk writes, *"Shall slaughter it [Korban Pesach] in the afternoon"* (Shemos 12:6).

Why were the Yidden obligated to bring the korban in the afternoon?

If they brought it at night, the Egyptians would argue that the Yidden could not bring it by day as the Egyptians worshiped the sun, and the sun would not have permitted it. Similarly, if the Yidden would have brought it during the day, the Egyptians would contend that they could not bring it at night because the Egyptians worshiped the moon, and the moon would not have permitted it. Therefore, the Yidden were told to bring it in the afternoon when both the sun and the moon were active and the Yidden were able to bring their korban.

That is why the Korban Pesach is eaten together with matzah and maror. The posuk states, *"And with the sweetness of the produce of the sun and with the sweetness of the moon's yield"* (Devorim 33:14).

Grain grows by the sun; maror, which is a vegetable, grows by the moon. When we eat these two types of food, we are reminded of the miracle that occurred when the Yidden brought the Korban Pesach in Egypt.

(Ahavat Yehonatan)

Lomdus

The posuk says, *"And this is how you shall eat it . . . your shoes on your feet . . . and you shall eat it in haste"* (Shemos 12:11).

The Midrash explains, *"your shoes on your feet"*—the Yidden considered the korban to be chulin. *"And you shall eat it in haste"*—the Yidden ate the korban until the time they had to escape, which was midnight. The Midrash seems to imply that there is a link between the korban being unsanctified and its being eaten until midnight.

What is the connection? The connection can be understood by understanding why the korban could only be eaten until midnight.

Egyptian firstborn had been placed in Jewish homes. When the plague began, they died, causing the Jewish homes to become tamei, and as a result, they had to stop eating the korban.

When did the plague begin?

Moshe had told Pharaoh that the plague would begin at *"about midnight."* Since Moshe did not say that the plague would begin at *"exactly midnight,"* the Yidden should have had to stop eating the korban prior to midnight, as perhaps some of the Egyptian firstborn may have begun to die prior to midnight. Why did the Yidden eat the korban until actual midnight?

There is a distinction between kodshim and chulin as it relates to a questionable interaction with tumah. If we are dealing with kodshim, we will err on the side of stringency, but if we are dealing with chulin, we will be lenient.

The plague definitely began by midnight. The question is whether it began earlier. If we view the korban as being kodshim, the Yidden would have had to err on the side of stringency and consider that the plague began before midnight. And they would have had to cease eating the korban prior to midnight. However, if the korban was chulin, then they did not have to be concerned that perhaps the plague commenced before midnight, and they could eat the korban until midnight.

The Midrash stating that the korban was chulin explains why the Yidden were lenient and ate it until exactly midnight. (Chasdei Yehonatan Bo)

Leil Shimurim—The Night Is Protected

Lomdus

The posuk writes, "*It is a night of anticipation*" (Shemos 12:42). The Hebrew word for *anticipation*—שִׁמּוּרִים—can also be translated to mean "protected." The Zohar writes, "The sun shone bright and strong on the night of the Exodus as if it were daytime during the month of Tammuz.

On what basis does the Zohar draw its conclusion as to what occurred on the night of the Exodus? Furthermore, what is the significance that the sun shone as if it was in the month of Tammuz?

The Midrash asks, "Why does the posuk read, '*And Hashem called light day and darkness night.*' Why didn't it say, '*And Hashem called light day and Hashem called darkness night*'?"

Darkness symbolizes evil, and Hashem does not link His name with evil.

The Talmud (Pesochim 109b) explains the phrase *leil shimurim* to mean that the night of Pesach is protected from harmful spirits. It is known that, during the day, we don't need to be guarded from evil spirits. However, the Talmud (Pesochim 11a) writes that during the month of Tammuz, a certain demon called Ketev Meriri can cause harm during the day.

We can now understand the basis for the Zohar's understanding.

The posuk reads, "*A night of protection for Hashem.*" How can Hashem attach His name to the night. Therefore, says the Zohar, while it may have been night, the sun shone brightly; as such, the night of the Exodus did not symbolize wickedness.

If the sun was shining, why was there a need for protection from the evil spirits if these spirits only cause harm when it is dark? The Zohar explains that the sun was shining like in the month of Tammuz, and in the month of Tammuz, even during the day, we need protection form the evil spirits.

(Pardes Reb Yehonatan)

When Hashem sits in judgment, the evil spirits cannot cause harm. They are allowed to cause harm when Hashem is not sitting in judgment. Hashem sits in judgment during the day, not at night. Therefore, the evil spirits can cause harm only at night, not during the day.

It is known that Hashem sat in judgment on the night of the Exodus; as such, the evil spirits could not cause harm. Hence, that night was protected.

If judgment can take place only during the day, how did Hashem sit in judgment on the night of the Exodus? According to the Zohar's understanding, on the night of the Exodus, the sun shone bright; therefore, Hashem was able to sit in judgment.

(Divrei Yehonatan)

עֶרֶב פֶּסַח

Erev Pesach

בְּדִיקַת חָמֵץ

On the night of the fourteenth of Nissan, a search for chametz is conducted by the light of a candle. Before the search, the following declaration of intent and blessing is recited:

הֲרֵינִי מוּכָן וּמְזוּמָן לְקַיֵּם מִצְוַת עֲשֵׂה וְלֹא תַעֲשֶׂה שֶׁל בְּדִיקַת חָמֵץ לְשֵׁם יִחוּד קוּדְשָׁא בְּרִיךְ הוּא וּשְׁכִינְתֵּיהּ עַל יְדֵי הַהוּא טָמִיר וְנֶעְלָם בְּשֵׁם כָּל יִשְׂרָאֵל. וִיהִי נוֹעַם אֲדֹנָי אֱלֹהֵינוּ עָלֵינוּ וּמַעֲשֵׂה יָדֵינוּ כּוֹנְנָה עָלֵינוּ וּמַעֲשֵׂה יָדֵינוּ כּוֹנְנֵהוּ.

בָּרוּךְ אַתָּה יְהֹוָה אֱלֹהֵינוּ מֶלֶךְ הָעוֹלָם, אֲשֶׁר קִדְּשָׁנוּ בְּמִצְוֹתָיו וְצִוָּנוּ עַל בִּיעוּר חָמֵץ.

Conversation not relating to the search should be avoided until the search is completed. Upon completion of the chametz search, the chametz is wrapped well and set aside to be burned the next morning and the following declaration is made. The declaration must be understood in order to take effect; one who does not understand the Aramaic text may recite it in English. Any chametz that will be used for that evening's supper or the next day's breakfast or for any other purpose prior to the final removal of chametz the next morning is not included in this declaration.

כָּל חֲמִירָא וַחֲמִיעָא דְּאִיכָּא בִרְשׁוּתִי, דְּלָא חֲמִתֵּיהּ, וּדְלָא בְעַרְתֵּיהּ, וּדְלָא יְדַעְנָא לֵיהּ, לִבַּטֵל וְלֶהֱוֵי הֶפְקֵר כְּעַפְרָא דְאַרְעָא

בִּיעוּר חָמֵץ

The chametz is burned on the morning of the fourteenth of Nissan, before the end of the fifth hour of daylight.

הֲרֵינִי מוּכָן וּמְזוּמָן לְקַיֵּם מִצְוַת עֲשֵׂה וְלֹא תַעֲשֶׂה שֶׁל שְׂרֵפַת חָמֵץ לְשֵׁם יִחוּד קוּדְשָׁא בְּרִיךְ הוּא וּשְׁכִינְתֵּיהּ עַל יְדֵי הַהוּא טָמִיר וְנֶעְלָם בְּשֵׁם כָּל יִשְׂרָאֵל. וִיהִי נוֹעַם אֲדֹנָי אֱלֹהֵינוּ עָלֵינוּ וּמַעֲשֵׂה יָדֵינוּ כּוֹנְנָה עָלֵינוּ וּמַעֲשֵׂה יָדֵינוּ כּוֹנְנֵהוּ

THE SEARCH FOR CHAMETZ

On the night of the fourteenth of Nissan, a search for chametz is conducted by the light of a candle. Before the search, the following declaration of intent and blessing is recited:

Behold, I am prepared and ready to fulfill the positive and prohibitive mitzvos of searching for chametz. For the sake of the unification of the Holy One Blessed is He, and His presence, through Him Who is hidden and inscrutable. [I pray] in the name of all Israel. May the pleasantness of Hashem, our God be upon us, and may He establish our handiwork for us; our handiwork, may He establish.

Blessed are You, Hashem, our God, King of the universe, who has sanctified us with His commandments, and commanded us concerning the removal of *chametz*.

Conversation not relating to the search should be avoided until the search is completed. Upon completion of the chametz search, the chametz is wrapped well and set aside to be burned the next morning and the following declaration is made. The declaration must be understood in order to take effect; one who does not understand the Aramaic text may recite it in English. Any chametz that will be used for that evening's supper or the next day's breakfast or for any other purpose prior to the final removal of chametz the next morning is not included in this declaration.

All leavening and chametz that is in my possession, which I have not seen nor disposed of, and about which I am unaware, is hereby nullified, and shall be ownerless as the dust of the earth.

BURNING THE CHAMETZ

The chametz is burned on the morning of the fourteenth of Nissan, before the end of the fifth hour of daylight.

Behold, I am prepared and ready to fulfill the positive and prohibitive mitzvos of burning chametz. For the sake of the unification of the Holy One Blessed is He, and His presence, through Him Who is hidden and inscrutable. [I pray] in the name of all Israel. May the pleasantness of Hashem, our God be upon us, and may He establish our handiwork for us; our handiwork, may He establish.

When the chametz is burning, the following declaration is recited:

יְהִי רָצוֹן מִלְּפָנֶיךָ יְהוָה אֱלֹהֵינוּ וֵאלֹהֵי אֲבוֹתֵינוּ כְּשֵׁם שֶׁאֲנִי מְבַעֵר חָמֵץ מִבֵּיתִי וּמֵרְשׁוּתִי כַּךְ יְהוָה אֱלֹהַי וֵאלֹהֵי אֲבוֹתַי תְּבַעֵר אֶת כָּל הַחִיצוֹנִים וְאֶת רוּחַ הַטֻּמְאָה תְּבַעֵר מִן הָאָרֶץ וְאֶת יִצְרֵנוּ הָרָע תְּבַעֲרֵהוּ מֵאִתָּנוּ וְתִתֶּן לָנוּ לֵב בָּשָׂר וְכָל הַסִּטְרָא אַחֲרָא וְכָל הָרִשְׁעָה כְּעָשָׁן תִּכְלֶה וְתַעֲבִיר מֶמְשֶׁלֶת זָדוֹן מִן הָאָרֶץ וְכָל הַמְּעִיקִים לַשְּׁכִינָה תְּבַעֲרֵם בְּרוּחַ בָּעֵר וּבְרוּחַ מִשְׁפָּט כְּשֵׁם שֶׁבִּעַרְתָּ אֶת מִצְרַיִם וְאֶת אֱלֹהֵיהֶם בַּיָּמִים הָהֵם וּבִזְמַן הַזֶּה

After burning the chametz, the following declaration is made:
It should be recited in a language that one understands. When Pesach begins on Motzei Shabbos, this declaration is made on Shabbos morning. Any chametz remaining from the Shabbos morning meal is flushed down the drain before the declaration is made.

כָּל חֲמִירָא וַחֲמִיעָא דְּאִכָּא בִרְשׁוּתִי דַּחֲזִתֵּהּ וּדְלָא חֲזִתֵּהּ דַּחֲמִתֵּהּ וּדְלָא חֲמִתֵּהּ דְּבִעַרְתֵּהּ וּדְלָא בִעַרְתֵּהּ לִבָּטֵל וְלֶהֱוֵי הֶפְקֵר כְּעַפְרָא דְאַרְעָא

עֵרוּב תַּבְשִׁילִין

When Yom Tov occurs on Thursday and Friday, an eruv tavshilin must be prepared on the preceding Wednesday. The head of the family should take a matzah and an item of cooked food such as meat, fish, or an egg, and put them on a plate and say the following blessing:

בָּרוּךְ אַתָּה יְהוָה אֱלֹהֵינוּ מֶלֶךְ הָעוֹלָם אֲשֶׁר קִדְּשָׁנוּ בְּמִצְוֹתָיו וְצִוָּנוּ עַל מִצְוַת עֵירוּב.

בְּדֵין עֵרוּבָא. יְהֵא שָׁרֵא לָנָא. לְאַפוּיֵי וּלְבַשׁוּלֵי וּלְאַטְמוּנֵי וּלְאַדְלוּקֵי שְׁרָגָא וּלְתַקָּנָא וּלְמֶעְבַּד כָּל צָרְכָנָא. מִיּוֹמָא טָבָא לְשַׁבַּתָּא. לָנָא וּלְכָל יִשְׂרָאֵל הַדָּרִים בָּעִיר הַזֹּאת:

The food of the Eruv should be eaten at one of the Shabbos meals.

When the chametz is burning, the following declaration is recited:

Let it be your will, Hashem our God and God of our fathers, that just as I rid my home and my property of chametz, so may you rid all the *chitzonim* and the impure forces from the land, and destroy the Evil Inclination from our midst, and grant us a heart of flesh. Let all the forces of the *Sitra Achra*, and all the *klippos* and all the wickedness, disperse, like smoke. Sweep the kingdom of evil away from the land and all those who cause pain to the *Shechinah*, destroy them with a spirit of destruction and a spirit of justice, as you destroyed Egypt and its deities in those days and at this time.

After burning the chametz, the following declaration is made:
It should be recited in a language that one understands. When Pesach begins on Motzei
Shabbos, this declaration is made on Shabbos morning. Any chametz remaining from
the Shabbos morning meal is flushed down the drain before the declaration is made.

All leavening and *chametz* that is in my possession, whether I have seen it or not, whether I have disposed of it or not, is hereby nullified, and shall be ownerless as the dust of the earth.

ERUV TAVSHILIN

When Yom Tov occurs on Thursday and Friday, an eruv tavshilin must be prepared on the
preceding Wednesday. The head of the family should take a matzah and an item of cooked
food such as meat, fish, or an egg, and put them on a plate and say the following blessing:

Blessed are You, Hashem our God, King of the Universe, Who sanctified us with His commandments and commanded us concerning the commandment of Eruv.

By means of this Eruv, it will be permissible for us to bake, cook, keep dishes warm, to kindle a light (from an existing flame), and to prepare and do all our necessities on the Festival for the needs of Shabbos, for us and for all Jews who live in this city.

The food of the Eruv should be eaten at one of the Shabbos meals.

סֵדֶר אֲמִירַת קָרְבַּן פֶּסַח

Following Minchah, many people have the custom to recite the
verses that relate to the bringing of the Pesach offering.
The order of the Korban Pesach is preceded by the following prayer:

רִבּוֹן הָעוֹלָמִים. אַתָּה צִוִּיתָנוּ לְהַקְרִיב קָרְבַּן הַפֶּסַח בְּמוֹעֲדוֹ
בְּאַרְבָּעָה עָשָׂר לַחֹדֶשׁ הָרִאשׁוֹן וְלִהְיוֹת כֹּהֲנִים בַּעֲבוֹדָתָם וּלְוִיִּם
בְּדוּכָנָם וְיִשְׂרָאֵל בְּמַעֲמָדָם קוֹרְאִים אֶת הַהַלֵּל, וְעַתָּה בַּעֲוֹנוֹתֵינוּ
חָרַב בֵּית הַמִּקְדָּשׁ וּבָטֵל הַקְרָבַת הַפֶּסַח. וְאֵין לָנוּ לֹא כֹהֵן בַּעֲבוֹדָתוֹ
וְלֹא לֵוִי בְּדוּכָנוּ וְלֹא יִשְׂרָאֵל בְּמַעֲמָדוֹ. וְאַתָּה אָמַרְתָּ וּנְשַׁלְּמָה פָרִים
שְׂפָתֵינוּ. לָכֵן יְהִי רָצוֹן מִלְּפָנֶיךָ יְהֹוָה אֱלֹהֵינוּ וֵאלֹהֵי אֲבוֹתֵינוּ
שֶׁיְּהֵא שִׂיחַ שִׂפְתוֹתֵינוּ חָשׁוּב וּמְקֻבָּל וּמְרֻצֶה לְפָנֶיךָ כְּאִלּוּ הִקְרַבְנוּ
אֶת הַפֶּסַח בְּמוֹעֲדוֹ וְעָמַדְנוּ עַל מַעֲמָדוֹ וְדִבְּרוּ הַלְוִיִּם בְּשִׁיר וְהַלֵּל
לְהוֹדוֹת לַיהֹוָה וְאַתָּה תְּכוֹנֵן מִקְדָּשְׁךָ עַל מְכוֹנוֹ וְנַעֲלֶה וְנַקְרִיב
לְפָנֶיךָ אֶת הַפֶּסַח בְּמוֹעֲדוֹ כְּמוֹ שֶׁכָּתַבְתָּ עָלֵינוּ בְּתוֹרָתֶךָ עַל יְדֵי
מֹשֶׁה עַבְדְּךָ כָּאָמוּר:

וַיֹּאמֶר יְהֹוָה אֶל מֹשֶׁה וְאֶל אַהֲרֹן בְּאֶרֶץ מִצְרַיִם לֵאמֹר: הַחֹדֶשׁ הַזֶּה
לָכֶם רֹאשׁ חֳדָשִׁים רִאשׁוֹן הוּא לָכֶם לְחָדְשֵׁי הַשָּׁנָה: דַּבְּרוּ אֶל כָּל
עֲדַת יִשְׂרָאֵל לֵאמֹר בֶּעָשֹׂר לַחֹדֶשׁ הַזֶּה וְיִקְחוּ לָהֶם אִישׁ שֶׂה לְבֵית
אָבֹת שֶׂה לַבָּיִת: וְאִם יִמְעַט הַבַּיִת מִהְיוֹת מִשֶּׂה וְלָקַח הוּא וּשְׁכֵנוֹ
הַקָּרֹב אֶל בֵּיתוֹ בְּמִכְסַת נְפָשֹׁת אִישׁ לְפִי אָכְלוֹ תָּכֹסּוּ עַל הַשֶּׂה:
שֶׂה תָמִים זָכָר בֶּן שָׁנָה יִהְיֶה לָכֶם מִן הַכְּבָשִׂים וּמִן הָעִזִּים תִּקָּחוּ:
וְהָיָה לָכֶם לְמִשְׁמֶרֶת עַד אַרְבָּעָה עָשָׂר יוֹם לַחֹדֶשׁ הַזֶּה וְשָׁחֲטוּ אֹתוֹ
כֹּל קְהַל עֲדַת יִשְׂרָאֵל בֵּין הָעַרְבָּיִם: וְלָקְחוּ מִן הַדָּם וְנָתְנוּ עַל שְׁתֵּי
הַמְּזוּזֹת וְעַל הַמַּשְׁקוֹף עַל הַבָּתִּים אֲשֶׁר יֹאכְלוּ אֹתוֹ בָּהֶם: וְאָכְלוּ
אֶת הַבָּשָׂר בַּלַּיְלָה הַזֶּה צְלִי אֵשׁ וּמַצּוֹת עַל מְרֹרִים יֹאכְלֻהוּ: אַל
תֹּאכְלוּ מִמֶּנּוּ נָא וּבָשֵׁל מְבֻשָּׁל בַּמָּיִם כִּי אִם צְלִי אֵשׁ רֹאשׁוֹ עַל
כְּרָעָיו וְעַל קִרְבּוֹ: וְלֹא תוֹתִירוּ מִמֶּנּוּ עַד בֹּקֶר וְהַנֹּתָר מִמֶּנּוּ עַד בֹּקֶר
בָּאֵשׁ תִּשְׂרֹפוּ: וְכָכָה תֹּאכְלוּ אֹתוֹ מָתְנֵיכֶם חֲגֻרִים נַעֲלֵיכֶם בְּרַגְלֵיכֶם
וּמַקֶּלְכֶם בְּיֶדְכֶם וַאֲכַלְתֶּם אֹתוֹ בְּחִפָּזוֹן פֶּסַח הוּא לַיהֹוָה:

KORBAN PESACH

*Following Minchah, many people have the custom to recite the
verses that relate to the bringing of the Pesach offering.
The order of the Korban Pesach is preceded by the following prayer:*

Master of the universe, You have commanded us to offer the Korban Pesach at its proper time on the fourteenth of the first month, with the Kohanim carrying out the service, the Leviim standing on their platform, and the *Yisraelim* in their positions, all singing Your praise. But now, because of our sins, the Beis Hamikdosh has been destroyed, the Korban Pesach has been annulled, we have no Kohen performing the service, no Levi standing atop the platform, no Yisroel in his position. Let the offerings of our lips take the place of the oxen. May it therefore be Your will, Hashem our God, and God of our fathers, that the words that we may come up and offer the Korban Pesach before You at its proper time, as You have written in Your Torah, given to us by Moshe, Your servant.

And Hashem said to Moshe and Aaron in the land of Egypt saying, "This month shall mark for you the beginning of the months; it shall be the first of the months of the year for you. Speak to the entire congregation of Israel and say that on the tenth of this month each of them shall take a lamb to a family, a lamb to a household. But if the household is too small for a lamb, let it share one with a neighbor who dwells nearby, in proportion to the number of persons: you shall contribute for the lamb according to what each household will eat. Your lamb shall be without blemish, a yearling male; you may take it from the sheep or from the goats. You shall keep watch over it until the fourteenth day of this month; and all the congregation of the Israelites shall slaughter it in the afternoon. They shall take some of the blood and put it on the two doorposts and the lintel of the houses in which they are to eat it. They shall eat the flesh that same night; they shall eat it roasted over the fire, with matzos and with bitter herbs. Do not eat any of it raw, or cooked in any way with water, but roasted—head, legs, and entrails—over the fire. You shall not leave any of it over until morning; if any of it is left until morning, you shall burn it. This is how you shall eat it: your loins girded, your sandals on your feet, and your staff in your hand; and you shall eat it hurriedly: it is a Pesach offering to Hashem."

The following description of the Korban Pesach appears in the Siddur of the Yaavetz:

כָּךְ הָיְתָה עֲבוֹדַת קָרְבַּן פֶּסַח בְּאַרְבָּעָה עָשָׂר בְּנִיסָן, אֵין שׁוֹחֲטִין אוֹתוֹ אֶלָּא אַחַר תָּמִיד שֶׁל בֵּין הָעַרְבַּיִם, עֶרֶב פֶּסַח בֵּין בְּחוֹל בֵּין בְּשַׁבָּת הָיָה הַתָּמִיד נִשְׁחַט בְּשֶׁבַע וּמֶחֱצָה, וְקָרֵב בִּשְׁמוֹנָה וּמֶחֱצָה, וְאִם חָל עֶרֶב פֶּסַח לִהְיוֹת עֶרֶב שַׁבָּת הָיוּ שׁוֹחֲטִין אוֹתוֹ בְּשֵׁשׁ וּמֶחֱצָה וְקָרֵב בְּשֶׁבַע וּמֶחֱצָה וְהַפֶּסַח אַחֲרָיו, כָּל אָדָם מִיִּשְׂרָאֵל אֶחָד הָאִישׁ וְאֶחָד הָאִשָּׁה בְּנֵי בֵיתוֹ הַגְּדוֹלִים וְהַטְּהוֹרִים וְנִמּוֹלִים (וּכְשֵׁם שְׂמִילָתוֹ מְעַכֶּבֶת מִלַּעֲשׂוֹת הַפֶּסַח וּמִלֶּאֱכוֹל בּוֹ, כָּךְ מִילַת בָּנָיו הַקְּטַנִּים וּמִילַת עֲבָדָיו בֵּין גְּדוֹלִים בֵּין קְטַנִּים וּטְבִילַת אִמְּהוֹתָיו מְעַכֶּבֶת) כָּל שֶׁיָּכוֹל לְהַגִּיעַ לִירוּשָׁלַיִם בִּשְׁעַת שְׁחִיטַת הַפֶּסַח חַיָּב בְּקָרְבַּן פֶּסַח:

מְבִיאוֹ מִן הַכְּבָשִׂים אוֹ מִן הָעִזִּים זָכָר תָּמִים בֶּן שָׁנָה (אֵינוֹ טָעוּן סְמִיכָה) וְשׁוֹחֲטוֹ בְּכָל מָקוֹם בָּעֲזָרָה אַחַר גְּמַר עֲבוֹדַת תָּמִיד הָעֶרֶב וְאַחַר הֲטָבַת הַנֵּרוֹת, וְאֵין שׁוֹחֲטִין הַפֶּסַח וְלֹא זוֹרְקִין הַדָּם וְלֹא מַקְטִירִין הַחֵלֶב עַל הֶחָמֵץ (אֲפִילוּ הָיָה כַּזַּיִת בִּרְשׁוּתוֹ שֶׁל אֶחָד מִבְּנֵי הַחֲבוּרָה:) בִּשְׁעַת אַחַת מֵהָעֲבוֹדוֹת שֶׁל קָרְבַּן פֶּסַח, הוּא לוֹקֶה וְהַפֶּסַח כָּשֵׁר:

שָׁחַט הַשּׁוֹחֵט (אֲפִילוּ זָר) וְקִבֵּל דָּמוֹ כֹּהֵן שֶׁבָּרֹאשׁ הַשּׁוּרָה בִּכְלִי שָׁרֵת וְנוֹתֵן לַחֲבֵירוֹ, וַחֲבֵירוֹ לַחֲבֵירוֹ, כֹּהֵן הַקָּרוֹב אֵצֶל הַמִּזְבֵּחַ זוֹרְקוֹ זְרִיקָה אַחַת כְּנֶגֶד הַיְסוֹד וְחוֹזֵר הַכְּלִי רֵיקָן לַחֲבֵירוֹ וַחֲבֵירוֹ לַחֲבֵירוֹ, מְקַבֵּל אֶת הַמָּלֵא וּמַחֲזִיר אֶת הָרֵיקָן, וְהָיוּ הַכֹּהֲנִים עוֹמְדִים שׁוּרוֹת וּבִידֵיהֶם בָּזִיכִין שֶׁכּוּלָּן כֶּסֶף אוֹ כוּלָּן זָהָב וְלֹא הָיוּ מְעוֹרָבִים, וְלֹא הָיוּ לַבָּזִיכִין שׁוּלַיִם שֶׁלֹּא יַנִּיחוּם וְיִקְרֹשׁ הַדָּם, אַחַר כָּךְ תּוֹלִין אֶת הַפֶּסַח בְּאוּנְקְלָיוֹת (אוֹ בְּמַקְלוֹת דַּקִּים מֵנִיחַ עַל כְּתֵפוֹ וְעַל כֶּתֶף חֲבֵירוֹ, תּוֹלֶה) וּמַפְשִׁיט אוֹתוֹ כּוּלּוֹ (וּבְשַׁבָּת עַד הֶחָזֶה וּמִשָּׁם לְמַטָּה שָׁקַל לֵיהּ בְּבַרְזָא) וְקוֹרְעִין בִּטְנוֹ וּמוֹצִיאִין אֵימוּרִים הַחֵלֶב שֶׁעַל הַקֶּרֶב וְיוֹתֶרֶת הַכָּבֵד וּשְׁתֵּי הַכְּלָיוֹת וְחֵלֶב שֶׁעֲלֵיהֶן וְהָאַלְיָה, אִם הָיָה מִמִּין הַכְּבָשִׂים לְעוּמַת הֶעָצֶה, נוֹתֵן בִּכְלִי שָׁרֵת וּמוֹלְחָן וּמַקְטִירָן הַכֹּהֵן עַל הַמַּעֲרָכָה, חֶלְבֵי כָּל זֶבַח וְזֶבַח לְבַדּוֹ, בְּחוֹל בַּיּוֹם, וְלֹא בַּלַּיְלָה שֶׁהוּא יוֹם טוֹב, אֲבָל אִם חָל עֶרֶב פֶּסַח בְּשַׁבָּת מַקְטִירִין וְהוֹלְכִין כָּל הַלַּיְלָה, וּמוֹצִיא קְרָבָיו וּמְמַחֶה אוֹתָן עַד שֶׁמֵּסִיר מֵהֶן הַפֶּרֶשׁ (כְּדֵי שֶׁיִּהְיוּ נְקִיִּים כְּשֶׁצּוֹלֵהוּ עִמָּם), שְׁחִיטָתוֹ וּזְרִיקַת דָּמוֹ וּמִיחוּי קְרָבָיו וְהַקְטֵר חֲלָבָיו דּוֹחִין אֶת הַשַּׁבָּת, וּשְׁאָר עִנְיָנָיו אֵין דּוֹחִין:

This was how the *Korban Pesach* was offered on the fourteenth of Nissan. It was slaughtered only after the daily afternoon offering. When Erev Pesach occurred on a weekday or on Shabbos, the daily afternoon offering was slaughtered at seven and a half hours after dawn and offered at eight and a half. If Erev Pesach occurred on Erev Shabbos, they would slaughter it at six and a half and offer it at seven and a half with the Pesach following it. Every Jewish person, man or woman, who was able to come to Yerushalayim by the time the Pesach was slaughtered is obligated in the mitzvah of Korban Pesach.

It may be offered from the lambs or from the kid goats, that are male, unblemished, and less than one year old. It may be slaughtered anywhere in the Temple Courtyard, after the service of the afternoon offering and after the Menorah was prepared. The Pesach may not be slaughtered nor may its blood be thrown upon the altar nor may its fats be burned upon the altar if chametz is still in one's possession.

The shochet slaughtered it, and the Kohen at the front of the line caught its blood in the sanctified vessel and passed it to his fellow Kohen, who would pass it to the next Kohen, and him to the next Kohen. The Kohen closest to the altar would throw its blood upon the altar in one shot, above the foundation of the altar. He would then return the empty vessel to his fellow Kohen, who would pass it to the next Kohen, and him to the next. As each Kohen received a vessel filled with blood, he would then pass back in its place an empty one. The Kohanim would stand in lines. Some lines used only silver vessels, while other lines used only gold vessels. They did not mix silver with gold in one line. The vessels did not have flat bottoms so that they would not be put down and the blood would then congeal.

Afterward, the *Korban Pesach* would be hung on hooks. Its entire body would be stripped of its skin. The stomach was cut open and the portions of meat for the altar removed, the fat above the intestines, the diaphragm, with the liver, the two kidneys, and the fat above them, and the tail across from the bone would all be placed in a sanctified vessel salted, and a Kohen would offer it upon the fire on [the altar], placing the fats of each offering separately. [When Erev Pesach occurred] on a weekday [the fats were only offered] by day and not by night, which was Yom Tov. When Erev Pesach occurred on Shabbos, the fats could be offered all night long. The intestines were removed and then squeezed to remove their waste. Slaughtering [the Korban Pesach], throwing its blood [on the altar], squeezing out the intestines, and burning the fats all may be performed on Shabbos. The other tasks [involved in processing the korban] do not supersede Shabbos.

בְּשָׁלֹשׁ כִּתּוֹת הַפֶּסַח נִשְׁחָט, וְאֵין כַּת פְּחוּתָה מִשְּׁלֹשִׁים אֲנָשִׁים, נִכְנְסָה כַּת אַחַת נִתְמַלְאָה הָעֲזָרָה, נוֹעֲלִין אוֹתָהּ, וּבְעוֹד שֶׁהֵן שׁוֹחֲטִין וּמַקְרִיבִין, הַלְוִיִּם קוֹרִין אֶת הַהַלֵּל, אִם גָּמְרוּ קֹדֶם שֶׁיַּקְרִיבוּ אֶת כֻּלָּם, שָׁנוּ, אִם שָׁנוּ, שִׁלֵּשׁוּ, עַל כָּל קְרִיאָה תָּקְעוּ הֵרִיעוּ וְתָקְעוּ, גָּמְרָה כַּת אַחַת לְהַקְרִיב, פּוֹתְחִין הָעֲזָרָה יָצְאָה כַּת רִאשׁוֹנָה, נִכְנְסָה כַּת שְׁנִיָּה נָעֲלוּ דַלְתוֹת הָעֲזָרָה, גָּמְרָה, יָצְאָה שְׁנִיָּה, נִכְנְסָה שְׁלִישִׁית, כְּמַעֲשֵׂה הָרִאשׁוֹנָה, כָּךְ מַעֲשֵׂה הַשְּׁנִיָּה וְהַשְּׁלִישִׁית, אַחַר שֶׁיָּצְאוּ כֻּלָּן רוֹחֲצִין הָעֲזָרָה מִלִּכְלוּכֵי הַדָּם וַאֲפִילוּ בְּשַׁבָּת, אַמַּת הַמַּיִם הָיְתָה עוֹבֶרֶת בָּעֲזָרָה, שֶׁכְּשֶׁרוֹצִין לְהָדִיחַ הָרִצְפָּה סוֹתְמִין מְקוֹם יְצִיאַת הַמַּיִם וְהִיא מִתְמַלְּאָה עַל כָּל גְּדוֹתֶיהָ עַד שֶׁהַמַּיִם עוֹלִין וְצָפִין וּמְקַבְּצִין אֲלֵיהֶם כָּל דָּם וְלִכְלוּךְ שֶׁבָּעֲזָרָה, אַחַר כָּךְ פּוֹתְחִין הַסְּתִימָה וְיוֹצְאִין הַמַּיִם עִם הַלִּכְלוּךְ, נִמְצָאת הָרִצְפָּה מְנוּקָה, זֶהוּ כְּבוֹד הַבַּיִת, יָצְאוּ כָּל אֶחָד עִם פִּסְחוֹ (וְעוֹר שֶׁלוֹ) וְצָלוּ אוֹתָם, כֵּיצַד צוֹלִין אוֹתוֹ מְבִיאִין שַׁפּוּד שֶׁל רִמּוֹן תּוֹחֲבוֹ מִתּוֹךְ פִּיו עַד בֵּית נְקוּבָתוֹ, וְתוֹלֵהוּ לְתוֹךְ הַתַּנּוּר וְהָאֵשׁ לְמַטָּה, וְתוֹלֶה כְּרָעָיו וּבְנֵי מֵעָיו חוּצָה לוֹ. וְאֵין מְנַקְּרִין אֶת הַפֶּסַח כִּשְׁאָר בָּשָׂר, בְּשַׁבָּת אֵין מוֹלִיכִין אֶת הַפֶּסַח לְבֵיתָם, אֶלָּא כַּת הָרִאשׁוֹנָה יוֹצְאִין בְּפִסְחֵיהֶן וְיוֹשְׁבִין בְּהַר הַבַּיִת, הַשְּׁנִיָּה יוֹצְאִין עִם פִּסְחֵיהֶן וְיוֹשְׁבִין בַּחֵיל, הַשְּׁלִישִׁית בִּמְקוֹמָהּ עוֹמֶדֶת, חֲשֵׁכָה יָצְאוּ וְצָלוּ אֶת פִּסְחֵיהֶן:

כְּשֶׁמַּקְרִיבִין אֶת הַפֶּסַח בָּרִאשׁוֹן, מַקְרִיבִין עִמּוֹ בְּיוֹם י"ד זֶבַח שְׁלָמִים, מִן הַבָּקָר אוֹ מִן הַצֹּאן, גְּדוֹלִים אוֹ קְטַנִּים, זְכָרִים אוֹ נְקֵבוֹת, וְהִיא נִקְרֵאת חֲגִיגַת אַרְבָּעָה עָשָׂר, עַל זֶה נֶאֱמַר בַּתּוֹרָה וְזָבַחְתָּ פֶּסַח לַיהוה אֱלֹהֶיךָ צֹאן וּבָקָר, וְלֹא קְבָעָהּ הַכָּתוּב חוֹבָה אֶלָּא רְשׁוּת בִּלְבָד, מִכָּל מָקוֹם הִיא כְחוֹבָה מִדִּבְרֵי סוֹפְרִים, כְּדֵי שֶׁיְּהֵא הַפֶּסַח נֶאֱכָל עַל הַשּׂוֹבַע, אֵימָתַי מְבִיאִין עִמּוֹ חֲגִיגָה, בִּזְמַן שֶׁהוּא בָּא בְּחוֹל, בְּטָהֳרָה, וּבְמוּעָט, וְנֶאֱכֶלֶת לִשְׁנֵי יָמִים וְלַיְלָה אֶחָד, וְדִינָהּ כְּכָל תּוֹרַת זִבְחֵי שְׁלָמִים, טְעוּנָה סְמִיכָה וּנְסָכִים וּמַתַּן דָּמִים שֶׁהֵן שְׁתַּיִם שֶׁהֵן אַרְבַּע, וּשְׁפִיכַת שִׁירַיִם לַיְסוֹד, זֶהוּ סֵדֶר עֲבוֹדַת קָרְבַּן פֶּסַח וַחֲגִיגָה שֶׁעִמּוֹ בְּבֵית אֱלֹהֵינוּ שֶׁיִּבָּנֶה בִּמְהֵרָה בְּיָמֵינוּ אָמֵן:

The Jewish people were divided into three groups when slaughtering their Pesach offerings. Each group had at least thirty people. The first group entered the Temple Courtyard until it was filled, and then the gates were shut. As they slaughtered and offered, the Kohanim blew the trumpets, a flute was played before the altar, and the Leviim sang Hallel. If they completed singing Hallel before everyone had a chance to offer his korban, they would repeat it two or three times.

With every repetition, the trumpets were blown with *tekiah*, *teruah*, and *tekiah*. After the first group completed their offerings, the courtyard was opened; the first group left, and the second group entered. The gates of the Courtyard were shut. As the first group performed their offerings, so did the second and third.

After everyone had left, the Courtyard was cleansed of the filth and blood, even on Shabbos. A water canal passed through the Courtyard. When they wished to wash the floor, they would seal off its exit. And the Courtyard would fill with water. The water level would rise and pick up all the blood and filth in the Courtyard. Then they would open the canal, and the filthy water would stream out. Thereby, the floor was kept clean to honor the Beis Hamikdosh.

Each person would then leave with his Korban Pesach and roast it. How would they roast it? They would bring a spit made from the wood of a pomegranate tree, skewer it from its mouth to its bottom, and hang it in an oven with a fire beneath it. Its legs and innards would hang out of it. *Nikkur* was not performed on the Pesach as it was performed on other meat.

On Shabbos, they did not carry the Pesach to their homes; rather the first group would exit the Courtyard with their Korban Pesach and wait on the Temple Mount. The second group would leave with their Korban Pesach and wait in the area surrounding the Beis Hamikdosh. The third group would wait in their place in the Beis Hamikdosh. When night fell, they would leave and roast their Korban Pesach.

When the Pesach was offered in the first month [Nissan], they would offer together with it on the fourteenth day a *shelamim* offering, whether cattle or sheep, old or young, male or female. This was called the Chagigah of the Fourteenth. In regard to this, the Torah states. "You shall slaughter a Pesach to your God from sheep or cattle." The Torah does not require this, leaving it optional. Nevertheless, it was made into a Rabbinic obligation so that the Korban Pesach would be eaten afterward on a full stomach.

When was the Chagigah offered with the Korban Pesach? When the Korban Pesach was brought on a weekday, in ritual purity, with insufficient meat. The Chagigah may be eaten for two days and one night. Its laws are the same as for those of all other offerings. It requires *semichah* (leaning on the korban) and *nesachim* (accompanying wine libations). Its blood is thrown on two corners of the altar, spreading across to reach all four sides. And the remaining blood is poured over the foundation.

This was how the Korban Pesach was offered, and the Chagigah that accompanied it, in the House of Our Lord, may it be rebuilt soon in our days.

הַדְלָקַת נֵרוֹת

On Yom Tov, the blessings are recited before the candles are lit. When Yom Tov falls on Shabbos, the candles are lit first and then the blessings are recited. (On Shabbos, the words in parentheses are added.)

בָּרוּךְ אַתָּה יְהֹוָה אֱלֹהֵינוּ מֶלֶךְ הָעוֹלָם, אֲשֶׁר קִדְּשָׁנוּ בְּמִצְוֹתָיו וְצִוָּנוּ לְהַדְלִיק נֵר שֶׁל [שַׁבָּת וְשֶׁל] יוֹם טוֹב

בָּרוּךְ אַתָּה יְהֹוָה. אֱלֹהֵינוּ מֶלֶךְ הָעוֹלָם, שֶׁהֶחֱיָנוּ וְקִיְּמָנוּ וְהִגִּיעָנוּ לַזְּמַן הַזֶּה.

It is customary for women to recite the following prayer after lighting the candles:

יְהִי רָצוֹן מִלְּפָנֶיךָ יְהֹוָה אֱלֹהַי וֵאלֹהֵי אֲבוֹתַי. שֶׁתְּחוֹנֵן אוֹתִי (וְאֶת אִישִׁי וְאֶת בָּנַי וְאֶת אָבִי וְאֶת אִמִּי) וְאֶת כָּל קְרוֹבַי. וְתִתֶּן לָנוּ וּלְכָל יִשְׂרָאֵל חַיִּים טוֹבִים וַאֲרֻכִּים. וְתִזְכְּרֵנוּ בְּזִכְרוֹן טוֹבָה וּבְרָכָה. וְתִפְקְדֵנוּ בִּפְקֻדַּת יְשׁוּעָה וְרַחֲמִים וּתְבָרְכֵנוּ בְּרָכוֹת גְּדוֹלוֹת. וְתַשְׁלִים בָּתֵּינוּ. וְתַשְׁכֵּן שְׁכִינָתְךָ בֵּינֵינוּ. וְזַכֵּנִי לְגַדֵּל בָּנִים וּבְנֵי בָנִים חֲכָמִים וּנְבוֹנִים. אוֹהֲבֵי יְהֹוָה יִרְאֵי אֱלֹהִים. אַנְשֵׁי אֱמֶת. זֶרַע קֹדֶשׁ בַּיהֹוָה. דְּבֵקִים וּמְאִירִים אֶת הָעוֹלָם בַּתּוֹרָה וּבְמַעֲשִׂים טוֹבִים וּבְכָל מְלֶאכֶת עֲבוֹדַת הַבּוֹרֵא. אָנָּא שְׁמַע אֶת תְּחִנָּתִי בָּעֵת הַזֹּאת. בִּזְכוּת שָׂרָה וְרִבְקָה וְרָחֵל וְלֵאָה אִמּוֹתֵינוּ. וְהָאֵר נֵרֵנוּ שֶׁלֹּא יִכְבֶּה לְעוֹלָם וָעֶד וְהָאֵר פָּנֶיךָ וְנִוָּשֵׁעָה. אָמֵן

LIGHTING THE CANDLES

On Yom Tov, the blessings are recited before the candles are lit. When
Yom Tov falls on Shabbos, the candles are lit first and then the blessings
are recited. (On Shabbos, the words in parentheses are added.)

Blessed are You, Hashem, our God, King of the universe, Who has sanctified us through His commandments, and commanded us to kindle the candle of (the Sabbath and) the festival.

Blessed are You, Hashem, our God, King of the universe, Who has granted us life and sustained us and allowed us to reach this occasion.

It is customary for women to recite the following prayer after lighting
the candles (insert the words in brackets as applicable):

May it be your will Hashem, my God and God of my forefathers, that You show favor to me [My husband, my sons, my daughters, my father, my mother] and all my relatives; and that you grant us and all Israel, a good and long life. That you remember us with a beneficent memory and blessing. That You consider us with a consideration of salvation and compassion. That You bless us with great blessings; that You make our households complete; that You cause Your presence to dwell among us. Privilege me to raise children and grandchildren, who are wise and understanding, who love Hashem and fear God. People of truth holy offspring attached to Hashem, who illuminate the world with Torah and good deeds and with every labor in the service of the Creator. Please hear my supplication at this time. In the merit of Sarah, Rebecca, Rachel, and Leah, our mothers, and cause our light to illuminate that it not be extinguished forever, and let Your countenance shine so that we are saved. Amen.

הַסֵּדֶר

THE SEDER

סִימָנֵי הַסֵּדֶר

The fifteen steps of the Seder

קַדֵּשׁ

וּרְחַץ

כַּרְפַּס

יַחַץ

מַגִּיד

רָחְצָה

מוֹצִיא

מַצָּה

מָרוֹר

כּוֹרֵךְ

שֻׁלְחָן עוֹרֵךְ

צָפוּן

בָּרֵךְ

הַלֵּל

נִרְצָה

THE ORDER OF THE SEDER

The fifteen steps of the Seder

Kaddesh   *Reciting Kiddush*

Urchatz   *Washing the hands in preparation for Karpas*

Karpas   *Dipping a vegetable in salt water and eating it*

Yachatz   *Breaking the middle matzah. Put away larger half for Afikomen*

Maggid   *Telling the story of the Exodus*

Rachtzah   *Washing the hands before the meal*

Motzi   *Reciting the Hamotzi blessing*

Matzah   *Reciting the blessing over the matzah and eating it*

Maror   *Eating the maror*

Korech   *Eating a sandwich of matzah and maror*

Shulchan Orech   *Eating the festive meal*

Tzafun   *Eating the Afikomen*

Barech   *Reciting Grace after Meals*

Hallel   *Reciting the remainder of Hallel*

Nirtzah   *Concluding the Seder with the hope that it was pleasing to Hashem!*

PREPARING FOR THE SEDER

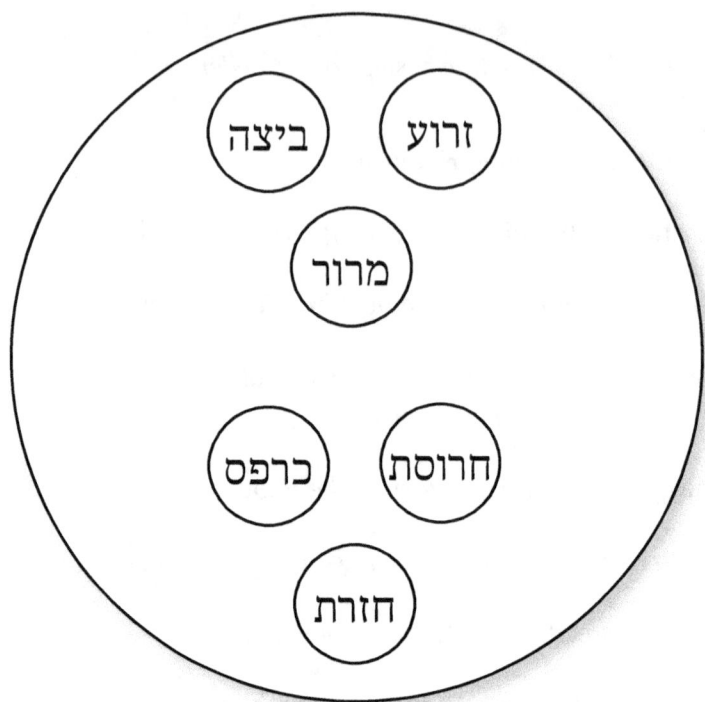

מַצָּה—Three whole matzos are placed one atop the other separated by a cloth or napkin. Matzah is eaten three times during the Seder, by itself, together with maror as korach, and as the Afikomen. Each time the minimum portion of matzah for each person should have a volume equivalent to half an egg.

זְרוֹעַ—Roasted bone

בֵּיצָה—Hard-boiled egg

מָרוֹר וַחֲזֶרֶת—Bitter herbs are eaten twice during the Seder, once by themselves and together with matzah as korech. Each time a minimum portion equal to the volume of half an egg should be eaten. The custom is to use grated horseradish for maror and romaine lettuce for chazeres.

חֲרוֹסֶת—The bitter herbs are dipped into charoses. The charoses is a mixture of grated apples, walnuts, and wine.

כַּרְפַּס—A vegetable such as a potato, parsley, or celery

PREPARING FOR THE SEDER

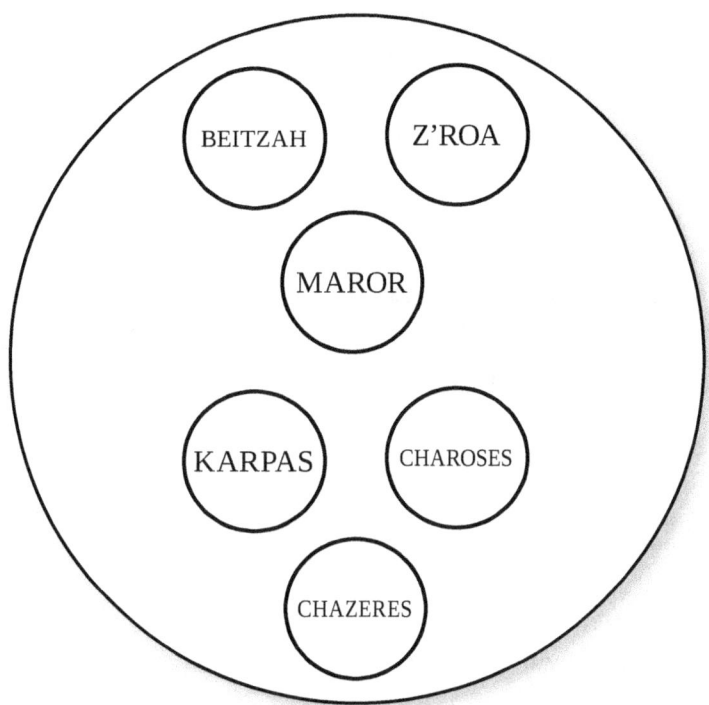

Matzah—Three whole matzos are placed one atop the other separated by a cloth or napkin. Matzah is eaten three times during the Seder, by itself, together with maror as korach, and as the Afikomen. Each time the minimum portion of matzah for each person should have a volume equivalent to half an egg.

Z'roa—Roasted bone

Beitzah—Hard-boiled egg

Maror and Chazeres—Bitter herbs are eaten twice during the Seder, once by themselves and together with matzah as korech. Each time a minimum portion equal to the volume of half an egg should be eaten. The custom is to use grated horseradish for maror and romaine lettuce for chazeres.

Charoses—The bitter herbs are dipped into charoses. The charoses is a mixture of grated apples, walnuts, and wine.

Karpas—A vegetable such as a potato, parsley, or celery

קַדֵּשׁ

*Kiddush should be recited and the Seder begun as soon after
synagogue services as possible, after nightfall.
The first of the four cups of wine is poured. The leader should have another
person pour the wine for him, as a gesture of leisure and freedom. As he is
about to recite Kiddush, one should bear in mind that he is about to fulfill the
mitzvah of Kiddush and the mitzvah of the first of the four cups of wine.
(On Friday night, add the words in parentheses.)*

[וַיְהִי עֶרֶב וַיְהִי בֹקֶר]

יוֹם הַשִּׁשִּׁי. וַיְכֻלּוּ הַשָּׁמַיִם וְהָאָרֶץ וְכָל צְבָאָם. וַיְכַל אֱלֹהִים בַּיּוֹם
הַשְּׁבִיעִי מְלַאכְתּוֹ אֲשֶׁר עָשָׂה וַיִּשְׁבֹּת בַּיּוֹם הַשְּׁבִיעִי מִכָּל מְלַאכְתּוֹ אֲשֶׁר
עָשָׂה. וַיְבָרֶךְ אֱלֹהִים אֶת יוֹם הַשְּׁבִיעִי וַיְקַדֵּשׁ אֹתוֹ כִּי בוֹ שָׁבַת מִכָּל
מְלַאכְתּוֹ אֲשֶׁר בָּרָא אֱלֹהִים לַעֲשׂוֹת

Kaddesh קַדֵּשׁ

וַיְהִי עֶרֶב וַיְהִי בֹקֶר יוֹם הַשִּׁשִּׁי

"And it was evening, and it was morning, the sixth day."

If we would have existed at the moment the world came into being, would we
have experienced the sun shining or would it have been in the middle of the night?

Hashem first created night, and it was followed by day, as the posuk says, *"It
was evening, and it was morning, day one"* (Bereishis 1:5).

The word *evening* implies that there was a sunset, meaning the sun had been
shining and then it set. If existence began with the night and, prior to the first night
of creation, there was no day and no sun, how do we understand the phrase *"It was
evening,"* inferring there was a sun and it had set?

Chazal writes, "The Torah preceded the world by two thousand years." In *Moreh
Nevuchim,* the Rambam asks, "If prior to creation there was no movement of the
sun and moon, how do we understand the passage of time and declare the Torah
preexisted the world by two thousand years?"

Rambam answers that, prior to the creation of our world, Hashem created the
movement of celestial beings that defined a day and three hundred and sixty-five
of such movements gave us a year.

Therefore, on the first day of creation when the posuk said, *"It was evening,"*
it implies that a day had just concluded. It was referring to the movement of the
celestial beings.

KADDESH

*Kiddush should be recited and the Seder begun as soon after
synagogue services as possible, after nightfall.
The first of the four cups of wine is poured. The leader should have another
person pour the wine for him, as a gesture of leisure and freedom. As he is
about to recite Kiddush, one should bear in mind that he is about to fulfill the
mitzvah of Kiddush and the mitzvah of the first of the four cups of wine.
On Friday night add:*

[And it was evening, and it was morning]

The sixth day. Then the heavens and the earth were completed, and all their array.

With the seventh day, God completed the work He had done. He ceased on
the seventh day from all the work He had done. God blessed the seventh day
and declared it holy, because on it

He ceased from all His work He had created to do.

The first day of creation was distinct from the other six days of creation. The last
six days of creation were divided into distinct segments of night and day. The terms
evening and *morning* are to be taken literally.

Concerning the first day of creation, the words *evening* and *morning* in the
posuk *"And it was evening, and it was morning, day one"* are to be taken figuratively.
Evening represents darkness and *morning* represents light. The posuk now reads,
"It was dark, and it was light, day one," meaning that darkness and light coexisted
during the first day of creation.

On the first day of creation, the word *evening* means "darkness." As such, it
need not be preceded by the setting of the sun.

(Yaaros Dvash 4,2)

וַיְכֻלּוּ הַשָּׁמַיִם וְהָאָרֶץ וְכָל־צְבָאָם וַיְכַל אֱלֹהִים בַּיּוֹם הַשְּׁבִיעִי מְלַאכְתּוֹ
אֲשֶׁר עָשָׂה וַיִּשְׁבֹּת בַּיּוֹם הַשְּׁבִיעִי מִכָּל מְלַאכְתּוֹ אֲשֶׁר עָשָׂה

**"And Hashem completed on the seventh day His work that He did, and He
abstained on the seventh day from all His work that He did."**

The Midrash brings an interesting conversation that took place between Hashem
and the Torah. The Torah complained that the Yidden would be preoccupied with
making a living, so when would they have time to study the Torah?

On other evenings Kiddush starts here:
(On Friday night, add the words in parentheses.)

סַבְרִי מָרָנָן וְרַבָּנָן וְרַבּוֹתַי.

בָּרוּךְ אַתָּה יְהֹוָה, אֱלֹהֵינוּ מֶלֶךְ הָעוֹלָם, בּוֹרֵא פְּרִי הַגָּפֶן.

בָּרוּךְ אַתָּה יְהֹוָה, אֱלֹהֵינוּ מֶלֶךְ הָעוֹלָם אֲשֶׁר בָּחַר בָּנוּ מִכָּל עָם
וְרוֹמְמָנוּ מִכָּל לָשׁוֹן וְקִדְּשָׁנוּ בְּמִצְוֹתָיו. וַתִּתֶּן לָנוּ יְהֹוָה אֱלֹהֵינוּ בְּאַהֲבָה
(שַׁבָּתוֹת לִמְנוּחָה וּ) מוֹעֲדִים לְשִׂמְחָה, חַגִּים וּזְמַנִּים לְשָׂשׂוֹן, (אֶת יוֹם
הַשַּׁבָּת הַזֶּה וְ) אֶת יוֹם חַג הַמַּצּוֹת הַזֶּה זְמַן חֵרוּתֵנוּ, (בְּאַהֲבָה) מִקְרָא
קֹדֶשׁ זֵכֶר לִיצִיאַת מִצְרָיִם. כִּי בָנוּ בָחַרְתָּ וְאוֹתָנוּ קִדַּשְׁתָּ מִכָּל הָעַמִּים,
(וְשַׁבָּת) וּמוֹעֲדֵי קָדְשֶׁךָ (בְּאַהֲבָה וּבְרָצוֹן) בְּשִׂמְחָה וּבְשָׂשׂוֹן הִנְחַלְתָּנוּ.

בָּרוּךְ אַתָּה יְהֹוָה, מְקַדֵּשׁ (הַשַּׁבָּת וְ)יִשְׂרָאֵל וְהַזְּמַנִּים.

Hashem responded, "I will give them the day of Shabbos. On Shabbos, when the Yidden will not be going to work, they will have sufficient time to study My Torah." Shabbos is the fulfilment of creation.

(Tiferet Yehonat Bereishis)

Is the seventh day holy because it is intrinsically holy, or did it become holy because on that day Hashem stopped working? And if Hashem had ceased working on a Wednesday, then would Wednesday have become a holy day?

The posuk says, *"For thereon He abstained from all His work that Hashem created to do."* (Bereishis 2:3)

This seems to imply that Hashem had more work to do, yet He stopped because of the sanctity of the seventh day.

The cessation of work did not create the day of holiness. Shabbos was always vested with holiness. Its sanctity was such that even Hashem rested on that day.

(Tiferet Yehonat Bereishis)

Blessed are You, Hashem our God, King of the Universe, who creates the fruit of the vine.

Blessed are You, Hashem our God, King of the Universe, who has chosen us from among all peoples, raised us above all tongues, and made us holy through His commandments.

You have given us, Hashem our God, in love (Sabbaths for rest), festivals for rejoicing, holy days and seasons for joy, (this Sabbath day and) this day of the festival of Matzos, (with love), a holy assembly in memory of the Exodus from Egypt.

For You have chosen us and sanctified us above all peoples, and given us as our heritage (Your holy Shabbos in love and favor and) Your holy festivals for joy and gladness.

Blessed are you, Hashem, who sanctifies (the Sabbath,) Israel and the festivals.

זֵכֶר לִיצִיאַת מִצְרָיִם

"Keeping Shabbos reminds us of the Exodus from Egypt."

Tosfos asks, "What is the link between Shabbos and the Exodus?"

The Torah writes, *"And the habitation of the Yidden, that they dwelled in Egypt was four hundred and thirty years"* (Shemos 12:40).

The Yidden were in Egypt for two hundred ten years. Where are the missing two hundred twenty years?

If we calculate the exile as beginning from the birth of Yitzchok, we will have four hundred years. However, we are still missing thirty years.

During the exile in Egypt, Shabbos was to be designated as a day of rest. However, the Egyptians forced the Yidden to desecrate the Shabbos.

Each week, when the Yidden worked on Shabbos, they worked a seventh more than they were meant to. A seventh of two hundred ten years is thirty years.

At the time of the Exodus, the Yidden had reached the forty-ninth level of impurity. If they had remained any longer, they would not have been able to leave.

It was in the merit of Shabbos that the Yidden were able to escape prior to the designated time. Therefore, on Shabbos, we remember the Exodus from Egypt.

(Yaaros Dvash 2:8)

On Saturday night, add the following two paragraphs:

בָּרוּךְ אַתָּה יְהוָֹה אֱלֹהֵינוּ מֶלֶךְ הָעוֹלָם, בּוֹרֵא מְאוֹרֵי הָאֵשׁ.

בָּרוּךְ אַתָּה יְהוָֹה, אֱלֹהֵינוּ מֶלֶךְ הָעוֹלָם, הַמַּבְדִּיל בֵּין קֹדֶשׁ לְחֹל, בֵּין אוֹר לְחֹשֶׁךְ, בֵּין יִשְׂרָאֵל לָעַמִּים, בֵּין יוֹם הַשְּׁבִיעִי לְשֵׁשֶׁת יְמֵי הַמַּעֲשֶׂה. בֵּין קְדֻשַּׁת שַׁבָּת לִקְדֻשַּׁת יוֹם טוֹב הִבְדַּלְתָּ, וְאֶת יוֹם הַשְּׁבִיעִי מִשֵּׁשֶׁת יְמֵי הַמַּעֲשֶׂה קִדַּשְׁתָּ. הִבְדַּלְתָּ וְקִדַּשְׁתָּ אֶת עַמְּךָ יִשְׂרָאֵל בִּקְדֻשָּׁתֶךָ. בָּרוּךְ אַתָּה יְהוָֹה, הַמַּבְדִּיל בֵּין קֹדֶשׁ לְקֹדֶשׁ.

On all nights conclude here:

בָּרוּךְ אַתָּה יְהוָֹה אֱלֹהֵינוּ מֶלֶךְ הָעוֹלָם, שֶׁהֶחֱיָנוּ וְקִיְּמָנוּ וְהִגִּיעָנוּ לַזְּמַן הַזֶּה.

Drink while reclining to the left. It is preferable to drink the entire cup, but at the very least most of the cup should be drunk.

וּרְחַץ

The hands are washed with a cup of water. No blessing is recited.

כַּרְפַּס

A small piece of vegetable (commonly used are potatoes, parsley, or celery) is dipped in salt water. A piece smaller in volume than half an egg should be eaten. The following blessing is recited (while reciting this blessing one should bear in mind that it also covers the maror, which will be eaten later at the Seder):

בָּרוּךְ אַתָּה יְהוָֹה, אֱלֹהֵינוּ מֶלֶךְ הָעוֹלָם, בּוֹרֵא פְּרִי הָאֲדָמָה

Eat without reclining.

יַחַץ

The middle matzah is broken into two pieces, in such a manner that one piece is larger than the other. The larger piece is set aside to be eaten later as the Afikomen. The smaller half is placed back between the other two, and the Haggadah is recited over it.

On Saturday night add the following two paragraphs:

Blessed are You, Hashem our God, King of the Universe, who creates the lights of fire.

Blessed are You, Hashem our God, King of the Universe, who distinguishes between sacred and secular, between light and darkness, between Israel and the nations, between the seventh day and the six days of work. You have made a distinction between the holiness of the Sabbath and the holiness of festivals, and have sanctified the seventh day above the six days of work.

You have distinguished and sanctified Your people Israel with Your holiness.

Blessed are You, Hashem, who distinguishes between sacred and sacred.

On all nights conclude here:

Blessed are You, Hashem our God, King of the Universe, who has given us life, sustained us, and brought us to this time.

Drink while reclining to the left. It is preferable to drink the entire cup, but at the very least most of the cup should be drunk.

URCHATZ

The hands are washed with a cup of water. No blessing is recited.

KARPAS

A small piece of vegetable (commonly used are potatoes, parsley, or celery) is dipped in salt water. A piece smaller in volume than half an egg should be eaten. The following blessing is recited (while reciting this blessing one should bear in mind that it also covers the maror, which will be eaten later at the Seder):

Blessed are You, Hashem our God, King of the Universe, who creates the fruit of the ground.

Eat without reclining.

YACHATZ

The middle matzah is broken into two pieces, in such a manner that one piece is larger than the other. The larger piece is set aside to be eaten later as the Afikomen. The smaller half is placed back between the other two, and the Haggadah is recited over it.

מַגִּיד

Throughout the Maggid section, the matzah should be uncovered, in plain view, in fulfillment of the description of matzah as "bread over which much discussion [of the Exodus] is held." The plate with the matzos is raised as the following paragraph is said:

הָא לַחְמָא עַנְיָא דִי אֲכָלוּ אַבְהָתָנָא בְּאַרְעָא דְמִצְרַיִם כָּל דִכְפִין יֵיתֵי
וְיֵיכוֹל כָּל דִּצְרִיךְ יֵיתֵי וְיִפְסַח הָשַׁתָּא הָכָא, לְשָׁנָה הַבָּאָה בְּאַרְעָא
דְיִשְׂרָאֵל הָשַׁתָּא עַבְדֵי, לְשָׁנָה הַבָּאָה בְּנֵי חוֹרִין

הָא לַחְמָא עַנְיָא דִי אֲכָלוּ אַבְהָתָנָא בְּאַרְעָא דְמִצְרַיִם

"This is the bread of affliction that our fathers ate in the land of Egypt."

The Hebrew phrase can be translated to mean, *"This is the poor man's bread that our forefathers ate in Egypt."*

The Yidden ate matzah after they left Egypt. However, this phrase seems to imply that the Yidden ate matzah while still in Egypt.

Every nation is represented by a star or a planet. The Yidden's heavenly luminary is the moon. As the posuk says, "As the sweetness of the moon's yield" (Devorim 33:14). Likewise, the Seven Nations established their capital in Jericho, יְרִיחוֹ. The word יְרִיחוֹ is the same word as יֶרַח, which means "moon."

The moon is referred to as the poor one because it has no independent light, as its light is drawn from the sun.

While enslaved in Egypt, the Yidden lived in Goshen. The Kuzari writes that the land of Goshen is considered part of Israel in respect to the moon being its heavenly star.

"This is the poor man's bread that our forefathers ate in Egypt" refers to the matzah that the Yidden ate in Goshen, as Goshen's heavenly planet was the moon.

(Ahavat Yehonatan Vayetze)

Lomdus

"This is the poor man's bread; whoever is hungry let him come and eat."

This statement seems to imply the reason the hungry person can come and eat is because the food belongs to a poor person. Does this mean that if it wasn't the food of the poor, the hungry could not eat it?

The posuk says, הֲלוֹא פָרֹס לָרָעֵב לַחְמֶךָ *"Is it not to share your bread with the hungry?"* (Yeshayahu 58:7).

MAGGID

This is the bread of affliction that our fathers ate in the land of Egypt. Whoever is hungry, let him come and eat; whoever is in need, let him come and celebrate Pesach. This year [we are] here, next year in the land of Israel! This year [we are] slaves, next year freed men!

The understanding of this posuk is illustrated by an argument between Rav Huna and Rav Yehuda. The Talmud (Bava Basra 9a) records an argument that debates whether a person who distributes tzedakah needs to examine whether the individual asking for food is poor and in need of funds.

Rav Huna is of the opinion that, before we give a person food, we need to ensure that they are needy. As the posuk says, *"Is it not to share [paros] your bread with the hungry?"* The word *paros* is written with a shin פרש (parosh) meaning "to examine." *"Only after examining and investigating the credibility of the poor person should you give him bread."*

Rav Huna focuses on how the word *paros* is written.

Rav Yehuda disagrees and is of the view that when distributing tzedakah, we do not examine the level of poverty of the one who asks for food. He understands the posuk *"Is it not to share your bread with the hungry?"* to mean share it immediately and do not examine whether the person requesting is poor, as the word *paros* is read as if it were spelled with a *samech* פרס (paros), which means "immediately."

Rav Yehuda focuses on how the word *paros* is read.

The Talmud rules that on the night of the Seder, we need to eat *"the poor man's bread."* The Talmud asks, "What is considered the poor man's bread?" and it answers, מַה דַּרְכּוֹ שֶׁל עָנִי בִּפְרוּסָה, *"a poor man eats a broken piece of matzah."*

The word used for a broken piece is פְּרוּס, written with a ס. Rav Yehuda uses the same word פְּרוּס to teach that we must immediately feed the poor, and we don't tell the poor person to first bring proof that he is poor.

According to Rav Yehuda's opinion, we can understand the link between the poor man's bread and feeding the poor. The word used to describe a poor man's bread is פְּרוּס. The word פְּרוּס also means to immediately feed the poor, not to first verify their financial situation. The Haggadah is saying, *"Whoever claims to be poor, they can immediately partake, and no questions will be asked."*

(Brocho Mishuleshes 100)

The plate with the matzos is temporarily removed to the far end of the table.
The second cup of wine is poured, after which the youngest
present asks the following four questions:

In this section, we make three declarations:

"Whoever is hungry, let him come and eat."

"Whoever is in need, let him come and conduct the Pesach Seder."

"This year [we are] here; next year in the Land of Israel."

What is the link between the three?

The Talmud Yerushalmi states, "The Korban Pesach brought in the Beis Hamikdosh could not be eaten on an empty stomach. The reason for this is that the Torah states that, when eating from the korban, we are not allowed to break any of the animal's bones." The Rabbis were concerned that a person who is famished may break a bone in their haste to eat the meat. However, if a person is no longer hungry and is eating the meat for dessert, they won't eat frantically, and we are not concerned that they may break a bone.

Since the destruction of the Beis Hamikdosh, we are unable to bring the Korban Pesach. As a reminder of the korban, the Rabbis instituted the eating of the afikomen at the conclusion of the meal.

The Talmud asks, "When eating matzah, there is no concern of breaking bones. Why then does it have to be eaten at the end of the meal when we are no longer hungry?"

The Talmud answers that the Beis Hamikdosh will be rebuilt speedily in our days, and as a result, people may err as it relates to the eating of the Korban Pesach. They will say, "Last Pesach when we ate the afikomen as a substitute for the korban, we ate it while we were hungry. This year, when we eat the actual korban, we can also eat it at the beginning of our meal while still hungry." Therefore, to ensure we don't make that mistake, we eat the afikomen at the end of the meal.

We now can understand the connection between the three points in this section.

"Whoever is hungry, let him come and eat."

Initially, we need to eat a meal so we will not be hungry.

"Whoever is in need, let him come and conduct the Pesach Seder."

Being that we are not hungry, we can conduct the Pesach Seder. As part of the Seder, we eat the afikomen at its conclusion. The question that needs to be addressed is why can the matzah only be eaten at the end of the Seder?

The plate with the matzos is temporarily removed to the far end of the table.
The second cup of wine is poured, after which the youngest
present asks the following four questions:

Why is this night different from all other nights?

"This year [we are] here; next year in the Land of Israel."

This year, while still in golus, we eat the afikomen at the end of the meal, thus ensuring that next year, when we are in Jerusalem and we bring the Korban Pesach, we will eat it at the correct time at the end of our meal.

(Divrei Yehonatan)

מַה נִּשְׁתַּנָּה

Ma Nishtana

Is there a connection between the question concerning the matzah and the maror?

The Midrash gives two reasons the Yidden left Egypt prior to the designated time, either due to the severity of the enslavement or as a result of having to work at night.

If it was because of the strenuous work, then we should also have to eat matzah during the day. However, if it was because we worked at night, that would explain why the obligation is to eat matzah only at night.

There are two reasons given why we eat maror: One reason is because the Egyptians made our lives bitter; the other is because Hashem has mercy on us. As the Talmud (Pesochim 39a) writes, "One should use חֲסָא for the maror as the word חַס means 'pity,' and Hashem has pity on us."

We begin by asking why we specifically eat the matzah at night. The reason is because we were also enslaved at night (not because of the hard labor).

As such, why do we eat the maror?

Since we eat maror, it must be because the Egyptians made the lives of the Yidden bitter. Hence, it was the hard labor that resulted in our early Exodus. Why then do we eat matzah only at night?

The answer is given in the section of "Avodim Hayinu," where we say that if Hashem had not had pity upon us, we would still be enslaved in Egypt. As such, we eat maror because Hashem had pity on the Yidden (not because of the hard labor).

We eat matzah at night because we were enslaved at night, and we eat maror because Hashem had pity on us.

(Pardes Reb Yehonatan)

שֶׁבְּכָל הַלֵּילוֹת אָנוּ אוֹכְלִין חָמֵץ וּמַצָּה, הַלַּיְלָה הַזֶּה—כֻּלּוֹ מַצָּה.

שֶׁבְּכָל הַלֵּילוֹת אָנוּ אוֹכְלִין שְׁאָר יְרָקוֹת—הַלַּיְלָה הַזֶּה מָרוֹר.

שֶׁבְּכָל הַלֵּילוֹת אֵין אָנוּ מַטְבִּילִין אֲפִילוּ פַּעַם אֶחָת—הַלַּיְלָה הַזֶּה שְׁתֵּי פְעָמִים.

שֶׁבְּכָל הַלֵּילוֹת אָנוּ אוֹכְלִין בֵּין יוֹשְׁבִין וּבֵין מְסֻבִּין—הַלַּיְלָה הַזֶּה כֻּלָּנוּ מְסֻבִּין

The plate with the matzos is returned to the table and the matzos are uncovered.
The Haggadah should be translated if necessary.

עֲבָדִים הָיִינוּ לְפַרְעֹה בְּמִצְרַיִם, וַיּוֹצִיאֵנוּ יְהֹוָה אֱלֹהֵינוּ מִשָּׁם בְּיָד חֲזָקָה וּבִזְרֹעַ נְטוּיָה. וְאִלּוּ לֹא הוֹצִיא הַקָּדוֹשׁ בָּרוּךְ הוּא אֶת אֲבוֹתֵינוּ מִמִּצְרַיִם,

עֲבָדִים הָיִינוּ לְפַרְעֹה בְּמִצְרַיִם

"We were slaves to Pharaoh in Egypt."

This section is the response given in the Torah to the wise son. The wise son is troubled by three things:

If the Yom Tov of Pesach marks the Exodus from Egypt, and the Exodus occurred on one day, why then do we celebrate it for seven? And if we do celebrate it for seven, then it cannot be considered a remembrance of what occurred at the time of the Exodus.

The main redemption occurred during the day. Why then does the Seder take place at night?

We traditionally sing songs of gratitude for miracles that occurred in Israel. Why are we celebrating a miracle that occurred in the diaspora?

On the fifteenth of Nissan, when the Yidden left Egypt, they had not witnessed the death of the Egyptian's firstborn, as they were not permitted to leave their homes until the plague had concluded.

However, on the twenty-first of Nissan, the Yidden witnessed the miracle of Krias Yam Suf and the death of the Egyptians.

We, therefore, celebrate Pesach for seven days to include the miracle of Krias Yam Suf where the Yidden saw the death of the Egyptians.

The purpose of the Exodus was to inherit the Land of Israel. The Midrash writes,

For on all nights, we eat chametz and matzah, but on this night only matzah!

For on all nights, we eat other vegetables, and on this night bitter herbs!

For on all nights, we do not dip our food even once, on this night we do it twice!

For on all nights, we eat either sitting upright or reclining, and on this night we all recline!

The plate with the matzos is returned to the table and the matzos are uncovered.
The Haggadah should be translated if necessary.

We were slaves to Pharaoh in Egypt, and Hashem our God brought us out of there with a strong hand and an outstretched arm. And if the Holy One, blessed be He, had not brought our fathers out of Egypt,

on the night of the fifteenth, the Yidden traveled on the wings of eagles to Israel and brought the Korban Pesach. It is fitting that we mark the miracle of traveling on the wings of eagles that occurred at night by celebrating the Seder at night.

The miracle of traveling on the wings of eagles to Israel is deemed to be a miracle that occurred in Israel, as the miracle enabled the Yidden to conquer the land in an easier manner.

(Tiferet Yehonatan Voeschanon)

וַיּוֹצִיאֵנוּ יְהוָֹה אֱלֹהֵינוּ מִשָּׁם בְּיָד חֲזָקָה וּבִזְרֹעַ נְטוּיָה

"And Hashem our God brought us out of there with a strong hand and an outstretched arm."

How are we to understand the phrase *"with a strong hand and with an outstretched arm"*?

Hashem is constantly recreating the world. Is there than anything difficult for Him that He needs a strong hand to accomplish?

Hashem created the world to follow certain rules and guidelines. When Hashem changes a rule or protocol, it is to be considered as if Hashem had used a strong hand.

(Tiferet Yehonatan Voeschanon)

הֲרֵי אָנוּ וּבָנֵינוּ וּבְנֵי בָנֵינוּ מְשֻׁעְבָּדִים הָיִינוּ לְפַרְעֹה בְּמִצְרָיִם. וַאֲפִילוּ כֻלָּנוּ חֲכָמִים כֻּלָּנוּ נְבוֹנִים כֻּלָּנוּ זְקֵנִים כֻּלָּנוּ יוֹדְעִים אֶת הַתּוֹרָה מִצְוָה עָלֵינוּ לְסַפֵּר בִּיצִיאַת מִצְרָיִם. וְכָל הַמַּרְבֶּה לְסַפֵּר בִּיצִיאַת מִצְרַיִם הֲרֵי זֶה מְשֻׁבָּח.

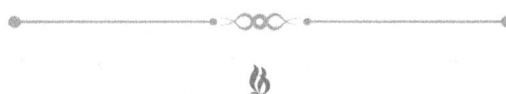

Hashem created mankind with free choice. He can choose between good and evil, right and wrong. This allows for reward and punishment.

Hashem took the Yidden *"out of there with a strong hand"* is not referring to the Egyptians who did not want the Yidden to leave. Rather, it is referring to the Yidden who were not worthy of being freed.

The Midrash writes that the Heavenly Court asked why the Yidden were being allowed to leave; they were no better than the Egyptians, as both were idol worshippers.

Hashem demonstrated His strong hand by silencing the Heavenly Court and taking the Yidden out of Egypt even though they were not worthy.

(Yaaros Dvash 1:17)

Hashem told the Heavenly Court that the Yidden are the descendants of the Avos; they are like a holy staff that has turned into a snake.

Rambam writes, "A miracle cannot be constant and everlasting as then it could no longer be viewed as miraculous and it would be described as a new reality."

When the Yidden left Egypt, they were not worthy. Hashem performed a miracle by removing their ability to choose, thus enabling them to leave. When the miracle concluded, the Yidden reverted back to how they had been living for hundreds of years in Egypt. And the holy staff reverted back to being a snake.

After the Yidden sinned with the Golden Calf, Hashem wanted to punish them. Moshe responded, "You took the Yidden out with great might and a strong hand." What was Moshe trying to convey with this statement?

Moshe was saying to Hashem, "You performed a miracle by changing the Yidden's capability to choose, and once the miracle concluded, they would eventually revert back to their former lifestyle." Hence, the Yidden should not be punished for the sin of the Golden Calf.

(Yaaros Dvash 1,17)

then we, and our children, and the children of our children, would still be enslaved to Pharaoh in Egypt. And even were we all wise, all intelligent, all aged, and all knowledgeable in the Torah, still the command would be upon us to tell of the Exodus out of Egypt; and whoever expands upon the recounting of the story of the Exodus from Egypt is praiseworthy.

וְאִלּוּ לֹא הוֹצִיא הַקָּדוֹשׁ בָּרוּךְ הוּא אֶת אֲבוֹתֵינוּ מִמִּצְרָיִם

"If Hashem had not taken our fathers out of Egypt . . ."

The posuk reads, *"Our fathers went down to Egypt, and we lived in Egypt for a long time. And the Egyptians mistreated us and our forefathers"* (Bamidbar 20:15).

When the posuk says, "Our fathers," it is not referring to our ancestors who were enslaved in Egypt. Rather, it is referring to Avrohom, Yitzchok, and Yaakov. They endured tremendous suffering, knowing that their descendants were enslaved in Egypt.

(Tiferet Yehonatan Chukas)

וְאִלּוּ לֹא הוֹצִיא הַקָּדוֹשׁ בָּרוּךְ הוּא אֶת אֲבוֹתֵינוּ מִמִּצְרַיִם הֲרֵי אָנוּ וּבָנֵינוּ וּבְנֵי בָנֵינוּ מְשֻׁעְבָּדִים הָיִינוּ לְפַרְעֹה בְּמִצְרָיִם

"If Hashem had not taken our fathers out of Egypt, then we, our children and our children's children, would have remained enslaved to Pharaoh in Egypt."

Lomdus

It seems the Haggadah is telling us the obvious. If Hashem had not taken us out, who then would have been capable of doing so?

The Talmud relates that the Prophet Elisha brought the Shunammite woman back to life. Tosfos asks, "Elisha was a Kohen, and a Kohen cannot come in contact with a corpse. How was Elisha able to do so?"

Tosfos answers that since Elisha was saving the life of this women, it was permitted for him to contaminate himself.

The Talmud records a question posed by an apostate. He asked, "The God of the Jews has the status of a Kohen. How then was He able to bury Moshe?"

Why didn't the apostate pose the question based on the events that occurred many years earlier by the Exodus from Egypt? Egypt was full of impurity and idols. How was Hashem able to enter Egypt to save the Jewish people?

At the time of the Exodus, the Yidden had reached the forty-ninth level of

מַעֲשֶׂה בְּרַבִּי אֱלִיעֶזֶר וְרַבִּי יְהוֹשֻׁעַ וְרַבִּי אֶלְעָזָר בֶּן עֲזַרְיָה וְרַבִּי עֲקִיבָא
וְרַבִּי טַרְפוֹן שֶׁהָיוּ מְסֻבִּין בִּבְנֵי בְרַק וְהָיוּ מְסַפְּרִים בִּיצִיאַת מִצְרַיִם כָּל
אוֹתוֹ הַלַּיְלָה, עַד שֶׁבָּאוּ תַלְמִידֵיהֶם וְאָמְרוּ לָהֶם רַבּוֹתֵינוּ הִגִּיעַ זְמַן
קְרִיאַת שְׁמַע שֶׁל שַׁחֲרִית.

אָמַר רַבִּי אֶלְעָזָר בֶּן עֲזַרְיָה הֲרֵי אֲנִי כְּבֶן שִׁבְעִים שָׁנָה, וְלֹא זָכִיתִי
שֶׁתֵּאָמֵר יְצִיאַת מִצְרַיִם בַּלֵּילוֹת עַד שֶׁדְּרָשָׁהּ בֶּן-זוֹמָא, שֶׁנֶּאֱמַר;

impurity. If they had remained any longer, they would have reached the fiftieth level, and they could no longer have been redeemed.

Tosfos has established that a Kohen can become impure if it is to save life. Likewise, Hashem was able to become impure as He was saving the lives of the Jewish people.

We now can appreciate the flow of the Haggadah.

"*We were slaves to Pharaoh in Egypt, and Hashem took us out.*"

If you ask, "Hashem is a Kohen. How could He enter an impure place?"

"*If Hashem had not taken our fathers out of Egypt, then we, our children and our children's children would have remained enslaved to Pharaoh in Egypt.*"

And the law is a Kohen is permitted to become impure to save life.

The Haggadah's intent is not to teach us the obvious. Rather, it is to explain how Hashem, who is a Kohen, could have acted in the manner that He did.

(Divrei Yehonatan)

מַעֲשֶׂה בְּרַבִּי אֱלִיעֶזֶר

"It happened that Reb Eliezer . . ."

Why is it significant to be aware of which rabbis were participating at the Seder? Furthermore, why does the Haggadah inform us that it took place in Bnei Brak?

The previous section concluded with the statement, "And the more one tells of the coming out of Egypt, the more admirable it is." Even though we were personally not enslaved in Egypt, we are obligated in retelling the story.

This story supports this position: Reb Eliezer and Reb Yehoshua were Leviim, and Reb Elazar ben Azaria and Reb Tarfon were Kohanim. The tribe of Levi were not enslaved in Egypt, yet these chachomim participated at the Seder.

Once Rabbi Eliezer and Rabbi Yehoshua and Rabbi Elazar ben Azaria and Rabbi Akiva and Rabbi Tarfon were gathered [for the seder] in Bnei Brak. And they told of the Exodus from Egypt all that night; until their students came in and said, "Teachers, the time for saying the *Shema* of the morning has come."

Rabbi Elazar ben Azaria said: I am like a seventy-year-old, but I could not accomplish that the Exodus from Egypt be mentioned every night. Until Ben Zoma interpreted: It is written,

Bnei Brak had many converts, as such they did not descend from those enslaved in Egypt, yet they also participated at the Seder.

Why, in fact, do converts need to participate in the mitzvah?

Second, shouldn't we be obligated in the mitzvah of retelling the story on the night we crossed the Yam Suf, not when we began to leave Egypt?

Moshe informed Pharaoh that the Yidden were leaving for only three days. The reason he misled Pharaoh and did not tell him directly that they were leaving permanently was to enable non-Jews to join them in the Exodus, resulting in the non-Jews being able to receive the Torah on Har Sinai.

Therefore, the gathering was in Bnei Brak, as the converts were rejoicing in having received the Torah.

(Pardes Reb Yehonatan)

אָמַר רַבִּי אֶלְעָזָר בֶּן עֲזַרְיָה

"Rabbi Elazar ben Azaria said . . ."

הֲרֵי אֲנִי כְּבֶן שִׁבְעִים שָׁנָה

"I am like a man of seventy."

What is the significance of being seventy years old?

When a person reaches seventy, he enters the best years of his life. At seventy, a person no longer has a desire or is interested in worldly pleasures. Therefore, it has always been the practice to appoint a person to a position of leadership when they are seventy, as then their actions will be for the sake of heaven.

(Pardes Reb Yehonatan)

לְמַעַן תִּזְכֹּר אֶת יוֹם צֵאתְךָ מֵאֶרֶץ מִצְרַיִם כֹּל יְמֵי חַיֶּיךָ יְמֵי חַיֶּיךָ הַיָּמִים.
כֹּל יְמֵי חַיֶּיךָ - הַלֵּילוֹת וַחֲכָמִים אוֹמְרִים; יְמֵי חַיֶּיךָ - הָעוֹלָם הַזֶּה. כֹּל
יְמֵי חַיֶּיךָ - לְהָבִיא לִימוֹת הַמָּשִׁיחַ

וְלֹא זָכִיתִי שֶׁתֵּאָמֵר יְצִיאַת מִצְרַיִם בַּלֵּילוֹת

"And never have I merited to find the command to speak of the Exodus from Egypt at night."

Hashem told Avrohom that the fourth generation would return to Israel. Therefore, the Yidden would be in Egypt for three generations. A generation is seventy years. Hence, three generations is two hundred ten years. And that was the number of years the Yidden were in Egypt.

As such, there is no need to count the nights of their enslavement to justify why the Yidden left earlier than the designated time, since they were not meant to be in Egypt for more than three generations. Therefore, there would be no need to mention the Exodus from Egypt at night. It was only as a result of Ben Zoma's interpretation did Reb Elazar come to the understanding that the exodus must be mentioned at night as well.

(Pardes Reb Yehonatan)

כֹּל יְמֵי חַיֶּיךָ

"All the days of your life . . ."

Ben Zoma is of the opinion that [the additional word] *all* teaches us that we are obligated to remember the Exodus from Egypt at night.

The chachomim argue and learn that the word *all* teaches us that we will be obligated in remembering the Exodus even after the coming of Moshiach.

Rabbi Elazar ben Azaria sides with Ben Zoma. Why didn't he follow the opinion of the chachomim?

Rabbi Elazar ben Azaria is of the opinion that the mitzvos will remain obligatory even during the times of Moshiach. Therefore, we don't need the word *all* to teach us that we are obligated in mentioning the Exodus during the Messianic era.

As such, he accepted the opinion of Ben Zoma that the word *all* comes to include the nights.

(Yaaros Dvash 2, 18)

"So that you remember the day of your exodus from Egypt all the days of your life."

"The days of your life" would mean only during the days; "all the days of your life" includes the nights.

But the sages say, "The days of your life" would mean only in this world; "all the days of your life" brings in the time of Moshiach.

כֹּל יְמֵי חַיֶּיךָ הַלֵּילוֹת

"The days of your life" refers to the days, [and the additional word] "all" indicates the inclusion of the nights.

A person is alive during the day and at night. Therefore, when the Torah writes, *"The days of your life,"* it must be referring to the twenty-four-hour period of both day and night. Why then do we need the word *all* to include the night?

The Talmud (Brochos 57a) writes that sleep is one-sixtieth of death. When a person sleeps, he is experiencing one-sixtieth of death. As such, it cannot be included in the words *"the days of your life,"* and as such, we need the additional word *all* to include the night.

(Tiferet Yehonatan Chayei Sarah)

🔥

Sleep is one-sixtieth of death. Therefore, *"The days of your life"* could not include the night, as night possesses an element of death, and we need the word *all* to include night.

As there will be no death with the coming of Moshiach, there will be no need for sleep. Based on this, we can offer the following understanding to the chachomim's opinion.

The chachomim interpret the phrase, *"All the days of your life"* in the following manner:

"The days of your life" refer to this world and only during the day. The Shema need only be recited during the day. And the word *all* includes the times of Moshiach, when the obligation of reciting the Shema will be by day and by night since, in the times of Moshiach, people will have no need to sleep and the phrase *"your life"* can include the night.

This is the understanding of the posuk, *"Avrohom was old advanced in days"* (Bereishis 24:1). The Hebrew word בָּא, which is translated to mean "advanced," can also

בָּרוּךְ הַמָּקוֹם, בָּרוּךְ הוּא, בָּרוּךְ שֶׁנָּתַן תּוֹרָה לְעַמּוֹ יִשְׂרָאֵל, בָּרוּךְ הוּא.
כְּנֶגֶד אַרְבָּעָה בָנִים דִּבְּרָה תוֹרָה: אֶחָד חָכָם, וְאֶחָד רָשָׁע, וְאֶחָד תָּם,
וְאֶחָד שֶׁאֵינוֹ יוֹדֵעַ לִשְׁאוֹל.

חָכָם מָה הוּא אוֹמֵר?

be translated to mean "coming close." The posuk now reads, *"Avrohom was old and coming close to days,"* meaning Avrohom would soon be passing away and he would enter a realm where there would only be day as there would be no need for sleep.

(Tiferet Yehonatan Chayei Sarah)

בָּרוּךְ הַמָּקוֹם, בָּרוּךְ הוּא, בָּרוּךְ שֶׁנָּתַן תּוֹרָה לְעַמּוֹ יִשְׂרָאֵל

"Blessed is the Omnipresent One, blessed be He! Blessed is He who gave the Torah to His people Israel, blessed be He!"

Lomdus

Why is the section where we thank Hashem for giving us the Torah at Har Sinai written immediately after being taught that we need to remember the Exodus from Egypt even at night?

Hashem had informed Avrohom that the Yidden would be exiled for four hundred years. There are two reasons given why the Yidden did not remain in Egypt for that amount of time. First, the angels were also exiled to Egypt and their presence reduced the years of slavery. Second, the Yidden were made to work at night, and this curtailed the years of slavery.

When Moshe went to heaven to receive the Torah, the Midrash records a three-way conversation that took place between Hashem, the angels, and Moshe. The angels protested and felt the Torah should remain in heaven. Hashem instructed Moshe to rebut their challenge. Moshe said to the angels, "The Torah does not speak to you. As the Torah writes, *'I took you out of Egypt.'* Were you then enslaved in Egypt that Hashem needed to redeem you?"

Clearly, the Midrash is of the opinion that the angels were *not* enslaved in Egypt. Therefore, the reason the Yidden's stay in Egypt was shortened was because they were enslaved at night. Hence, we mention the Exodus at night.

Blessed is the Omnipresent—blessed is He. Blessed is the One who gave His people Israel, the Torah—blessed is He.

The Torah relates to four types of sons—one who is wise, one who is wicked, one with a simple nature, and one who does not know how to ask.

The wise son, what does he say?

If the Yidden had remained any longer in Egypt, we would have fallen to the fiftieth level of impurity and we would never have been redeemed and we would not have received the Torah on Mount Sinai. We were able to leave prior to the designated time since we also worked at night and that is why we are obligated in remembering the Exodus at night. Hence, after learning of the obligation to remember the Exodus at night, we immediately bless Hashem for giving us the Torah. Because if we would not have worked at night, we would never have been able to leave Egypt to receive the Torah.

(Midrash Yehonatan)

חָכָם מָה הוּא אוֹמֵר?

The wise one, what does he say?

Lomdus

What is the connection between the section *"Blessed is Hashem who gave the Torah to His nation the Yidden"* and the question posed by the chochom?

The meforshim ask, "The halocho is that all korbonos have to be brought in the Beis Hamikdosh. How then could the Yidden bring the Korban Pesach in Egypt?"

They answer that since Hashem was with them, it was as if the Yidden were in the Beis Hamikdosh.

While the Yidden were in Egypt, Hashem had the status of a lender, and a lender is not permitted to enter the home of the borrower to take a security, as the posuk says, *"You shall stand outside and the man to whom you are extending the loan shall bring the security to you outside."* (Devorim 24:11). As such, Hashem could not have been in Egypt.

The halocho forbidding the lender from entering the home of the borrower is for when the loan is not yet due; however, if the loan is outstanding, the lender is granted permission.

This distinction would justify Hashem being in Egypt only if the Yidden had been enslaved for four hundred years, as Hashem had told Avrohom that would be the length of their servitude. However, the Yidden were in Egypt only for two hundred and ten years. How then was Hashem able to enter Egypt?

There is an opinion that the angels were also enslaved. Adding their years to the years that the Yidden were enslaved totals four hundred years, thus allowing Hashem to enter Egypt.

The Talmud (Shabbos 88b) records that, when Moshe went up to heaven to receive the Torah, the angels wanted the Torah to remain with them in heaven. Hashem told them, the posuk says, *"I am the Lord your God who has taken you out of Egypt* (Shemos 20:2), did you then descend to Egypt?" From this conversation, it is evident that the angels were not enslaved in Egypt.

Based on the above, we can appreciate the order of the Seder. *"Blessed is Hashem who gave the Torah to the Yidden,"* and He did not give it to the angels. The reason He did not give it to the angels is because they were not enslaved.

As such, we do not have four hundred years of slavery. Hence, the Yidden left early, thus not allowing Hashem to enter Egypt. If Hashem was not in Egypt, how did the Yidden bring the Korban Pesach outside the Beis Hamikdosh?

That is the question posed by the chochom when he asks, *"What is the eidus?"* The *eidus* refers to the Korban Pesach, and he is asking, "How could the Yidden bring the Korban Pesach outside of the Beis Hamikdosh?"

(Pardes Reb Yehonatan)

There are three categories of mitzvos: eidus, chukim, and mishpatim. At the Seder, we have mitzvos in all three categories.

Eating the matzah is part of eidus, or testimony, as the posuk says, *"They were driven out of Egypt and they could not tarry"* (Shemos 12:39). Eating the matzah reminds us how we escaped.

The Korban Pesach is part of chukim, or statute, as the posuk says, *"This is the statute [chukas] of the Korban Pesach"* (Shemos 12:43).

Eating the maror is part of mishpatim, or judgment; it reminds us of the judgment the Egyptians inflicted on the Yidden, as the posuk says, *"And they made their lives bitter"* (Shemos 1:14).

The chochom asks why it is necessary to have three different types of reminders at the Seder. It should be sufficient with one.

The answer we give the chochom is *"After eating the Korban Pesach, one does not eat anything more."* The reason we don't eat after eating the meat of the korban is to ensure that the taste of the meat remains until the morning.

This halocho and the reason given answer the chochom's question about why we need three different types of reminders.

Our Rabbis teach that a person remembers something that is unusual, and doing something three different ways is unusual and will cause a person to remember.

As such, we do three different things at the Seder to remember the Exodus.

(Ahavat Yehonatan)

&

The posuk says, *"I remember to you the kindness of your youth, the love of your nuptials, your following Me in the desert, in a land not sown"* (Yirmiyahu 2:2).

The three mitzvos the Yidden fulfilled on the night of the Exodus demonstrated their complete faith in Hashem. They did not take any food supplies, nor did they allow their dough to rise to bake bread. They were content with eating only matzah.

Eating maror helps the digestive process. The Yidden ate maror on the night of the Exodus even though it would cause them to become hungrier faster. They also ate the Korban Pesach. The korban was roasted. Meat that is roasted is digested quicker than meat that is cooked in a pot of water.

We too commemorate on the night of the Seder the matzah, maror, and Korban Pesach that the Yidden ate when they left Egypt to remind Hashem of *"the loving kindness of our youth."*

However, if the Yidden would have known that Hashem would soon be performing a miracle and they would receive the manna on a daily basis, then eating the matzah, Korban Pesach, and maror would not be considered virtuous.

This is the question posed by the chochom. The chochom is under the impression that the Yidden knew they would be receiving the manna. He therefore asks, "What are the testimonies, the statutes, and the laws which Hashem has commanded you?" By this, he means, why do we need to perform at the Seder testimonies (eating the matzah), statutes (eating the Korban Pesach), and laws (eating the maror)?

We therefore answer him, *"After eating the Korban Pesach one does not eat anything more."* The word אֲפִיקוֹמָן can be divided into two words מָן אָפִיק excluding the manna.

The answer we give the chochom is, *"After eating the Korban Pesach [in Egypt the Yidden did not know that] they would be eating manna."* Therefore, eating the matzah, Korban Pesach, and maror does show the Yidden's absolute faith in Hashem.

(Ahavat Yehonatan Pesach)

מָה הָעֵדוֹת וְהַחֻקִּים וְהַמִּשְׁפָּטִים אֲשֶׁר צִוָּה יְהֹוָה אֱלֹהֵינוּ אֶתְכֶם. וְאַף אַתָּה אֱמוֹר לוֹ כְּהִלְכוֹת הַפֶּסַח: אֵין מַפְטִירִין אַחַר הַפֶּסַח אֲפִיקוֹמָן:

The wise son asks, *"What are the testimonies, the statutes, and the laws which Hashem has commanded you?"*

The wicked son asks, *"What is this service to you?"* He says, "to you," not "to him," thus excluding himself from the community. He has denied that which is fundamental.

The wise son seems to be posing the same question as the wicked son. He, too, seems to exclude himself from the community when he asks, *"which Hashem has commanded you?"* Why is he not considered wicked?

The wise son has no questions. He is comfortable and accepting of all that Hashem asks of him. However, he seeks answers to be able to respond to the challenges he will encounter. This understanding of the wise son's position is reflected in the manner the wise son's question is introduced in the Torah.

The posuk states, וְהָיָה כִּי יִשְׁאָלְךָ בִנְךָ מָחָר לֵאמֹר *"When your son will ask you in the future, saying"* (Shemos 13:14). The word *saying* generally means "to convey the information to others." The posuk reads, *"When your* wise *son will ask you tomorrow"* about the Exodus from Egypt *"saying"* because he wants to share it with others who are questioning Hashem and His Torah.

Therefore, in the Haggadah, when the wise son asks, *"What are the testimonies, the statutes, and the laws which Hashem has commanded you?"* the wise son is not excluding himself from the community. Rather, the question *"which Hashem has commanded you?"* is the question the wise son is asked by others, and their question is posed in a manner similar to the wicked son, who removes himself from the rest of the community.

(Tiferet Yehonatan Voetchanan)

אֵין מַפְטִירִין אַחַר הַפֶּסַח אֲפִיקוֹמָן

"After eating the Korban Pesach one does not eat anything more."

Lomdus

The Talmud Yerushalmi (Pesochim 10:4) offers another answer posed by the chochom. It answers by quoting the posuk, *"Hashem took us out of Egypt with a strong hand"* (Shemos 13:14).

"What are the testimonies, the statutes and laws, that Hashem our God commanded you?"

And you must tell him the laws of the Pesaḥ offering: "After eating the Pesach offering one does not eat anything more."

Why does the Talmud Yerushalmi offer a different answer to the question posed by the chochom?

They do so because of the diverging reasons as to why the Korban Pesach must be eaten when one is already satiated.

The Talmud Yerushalmi (Pesochim 6:4) explains that the Torah prohibits a person from breaking a bone of the korban. The Rabbis were concerned that if a person is very hungry, in his haste, he may inadvertently come to break a bone while eating the meat. They, therefore, established that the Korban Pesach should be eaten when a person is no longer hungry. The Talmud Bavli (Pesochim 119b) explains that eating the Korban Pesach at the end of the meal will ensure that the taste of the korban will remain in his mouth.

The difference between the two opinions is apparent when eating matzah for the afikomen. If the reason we must eat the korban when we are already satiated is to ensure that the taste of the korban will linger in our mouth, then the afikomen must also be eaten at the end of the meal. If, however, the reason is to ensure we don't break any bones, since we are eating matzah as a remembrance and there are no bones in matzah, then we would not need to eat the afikomen at the end of the meal.

We can now understand the different answers given by the Talmud Yerushalmi and the Haggadah to the question posed by the chochom.

The Talmud Yerushalmi is consistent. It states that the reason the Korban Pesach is eaten at the end of the meal is to ensure that we don't break any bones. That reason is not applicable to why we eat the afikomen at the end of the meal; therefore, the Talmud Yerushalmi could not answer the chochom by telling him "we cannot eat anything after the afikomen" and it therefore answers, "Hashem took us out with a strong hand."

The Haggadah is in agreement with the Talmud Bavli and the reason we are to eat the Korban Pesach at the end is to ensure the taste remains in our mouth. That reason is equally applicable to when we eat the matzah as the afikomen. Therefore, the Haggadah answers the chochom by telling him that "We do not eat any foods after eating the afikomen."

(Pardas Reb Yehonatan)

רָשָׁע מָה הוּא אוֹמֵר?

The chochom possess a number of questions. If we are celebrating Pesach as a remembrance of the Exodus, shouldn't we celebrate it for one day, as was the case in Egypt?

The beginning of the Exodus occurred on the fifteenth of Nissan with the killing of the firstborn. The Yidden did not see and experience this miracle as they were not permitted to leave their homes. However, through the splitting the sea when all the Egyptians died, the Yidden saw Hashem's mighty hand, as the posuk says, *"And the Yidden saw Hashem's mighty hand"* (Shemos 14:31).

When discussing the Exodus, the Torah says, *"You shall say to your son, we were slaves to Pharaoh in Egypt, and Hashem took us out of Egypt with a strong hand"* (Devorim 6:21). The next posuk says, *"And Hashem gave signs and wonders."* The first posuk is referring to the plague of the slaying of the firstborn and the Exodus. The second posuk is referring to the miracle of Krias Yam Suf.

Since we only experienced signs and wonders by Krias Yam Suf, we celebrate Pesach for seven days.

(Tiferet Yehonatan Voetchanan)

רָשָׁע מָה הוּא אוֹמֵר? מָה הָעֲבוֹדָה הַזֹּאת לָכֶם

**The wicked one, what does he say? The wicked son asks,
"What is this service to you?!"**

He cannot understand why we continue to remember the Exodus from Egypt if we are still in exile.

We answer the wicked son that remembering the Exodus from Egypt gives us hope and encouragement that we, too, will be redeemed and merit the final redemption.

(Alon Bachut 1:7)

If the rosho participated in the Korban Pesach, why does he exclude himself by stating, *"What is this service to you?"* If he did not participate, then he is punished with kares, not just having his teeth blunted?

The Haggadah states that since he removed himself from the rest of the community, he is deemed to be a denier of Hashem. Why is he called a denier of

The wicked son, what does he say?

Hashem? The rosho failed to bring the Korban Pesach. Why does that warrant that he be labeled a nonbeliever?

Finally, how do we know that this rosho would not have been redeemed from Egypt?

The Midrash writes that when the Yidden were crossing the sea, the angels challenged Hashem, questioning why He was drowning the Egyptians but saving the Yidden, as both nations were idol worshippers.

Based on the Midrash that the Yidden and the Egyptians were idol worshippers, we can understand the question posed by the rosho. He asks, *"What is this service?"* meaning why was it necessary to bring a Korban Pesach and place the blood on the doorpost? And when the rosho adds, *"To you,"* he is referring to the tzaddik, meaning a tzaddik should not need to place blood on the doorpost to identify the home as belonging to a Yid, as a tzaddik believes that Hashem examines the hearts of mankind. And if Hashem does so, then Hashem would know which homes belong to the Yidden, even without the blood on the doorposts.

The rosho is a heretic, not because he did not bring the korban; it is because he believes that Hashem doesn't examine the hearts of man.

When the angels questioned why the Yidden were saved and the Egyptians drowned, the Yidden had a valid explanation: they served the idols out of fear, while the Egyptians served them based on love. And since Hashem examines the hearts of man, he would see the clear distinction.

However, the rosho, who does not believe Hashem examines our hearts, sees no apparent difference between the Jewish people and the Egyptians, and as such the Yidden, including this rosho, should have perished as well.

(Pardes Reb Yehonatan)

A fool considers Hashem's mitzvos hard labor; a wise person doesn't see it as work at all.

If we know the reason for the mitzvos—for example, if we were informed that eating non-kosher food is harmful to our health, how could we consider not eating non-kosher a burden. If we were told that a certain food is poisonous, would we find it difficult and challenging to refrain from eating it?

Hashem did not inform us of the reason for each particular mitzva; therefore, fulfilling the mitzvos is considered an avodah. As the Midrash points out, a person

מָה הָעֲבוֹדָה הַזֹּאת לָכֶם. לָכֶם—וְלֹא לוֹ. וּלְפִי שֶׁהוֹצִיא אֶת עַצְמוֹ מִן הַכְּלָל כָּפַר בְּעִקָּר. וְאַף אַתָּה הַקְהֵה אֶת שִׁנָּיו וֶאֱמוֹר לוֹ: "בַּעֲבוּר זֶה עָשָׂה יְהֹוָה לִי בְּצֵאתִי מִמִּצְרָיִם". לִי וְלֹא לוֹ. אִלּוּ הָיָה שָׁם, לֹא הָיָה נִגְאָל:

תָּם מָה הוּא אוֹמֵר?

מָה זֹּאת. וְאָמַרְתָּ אֵלָיו "בְּחוֹזֶק יָד הוֹצִיאָנוּ יְהֹוָה מִמִּצְרַיִם מִבֵּית עֲבָדִים".

וְשֶׁאֵינוֹ יוֹדֵעַ לִשְׁאוֹל—אַתְּ פְּתַח לוֹ, שֶׁנֶּאֱמַר, וְהִגַּדְתָּ לְבִנְךָ בַּיוֹם הַהוּא לֵאמֹר, בַּעֲבוּר זֶה עָשָׂה יְהֹוָה לִי בְּצֵאתִי מִמִּצְרָיִם.

יָכוֹל מֵרֹאשׁ חֹדֶשׁ?

should not say, "I will not eat pig because it is bad and I find it despicable"; rather, he should say that the reason he doesn't eat pig is because it is Hashem's will.

This understanding is further seen in the fact that during the first fourteen years after the Yidden entered the Land of Israel, they were permitted to eat any foods that would normally be prohibited. If such foods were deemed harmful to the person, how could Hashem permit the Yidden to eat them?

Rather, the reason we fulfill the mitzvos is because it is the will of Hashem. And, at times, He permitted us to eat non-kosher and at times He prohibited it.

With this approach to why we keep Hashem's mitzvos, we can appreciate the question posed by the rosho. He asks, "What is this service?" He questions, if we fulfill the mitzvos because that is the will of Hashem, what then is the difference between having to follow the instructions of Pharaoh and having to follow the laws enacted by Hashem? Moreover, he questions whether the mitzvos of Hashem are more difficult and severe then the decrees of Pharaoh.

The rosho's mistake is equating Hashem's laws to Pharaoh's decrees. While we perform Hashem's mitzvos because that is His will, all Hashem's mitzvos are beneficial to the person unlike the harsh decrees of Pharaoh.

(Tiferet Yehonatan Voeschanan)

"What is this service to you?"

"To you," he says, not to him. When he sets himself apart from the community, he denies the very core of our beliefs. And you must blunt his teeth and tell him, "Because of this Hashem acted for me when I came out of Egypt." "For me," and not for *him;* had he been there, he would not have been redeemed.

The simple son, what does he say?

"What is this?"

And you must tell him, "With a strong hand Hashem brought us out of Egypt, from the grip of slavery."

And the one who does not know how to ask, you must open [the story] for him, as it is said:

"And you shall tell your child on that day, 'Because of this Hashem acted for me when I came out of Egypt.'"

One might have thought that the obligation to discuss the Exodus commences with the first day of the month.

יָכוֹל מֵרֹאש חֹדֶשׁ?

One might have thought that the obligation to discuss the Exodus commences with the first day of the month.

Why would we contemplate retelling the story of the Exodus on Rosh Chodesh?

The Talmud writes (Shabbos 156a) that Avrohom was a great astrologer, and he was able to demonstrate how the planets were not gods and there was a power that controlled them: Hashem.

One of the ways he came to this conclusion was, since a person can calculate when the next solar or lunar eclipse will occur, this proves that the planets are not gods. For if they were, how could mankind predict the exact paths of the solar system? Being a god, they could change their minds rather than follow a preordained path.

תַּלְמוּד לוֹמַר בַּיּוֹם הַהוּא. אִי בַּיּוֹם הַהוּא יָכוֹל מִבְּעוֹד יוֹם? תַּלְמוּד לוֹמַר בַּעֲבוּר זֶה בַּעֲבוּר זֶה לֹא אָמַרְתִּי, אֶלָּא בְּשָׁעָה שֶׁיֵּשׁ מַצָּה וּמָרוֹר מֻנָּחִים לְפָנֶיךָ.

מִתְּחִלָּה עוֹבְדֵי עֲבוֹדָה זָרָה הָיוּ אֲבוֹתֵינוּ, וְעַכְשָׁיו קֵרְבָנוּ הַמָּקוֹם לַעֲבוֹדָתוֹ, שֶׁנֶּאֱמַר: וַיֹּאמֶר יְהוֹשֻׁעַ אֶל כָּל הָעָם, כֹּה אָמַר יְהֹוָה אֱלֹהֵי יִשְׂרָאֵל, בְּעֵבֶר הַנָּהָר יָשְׁבוּ אֲבוֹתֵיכֶם מֵעוֹלָם, תֶּרַח אֲבִי אַבְרָהָם וַאֲבִי נָחוֹר, וַיַּעַבְדוּ

The movement of the celestial bodies prove Hashem's existence; hence, we may have thought to retell the story on Rosh Chodesh, a day that demonstrates Hashem's existence and that He is the Master of the universe.

(Pardes Reb Yehonatan)

מִתְּחִלָּה עוֹבְדֵי עֲבוֹדָה זָרָה הָיוּ אֲבוֹתֵינוּ

"In the beginning, our fathers served idols."

בְּעֵבֶר הַנָּהָר יָשְׁבוּ אֲבוֹתֵיכֶם מֵעוֹלָם

"Your fathers used to live on the other side of the river."

The Torah writes, *"Hashem instructed Avrohom, you should leave your land, your birthplace, and your father's home"* (Bereishis 12:1).

A person is very much influenced by where they were born, when they were born, and the zodiac sign they were born under.

Hashem informed Avrohom that he was being removed from these three influencers. *"Leave your land,"* and you will not be influenced by where you were born. *"Leave your birthplace,"* and you will not be influenced by when you were born. *"Leave your father's home,"* and you won't be influenced by the zodiac sign you were born under.

Hashem blessed Avrohom with three distinct blessings, each corresponding to one of the three influencers in a person's life.

The posuk reads, *"I will make you into a great nation, I will bless you, I will make your name great and you shall be a blessing"* (Bereishis 12:2).

"I will make you into a great nation"—this promise is connected to *"you should leave your birthplace."* Hashem tells Avrohom he will no longer be linked to his past. It will be a new beginning, the start of a great nation. As the Midrash writes, when

Therefore, the Torah says, "on that day." But based on the expression "on that *day*" one might think that it should be done while it is still daytime. Therefore, the Torah says, "Because of this"—implying that "I am speaking only of the time when matzah and maror are placed before you."

Originally our fathers were idol worshippers, but now the Omnipresent has drawn us close in His service, as it is said: "Yehoshua said to all the people, 'This is what Hashem God of Israel has said: Beyond the river your fathers always dwelled—Terach the father of Avraham, the father of Nachor—and

Avrohom left his birthplace, it was as if he was reborn. That is why the Yidden are called the children of Avrohom, and they are not known as the children of Noach.

"I will bless you"— this promise is linked to *"you shall leave your father's home."*

The custom was for a father to bless his children prior to his demise. Avrohom left prior to his father, Terach, passing away. As such, he would not be receiving his father's blessings. Hashem, therefore, informs Avrohom that he should not be concerned as He will bless him.

"I will make your name great" is aligned with *"you shall leave your land."*

Initially he was called Avrom, meaning that he was the master of only his land. Hashem promised him, *"I will make your name great. You will now be called Avrohom; you will be the father of all, including the sinners who will return."*

(Tiferet Yehonatan)

Why was it necessary for the Haggadah to inform us where they were living?

Living outside of Israel, they were influenced by the mazal of that particular country and that led them to serve idols. Therefore, Hashem instructed Avrohom to move to the Land of Israel. In Israel, a person is under the direct influence of Hashem, as the posuk says, *"The eyes of Hashem your God are always upon it"* (Devorim 11:12).

(Pardes Reb Yehonatan)

Avrohom is known as Avrohom Ivri. The word *Ivri* means "other side" as the Haggadah writes, *"Your father Avrohom used to live on the other side of the river."*

When Hashem commanded Moshe to go to Pharaoh, the posuk says, "So Moshe

אֱלֹהִים אֲחֵרִים. וָאֶקַּח אֶת אֲבִיכֶם אֶת אַבְרָהָם מֵעֵבֶר הַנָּהָר וָאוֹלֵךְ אוֹתוֹ בְּכָל אֶרֶץ כְּנָעַן, וָאַרְבֶּה אֶת זַרְעוֹ וָאֶתֶּן לוֹ אֶת יִצְחָק. וָאֶתֵּן לְיִצְחָק אֶת

and Aaron came to Pharaoh and said to him, 'So said the Lord, the God of the Ivrim [Hebrews]'" (Shemos 10:3).

Why does Moshe refer to Hashem as the God of the Ivrim?

The Kuzari writes that humanity is like a tree. The roots are a person's forebearers while the branches are the person's offspring.

Avrohom was a descendant of Ever. Ever was a tzaddik, and he chastised the people for wanting to build the Tower of Bavel.

Ever was the root and his root remained concealed until the birth of Avrohom.

Since Avrohom's roots take him back to Ever, he was called Avrohom Ivri.

(Tiferet Yehonatan Bo)

Pharaoh used the Yidden as slaves to build large, fortified cities. He felt the reason the Tower of Bavel was not completed was because they did not speak lashon hakodesh. By speaking lashon hakodesh, they could have used special Hebrew words and phrases that would have caused the angels to help in the building of the tower.

Pharaoh knew that the Yidden spoke only Hebrew. Hence, he would be successful in building his cities.

Ever was opposed to the building of the tower. Therefore, Moshe referred to Hashem as the God of the Ivri. To remind Pharaoh just as the people were unsuccessful in building the tower, so too Pharaoh would be unsuccessful in building his cities.

(Tiferet Yehonatan Bo)

תֶּרַח אֲבִי אַבְרָהָם

"Terach, the father of Avrohom"

Terach and his ancestors were idol worshippers; therefore, the Yidden who were his descendants needed to be enslaved in Egypt.

(Tiferet Yehonatan Mishpotim)

they served other gods. But I took your father Avraham from beyond the river, and I led him all the way across the land of Canaan, and I multiplied his offspring and gave him Yitzchak. And to Yitzchok I gave

---

וָאוֹלֵךְ אוֹתוֹ בְּכָל־אֶרֶץ כְּנָעַן

"I led him throughout the whole land of Canaan."

This statement is based on the posuk, *"And Abram passed through the land, until the place of Shechem, until the plain of Moreh, and the Canaanites were then in the land"* (Bereishis 12:6).

Why was it necessary for the Torah to tell us that the land was occupied by the Canaanites?

Rashi writes that Noach divided the lands amongst his sons, and he gave Shem the Land of Israel. As such, what right did Avrohom have to conquer the land from the descendants of Shem?

The Torah writes that the Canaanites were living in Israel to justify Avrohom's actions. The Canaanites were not Shem's offspring. They had stolen the land from Shem's descendants. Therefore, Avrohom who was a descendant of Shem was within his rights to take the land back from the Canaanites.

(Tiferet Yehonatan)

From a different perspective, stating that the Canaanites were living in Israel explains why Avrohom only traveled to Shechem and did not travel throughout Israel.

Hashem had designated that the Canaanites would occupy the land for a specific period of time and that time had not yet elapsed therefore Avrohom was unable to retake all of the land and was only able to reach Shechem.

(Tiferet Yehonatan)

וָאֶתֵּן לוֹ אֶת יִצְחָק

"Gave him Yitzchok"

When the three angels came to visit Avrohom, Sarah overheard them saying that she and her husband would be blessed with a son. Her reaction was to laugh and question their assurance.

That we don't err and assume that Sarah's reaction was inappropriate, they named their son Yitzchok, which means "laughter," as Avrohom and Sarah

יַעֲקֹב וְאֶת עֵשָׂו, וָאֶתֵּן לְעֵשָׂו אֶת הַר שֵׂעִיר לָרֶשֶׁת אוֹתוֹ, וְיַעֲקֹב וּבָנָיו יָרְדוּ מִצְרָיִם.

would not have named their son *laughter* to be a constant reminder of Sarah's inappropriate reaction when first hearing she was to be blessed with a child.

(Tiferet Yehonatan Vayero)

The Midrash writes the name יִצְחָק is spelled י, which has a numerical value of ten, corresponding to the Ten Commandments. The letter צ, which has a numerical value of ninety corresponds to Sarah's age when she gave birth to her son. The letter ח, which has a numerical value of eight, corresponds to the bris milah that takes place on the eighth day. Yitzchok was the first to have a bris at eight days. And the letter ק, which has a numerical value of one hundred corresponds to Avrohom's age when Yitzchok was born.

(Tiferet Yehonatan Vayero)

Sarah's name at birth was שָׂרַי. While she was called Sarai, she was unable to bare children. It was only after her name was changed to שָׂרָה was she able to become pregnant.

The letter *yud* was upset that it was removed from the righteous woman, Sarai. Hashem pacified the *yud* by placing it as the first letter of Avrohom and Sarah's son, Yitzchok.

The posuk detailing the birth of Yitzchok says, אֲשֶׁר יָלְדָה לּוֹ שָׂרָה יִצְחָק. *"Whom Sarah had borne to him, Yitzchok"* (Bereishis 21:3). The posuk can be understood to mean that *Sarah* conceived after her name was changed from Sarai and *"had borne to him, Yitzchok"*. And his name received the letter *yud* after the letter *yud* had complained about being removed from the name Sarai.

(Tiferet Yehonatan Vayero)

וָאֶתֵּן לְיִצְחָק אֶת יַעֲקֹב

"And to Yitzchok I gave Yaakov..."

The posuk reads, *"And afterward, his brother emerged, and his hand was grasping Esov's heel, and he named him Yaakov. Now Yitzchok was sixty years old when she gave birth to them"* (Bereishis 25:26).

Yaakov and Esov, and I gave Esov Mount Seir as an inheritance, while Yaakov and his children went down to Egypt."

There is a correlation between Yitzchok's being sixty and the name Yaakov.

The word עָקֵב means "heel." If Yaakov was given his name because, at birth, he was holding Esov's heel, then he should have been simply named עָקֵב. Why was the letter י added such that his name was יַעֲקֹב?

When Yitzchok was fifty, his wife Rivkah was thirteen. She was at an age where she could bear children. Why then did they have to wait another ten years to be blessed with children?

The Land of Israel has ten spiritual levels; each level corresponds to a year. The ten levels are reached after a period of ten years. Prior to the birth of Yaakov, Yitzchok wanted to attain the ten levels of spirituality and therefore was blessed once the ten years had elapsed.

Hence, his son's name was Yaakov עָקֵב, and the additional letter י, whose numerical value is ten, alluded to the ten levels of spirituality that was reached by waiting ten years prior to bearing children.

(Tiferet Yehonatan Vayero)

וָאֶתֵּן לְיִצְחָק אֶת יַעֲקֹב וְאֶת עֵשָׂו

"And to Yitzchok I gave Yaakov and Esov."

Regarding the shirah the Yidden sang after the miracle of Krias Yam Suf, the posuk says, *"Then the chieftains of Edom were startled; [as for] the powerful men of Moab, trembling seized them; all the inhabitants of Canaan melted"* (Shemos 15:15).

What caused the three nations—Edom, Moab, and Canaan—to become so frightened?

Edom was a descendant of Esov. They assumed that the blessings Hashem gave Yaakov when he was fleeing from his brother, Esov, and the blessings he received from his father, Yitzchok, had not come to fruition. The Yidden had been enslaved in Egypt. They believed the Yidden were a nation of sinners, unworthy of these blessings.

Hashem's blessing to Yaakov was that his descendants achieve *"And you shall spread westward and eastward . . ."* (Bereishis 28:14). When the Yidden merited the miracle of splitting the Yam Suf, they realized that Hashem's blessing had been fulfilled.

What led them to this realization?

בָּרוּךְ שׁוֹמֵר הַבְטָחָתוֹ לְיִשְׂרָאֵל, בָּרוּךְ הוּא. שֶׁהַקָּדוֹשׁ בָּרוּךְ הוּא חִשַּׁב
אֶת הַקֵּץ, לַעֲשׂוֹת כְּמוֹ שֶׁאָמַר לְאַבְרָהָם אָבִינוּ בִּבְרִית בֵּין הַבְּתָרִים,

The blessing וּפָרַצְתָּ יָמָה וָקֵדְמָה "and you shall spread westward and eastward" can be understood to be referring to water. As the word יָמָה means "water" and the blessing is the waters split, creating a dry path for the Yidden to cross.

Esov's strength came from water. The Romans were descendants of Esov. The Midrash relates that the angel Gavriel took a staff, plunged it into the sea, and built on it the great city of Rome.

When Edom saw that the Yidden were more powerful than water and were able to drive it away, they became extremely fearful.

Moab were descendants of Avimelech. They believed that Yitzchok was the son of Avimelech, not the son of Avrohom. As such, they are the legitimate heirs of Yitzchok.

There is a tradition that a mamzer will die prematurely by drowning. And that is why Pharaoh instructed that all the Jewish males born be cast into the sea, as Pharaoh believed that the married Jewish women were impregnated by the Egyptians and, as such, the offspring were illegitimate.

Likewise, Moab thought that Yitzchok was illegitimate, as his real father was Avimelech. As such, the Yidden should have drowned in the sea. When they saw that the sea split for them, they realized that Yitzchok was the son of the Avrohom and the Yidden were his legitimate descendants. As such, they became extremely frightened.

Canaan felt that since Hashem did not lead the Yidden on a direct course to the Land of Israel, it must be because the time of their entry into the land had not yet arrived. However, after the miracle of Krias Yam Suf, they understood that the Yidden went on a longer route to show the world that Hashem is all powerful, both on dry land and in the sea.

Canaan was now fearful as the Yidden were indeed marching toward the land of Canaan.

(Tiferet Yehonatan Vayigash)

Why does the Haggadah inform us that Hashem gave Mount Seir to Esov as an inheritance?

Blessed is the One Who has kept His promise to Israel! Blessed is He.

For the Holy One calculated the end and fulfilled what He had spoken to our father Avraham in the Covenant Between the Parts.

The Land of Israel was to be given to the nation that would experience exile. Esov wanted to be exiled to Mount Seir, as then he would be entitled to inherit the Land of Israel.

Therefore, the Haggadah informs us of Hashem's kindness that he gave Mount Seir to Esov as an inheritance. Because it was an inheritance, he would not be entitled to claim the Land of Israel.

(Pardes Reb Yehonatan)

בָּרוּךְ שׁוֹמֵר הַבְטָחָתוֹ לְיִשְׂרָאֵל בָּרוּךְ הוּא

"Blessed is He who keeps His promise to Israel, blessed be He."

שֶׁהַקָּדוֹשׁ בָּרוּךְ הוּא חִשַּׁב אֶת הַקֵּץ

"For the Holy One calculated the end."

What is the Haggadah emphasizing by stating that Hashem *"calculated the end"*?

The Talmud (Yoma 9b) writes, "The Yidden were told the reason for the destruction of the first Beis Hamikdosh; therefore, they were also informed that they would return to their land in seventy years. By the second Beis Hamikdosh where their sins were not revealed, how long the golus would last was also not revealed."

Since the Torah does not explain why the Yidden had to be enslaved in Egypt, why does the Torah give the number of years that we were to be enslaved in Egypt? By doing so, Hashem is showing His love of the Yidden.

The years of exile were calculated from the birth of Yitzchok. When Yitzchok was sixty, Yaakov was born. Yaakov was one hundred and thirty when he went down to Egypt. The Yidden were in Egypt for two hundred ten years, giving us a total of four hundred years.

The calculation is seemingly not accurate, as Yaakov was born during Yitzchok's sixtieth year, which was the first year of Yaakov's life. Likewise, the one hundred and thirtieth year of Yaakov's life was also the first year of the exile. That said, two years are missing from the total of four hundred years.

שֶׁנֶּאֱמַר: וַיֹּאמֶר לְאַבְרָם, יָדֹעַ תֵּדַע כִּי גֵר יִהְיֶה זַרְעֲךָ בְּאֶרֶץ לֹא לָהֶם,
וַעֲבָדוּם וְעִנּוּ אֹתָם אַרְבַּע מֵאוֹת שָׁנָה.

Yitzchok's sixtieth year and Yaakov's first year are counted as two years.

The year the Yidden left Egypt was added to the total. This gives us the two missing years.

That Hashem calculated the end, meaning while certain events happened in the same calendar year, Hashem counted them as separate years, showing us Hashem's kindness. If the year of the Exodus were not counted, we would have had to remain in Egypt an extra year. Then we would have sunk to a level of impurity, and we would not have been able to be redeemed.

(Pardes Reb Yehonatan)

כִּי גֵר יִהְיֶה זַרְעֲךָ בְּאֶרֶץ לֹא לָהֶם

"You shall know that your seed will be strangers in a land that is not theirs."

"In a land that is not theirs" can refer to the Yidden meaning they will be enslaved in a land that is not theirs. Or it may be referring to the captors, that the Yidden will be strangers in a land that has been occupied by a foreign entity.

The second approach is consistent with the fact that Yoseph resettled the citizens of the land. He would transfer people from one city to the next. Therefore, people were no longer living in their ancestral homes.

(Tiferet Yehonatan Beshalach)

וַעֲבָדוּם וְעִנּוּ אֹתָם אַרְבַּע מֵאוֹת שָׁנָה

"And they will be enslaved and oppressed for four hundred years."

According to a number of opinions, the exile began with the birth of Yitzchok. There are a number of similarities between Yitzchok's experiences and what the Yidden endured.

They include:

There was a famine in the land, and Yitzchok and Rivka traveled to Gerar. While in Gerar, the posuk states, *"Avimelech commanded all the people, saying, 'Whoever touches this man or his wife shall be put to death'* (Bereishis 26:11).

Avimelech was aware through sorcery that the Jewish people's exile began with the birth of Yitzchok. Avimelech also knew that Hashem would judge the people

As it is said: "He said to Avram, 'Know that your descendants will be strangers in a land not their own, and they will be enslaved and oppressed for four hundred years;

who persecuted Yitzchok and Rivka as He did with the Egyptians. Therefore, he warned his nation not to harm Yitzchok and Rivka.

When the Yidden left Egypt, they left with great wealth. Similarly, once Yitzchok had attained financial success, Avimelech insisted that he leave, just as his descendants did four hundred years later.

When Avimelech saw Yitzchok's successes, he became frightened. He thought that Yitzchok would rise up and overthrow the king, as the posuk says, *"And Avimelech said to Yitzchok, 'Go away from us, for you have become much stronger than we'"* (Bereishis 26:16). Likewise, Pharaoh shared the same fear as Avimelech. As the posuk says, *"Get ready, let us deal shrewdly with them, lest they increase, and a war befall us, and they join our enemies and wage war against us and depart from the land"* (Shemos 1:10).

(Tiferet Yehonatan Toldos)

Hashem informed Avrohom that his children would be strangers in a foreign land for four hundred thirty years. The Yidden were only in Egypt for two hundred ten years, what happened to the missing years?

There are many answers given, including the following:

The four hundred thirty years began either at the birth of Yitzchok or from the time Hashem made His covenant with Avrohom.

This answer seems inadequate, as Avrohom, Yitzchok, and Yaakov were not living in a foreign country; they were residing in their homeland.

How can we begin calculating the Jewish exile while they were still living in Israel?

While it is true that they were living in Israel, they were in constant fear of being attacked by other nations. The nations did not appreciate that Avrohom's family was teaching the world that there is a God who is the master of the universe.

Furthermore, Yitzchok suffered at the hands of Yishmoel, and Esov sought to kill Yaakov.

As such, it was considered as if they were living in a foreign land.

(Midrash Yehonatan)

Only the Yidden were meant to be exiled; however, Hashem joined them in their exile. Hashem's participation caused the duration of the exile to be shortened.

How is this answer consistent with Rashi's understanding of why Moshe needed to pray to Hashem outside of the metropolis? The Torah writes that Moshe left the city to pray to Hashem, and Rashi explains that Moshe had to leave the city since Hashem was not present in the city, as it was full of idols.

If so, how was Hashem together with the Yidden during their exile in Egypt?

The Yidden are called Hashem's children, and the law is that one can become impure for the sake of one's relatives. As such, Hashem was allowed to be exiled in a place of impurity.

This understanding is alluded to in the sequence of the posukim. The last posuk of Parshas Bo reads, *"With a strong hand Hashem took us out of Egypt"* (Shemos 13:16). The first posuk of Parshas Beshalach reads, *"And it was when Pharaoh sent the nation and Hashem did not lead them . . . because it was close"* (Shemos 13:17).

The posuk is explaining why Hashem led the Yidden in a roundabout way. This understanding is based on translating the word קָרוֹב to mean "close." However, it can also be understood to mean "a relative." By translating the word to mean "relative," the posukim are explaining why Hashem allowed Himself to become impure.

The posukim now read, *"Hashem took the Yidden out with a strong hand."* How could Hashem enter a place of such impurity? The answer is given in the next posuk: Since the Yidden are Hashem's relatives, He was allowed to become impure.

(Midrash Yehonatan)

Only six hundred thousand Yidden were meant to be enslaved. The Torah tells us that the Yidden multiplied greatly. As such, there were many more enslaved Yidden. The increase in the number of Yidden compensated for the reduced years of slavery.

(Tiferet Yehonatan Lech Lecha)

The missing years were made up by the other four exiles the Yidden will endure until the Messianic era.

This answer seems inadequate as the Yidden have been exiled for a lot more than the missing one hundred ninety years.

The posuk says, *"They will enslave them for four hundred years"* (Bereishis 15:13). The next posuk reads, וְגַם אֶת הַגּוֹי *"And also the nation."* Take the first word of the second posuk and add it to the previous posuk. The word to be added is וְגַם, which also means *"and more."*

We can now read the phrase to mean, "The Yidden will be exiled for *more* than four hundred years."

(Keshet Yehonatan)

۞

Hashem had promised Avrohom that after being in exile for four hundred years, his children would return to Eretz Yisroel, as the posuk says, *"They shall return **here** in the fourth generation"* (Bereishis 15:13). This did not occur, as after the Exodus from Egypt, the Yidden wandered in the desert for another forty years.

Second, how were the Yidden permitted to slaughter the Korban Pesach in Egypt when the lamb had to be slaughtered at the site of the Beis Hamikdosh?

The answer given is that Hashem miraculously transported the Yidden on the wings of eagles on the fourteenth of Nissan to the site of the Beis Hamikdosh to bring the korban.

Consequently, Hashem did fulfill His promise of returning the Yidden to Israel after the four hundred years when He returned the Yidden to bring their sacrifice.

(Tiferet Yehonatan Beshalach)

וְגַם אֶת הַגּוֹי אֲשֶׁר יַעֲבֹדוּ דָן אָנֹכִי וְאַחֲרֵי כֵן יֵצְאוּ בִּרְכֻשׁ גָּדוֹל.

וְאַחֲרֵי כֵן יֵצְאוּ בִּרְכֻשׁ גָּדוֹל

"And then they will leave with great wealth."

Why does Hashem preface His instruction by saying *"please"*? It stands to reason that the Yidden would follow the request even without Hashem saying please.

There are two reasons Hashem prefaced His remarks with "please."

First, the Yidden were scared that if they borrowed items of value from the Egyptians and then left, the Egyptians would chase after them to retrieve their possessions. Indeed, Hashem wanted the Egyptians to chase after the Yidden, and by the Yidden taking their belongings, this would be an added incentive to do so.

Second, it was to placate the tzaddikim who felt that leaving Egypt with great wealth would indicate that they were fleeing for an ulterior motive and they were not escaping to fulfill the word of Hashem but rather because they wanted to keep their new found wealth.

Therefore, Hashem had said *please,* thereby honoring His commitment to Avrohom that the Yidden would leave Egypt with great wealth.

(Tiferet Yehonatan)

Shlomo Hamelech writes, *"A tzaddik eats to satisfy his appetite"* (Mishlei 13:25). The tzaddik is content if he has sufficient monies to ensure that he does not go hungry.

Seemingly wealth is not considered a virtue worth striving for.

Why then does Hashem promise Avrohom that his offspring will leave Egypt extremely rich?

The answer is that anyone who subjugates the Yidden the way the Egyptians did deserves the death penalty.

The attribute of strict justice was responsible for imposing this decree. However, there was a caveat that the sentence could not be enforced unless the person or nation had reached their limit in terms of sin.

Since the Yidden had concluded their years of slavery prematurely, the attribute of strict justice could not enforce the death penalty.

Therefore, Hashem instructed the Yidden to take the Egyptians' wealth, thus reducing them to paupers. The halocho is that from a certain perspective a poor

but know that I shall judge the nation that enslaves them, and then they will leave with great wealth.'"

person has the status of a dead person. As such, the attribute of strict justice could not complain to Hashem and demand that the Yidden remain in Egypt in order for it to be able to eventually punish the Egyptians. The Egyptians had already received their punishment, as a poor man is a dead man.

The purpose of taking the Egyptians wealth was not to enrich the Yidden; it was to impoverish the Egyptians.

(Ahavat Yehonatan Shoftim)

Prior to the Yidden leaving Egypt, Hashem instructed them, *"And let them borrow, each man from his friend and each woman from her friend, silver vessels and golden vessels."*

Why did Hashem instruct the Yidden to take items of value from the Egyptians?

The surrounding nations spread a false rumor that the Egyptians despised the Jewish people to such an extent that they simply banished them from their country.

To disprove this rumor, the Yidden were told to take the Egyptians' gold and silver. For if there was any truth to this claim, the Egyptians would have retaken all of their possessions. Since they did not do so clearly demonstrates that it was Hashem who led the Yidden out of Egypt, much to the chagrin of Pharaoh and the Egyptians.

(Tiferet Yehonatan)

The two posukim on which this section of the Haggadah is based reads in full:

"And He said to Avram, 'You shall surely know that your seed will be strangers in a land that is not theirs, and they will enslave them and oppress them, for four hundred years.' (Bereishis 15:134)

'And also the nation that they will serve will I judge, and afterwards they will go forth with great possessions.' (Bereishis 15:14)

Let us focus on five phrases in these two posukim:

כִּי גֵר *"Strangers."* The Baal Haturim writes that the last letter of these two words are the letters י and ר, which have a numerical value of two hundred ten. This is the number of years the Yidden were enslaved in Egypt.

אַרְבַּע מֵאוֹת שָׁנָה *"Four hundred years."* The Yidden were meant to be enslaved in Egypt for four hundred years.

וְגַם אֶת הַגּוֹי *"And also the nations."* Rashi explains that the word *also* is

The matzos are covered and the wine cup is raised as the following paragraph is recited:

וְהִיא שֶׁעָמְדָה לַאֲבוֹתֵינוּ וְלָנוּ. שֶׁלֹּא אֶחָד בִּלְבַד עָמַד עָלֵינוּ לְכַלּוֹתֵנוּ,

unnecessary, and it is meant to teach us that the Yidden would be enslaved by other nations and that would complete the years the Yidden were not enslaved in Egypt.

וְאַחֲרֵי כֵן יֵצְאוּ בִּרְכֻשׁ גָּדוֹל *"The Yidden will leave Egypt with great wealth."*

The posuk can be understood to mean the following: The Yidden were strangers in Egypt for only two hundred ten years. The question then is why did Hashem say they would be strangers in Egypt for four hundred years?

The posuk adds the word *also*, meaning that the Yidden would experience exile at the hands of other nations, thereby fulfilling the quota of four hundred years and deserving the reward of leaving with great wealth.

(Ahavat Yehonatan)

🔥

The Midrash (Bereishis Rabah 44:21) writes that Hashem gave Avrohom the choice—either his children would be exiled and placed in servitude, or they would have to experience gehenom. Hashem advised him to choose exile.

Avrohom's dilemma was perhaps the Yidden would not be able to bear the exile and they would assimilate amongst the non-Jewish nations and become idol worshippers. And due to their sins during their exile, they would also endure gehenom.

Hashem told him to choose exile, as Hashem was sure that the Yidden would not rebel against Him and all their years in exile would not affect their eternal bond with Hashem. Hashem reassured Avrohom, telling him that the Yidden would leave Egypt with great wealth not just with financial wealth but also with great spiritual wealth and would merit to receive the Torah.

Hashem also promised Avrohom that the wicked of the Jewish people would perish in Egypt and as such they would not cause the Yidden to sin after the Exodus. This is alluded to in the words וְגַם אֶת הַגּוֹי and also the nation that caused harm to the Yidden would be punished. The word וְגַם *also* comes to include the wicked of the Bnei Yisroel.

(Ahavat Yehonatan Lech Lecha)

The matzos are covered and the wine cup is raised as the following paragraph is recited:

And this [promise] is what has stood by our fathers and us; for it was not only one man who rose up to destroy us:

Why did the Egyptian exile begin with the birth of Yitzchok?

The Yidden were to be exiled for four hundred years. Two hundred ten of those years were in Egypt. At their conclusion, Hashem had to take the Yidden out with great haste, for if they had stayed even a moment longer, they would not have been able to be redeemed.

If the exile had not commenced from Yitzchok's birth, their time in Egypt would have had to be lengthened, and as a result, they would have reached the fiftieth gate of impurity.

(Ahavat Yehonatan Lech Lecha)

Avrohom was a hundred when Yitzchak was born, and he passed away at one hundred seventy-five. Since the exile began with Yitzchok's birth, Avrohom experienced seventy-five years of exile. Avrohom was worried whether he could maintain his holiness and spirituality for such a lengthy period. Therefore, Hashem promised him that he would return to his fathers in peace.

(Ahavat Yehonatan Lech Lecha)

וְהִיא שֶׁעָמְדָה לַאֲבוֹתֵינוּ וְלָנוּ

"And this [promise] is what has stood by our ancestors and us."

The Haggadah does not mention what the "this" is.

The previous section concluded by quoting the posuk "and then they will leave with great wealth." What is the significance of being told that the Yidden left wealthy?

"And this is what stood by our ancestors [in Egypt]" was their lack of desire to become wealthy. And in that merit, the Yidden were redeemed.

(Tiferet Yehonatan Voera)

אֶלָּא שֶׁבְּכָל דּוֹר וָדוֹר עוֹמְדִים עָלֵינוּ לְכַלּוֹתֵנוּ, וְהַקָּדוֹשׁ בָּרוּךְ הוּא מַצִּילֵנוּ מִיָּדָם.

The cup is put down and the matzos are uncovered.

צֵא וּלְמַד מַה בִּקֵּשׁ לָבָן הָאֲרַמִּי לַעֲשׂוֹת לְיַעֲקֹב אָבִינוּ: שֶׁפַּרְעֹה לֹא גָזַר אֶלָּא עַל הַזְּכָרִים, וְלָבָן בִּקֵּשׁ לַעֲקֹר אֶת הַכֹּל. שֶׁנֶּאֱמַר: אֲרַמִּי אֹבֵד אָבִי, וַיֵּרֶד מִצְרַיְמָה וַיָּגָר שָׁם בִּמְתֵי מְעָט, וַיְהִי שָׁם לְגוֹי גָּדוֹל עָצוּם וָרָב.

When the Haggadah says, "And this," the *this* is referring to the posuk, *"Hashem spoke to Moshe and Aaron and He commanded them concerning the Bnei Yisroel . . . To let the Bnei Yisroel out of the land of Egypt"* (Shemos 6:13).

The Hebrew word for *command them* is וַיְצַוֵּם, which is similar to the word צוּתָא, which means "to join, to connect." The Haggadah is teaching that when the Yidden are united as one, *this* display of unity will ensure their protection.

(Tiferet Yehonatan Voera)

צֵא וּלְמַד

"Go [to the posuk] and learn."

The years Yaakov spent with his father-in-law, Lavan, were considered years of exile. Lavan was the source of all impurity, and if Yaakov had remained living with him, he would have descended into the impurity.

Therefore, Hashem removed him from Lavan, and Yaakov continued his exile in Egypt.

(Tiferet Yehonatan)

וַיֵּרֶד מִצְרַיְמָה – אָנוּס עַל פִּי הַדִּבּוּר.

"And he went down to Egypt" [compelled by Divine decree]."

The posuk reads, *"Moshe sent messengers from Kadesh to the king of Edom. So says your brother Israel, 'You know of all the hardship that has befallen us. Our*

in every single generation people rise up to destroy us—but the Holy One, Blessed be He, saves us from their hands.

The cup is put down and the matzos are uncovered.

Go [to the posuk] and learn what Lavan the Aramean sought to do to our father Yaakov: Pharaoh condemned only the boys to death, but Lavan sought to uproot everything, as it is written: "An Aramean sought my father's death, and he went down to Egypt and resided there, just a handful of souls; and there he became a nation—large, mighty, and great."

fathers went down to Egypt, and we lived in Egypt for a long time. And the Egyptians mistreated us and our forefathers'" (Bamidbar 20:14,15).

When Moshe said, "*You know of all the hardship that has befallen us,*" he is referring to the sale of Yoseph by his brothers. Moshe was impressing upon the king of Edom the graveness of sinas chinam and what it can cause.

(Tiferet Yehonatan Chukas)

וַיֵּרֶד מִצְרַיְמָה

"And he went down to Egypt . . ."

שֶׁלֹּא יָרַד יַעֲקֹב אָבִינוּ לְהִשְׁתַּקֵּעַ בְּמִצְרַיִם אֶלָּא לָגוּר שָׁם שֶׁנֶּאֱמַר: וַיֹּאמְרוּ אֶל פַּרְעֹה לָגוּר בָּאָרֶץ בָּאנוּ

"But only to live there temporarily. Thus, it is said, 'They said to Pharaoh, we have come to sojourn in the land."

The Torah writes, לֹא תְתַעֵב מִצְרִי כִּי גֵר הָיִיתָ בְאַרְצוֹ "*You shall not despise an Egyptian for you were a sojourner in his land"* (Devorim 23:8).

The Hebrew word for *despise* is תְתַעֵב, which can also mean "desire." The posuk can be understood to mean, "*You shall not desire to be as the Egyptians, for you were a sojourner in his land and you should not be drawn to his way of life.*" Egypt was a very immoral land steeped in idol worship and witchcraft. Hashem was concerned that the Yidden would want to assimilate with the Egyptians and copy their lifestyle, hence the warning.

(Tiferet Yehonatan Ki Teitzei)

וַיֵּרֶד מִצְרַיְמָה—אָנוּס עַל פִּי הַדִּבּוּר.

וַיָּגׇר שָׁם—מְלַמֵּד שֶׁלֹּא יָרַד יַעֲקֹב אָבִינוּ לְהִשְׁתַּקֵּעַ בְּמִצְרַיִם אֶלָּא לָגוּר שָׁם, שֶׁנֶּאֱמַר: וַיֹּאמְרוּ אֶל פַּרְעֹה, לָגוּר בָּאָרֶץ בָּאנוּ, כִּי אֵין מִרְעֶה לַצֹּאן אֲשֶׁר לַעֲבָדֶיךָ, כִּי כָבֵד הָרָעָב בְּאֶרֶץ כְּנָעַן, וְעַתָּה יֵשְׁבוּ נָא עֲבָדֶיךָ בְּאֶרֶץ גֹּשֶׁן.

בִּמְתֵי מְעַט—כְּמָה שֶׁנֶּאֱמַר: בְּשִׁבְעִים נֶפֶשׁ יָרְדוּ אֲבֹתֶיךָ מִצְרַיְמָה, וְעַתָּה שָׂמְךָ יְהֹוָה אֱלֹהֶיךָ כְּכוֹכְבֵי הַשָּׁמַיִם לָרֹב.

וַיְהִי שָׁם לְגוֹי—מְלַמֵּד שֶׁהָיוּ יִשְׂרָאֵל מְצֻיָּנִים שָׁם.

וְעַתָּה שָׂמְךָ יְהֹוָה אֱלֹהֶיךָ כְּכוֹכְבֵי הַשָּׁמַיִם לָרֹב

"And now Hashem has made you as many as the sky has stars."

Pharaoh understood that the way the Yidden were increasing in number was nothing short of miraculous, and without a doubt, it was caused by Hashem's direct intervention. He, therefore, sought a plan whereby Hashem would forsake His people and Pharaoh would be able to do with them as he pleased.

As part of this plan, Pharaoh appointed Jews to enforce his decrees. The Jews would have to ensure that the work quotas were filled. They would be responsible for collecting the taxes. Pharaoh was hoping this would lead to inner turmoil among the Yidden. And disunity, division, animosity, and hatred among the Jewish people would ensure.

Pharaoh knew this outcome would cause Hashem to remove His presence from among the Jewish people.

And he went down to Egypt—Compelled by Divine decree

And resided there—From this, we learn that our father Yaakov went down not to settle in Egypt but only to reside there for a time. "They said to Pharaoh, 'We have come to reside in this land, for there is no pasture for your servants' flocks, for the famine is heavy in the land of Canaan; and now, if you please, let your servants dwell in the land of Goshen.'"

With a small number of people—As it is said: "Your fathers were but seventy souls when they went down to Egypt—and now Hashem has made you as many as the sky has stars."

And there he became a nation—From this, we learn that Israel was distinct there.

What Pharaoh failed to realize is that, while it is true there may be times when the Jewish people do not see eye to eye, it will never be ongoing and everlasting. There is an unbreakable bond between one Jew and another. It is a bond fashioned by the unity of our souls.

What better example of this than Yoseph's relationship with his brothers. They wanted to kill him and eventually sold him into slavery, yet when they were reunited, Yoseph treated them with great love and respect.

When the posuk says, "*Pharaoh did not know about Yoseph,*" it wishes to impart that Pharaoh did not appreciate the kind of eternal bond that existed between Yoseph and his brothers. He did not recognize that their love was strong, deep, and eternal. And this love is part of the Jewish people's makeup. If Pharaoh would have realized this, he never would have accepted the advice of appointing Jewish taskmasters.

(Tiferet Yehonatan)

גָּדוֹל עָצוּם—כְּמָה שֶׁנֶּאֱמַר: וּבְנֵי יִשְׂרָאֵל פָּרוּ וַיִּשְׁרְצוּ וַיִּרְבּוּ וַיַּעַצְמוּ בִּמְאֹד מְאֹד, וַתִּמָּלֵא הָאָרֶץ אֹתָם.

וָרָב—כְּמוֹ שֶׁנֶּאֱמַר; רְבָבָה כְּצֶמַח הַשָּׂדֶה נְתַתִּיךְ, וַתִּרְבִּי וַתִּגְדְּלִי וַתָּבֹאִי

וּבְנֵי יִשְׂרָאֵל פָּרוּ וַיִּשְׁרְצוּ וַיִּרְבּוּ וַיַּעַצְמוּ בִּמְאֹד מְאֹד

"And the Bnei Yisroel were fertile, and they swarmed, and grew more and more numerous and strong . . ."

The Midrash shares an interesting episode that occurred with Rebbi Yehudah HaNasi. He was once giving a lecture, and he noticed that the listeners had begun to doze off. To grab their attention, he told them there was a woman in Egypt who had given birth to six hundred thousand children at one time.

Why did the audience let their minds drift and why did Rebbi Yehudah HaNasi specifically choose this ambiguous statement to pique their interest?

Obviously, the statement that a woman gave birth to six hundred thousand children at one time cannot be taken literally. The woman Reb Yehudah was referring to was Yocheved, who gave birth to Moshe Rabbeinu. And Moshe was comparable to six hundred thousand Yidden, as that is the number of Yidden he influenced in a positive manner.

Before his students had dozed off, Rebbi Yehudah had been elaborating on the posuk, *"Declare to my people their transgressions"* (Yeshayahu 58:1). He explained that the posuk was referring to the Talmidei Chachomim, who may sin unwittingly, yet they are judged as if they had sinned intentionally since they are very learned and, therefore, held to a higher standard.

When Rebbi Yehudah's students heard this, they felt it would be in their best interest to remain ignorant, as then they would not be held to a higher standard. As a result, they began to doze off as they no longer wanted to hear words of Torah.

Rebbi Yehudah understood the reason for their behavior. He knew that they

Great, mighty—"And the Bnei Yisrael were fertile, and they swarmed, and grew more and more numerous and strong, and the land was filled with them."

Numerous, as it is said, "I made you as numerous as the plants of the field; you increased and grew

weren't simply tired. He, therefore, needed to encourage them to continue learning and growing in Torah knowledge.

To do so, he shared with them a cryptic teaching that alludes to Moshe's greatness, hoping that his students would recognize the virtue in studying Torah and then they, too, would be in a position to influence their fellow Jew in coming closer to Hashem.

(Midrash Yehonatan Shemos)

רְבָבָה כְּצֶמַח הַשָּׂדֶה נְתַתִּיךְ

"I made you as numerous as the plants of the field."

The Yidden are compared to the plants of the field. Some plants are a source of nourishment, some are poisonous, and some are neither beneficial nor harmful for a human being.

Similarly, in Egypt, there were Yidden who were considered righteous and others who were viewed as simple. The simple Jew was referred to as the children of Yaakov and the righteous the children of Yisroel.

As the posuk says, *"Those who came* [to Egypt] *whom Yaakov caused to take root, Yisroel flourished and blossomed, and they filled the face of the world with fruitage"* (Yeshayahu 27:6).

The Yidden referred to as Yaakov only took root, while those designated as Yisroel flourished and blossomed. And then there were Yidden who filled the world with fruitage.

(Ahavat Yehonatan Shemos)

בַּעֲדִי עֲדָיִים שָׁדַיִם נָכֹנוּ וּשְׂעָרֵךְ צִמֵּחַ וְאַתְּ עֵרֹם וְעֶרְיָה וָאֶעֱבֹר עָלַיִךְ
וָאֶרְאֵךְ מִתְבּוֹסֶסֶת בְּדָמָיִךְ, וָאֹמַר לָךְ בְּדָמַיִךְ חֲיִי וָאֹמַר לָךְ בְּדָמַיִךְ חֲיִי

"Those who came [to Egypt] whom Yaakov caused to take root,
Yisroel flourished and blossomed, and they filled the face of
the world with fruitage."

The name Yaakov refers to the mixed multitude who did not have the same faith in Hashem as the Bnei Yisroel. The name Yaakov symbolizes the body that lusts after physical pleasures, while the name Yisroel represents the soul and refers to the Yidden who had complete trust in Hashem.

(Ahavat Yehonatan Shemos)

וְאַתְּ עֵרֹם וְעֶרְיָה

"However, you were naked and barren."

The Yidden were naked and barren from Torah and mitzvos, and they had attached themselves to idol worship. Moshe and the Elders found it difficult to believe that the time of redemption had arrived due to the Yidden's spiritual decline.

Hashem showed Moshe a snake; the snake symbolizes exile and servitude. Hashem was conveying to Moshe that the exile and enslavement would be the catalyst for the Yidden to do teshuvah and seek Hashem's salvation. As the posuk says, *"And the children of Israel sighed from the labor, and they cried out and their cry ascended to Hashem from the labor to embrace Hashem"* (Shemos 2:23).

Moshe was concerned that the Yidden would not be able to endure the suffering and he cries out to Hashem, *"Why have You harmed these people?"* (Shemos 5:22).

Hashem placates Moshe's concerns by instructing him to "stretch out your hand and grab its [the snakes] tail." What was Hashem imparting to Moshe with this instruction?

and you came to have great charm, beautiful of figure your hair grown, and you were naked and exposed."

"And I passed by you and saw you wallowing in your own blood—and I said to you, 'In your blood, live!' and I said, 'In your blood, live!'"

The Mishna writes, "It is better to be a tail unto lions then a head unto foxes" (Pirkei Avos 4:16).

Hashem was conveying to Moshe that if the Yidden would be truly humble, they would be able to overcome the hardships they were enduring.

This understanding is seen in the Talmud, as it writes, "Every wave that came on me I bowed my head" (Yevomos 121a). The waves that come crashing down on us represent life's challenges. By bowing our head in humility, we will be able to navigate the treacherous seas of the exile.

(Yaaros Dvash 1,3)

וָאֶעֱבֹר עָלַיִךְ וָאֶרְאֵךְ מִתְבּוֹסֶסֶת בְּדָמָיִךְ וָאֹמַר לָךְ בְּדָמַיִךְ חֲיִי וָאֹמַר לָךְ בְּדָמַיִךְ חֲיִי

"I passed over you and saw you wallowing in your bloods, and I said to you 'By your blood you shall live,' and I said to you 'By your blood you shall live!'"

This posuk mentions blood twice; it refers to the blood of bris milah and the blood of the Korban Pesach. The Yidden circumcised themselves and brought the Korban Erev Pesach. The blood of the circumcision and the sacrifice was then placed on the doorposts and the lintel of the Jewish home.

The Talmud writes that the child needs to be bathed on the third day of circumcision. The act of bathing a baby on the Shabbos may lead to desecrating the Shabbos. Therefore, the Tashbetz rules that if the bris does not occur when the baby is eight days old, it should not take place on a Thursday, as day three would be Shabbos and one should do their utmost to safeguard it.

The Yidden left Egypt on a Thursday; therefore, Erev Pesach was on a Wednesday. The third day was the Friday, thereby ensuring no desecration on the Shabbos.

(Midrash Yehonatan)

וַיָּרֵעוּ אֹתָנוּ הַמִּצְרִים וַיְעַנּוּנוּ, וַיִּתְּנוּ עָלֵינוּ עֲבֹדָה קָשָׁה.

וַיָּרֵעוּ אֹתָנוּ הַמִּצְרִים—כְּמָה שֶׁנֶּאֱמַר: הָבָה נִתְחַכְּמָה לוֹ פֶּן יִרְבֶּה, וְהָיָה כִּי תִקְרֶאנָה מִלְחָמָה וְנוֹסַף גַּם הוּא עַל שֹׂנְאֵינוּ וְנִלְחַם בָּנוּ, וְעָלָה מִן הָאָרֶץ.

וַיִּתְּנוּ עָלֵינוּ עֲבֹדָה קָשָׁה.

"And imposed hard labor upon us."

There are various opinions when the servitude began. One opinion is based on the posuk *"And Yoseph passed away . . . as did that whole generation . . ."*

The commentators explain that the whole generation passing away is referring to the Egyptians who were alive during the reign of Yoseph. And only after the generation had passed away did the servitude begin.

Why did the enslavement only begin with the next generation? Why didn't it commence as soon as Yoseph died?

The Egyptians were idol worshippers and never believed in Hashem. However, when Yoseph become viceroy, his actions caused them to believe in Hashem. They saw how Yoseph was able to predict the future, something their own leaders could not do. Yoseph had instructed the Egyptian men to have a bris. Those Egyptians who followed Yoseph's instructions saw their crops increase, while those who refused to be circumcised saw their produce wither.

Yoseph was a constant reminder that there must be a God in the world. The generation that saw and experienced this feared punishing God's nation. It was the next generation that persecuted the Yidden, as they no longer remembered Yoseph and all he epitomized.

(Tiferet Yehonatan)

The Egyptians did evil to us and afflicted us and imposed hard labor upon us.

The Egyptians did evil to us—"We must act wisely against [this people], in case it grows great, and when we are called to war they may join our enemies, fight against us, and rise up to leave the land."

הָבָה נִתְחַכְּמָה לוֹ פֶּן יִרְבֶּה וְהָיָה כִּי תִקְרֶאנָה מִלְחָמָה וְנוֹסַף גַּם הוּא עַל שֹׂנְאֵינוּ וְנִלְחַם בָּנוּ וְעָלָה מִן הָאָרֶץ

"Let us be wise toward him, lest he multiply, and it will be that when war is called, he too will join with our enemies and fight against us and go up from the land."

Pharaoh was intent on preventing the Yidden from multiplying. He, therefore, decreed that they should be enslaved. The Torah states that Pharaoh considered this approach as being one of great wisdom.

There are many different ways Pharaoh could have diminished the Jewish population. Why did he choose slavery and why was this considered an act of wisdom?

While the Yidden were living in Egypt, they actively encouraged the local population to embrace the Jewish faith. This was Pharaoh's fear—that his kingdom would convert to Judaism.

When the posuk says, *"lest he multiply,"* it is not referring to the Jewish people having many children; rather, it is speaking about the Egyptian population converting and becoming part of the Jewish people.

Enslaving the Yidden would discourage the Egyptians from wanting to convert. Pharaoh considered this an ingenious idea.

(Ahavat Yehonatan Shemos)

Who is *him* referring to?

If it is referring to the Yidden, how do we understand the continuation of the posuk that says, *"they join our enemies."* Who then are our enemies if not the Yidden?

וַיְעַנּוּנוּ—כְּמָה שֶׁנֶּאֱמַר: וַיָּשִׂימוּ עָלָיו שָׂרֵי מִסִּים לְמַעַן עַנֹּתוֹ בְּסִבְלֹתָם,
וַיִּבֶן עָרֵי מִסְכְּנוֹת לְפַרְעֹה אֶת פִּתֹם וְאֶת רַעַמְסֵס.

The word *him* is referring to the Egyptians who had circumcised themselves. Pharaoh felt that these Egyptians had shifted allegiance to the Jewish people. He feared they would instigate the revolt and would *"join our enemies,"* meaning the descendants of Yaakov, and attack them. He felt that if he taxed the Jewish people, which would include the circumcised Egyptians, they would renounce their Jewish connection and would rejoin their fellow Egyptians.

The posuk can now be understood to mean, *"Let us deal shrewdly with those Egyptians who circumcised themselves because they may join with the Jewish people who are our enemy. We will accomplish this by placing a tax on them all, and this will cause the circumcised Egyptians to separate themselves from the Jewish people."*

(Tiferet Yehonatan)

The Egyptians sought to kill the Yidden, yet they didn't want to kill them with their bare hands.

Pharoah consulted his sorcerers, who informed him that the Jewish leader would experience his downfall due to water. Therefore, the sorcerers contended that the best course of action to rid the country of the Jews would be to drown them in the sea.

When the Torah discusses the episode of Yoseph and his brothers, it writes that the brothers had decided to kill Yoseph. Reuven suggested that they throw him into a pit. Reuven felt that he would then be in a position to save him as the posuk says, *"So that I will be able to save him from their hands"* (Bereishis 37:22).

The Talmud writes that the pit was full of snakes and scorpions (Shabbos 22a). How then would Reuven be in a position to save Yoseph's life? Wouldn't the snakes and scorpions kill Yoseph? What is the difference between being killed by his brothers or by those deadly creatures?

Saving Yoseph from being killed by his brothers' hands necessitated a far greater miracle than the miracle needed to save him from the snakes and scorpions in the pit. The reason for this is that mankind has free will. Man can choose to take the life of another human being if he so desires. To stop the brothers from killing Yoseph, Hashem would have had to remove their free will.

And oppressed us—As it is said: "They placed taskmasters over [the people] to oppress them under their burdens; they built store cities for Pharaoh: Pisom and Raamses."

This was the dilemma that Pharaoh faced. On the one hand, drowning the Yidden was advantageous as they would not be directly killing them. However, it would take a far greater miracle to prevent the Egyptians from killing them directly, as Hashem would have to remove their free will.

However, once the sorcerers informed Pharaoh that the Jews would not be saved by water, Pharaoh decided the best way to deal with the Jews would be to cast them into the sea.

(Yaaros Dvash 2)

וַיְעַנּוּנוּ

"The Egyptians treated us badly."

לְמַעַן עַנֹּתוֹ בְּסִבְלֹתָם וַיִּבֶן עָרֵי מִסְכְּנוֹת לְפַרְעֹה אֶת פִּתֹם וְאֶת רַעַמְסֵס

"To afflict them with their burdens, and they built store cities for Pharaoh, namely Pithom and Ramses."

Pharaoh's advisors also suggested that the Yidden be made to build cities. One of the reasons for this was to force the Jewish men to leave their homes and move to the cities they were building. Their wives would be living alone, and the Egyptians could do as they pleased with them.

However, this did not occur. The Torah informs us the Jewish women were righteous, and they remained pure and holy. This is evident from the fact that they gave birth to six children at a time. Hashem would not perform a miracle of birthing six children if the women had been defiled.

This is the deeper understanding of the next posuk that reads, *"But as much as they would afflict them, so did they multiply."* The Egyptians *afflicted them* by sending them away to build cities, hoping to do as they please with their wives. Miraculously this did not occur, as is evident from the fact that *"so did they multiply."* They would not have multiplied if they had been contaminated by the Egyptian men.

It is well known that the Egyptian men were of a very low moral standing. How did the Jewish women preserve their holy standing?

וַיִּתְּנוּ עָלֵינוּ עֲבֹדָה קָשָׁה—כְּמָה שֶׁנֶּאֱמַר: וַיַּעֲבִדוּ מִצְרַיִם אֶת בְּנֵי יִשְׂרָאֵל בְּפָרֶךְ.

וַנִּצְעַק אֶל יְהֹוָה אֱלֹהֵי אֲבֹתֵינוּ, וַיִּשְׁמַע יְהֹוָה אֶת קֹלֵנוּ, וַיַּרְא אֶת עָנְיֵנוּ וְאֶת עֲמָלֵנוּ וְאֶת לַחֲצֵנוּ.

Hashem performed a miracle that the Egyptian men despised the Jewish women and found them repulsive, and as such, they left them alone. As the posuk says, *"And they [the Egyptians] despised the children of Israel"* (Shemos 1:12), including the Jewish women.

(Tiferet Yehonatan)

וַיִּתְּנוּ עָלֵינוּ עֲבֹדָה קָשָׁה

"And they put hard work upon us."

There are two reasons a person is made to experience pain and suffering. The attribute of justice is punishing the person for their transgressions. The other form of pain, as explained in the Talmud, is pain that stems from Hashem's love of the person, as Shlomo Hamelech writes, *"Hashem rebukes those that he loves"* (Mishlei 3:12).

When a person's physicality is weakened through suffering, this may result in his spirit coming to the fore and his mind being more conducive to comprehend loftier ideas. That is why prior to a person's passing, very often the body is weak, yet the mind is able to understand ideas that had previously been beyond the person's reach.

How does a person know the reason for their suffering? If the suffering curtails and infringes on their Torah study, then it cannot be considered suffering of love.

The Yidden were experiencing great suffering, and they wondered the reason for it.

The posuk says, וְלֹא שָׁמְעוּ אֶל מֹשֶׁה מִקֹּצֶר רוּחַ *"They did not listen to Moshe from shortness of breath"* (Shemos 6:9). The Hebrew word for shortness of breath is מִקֹּצֶר רוּחַ, which can also translate to "a reduced spirit."

The posuk now reads, *"They did not listen to Moshe because of a reduced spirit."*

And imposed hard labor on us—As it is said: "The Egyptians enslaved the Bnei Yisrael with hard labor."

"And we cried out to Hashem, god of our fathers, and Hashem heard our voice, and he saw our oppression and our labor and slavery."

The Yidden realized that since their suffering had impacted their spirituality, its source was not suffering of love.

(Tiferet Yehonatan Voera)

אֶת־בְּנֵי יִשְׂרָאֵל

"The children of Israel"

Yoseph instructed the Egyptians to undergo circumcision and many complied. When the Torah writes עַם יִשְׂרָאֵל *"the Jewish nation,"* it is including the Egyptians who had become circumcised. When the posuk writes, בְּנֵי יִשְׂרָאֵל *"the children of Israel,"* it refers only to Yaakov's descendants.

(Tiferet Yehonatan)

וַנִּצְעַק אֶל יְהֹוָה אֱלֹהֵי אֲבֹתֵינוּ וַיִּשְׁמַע יְהֹוָה אֶת קֹלֵנוּ

"And we cried out to Hashem, God of our fathers, and Hashem heard our voice."

The redemption took place in stages. The posuk reads, *"Therefore, say to the children of Israel, 'I am the Lord, and I will take you out from under the burdens of the Egyptians, and I will save you from their labor, and I will redeem you with an outstretched arm and with great judgments"* (Shemos 6:6).

The enslavement of the Jewish people ceased on Rosh Hashonoh, and the Exodus occurred six months later on Pesach.

"I will save you from their labor" refers to the end of the enslavement on Rosh Hashonoh, and the statement *"I will redeem you"* speaks of the Exodus on Pesach.

(Tiferet Yehonatan)

וַנִּצְעַק אֶל יְהֹוָה

"And we cried out to Hashem"

וַנִּצְעַק אֶל יְהֹוָה אֱלֹהֵי אֲבֹתֵינוּ—כְּמָה שֶׁנֶּאֱמַר: וַיְהִי בַיָּמִים הָרַבִּים הָהֵם וַיָּמָת מֶלֶךְ מִצְרַיִם, וַיֵּאָנְחוּ בְנֵי יִשְׂרָאֵל מִן הָעֲבוֹדָה וַיִּזְעָקוּ, וַתַּעַל שַׁוְעָתָם אֶל הָאֱלֹהִים מִן הָעֲבֹדָה.

וַיִּשְׁמַע יְהֹוָה אֶת קֹלֵנוּ. כְּמָה שֶׁנֶּאֱמַר: וַיִּשְׁמַע אֱלֹהִים אֶת נַאֲקָתָם, וַיִּזְכֹּר אֱלֹהִים אֶת בְּרִיתוֹ אֶת אַבְרָהָם, אֶת יִצְחָק וְאֶת יַעֲקֹב.

וַיַּרְא אֶת עָנְיֵנוּ—זוֹ פְּרִישׁוּת דֶּרֶךְ אֶרֶץ, כְּמָה שֶׁנֶּאֱמַר: וַיַּרְא אֱלֹהִים אֶת בְּנֵי יִשְׂרָאֵל וַיֵּדַע אֱלֹהִים

וַיְהִי בַיָּמִים הָרַבִּים הָהֵם וַיָּמָת מֶלֶךְ מִצְרַיִם

"During that long period, the king of Egypt died."

When the brothers came down to Egypt to buy supplies, Yoseph who had yet to reveal himself told them, *"With this you shall be tested, by Pharaoh's life you shall not leave this place unless your youngest brother [Binyomin] comes here"* (Bereishis 42:15).

Yoseph was alluding to the two things that need to occur prior to the Yidden leaving Egypt. "By Pharaoh's life," Pharaoh will need to have died, and "Unless your youngest brother [Binyomin] comes here," the Jewish people will have to experience servitude.

(Tiferet Yehonatan)

Rashi explains that Pharaoh did not die but had contracted tzoraas.
How does Rashi know that Pharaoh did not die?
Shlomo Hamelech writes, *"There is no ruling on the day of death"* (Kohelet 8:8).
Rashi explains this to mean, "[The power] of any king [is not] discernable on the day of his death. Everywhere [in Novi] you find [that Dovid is referred to as] 'King Dovid,' but on the day of his death [it states], *'And the days of Dovid drew near that*

And we cried out to Hashem, God of our fathers—As it is said: "It came to be, as a long time passed, that the king of Egypt died, and the Bnei Yisrael groaned under the burden of work, and they cried out, and their plea rose to God from amid the work."

And Hashem heard our voice—As it is said: "And God heard their groans, and God remembered His covenant with Avraham, Yitzchok, and Yaakov."

And he saw our oppression—The disruption of family life, as it is said: "And God saw the Bnei Yisrael, and God knew."

he should die' (Melochim I 2:1) and no kingship is mentioned. Since on the day that the king dies, he is no longer viewed as the king."

The posuk says, *"The king of Egypt died."* If he had indeed died, he would not have been referred to as a king. Therefore, Rashi is of the opinion that he was afflicted with tzoraas.

(Midrash Yehonatan Shemos)

וַיִּשְׁמַע יְהֹוָה אֶת קֹלֵנוּ

"And Hashem heard our voice."

וַיִּזְכֹּר אֱלֹהִים אֶת בְּרִיתוֹ

"Hashem remembered His covenant."

The Midrash explains that the reason the Yidden suffered in Egypt was because they no longer circumcised their sons. This is alluded to in the posuk, *"Hashem remembered His covenant."* The Hebrew word for *covenant* בְּרִית also means circumcision.

As such, the posuk can be understood to mean, *"Hashem remembered His* [mitzvah of] *bris"* that the Yidden did not fulfill, and therefore, He subjugated them to enslavement.

(Tiferet Yehonatan Vayera)

וְאֶת עֲמָלֵנוּ—אֵלּוּ הַבָּנִים. כְּמָה שֶׁנֶּאֱמַר: כָּל הַבֵּן הַיִּלּוֹד הַיְאֹרָה תַּשְׁלִיכֻהוּ וְכָל הַבַּת תְּחַיּוּן.

וְאֶת לַחֲצֵנוּ—זֶה הַדְּחַק, כְּמָה שֶׁנֶּאֱמַר: וְגַם רָאִיתִי אֶת הַלַּחַץ אֲשֶׁר מִצְרַיִם לֹחֲצִים אֹתָם.

The posuk states, *"And I also heard the moans of the Yidden whom the Egyptians are holding in bondage and I remembered my covenant"* (Shemos 6:5). The covenant is referring to the covenant between Hashem and Avrohom known as the *bris bein habsorim*, covenant of the parts.

Regarding the covenant of the parts, the posuk says, *"And also the nation that they [the Yidden] will serve will I judge"* (Bereishis 15:14). The word *also* is seemingly unnecessary. Rather, it is to inform that Hashem will also judge the Yidden at the same time.

(Tiferet Yehonatan Vayera)

וְאֶת עֲמָלֵנוּ

"And our labor ..."

The Torah writes, *"They did not hearken to Moshe because of [their] shortness of breath and because of [their] hard labor."*

The question begs to be asked, "On the contrary, should not their challenging servitude have been the impetus to want to believe that salvation was at hand?" Finally, after all these years of slavery their freedom has been proclaimed.

The Yidden had a tradition that the ultimate redeemer would be from the tribe of Yehuda, as the posuk says, *"The scepter will not depart [from the tribe of] Yehudah"* (Bereishis 49:10).

The Yidden were of the belief that the Exodus from Egypt would herald in the Messianic era. As Moshe was from the tribe of Levi, he could not be the redeemer. They, therefore, could not believe his declaration of their imminent redemption.

(Tiferet Yehonatan)

And our labor—This refers to the children, as it is said: "Throw every boy who is born into the river, and the girls let live."

And our oppression—This refers to the pressure expressed in the words: "I have also seen how the Egyptians are oppressing them."

כָּל הַבֵּן הַיִּלּוֹד הַיְאֹרָה תַּשְׁלִיכֻהוּ

"Throw every boy who is born into the river."

Pharaoh's evil decree stating that all male children be thrown into the Nile River was the impetus that led to the divorce of Moshe's parents, Amram and Yocheved. At the encouragement of their daughter, Miriam, they remarried. Yocheved was 130 years old at the time. The Talmud relates that a miracle occurred, and Yocheved appeared as a young lady. Six months after their wedding, Yocheved gave birth to Moshe. They were able to conceal him for three months, and then they had no choice and he had to be placed in the Yam Suf.

Why was it necessary for Hashem to turn back the clock, and Yocheved's appearance was that of a young lady? Couldn't Hashem have performed a miracle to allow an elderly woman of 130 years to give birth to a son?

There would have been no need to conceal Moshe's birth if Yocheved gave birth while physically showing her age, as the Egyptians would not be sending inspectors to see if Yocheved was pregnant or had given birth, as a lady of that age doesn't have children.

However, if Yocheved looked like a young lady, then she would be capable of having children, and the Egyptians would be sending officers to see whether, in fact, she had become pregnant. Therefore, there was no other option than to place Moshe in hiding.

(Pardes Reb Yehonatan)

Why did Pharaoh instruct the Egyptians to cast the Jewish male babies into the river. Why didn't he instruct that they be killed?

The Talmud (Sanhedrin 66b) records the story of an individual who came to Egypt to buy a donkey. The seller had used black magic, and it made a piece of

וַיּוֹצִאֵנוּ יְהֹוָה מִמִּצְרַיִם בְּיָד חֲזָקָה, וּבִזְרֹעַ נְטוּיָה, וּבְמֹרָא גָּדֹל, וּבְאֹתוֹת וּבְמֹפְתִים.

וַיּוֹצִאֵנוּ יְהֹוָה מִמִּצְרַיִם—לֹא עַל יְדֵי מַלְאָךְ, וְלֹא עַל יְדֵי שָׂרָף, וְלֹא עַל יְדֵי שָׁלִיחַ, אֶלָּא הַקָּדוֹשׁ בָּרוּךְ הוּא בִּכְבוֹדוֹ וּבְעַצְמוֹ. שֶׁנֶּאֱמַר: וְעָבַרְתִּי בְאֶרֶץ מִצְרַיִם בַּלַּיְלָה הַזֶּה, וְהִכֵּיתִי כָל בְּכוֹר בְּאֶרֶץ מִצְרַיִם מֵאָדָם וְעַד בְּהֵמָה, וּבְכָל אֱלֹהֵי מִצְרַיִם אֶעֱשֶׂה שְׁפָטִים, אֲנִי יְהֹוָה.

wood to appear as a donkey. The purchaser, believing that he had bought a donkey, gave it water to drink. When the donkey began to drink the water, it caused the image of the donkey to disappear and the reappearance of the wood, as water has the ability to thwart the magic.

Pharaoh was scared that the Yidden would use magic to trick the Egyptians into believing that they were killing Jewish babies when this was not the case. By forcing the Yidden to throw their babies into the water, it would confirm if, in fact, a baby was being drowned.

(Ahavat Yehonatan Voera)

וַיּוֹצִאֵנוּ יְהֹוָה מִמִּצְרַיִם בְּיָד חֲזָקָה

"And Hashem brought us out of Egypt with a strong hand . . ."

The Midrash (Shir Hashirim 4:4) writes that the Yidden were redeemed from Egypt in the merit that they did not change their names or their language. They did not mingle with the Egyptian women, and they did not speak lashon hara.

Why were these four things significant to warrant the redemption of the Bnei Yisroel?

The Midrash (Bereishis Rabbah 4:7) writes that Yoseph spoke lashon hara to their father, Yaakov, about his brothers. He said that they showed interest in Canaanite women and that they referred to their brothers who were the sons of the midwives as slaves, and they ate meat cut from a living animal.

It was due to the sins of Yoseph and the brothers that they descended to Egypt. Therefore, it was necessary for the Yidden to rectify these sins so they could be redeemed.

"And Hashem brought us out of Egypt with a strong hand and an out-stretched arm, in an awesome happening, with signs and with wonders."

"And Hashem brought us out of Egypt"—not through an angel, not through a seraph, not through any emissary. No, it was the Holy One, His glory, His own presence. As it is said: "I shall pass through the land of Egypt on that night; I shall kill every firstborn son in the land of Egypt, man and beast, and I shall pass judgment on all the gods of Egypt: I am Hashem."

That they didn't mingle with the non-Jewish women rectified the sin of the brothers who had shown interest in the daughters of Canaan. The brothers had called some of their siblings slaves when they should have called them by their Hebrew names. The Yidden rectified this by only calling one another by their Hebrew names.

Yoseph had spoken lashon hara about his brothers. The Yidden did not speak ill of one another.

The brothers had only eaten meat that had been shechted, and Yoseph erred in believing that it was meat from a living creature. As such, Yoseph had changed the language, meaning that he had spoken an untruth. Therefore, the Yidden in Egypt didn't change their language; they spoke the truth.

(Yaaros Dvash 1:16)

וַיּוֹצִאֵנוּ יְהֹוָה מִמִּצְרַיִם

"And Hashem took us out of Egypt . . ."

לֹא עַל יְדֵי מַלְאָךְ וְלֹא עַל יְדֵי שָׂרָף וְלֹא עַל יְדֵי שָׁלִיחַ

"Not through an angel, not through a seraph, and not through a messenger."

Why did Hashem redeem the Jewish people Himself? Why didn't He give this responsibility to an angel?

There are a number of reasons given:

The Zohar explains that if an angel had been tasked with redeeming the Yidden, the angel would have been negatively affected by the impurities of Egypt.

After the Akeida, Yitzchok became angelic and was prohibited from descending to Egypt. Similarly, an angel was not permitted to descend to Egypt.

(Tiferet Yehonatan Toldos)

🔥

All the Egyptians deserved to perish. However, Hashem displayed great compassion and punished only the firstborn. If Hashem had instructed an angel to kill all the firstborn, the angel would not have been able to differentiate between the firstborn and the rest of the population; therefore, Hashem had to carry out the task on His own.

However, when Hashem punishes a whole nation, He will send an angel, as the posuk states, *"For my angel will go before you to the Amorites . . . and I will destroy them"* (Shemos 23:23).

Since Hashem destroyed all of them, He was able to send an angel to fulfill this mission.

(Tiferet Yehonatan Mishpotim)

🔥

Pharaoh and his sorcerers questioned whether Hashem concerned Himself with trivial matters such as the dealings of mankind. When they saw the many miracles that occurred with the Exodus, they realized these miracles could only be performed by Hashem.

They now understood that Hashem was involved in all aspects of existence, no matter how trivial it may seem.

(Tiferet Yehonatan)

🔥

The Talmud writes that Pharaoh personally blasphemed Hashem; therefore, Hashem Himself exacted retribution. Sancheriv blasphemed Hashem by means of an agent; therefore, Hashem exacted retribution by means of an agent, as the posuk states, *"An angel of Hashem went forth and smote the Assyrian camp"* (Melachim II 19:35).

(Pardes Reb Yehonatan)

Hashem always uses an angel to lead the Yidden, as the novi writes, *"And the angel of His presence saved them"* (Yeshayahu 63:9). And this was the motivation of the Yidden when they made the golden calf. They did not want to replace Hashem; rather, they needed an emissary of Hashem to lead them. As the posuk says concerning the making of the golden calf, *"Come make us gods that will go before us"* (Shemos 32:1), meaning "make us an agent who will lead us."

However, in the desert, Hashem did not appoint an agent to lead them; rather, He led them Himself. The mixed multitude who attached themselves to the Jewish people were practitioners of black magic. Hashem was worried that they would be able to negatively influence the angel.

This is alluded to in the posuk *"I will take you to Me as a people, and I will be a God to you"* (Shemos 6:7), meaning Hashem Himself would lead the Yidden out of Egypt, not via an angel as was the norm.

(Tiferet Yehonatan Voera)

❀

There was a fundamental difference between Pharaoh and Sancheriv concerning their understanding of God. Pharaoh recognized that God created the world; he simply didn't believe He was involved in its daily running. As the posuk says, *"Who is Hashem that I should listen to His voice?"* (Shemos 5:2).

Pharaoh acknowledged the existence of Hashem but believed He was far removed from man's existence and did not concern Himself with trivial earthly matters. Hence, Pharaoh felt no obligation to heed Him. Therefore, he was punished in an extraordinary fashion that left no doubt that Hashem was truly running the world.

Sancheriv, however, did not believe in the existence of Hashem, as the posuk says, *"Who are they among the gods of the lands who saved their land from my hand?"* (Melachim II 18:35).

By sending an angel to smite Sancheriv's army, Sancheriv concluded that God does exist.

(Ahavat Yehonatan Voera)

וְעָבַרְתִּי בְאֶרֶץ מִצְרַיִם בַּלַּיְלָה הַזֶּה—אֲנִי וְלֹא מַלְאָךְ; וְהִכֵּיתִי כָל בְּכוֹר בְּאֶרֶץ מִצְרָיִם. אֲנִי וְלֹא שָׂרָף; וּבְכָל אֱלֹהֵי מִצְרַיִם אֶעֱשֶׂה שְׁפָטִים. אֲנִי וְלֹא הַשָּׁלִיחַ; אֲנִי יְהוָֹה. אֲנִי הוּא וְלֹא אַחֵר.

בְּיָד חֲזָקָה—זוֹ הַדֶּבֶר, כְּמָה שֶׁנֶּאֱמַר: הִנֵּה יַד יְהוָֹה הוֹיָה בְּמִקְנְךָ אֲשֶׁר בַּשָּׂדֶה, בַּסּוּסִים, בַּחֲמֹרִים, בַּגְּמַלִּים, בַּבָּקָר וּבַצֹּאן, דֶּבֶר כָּבֵד מְאֹד.

וּבִזְרֹעַ נְטוּיָה—זוֹ הַחֶרֶב, כְּמָה שֶׁנֶּאֱמַר: וְחַרְבּוֹ שְׁלוּפָה בְּיָדוֹ, נְטוּיָה עַל יְרוּשָׁלָיִם.

אֲנִי יְהוָֹה אֲנִי הוּא וְלֹא אַחֵר.

"I am Hashem, it is I, and no other."

"And the Egyptians shall know that I am Hashem when I stretch forth my hand over the Egyptians, and I will take the children of Israel out of their midst." (Shemos 7:5).

The Egyptians did not believe that Hashem was capable of doing good and bad simultaneously. When the Egyptians saw how Hashem punished them and saved the Yidden, they realized their error and that Hashem was capable of doing two contrasting actions at the same time.

Every name used to identify Hashem reflects a different quality that He is expressing at that moment. When the posuk uses the name Hashem, it means He is expressing the qualities of kindness and compassion.

Pharaoh asked Moshe, *"Who is Hashem?"*

The Zohar explains that Pharaoh was asserting that when Hashem is showing kindness, He cannot be displaying severity.

This was Pharaoh's mistake. The name Hashem means that He is all capable and that He is able to do both good and bad at the same time.

When the posuk says, *"And the Egyptians shall know that I am Hashem"* (Shemos 7:5), Hashem was stating that through My actions, the Egyptians will understand that the name Hashem is all capable and can express seemingly contradictory actions at the same time.

(Tiferet Yehonatan Voera)

"I shall pass through the land of Egypt on that night"—I and no angel. "I shall kill every firstborn son in the land of Egypt"—I and no seraph. "And I shall pass judgment on all the gods of Egypt"—I and no emissary. "I am Hashem"—It is I and no other.

With a strong hand—This refers to the pestilence, as it is said: "You shall see the hand of Hashem among your cattle in the field, among your horses and donkeys and camels, in the herd and in the flock, bringing harsh, heavy pestilence."

And an outstretched arm—This refers to the sword, as it is said: "And His sword was drawn in His hand, stretched out over Jerusalem."

וּבִזְרֹעַ נְטוּיָה

"With an outstretched hand"

The Yidden's redemption was experienced in stages. On the Rosh Hashonoh prior to their Exodus, they were no longer enslaved, as the posuk says, *"I will take you out from under the burdens of the Egyptians"* (Shemos 6:6).

The second part of the posuk reads, *"I will redeem you with an outstretched hand."* That occurred on Pesach when they experienced their complete redemption.

(Tiferet Yehonatan Voera)

🔥

The servitude in Egypt ceased during the month of Tishrei, and the Yidden were redeemed six months later in the month of Nissan.

Why was it necessary for the enslavement to have halted prior to the Exodus?

Avrohom saw that, according to the zodiac system, the Land of Israel would be conquered by an Egyptian slave. He, therefore, thought that his servant Eliezer who was a descendent of Cham who was an Egyptian would conquer the land. That is why he said, *"Hashem, what will You give me since I am going childless and the steward of my household is Eliezer of Damascus?"* (Bereishis 15:2).

Hashem informed Avrohom that his descendants would be enslaved in Egypt, and they would then conquer the Land of Israel.

Hashem caused the Yidden to be freed in Tishrei, and they no longer were

וּבְמוֹרָא גָּדֹל—זוֹ גִּלּוּי שְׁכִינָה, כְּמָה שֶׁנֶּאֱמַר: אוֹ הֲנִסָּה אֱלֹהִים לָבוֹא לָקַחַת לוֹ גוֹי מִקֶּרֶב גּוֹי בְּמַסֹּת בְּאֹתֹת וּבְמוֹפְתִים וּבְמִלְחָמָה וּבְיָד חֲזָקָה וּבִזְרוֹעַ נְטוּיָה וּבְמוֹרָאִים גְּדֹלִים כְּכֹל אֲשֶׁר עָשָׂה לָכֶם יְהֹוָה אֱלֹהֵיכֶם בְּמִצְרַיִם לְעֵינֶיךָ

considered slaves when they were redeemed from Egypt. Hashem wanted to show that the Yidden were freed, not because the alignment of the planets dictated as such, but rather because this was His will.

This idea offers insight into the words of the Ibn Ezra. The posuk reads, "*I will take you out from under the burdens of the Egyptians and I will save you from their labor and I will redeem you with an outstretched arm and with great judgment*" (Shemos 6:6).

The Ibn Ezra explains that the phrase "*with an outstretched hand*" refers to Hashem going against the heavenly bodies.

The phrase "*I will take you out from under the burdens of the Egyptians*" refers to Hashem stopping the actual servitude in the month of Tishrei. Hence the Yidden were no longer slaves, and according to the heavenly spheres, they should not be able to conquer the Land of Israel. Therefore, the posuk then says, "*with an outstretched hand.*" Hashem went against the heavenly bodies and gave the Land of Israel to the Yidden, even though they were no longer slaves.

(*Tiferet Yehonatan Voera*)

וּבְמוֹרָא גָּדֹל

"With a great manifestation . . ."

Moshe did not want to lead the Yidden out of Egypt. He wanted Hashem to. Hashem was concerned that if He would suddenly reveal Himself to the Yidden, they would die from the shock of encountering the Shechinah.

Therefore, Hashem initially sent Moshe and then He performed the miracles.

In an awesome happening—This refers to the revelation of His Presence, as it is said: "Has any god ever tried to come and take a nation out of the midst of another, with trials and with signs and wonders, in war and with a strong hand, with an outstretched arm, inspiring great awe, as Hashem your God has done all this for you in Egypt, before your eyes?"

This gradual process spiritually refined the Yidden so that Hashem was able to reveal Himself at the time of the redemption.

Yet with all of this, the Yidden still experienced a great manifestation. One can only imagine how they would have reacted if Hashem had appeared suddenly.

(Tiferet Yehonatan Haazinu)

The Talmud writes that the Yidden were redeemed due to their faith. As the posuk says, *"And they believed in Hashem"* (Shemos 14:31).

If a prophet informs someone that they will experience wonderful things in the near future, why would they not believe him?

Why was the Yidden's faith of such significance that it was the catalyst for their redemption?

The Yidden could no longer cope with their immense suffering, and they planned to flee even though they knew the time of their redemption had not yet arrived. While they were aware that the Egyptians practiced witchcraft and as a result no one had ever escaped the land, they were also practitioners of witchcraft and felt they would be able to overcome the Egyptian sorcerers.

However, Miriam, the prophetess, had told the Yidden they should not attempt to awaken Hashem's love until Hashem was ready to redeem them and had sent His prophet to take them out of their darkness. Their belief in Miriam's prophecy kept them in bondage and oppression, and it was due to this level of faith that they merited to be redeemed.

(Ahavat Yehonatan Haftora Vayetzei)

וּבְאֹתוֹת—זֶה הַמַּטֶּה, כְּמָה שֶׁנֶּאֱמַר: וְאֶת הַמַּטֶּה הַזֶּה תִּקַּח בְּיָדְךָ, אֲשֶׁר תַּעֲשֶׂה בּוֹ אֶת הָאֹתוֹת.

וּבְאֹתוֹת

With Signs

זֶה הַמַּטֶּה

"This refers to [Moshe's] staff"

Hashem instructed Moshe to perform a sign that would demonstrate that he had been sent by Hashem to redeem the Yidden when he presented himself to Pharaoh. He was told to cast his staff on the ground, and it would miraculously turn into a snake.

What was the significance of a staff becoming a snake and what message was being conveyed to Pharaoh as a result?

The consequence of Yidden experiencing exile is that they become downtrodden and subservient to their oppressors. If the Yidden took the nations who sought them ill to a Heavenly Court, the attribute of strict justice would come to the nation's defense, claiming that the Yidden's exile was due to their sins.

Therefore, Hashem told Moshe, "Your staff shall become a snake. This will be the Yidden's defense against the attribute of justice. A snake slithers on the ground; it can go no lower. Likewise, the Yidden in exile are like the snake, and their behavior is a direct consequence of what they are enduring. And they cannot be held accountable for their actions."

Seeing this, the force of justice changed its stance and sought retribution from the nations that had mistreated the Jewish people.

(Tiferet Yehonatan Voera)

❀

The posuk says, *"Cast it to the ground and he* [Moshe] *cast it to the ground and it became a serpent and Moshe fled from before it"* (Shemos 4:3).

Hashem had cursed the snake. Why then did Hashem choose the snake to be the sign?

With signs—This refers to the staff, as it is said: "Take this staff in your hand, and with it you shall perform the signs."

The Talmud writes (Bava Basra 16a) that the doe's womb is extremely narrow and has difficulty giving birth. Hashem directs a snake to bite her at the opening of her womb, and it is then able to give birth.

The Talmud writes that if the Yidden do not do teshuvah, they will not be redeemed. How then does Hashem cause the Yidden to do teshuvah?

The doe and the snake are a parable to the Jewish people in exile. Dovid Hamelech compares the Yidden to a doe that is having difficulty giving birth. The Yidden are struggling to bring into the world words of Torah, good deeds, and teshuvah. As the posuk says, *"For the children have come as far as the birthstool and there is no strength to give birth"* (Yeshayahu 37:3).

The posuk can be understood to mean that the Yidden are unable to give birth to teshuvah, redemption, and salvation. Therefore, Hashem brings a snake in the form of an evil individual such as Haman who causes the Yidden to suffer until they repent.

(Yaaros Dvash 2:3)

Moshe and the elders did not believe that the Yidden where righteous enough to be redeemed. Therefore, Hashem showed him the snake. The snake symbolizes the intense labor the Yidden suffered at the hands of the Egyptians. making their lives unbearable. As a result, the Yidden would do teshuvah and they would cry out to Hashem as the posuk says, *"The Yidden sighed from the labor and they cried out and their cry ascended to Hashem from the labor"* (Shemos 2:23).

(Yaaros Dvash 2,3)

וּבְמִפְּתִים—זֶה הַדָּם, כְּמָה שֶׁנֶּאֱמַר: וְנָתַתִּי מוֹפְתִים בַּשָּׁמַיִם וּבָאָרֶץ

*It is customary to spill out some wine from the cup while saying
the three terms: blood, fire, and pillars of smoke.*

דָּם וָאֵשׁ וְתִימְרוֹת עָשָׁן.

דָּבָר אַחֵר: בְּיָד חֲזָקָה—שְׁתַּיִם, וּבִזְרֹעַ נְטוּיָה—שְׁתַּיִם, וּבְמֹרָא גָּדֹל—
שְׁתַּיִם, וּבְאֹתוֹת—שְׁתַּיִם, וּבְמֹפְתִים—שְׁתַּיִם.

אֵלּוּ עֶשֶׂר מַכּוֹת שֶׁהֵבִיא הַקָּדוֹשׁ בָּרוּךְ הוּא עַל הַמִּצְרִים בְּמִצְרַיִם, וְאֵלּוּ הֵן:

עֶשֶׂר מַכּוֹת

The Ten Plagues

The Midrash writes that I [Hashem] placed upon them signs and wonders. The Hebrew word for *signs* is אוֹתוֹת. This teaches us that Hashem sent the plagues as they are written, meaning with their letters. The Hebrew for *word* is אוֹתִיוֹת. The two words, signs, and letters are similar.

How do we understand this Midrash?

The halocho is that one can only purchase an item from a non-Jew with a written contract. The Midrash writes that Hashem acquired the Yidden with the plagues. According to halocho, there needed to be a written contract. How then did Hashem obtain the Yidden?

Therefore, the Midrash says Hashem sent the plagues as they are written, meaning he sent a written document with each of the plagues, and thereby, Hashem was able to acquire the Yidden.

(Pardes Reb Yehonatan)

And with wonders—This refers to the blood, as it is said: "I shall make wonders in the sky and on the earth.

It is customary to spill out some wine from the cup while saying
the three terms: blood, fire, and pillars of smoke.

"Blood, fire, and pillars of smoke"

Another interpretation: "With a strong hand"—two. "And an outstretched arm"—two.

"In an awesome happening"—two. "With signs"—two. "And with wonders"—two.

These are the ten plagues that the Holy One brought upon Egypt, and these are they:

The Midrash asks, "By hardening Pharaoh's heart, wasn't this taking away Pharaoh's ability to choose and let the Yidden leave? Why then was Pharaoh punished?"

A person who despises someone has no interest in giving him a gift. However, if he is beaten badly, this will affect his resolve and he will give the gift. If the person is extremely strong, the beating will not have any impact and he will not give the gift.

Such was the case by Pharaoh. If his intent was to let the Yidden go, Hashem would not have hardened his heart to cause Pharaoh to change his mind. Rather, Pharaoh had declared that he had no intention of allowing the Yidden to leave. However, the many plagues would weaken Pharaoh and he would let the Yidden go.

Therefore, Hashem hardened his heart to give him the strength and resolve to withstand the plagues and not change his mind to let the Yidden leave.

(Tiferet Yehonatan Bo)

*Some wine is spilled with the mention of each of the ten plagues,
as well as the three words of Reb Yehuda's acronym.*

דָּם. צְפַרְדֵּעַ. כִּנִּים. עָרוֹב. דֶּבֶר. שְׁחִין. בָּרָד.

עָרוֹב

Wild Beasts

When describing the plague of the wild beasts, the posuk says, *"The houses of Egypt will be filled with wild animals as well as the land upon which they are"* (Shemos 8:20).

What does the Torah mean when it writes "as well as the land upon which they are?"

Sefer Melochim writes how the prophet Elisha incited the bears to attack the youth. As the posuk states, *"And two she-bears came out of the forest and tore forty-two children from them"* (Melochim II 2:24).

The Talmud (Sotah 47a) elaborates on this incident and quotes an opinion that there were no bears and no forest. Elisha had performed two miracles. He created two bears, and he created the forest. It asks why Elisha needed to create a forest, as the forest served no role in the story?

The Talmud explains that Elisha had to create a forest, as bears are frightened to venture into open areas but will attack people in their natural habitat, such as a forest.

When Pharaoh was informed that Egypt would be attacked by wild animals, he was not frightened. He knew that they would be too frightened to attack since they were not in their natural habitat.

Therefore, Pharaoh was told "as well as the land upon which they are." The wild animals would be transported together with their familiar surroundings. Hence, they would no longer be afraid to attack the human population.

(Midrash Yehonatan Shemos)

בָּרָד

Hail

After the plague of the hail, Hashem needed to explicitly instruct Moshe to confront Pharaoh as the posuk says, *"Come to Pharaoh"* (Shemos 10:1).

Why was this necessary?

Pharaoh had asked Moshe to partially remove the plague of hail. He wanted the

Blood. Frogs. Lice. Wild Animals. Pestilence. Boils. Hail.

hail and loud thunder to cease and the rain component to continue. The Egyptians were reliant on the Nile for water. If the rain remained, then they would not be dependent on the river. Moshe did not heed Pharaoh's request and he removed the rain as well. Pharaoh believed that if Moshe had brought the plague, he would have been able to halt parts of it and allow other facets such as the rain to continue. His inability to do so proved that the plague was a chance occurrence.

Therefore, Moshe was somewhat reluctant to once again approach Pharaoh, as he felt that Pharaoh would view him as a fraud. Hence, Hashem had to instruct Moshe to go to Pharaoh, and He calmed Moshe's fears by telling him that Pharaoh did not think he was a trickster; rather, He had hardened his heart, which is why Pharaoh was not listening to him.

(Tiferet Yehonatan Bo)

The Egyptians believed that the sun was the ultimate ruler and the source of all earthly experiences. The purpose of the plagues of locust and darkness was to debunk this theory. The locust would cover the face of the sun and the darkness would be so profound that there would be no sunrays. This would show the Egyptians that the sun was not all powerful and its function was to fulfill the wishes of Hashem.

Prior to the implementation of these two plagues, Hashem wanted to ensure that though the sun was shining bright, it would be unable to halt the onset of the plagues. Therefore, Hashem stopped the rain together with the hail, since the sun's strength is diminished when it rains, and the Egyptians would have been in a position to state that the reason for the plagues of locust and darkness was because the rain had weakened the strength of the sun.

(Tiferet Yehonatan Bo)

There was a distinct difference between the earlier plagues and the plagues that Hashem said would harden the heart of Pharaoh and the Egyptians.

The Egyptians wondered why there was a need for any of the plagues. If the

Jewish God really was more powerful than Pharaoh, He simply could instruct them to leave, and Pharaoh would not be able to stop them—and being that He didn't prove that, Pharaoh was mightier.

However, the Egyptians were not sure if this indeed was the case. Perhaps the following argument could be made why the Yidden didn't simply leave.

The Yidden had been subjugated and enslaved, and as a result, they were a frightened and weak nation. Even if they had left, once the Egyptians attacked them, they would have meekly returned to Egypt. As seen in the posuk, *"Hashem did not lead them by the way of the land of the Philishtim for it was near . . . When they see war and return to Egypt"* (Shemos 13:17). If the Yidden had been frightened by the Philishtim, they definitely would dread encountering the Egyptians. As such, the Yidden didn't want to leave.

However, the Egyptians were incapacitated by the plagues of locust and darkness and were not in a position to halt the Exodus, and yet the Yidden did not leave. The Egyptians assumed the reason for this was that the powers of witchcraft were such that Pharaoh had to agree to allow the Yidden to leave. This understanding strengthened their resolve to not allow the Yidden to leave and their hearts were hardened as a result.

(Tiferet Yehonatan Bo)

Prior to the last three plagues, the Torah writes, *"And in order that you tell into the ears of your son and your son's son how I made a mockery of the Egyptians"* (Shemos 10:2).

What are the Yidden obligated to convey to their future generations?

These plagues proved that the Egyptians were willing participants in Pharaoh's wish to subjugate and punish the Yidden—because, during these plagues, the Egyptians could have encouraged the Yidden to leave, and Pharaoh would not have known. As such, they deserved to be punished. We are obligated to teach our children that Hashem does not punish indiscriminately, and punishment is meted out to those who deserve it.

(Tiferet Yehonatan Bo)

What was the mockery?

Locusts.

The mockery was that the Egyptians were misled into believing that they wre all powerful. During the plague of the locust and darkness, the Yidden could have left, and no one could have stopped them. Seeing that the Yidden didn't leave, the Egyptians came to the conclusion that they could not leave without the consent of the Egyptians. This further strengthened their resolve to not allow the Yidden to leave.

(Tiferet Yehonatan Bo)

אַרְבֶּה

Locust

Pharaoh declared, "Who is Hashem that I should listen to Him?"

Pharaoh was well aware that there is a Creator. Why then was he asking, "Who is Hashem?"

Moshe had told Pharaoh that the name of Hashem is אהיה, which means "the God of compassion." Pharaoh couldn't reconcile how a God of compassion was capable of causing so much suffering and destruction. How is the source of goodness able to emit so much evil?

For a kosher species to be edible it must first be killed. The manner in which this needs to occur depends on the species. A mammal needs to have both its trachea and esophagus severed. A bird only needs one of its pipes cut, while fish or locust can be killed without a ritual slaughtering.

Why are there three distinct classes in the taking of the life of a kosher living creature?

A mammal is viewed as being evil; therefore, both pipes need to be cut. A bird is not as evil; therefore, cutting one pipe is sufficient. A fish and locust are considered good; therefore, no pipe needs to be cut.

The plague of locusts demonstrated that while the locust was deemed to be good, it still destroyed everything that remained after the plague of the hail.

(Tiferet Yehonatan Bo)

The nature of locust is that they travel en masse from one country to another or from city to city. They don't just suddenly appear in a particular place.

The posuk says, *"[By the time] it was morning the east wind had brought the locusts"* (Shemos 10:13).

Hashem performed a miracle for the locust to suddenly appear in Egypt without coming from a neighboring land. The reason for this is that Hashem did not want to give Pharaoh's sorcerers the opportunity to say that the arrival of the locust was an act of witchcraft, not an act of the hand of Hashem.

(Tiferet Yehonatan Bo)

❦

Moshe and Aaron informed Pharaoh that Hashem was about to bring the plague of locust. The Torah records how his servants reacted to this. *"Pharaoh's servants said to him, 'How long will this one be a stumbling block to us? Let the people go and they will worship their God. Don't you yet know that Egypt is lost?'"* (Shemos 10:7).

How were the Egyptians able to ascertain that their country was lost?

Yoseph had told Pharaoh that Egypt would have seven bounty years and then it would experience seven years of famine. Yaakov descended with his family to Egypt after two years of the famine had transpired. In the merit of Yaakov coming to Egypt, the famine ceased.

The Egyptians understood that they would still have to experience another five years of famine. They thought that since the locust would consume all the remaining crop, the five years of starvation would commence with the plague of the locust and Egypt would be lost.

The Egyptians viewed the plague of the locust as the beginning of the remaining five years of famine. Pharoah's servants understood that the locust would cause "Egypt to be lost," and it could not be viewed as a miraculous event to save the Jewish people.

The Egyptians had erred; the additional five years occurred during the times of Yermiyahu, the prophet. As such, the plague of the locust was meant to save the Yidden.

(Tiferet Yehonatan Bo)

❦

The Midrash writes that locust do not have a king; therefore, Hashem sent the plague of locust.

The understanding of the Midrash is that the Egyptians thought that all the plagues were done through sorcery, and as such, they could duplicate them by connecting with the plagues' heavenly source. However, the locust do not have a king, meaning they do not have a spiritual entity. As such, Moshe could not have brought the locust by using sorcery.

(Tiferet Yehonatan Bo)

§

There is a profound reason the plagues of locust and darkness came immediately after the plague of hail. When it is raining or hailing, the rays of the sun are somewhat diminished. After a spell of rain and the sun begins to shine, the contrast is very noticeable. The impression given is that the sun is then at its most powerful.

The purpose of the eighth and ninth plague was to debunk a long-held belief of Pharaoh and his advisors. They thought that the sun ruled the world. Therefore, Hashem wanted to show them that, even after rain when the sun is at its most powerful, Hashem is still in control, evidenced by the fact that the locust and darkness both caused the sun to be concealed.

(Tiferet Yehonatan Bo)

§

Moshe informed Pharaoh by the Nile of each subsequent plague. Why didn't he meet him at Pharaoh's palace? Since Pharaoh's advisors were located in the palace, Moshe was concerned that the advisors may convince Pharaoh to grant the Yidden their freedom. Therefore, Moshe felt it was prudent to meet him alone.

Why then, with regard to the plagues of locust and darkness, did Moshe appear in Pharaoh's palace? Wasn't Moshe afraid Pharaoh might be influenced by his advisors?

Moshe had no reason to be worried, as the posuk clearly states that *"Hashem hardened the hearts of Pharaoh and his servants"* (Shemos 7:13). As such, they would not be changing their minds. Therefore, Moshe felt that the proper place for Moshe to convey the command of the King of Kings was in the palace.

(Pardes Reb Yehonatan)

§

Each plague lasted a month—three weeks of warning and a week for the actual plague. The Ramban writes that the plague of hail began at the beginning of the month of Adar.

On the first of Nissan, the Yidden received the instruction to sanctify the new month. As such, the three plagues—hail, locust, and darkness—all occurred in the month of Adar.

Why specifically did the month of Adar have the most plagues?

The Egyptians worshipped the sheep, and the month of Nissan was considered their luckiest month. Being the month prior to Nissan, Adar was the Egyptian's least fortunate month.

The Egyptians assumed that the reason they suffered so severely during the month of Adar was not because of Hashem's divine intervention but because of the negative forces that impact them in the month of Adar. This is alluded to in the posuk, *"Hashem said to Moshe: 'Come to Pharaoh, for I have hardened his heart and the heart of his servants, in order that I may place these signs of Mine in his midst'"* (Shemos 7:13).

By placing *"these signs"*—the plagues of hail, locust, and darkness—*"of Mine in his midst,"* during the month of Adar, this will result in the hardening of Pharaoh's heart (*"I have hardened his heart and the heart of his servants"*) as they will mistakenly assume that the plagues were not a directive of Hashem but a result of the bad luck generated by the month of Adar. As such, Pharaoh did not grant the Yidden their freedom.

(Tiferet Yehonatan)

The posuk reads, *"Pharaoh's servants said to him, 'How long will this one be a stumbling block to us? Let the people go and they will worship their God. Don't you yet know that Egypt is lost?'"* (Shemos 10:7).

The Midrash writes that when Moshe was a child, he grabbed Pharaoh's crown. The Egyptian magicians told Pharaoh that his actions indicated that he would one day destroy Egypt. Therefore, Moshe needed to be killed. However, a miracle occurred, and his life was saved.

This is what the magicians meant when they said, *"Don't you yet know that Egypt is lost? . . .* You know what happened when Moshe was a child, and he grabbed the crown. The magicians warned you then that Moshe would be a thorn and is out to destroy us."

They further said to Pharaoh, "You told us that with your wisdom you would defeat Moshe and the Jewish people. You said that by enslaving them and forcing them into a life of hard labor, we would destroy them. However, since Rosh Hashonoh, the servitude has ceased; as such, we will not be able to defeat them."

(Tiferet Yehonatan Bo)

Darkness.

חֹשֶׁךְ

Darkness

Why were the Egyptian people punished? How could they be held responsible for the decrees enacted by Pharaoh?

If the Egyptians really wanted to see the Jewish people emancipated, then during the three days of darkness, they should have gone to the Yidden and told them that Pharaoh had decreed they were free, and they must leave immediately.

And if the Egyptians feared Pharoah's wrath, they could have responded that they were blinded and could not see, while the Jews could, and they could not have prevented their escape.

Since the Egyptians did not do this, it is clear that they were in full agreement with Pharaoh's decrees, and as such, they were also punished.

(Tiferet Yehonatan Bo)

The Midrash writes that the plague of darkness was doubled.

The understanding of this Midrash is that, for the Egyptians, it was dark even during the day, and for the Yidden, it was light even at night.

(Tiferet Yehonatan Bo)

The Egyptians wondered whether the Yidden who were living in Goshen were impacted by the plagues. They sent spies there to see what was happening. The Egyptians who had traveled to Goshen during the plague of darkness could not see. How would they know if the Yidden were also afflicted with the plague of darkness?

The plague of darkness not only blinded the individual but also made it impossible for a person to move about. The Egyptians who had traveled to Goshen were unable to see; however, they could hear the Yidden moving around freely and realized that the Yidden had not been smitten with the plague of darkness.

(Tiferet Yehonatan Bo)

An Egyptian who had traveled to Goshen was not afflicted with the plague of darkness. And if the plague had not inhibited the movement of the Egyptians, they would have all fled to Goshen.

(Tiferet Yehonatan Bo)

Why did the plague of darkness last for three days?

During the three days of darkness, the Yidden circumcised themselves. The third day of bris milah is the most painful. If the plague had lasted only two days, then on the third day, the Egyptians would have realized what the Yidden had done, and they would have taken up arms against them. They, therefore, had to experience at least three days of darkness.

(Tiferet Yehonatan Bo)

During the three days of darkness the Torah writes *"It was light in the homes of all the Yidden"* (Shemos 10:23).

The Arizal writes that when a bris is held in a shul, the shul needs to be well lit. It was light in the Yidden's homes as they were fulfilling the mitzvah of bris milah.

(Tiferet Yehonatan Bo)

During the day there is always natural light in a person's dwellings. What is the posuk highlighting when it says there was light in the dwellings of the Yidden?

Miraculously, during the three days, the Yidden didn't experience the night. For them, the sun shone for seventy-two hours, unlike the Egyptians who experienced darkness during the same seventy-two hours.

(Tiferet Yehonatan Bo)

After the plague of darkness, Pharaoh did not have a change of heart, and he refused to allow the Yidden to leave.

Pharaoh's rationale was a result of an erroneous assumption. He argued that during the three days of darkness, they were not in a position to stop the Yidden from escaping, and yet none of them left. The only explanation is that without Pharaoh's consent, they were unable to escape. Therefore, he refused to let them leave.

(Tiferet Yehonatan Bo)

When a delegation presented before a monarch, the first meeting was always in person. If there was a need for further discussions, it was via the king's appointed ministers.

After meeting Pharaoh in person, why did Moshe and Aaron feel it was necessary to continue having face-to-face discussions. Why didn't they convey their position via Pharaoh's officers?

Moshe and Aaron had to warn Pharaoh personally prior to each plague as Pharaoh also suffered through each of them.

However, After the plague of darkness, Pharaoh saw that the next plague would be the plague of the slaying of the firstborn, and while he was a firstborn, his life would be spared. Since he would not suffer during the last plague, he told Moshe and Aaron that there was no need for them to speak to him directly.

(Tiferet Yehonatan Bo)

Lomdus

There are two reasons given for why Hashem brought the plague of darkness. The first was so that the Egyptians would not see the death of those Yidden who would not merit the Exodus. The second was to enable the Yidden to take the Egyptian's treasures.

The Midrash writes that Hashem said to the angels that the Egyptians deserve to be punished with the plague of darkness, and the angels immediately agreed with Him.

According to one opinion, the plague of darkness would bring death to an untold number of Yidden. Why then were the angels so eager and quick to consent to Hashem's actions?

A Beis Din adjudicates both financial disputes and cases of corporeal punishment. There are distinct differences in the procedural conduct of a financial dispute and one that may result in a verdict of the death penalty.

In a monetary case, the head of the Beis Din gives his opinion first, and then the other judges either agree or disagree. However, when the Beis Din needs to decide if an individual will be sentenced to death, the procedure is reversed. The junior judge gives his ruling first and the head of the Beis Din gives his opinion last.

The angels were unsure why Hashem was bringing the plague of darkness. Was it to punish the Yidden or was it to financially benefit them?

Hashem did not seek the angels' opinion whether there should be a plague of darkness and then inform them of His opinion. Rather He informed the angels that He had come to the decision that there would be a plague of darkness. Since they weren't asked to first express their opinion, the angels knew that the plague was to benefit the Yidden financially; therefore, they immediately responded in the affirmative.

(Tiferet Yehonatan Bo)

Lomdus

Concerning the plague of darkness, the posuk writes, "*He sent darkness and it darkened and they did not disobey His word*" (Tehillim 105:28).

"He sent darkness and it darkened" seems repetitive.

The double expression teaches us that the Egyptians experienced two punishments during the plague of darkness. First, the actual darkness, and second, during the three days of darkness, they experienced the fires of gehenom. The fires of gehenom were not a punishment for the Egyptians but was for their benefit, as they would not need to experience gehenom in the world to come.

What did the Egyptians do to deserve this?

They had implored Pharaoh to "Let the people go and they will worship their God" (Shemos 10:7).

The posuk in Tehillim can be understood to mean, "He sent darkness and it darkened"—the Egyptians received two punishments, darkness and the fire of gehenom.

❖

Why did they merit to experience the fires of gehenom in this world?

Since "They did not disobey His word," the Egyptians listened to Hashem and wanted to let the Yidden leave.

Contrasting this understanding of the posuk in Tehillim with Rashi's explanation, the phrase "They did not disobey His words" means that "the plagues He commanded upon them came and they did not deviate from His word."

Rashi explains the word they is referring to the plagues, though it could be referring to the Egyptians.

(Tiferet Yehonatan Bo)

❖

The Midrash writes that Hashem consulted with the Heavenly Court to see if they were in agreement to bring the plague of darkness. The Heavenly Court immediately responded in the affirmative. Why did they all agree?

The plague of darkness was not a punishment for the Egyptians but rather for their benefit, as they would be punished in this world rather than in the world to come.

The Talmud (Sanhedrin 17b) writes that if all the presiding judges find the person guilty and deserving of the death penalty, he is freed and does not receive the death penalty.

With regard to the other plagues, if all the Heavenly Court would say the Egyptians were guilty, they could not be punished with the plague. However, the plague of darkness was not to be viewed as a punishment but rather as beneficial for them. As such, even if all the Heavenly Court said they deserved the darkness and the fire, they would receive it, as it was for their benefit and was not a punishment.

(Tiferet Yehonatan Bo)

✿

The Midrash explains that when the Torah says, "*Hashem called the light day*," it refers to the acts of the tzaddikim. And when it says, "*And the darkness He called night*" (Bereishis 1:5), it refers to the acts of the wicked.

During the three days of darkness, all the wicked perished. The posuk says, "*For all the Bnei Yisroel, there was light in their dwellings*" (Shemos 10:23).

The posuk can be understood to mean that not only was it light in their homes but also there was an added element of light as the wicked had perished.

(Tiferet Yehonatan Bo)

✿

During the three days of darkness, the Yidden searched the homes of the Egyptians to see where they had hidden their precious items. The Yidden then asked them to lend them these items, which they gladly did. Why did the Egyptians entrust the Yidden with their possessions?

The Egyptians saw that the Yidden didn't take any of their belongings during the three days of darkness. As such, "*The Yidden found favor in the Egyptians' eyes*" and they trusted them.

Likewise, Moshe the leader of the Jewish people, was extremely respected. He was viewed as an upright morale human being, and when he stated that he was taking his people for only three days, he was believed.

(Tiferet Yehonatan Bo)

✿

Why didn't Moshe warn Pharaoh before the plague of darkness?

For the Yidden to leave Egypt with great wealth, it was imperative that the Egyptians not be made aware of the plague of darkness.

Why?

If the Egyptians had been made aware that the next plague would plunge the populous into a state of darkness, they would have hidden all their gold and silver.

And when the Yidden asked to borrow their fine garments and their gold and silver, the Egyptians would not have known that they could trust them.

However, since Moshe did not warn Pharaoh, the Egyptians left their precious goods out in the open, and during the plague of darkness, the Yidden did not take any of it, even though they could have easily taken the items and fled. As such, the Egyptians trusted the Yidden, so that when they later asked to borrow their gold and silver, the Egyptians were forthcoming, thus enabling the Yidden to leave with great wealth.

(Tiferet Yehonatan Bo)

מַכַּת בְּכוֹרוֹת

Slaying of the Firstborn

Why was the plague of the slaying of the firstborn the only plague that Pharaoh was prewarned of in his palace?

With regard to the slaying of the firstborn, the Yidden were obligated to place the blood of the Korban Pesach on their doorposts and lintel to protect them from the angel of death.

Why did the Yidden need protection? Didn't the forces of evil know the difference between a Jewish and Egyptian firstborn?

The Talmud (Bava Kama 60a) answers that once permission has been granted to the evil force of destruction, it does not distinguish between the righteous and the wicked. While the Jewish firstborn were righteous, the evil forces do not differentiate. As such, they needed the protection afforded by the blood of the sacrifice.

Hashem showed Pharaoh compassion and allowed him to live, even though he was a firstborn. According to the Talmud, the evil forces did not distinguish. How then would Pharaoh be protected and not die with all the other Egyptian firstborn?

When Moshe went to the palace to tell Pharaoh about the upcoming plague, Hashem's presence accompanied him. And while it departed together with Moshe, part of it remained. The spirituality that remained created a shield of protection for Pharaoh, similar to the blood's role in protecting the Jewish people.

This is the reason Moshe had to go to Pharaoh's palace to warn him about the plague of the firstborn.

(Tiferet Yehonatan Voera)

Slaying of the Firstborn.

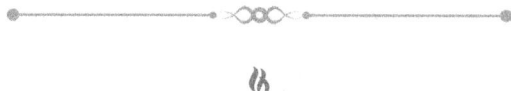

The posuk says, *"It came to pass on the day that Hashem spoke to Moshe in the land of Egypt"* (Shemos 6:28).

Why did Hashem speak to Moshe in Pharoah's palace with regard to the plague of the slaying of the firstborn?

Moshe knew that Egypt was full of idols, and as such, Hashem was unable to speak to him in Egypt. It was a result of the plagues that Egypt became purified from its idols. Prior to the plague of the slaying of the firstborn, Egypt had been cleansed of its idols, and as such, Hashem spoke to Moshe in Pharaoh's palace.

(Tiferet Yehonatan Voera)

Lomdus

In a home where there was no firstborn male, the oldest person in the house perished. Rashi points out that Pharaoh was a firstborn, and yet miraculously, he was saved. How does Rashi know that Pharaoh was a firstborn? Perhaps Pharaoh was not a firstborn; perhaps he was miraculously saved even though there were no firstborns in the palace and he was the oldest.

The posuk says, *"There was no house where there was not someone dead"* (Shemos 12:30).

This would imply that Pharaoh's palace also contained a corpse. If there was no firstborn in the palace at the time and Pharaoh was the oldest person (who should have died but did not), then we would have a home that did *not* contain a corpse. How then can the Torah write *"every home"*?

We must conclude that Pharaoh was a firstborn and there was another firstborn in the palace. The other firstborn died, as such the posuk says, *"There was no house where there was not someone dead,"* including the palace.

Being a firstborn, Pharaoh should have also died; however, miraculously his life was spared.

This explanation justifies Rashi's belief that Pharaoh was a firstborn and his not dying in the plague was miraculous.

(Pardes Reb Yehonatan)

רַבִּי יְהוּדָה הָיָה נוֹתֵן בָּהֶם סִמָּנִים: דְּצַ"ךְ עַדַ"שׁ בְּאַחַ"ב.

רַבִּי יוֹסֵי הַגְּלִילִי אוֹמֵר: מִנַּיִן אַתָּה אוֹמֵר שֶׁלָּקוּ הַמִּצְרַיִם בְּמִצְרַיִם עֶשֶׂר מַכּוֹת וְעַל הַיָּם לָקוּ חֲמִשִּׁים מַכּוֹת? בְּמִצְרַיִם מָה הוּא אוֹמֵר? וַיֹּאמְרוּ הַחַרְטֻמִּם אֶל פַּרְעֹה, אֶצְבַּע אֱלֹהִים הוּא. וְעַל הַיָּם מָה הוּא אוֹמֵר? וַיַּרְא יִשְׂרָאֵל אֶת הַיָּד הַגְּדֹלָה אֲשֶׁר עָשָׂה יְהֹוָה בְּמִצְרַיִם, וַיִּירְאוּ הָעָם אֶת יְהֹוָה, וַיַּאֲמִינוּ בַּיהֹוָה וּבְמֹשֶׁה עַבְדּוֹ. כַּמָּה לָקוּ בָאֶצְבַּע? עֶשֶׂר מַכּוֹת. אֱמוֹר מֵעַתָּה: בְּמִצְרַיִם לָקוּ עֶשֶׂר מַכּוֹת וְעַל הַיָּם לָקוּ חֲמִשִּׁים מַכּוֹת.

רַבִּי אֱלִיעֶזֶר אוֹמֵר: מִנַּיִן שֶׁכָּל מַכָּה וּמַכָּה שֶׁהֵבִיא הַקָּדוֹשׁ בָּרוּךְ הוּא עַל הַמִּצְרִים בְּמִצְרַיִם הָיְתָה שֶׁל אַרְבַּע מַכּוֹת? שֶׁנֶּאֱמַר: יְשַׁלַּח בָּם חֲרוֹן אַפּוֹ, עֶבְרָה וָזַעַם וְצָרָה, מִשְׁלַחַת מַלְאֲכֵי רָעִים. עֶבְרָה—אַחַת, וָזַעַם—שְׁתַּיִם, וְצָרָה—שָׁלֹשׁ, מִשְׁלַחַת מַלְאֲכֵי רָעִים—אַרְבַּע. אֱמוֹר מֵעַתָּה: בְּמִצְרַיִם לָקוּ אַרְבָּעִים מַכּוֹת וְעַל הַיָּם לָקוּ מָאתַיִם מַכּוֹת.

רַבִּי יוֹסֵי הַגְּלִילִי אוֹמֵר

"Rabbi Yossi Haglili said . . ."

וַיַּאֲמִינוּ בַּיָי וּבְמֹשֶׁה עַבְדּוֹ

"And they believed in Hashem and in His servant Moshe."

When Moshe was born, the posuk relates, *"They saw he [Moshe] was good"* (Shemos 2:2). One of the explanations offered in the Talmud is that after Moshe's birth, his whole surroundings were filled with light. This phenomenon can be understood to mean the following:

The Talmud writes that while a fetus is in its mother's womb, a lit candle hovers above his head. This, of course, should not be taken literally. Rather, it means that the fetus is surrounded by an abundance of light. This light refers to the light created on the first day of creation.

Rabbi Yehuda grouped these under acronyms: D'TZACH, ADASH, B'ACHAV.

Rabbi Yossi Haglili says: How can you know that the Egyptians were struck with ten plagues in Egypt and another fifty at the sea? For in Egypt it is said, "The astrologers said to Pharaoh, 'This is the finger of God,'" while at the sea it is said, "When Israel saw the great hand Hashem raised against the Egyptians, the people feared Hashem, and they believed in Hashem and in His servant Moshe." If a finger struck them with ten plagues, conclude from this that they were struck with ten plagues in Egypt and with fifty plagues at the sea.

Rabbi Eliezer says: How can you know that each and every plague the Holy One brought upon the Egyptians in Egypt was in fact made up of four plagues? For it is said, "His fury was sent down upon them, great anger, rage, and distress, a company of messengers of destruction."

"Great anger"—one; "rage"—two; "distress"—three; "a company of messengers of destruction"—four. Conclude from this that they were struck with forty plagues in Egypt and with two hundred plagues at the sea.

Moshe was born after a six-month pregnancy. As such, he did not experience a full nine months of being enveloped by this supernatural light. To compensate for that, after his birth and until he was three months old, he was surrounded by this unique light.

(Divrei Yehonatan)

Another understanding of the posuk is that Moshe was born circumcised. How do we infer this from the posuk?

Prior to a boy receiving a bris, he is deemed to be similar to grain that has not yet had terumah taken from it. Such grain is called tevel, meaning it contains both good and bad.

רַבִּי עֲקִיבָא אוֹמֵר: מִנַּיִן שֶׁכָּל מַכָּה וּמַכָּה שֶׁהֵבִיא הַקָּדוֹשׁ בָּרוּךְ הוּא עַל הַמִּצְרִים בְּמִצְרַיִם הָיְתָה שֶׁל חָמֵשׁ מַכּוֹת? שֶׁנֶּאֱמַר: יְשַׁלַּח בָּם חֲרוֹן אַפּוֹ, עֶבְרָה וָזַעַם וְצָרָה, מִשְׁלַחַת מַלְאֲכֵי רָעִים. חֲרוֹן אַפּוֹ – אַחַת, עֶבְרָה – שְׁתַּיִם, וָזַעַם – שָׁלוֹשׁ, וְצָרָה – אַרְבַּע, מִשְׁלַחַת מַלְאֲכֵי רָעִים – חָמֵשׁ. אֱמוֹר מֵעַתָּה: בְּמִצְרַיִם לָקוּ חֲמִשִּׁים מַכּוֹת וְעַל הַיָּם לָקוּ חֲמִשִּׁים וּמָאתַיִם מַכּוֹת.

By virtue of the fact that the posuk says that Moshe was born good, implying that he possessed no bad, must mean that he was born circumcised.

(Midrash Yehonatan)

On the 21st of Nissan, Moshe's mother, Yocheved, placed him into the basket on the water. Eighty years later, on the 21st of Nissan, the miracle of Krias Yam Suf occurred.

The Yidden were unsure whether they were saved in their own merit or in the merit of Moshe. There is a fascinating Midrash that relates that Moshe told the Jewish people that they were saved in his merit. Moshe informed them that since he had been placed into the water, it was an atonement for the Jewish people, which led to the miracle.

The posuk can be understood to mean *"and they believed in Hashem and in His servant Moshe* [when he informed them that they were saved in his merit]."

(Tiferet Yehonatan Beshalach)

רַבִּי עֲקִיבָא אוֹמֵר

"Reb Akiva said . . ."

Lomdus

The posuk says, לֹא יָדַעְתִּי אֶת יְהוָה, וְגַם אֶת יִשְׂרָאֵל לֹא אֲשַׁלֵּחַ "[And Pharaoh said], '*Who is Hashem that I should heed His voice to let Israel out? I do not know Hashem nor will I let Israel out'*" (Shemos 5:2).

Rabbi Akiva says: How can you know that each and every plague the Holy One brought upon the Egyptians in Egypt was in fact made up of five plagues? For it is said, "His fury was sent down upon them, great anger, rage, and distress, a company of messengers of destruction."

"His fury"—one; "great anger"—two; "rage"—three; "distress"—four; "a company of messengers of destruction"—five. Conclude from this that they were struck with fifty plagues in Egypt and with two hundred fifty plagues at the sea.

The Midrash writes that Pharaoh's response was "I will let the Yidden leave when Reb Akiva comes to redeem them." Why would Pharaoh release them only when Reb Akiva is the redeemer?

The Talmud (Bava Metzia 37a) writes that when two people deposit an item at the same time with a third person, the third person needs to return the item in the presence of both people.

The Yidden had been placed in Egypt. The Talmud (Pesochim 22b) writes, "Shimon HaAmmassoni would interpret all occurrences of the word אֶת *et* in the Torah, deriving additional laws with regard to the particular subject matter. Once he reached the verse 'You shall be in awe of [*et*] Hashem your God' (Devorim 10:20), he withdrew from this method of exposition, as how could one add to Hashem Himself?"

The word *et* in this verse was not explained until Rabbi Akiva expounded upon it:

"The word *et* comes to include a Talmid Chochom, that one is commanded to fear them just as one fears Hashem." As such, when Pharaoh declares לֹא יָדַעְתִּי אֶת יְהֹוָה *"I do not know [et] Hashem,"* it means "I do not know what we learn from the word *et* placed before the name of Hashem." The word *et* usually means "to add." We are adding to God and concluding that there are two Gods. If there are two Gods who placed the Jewish people in Egypt, then they must be returned to both Gods.

However, according to Reb Akiva, the word *et* is to include Talmidei Chachomim. As such, there aren't two Gods—and Pharaoh was now in a position to allow the Yidden to leave. When the Midrash states, "I will let the Yidden leave when Reb Akiva comes to redeem them," it is understood to mean, according to Reb Akiva's interpretation of the word *et*, "I can allow the Yidden to leave."

(Pardes Reb Yehonatan)

כַּמָּה מַעֲלוֹת טוֹבוֹת לַמָּקוֹם עָלֵינוּ!

אִלּוּ הוֹצִיאָנוּ מִמִּצְרַיִם וְלֹא עָשָׂה בָהֶם שְׁפָטִים, דַּיֵּנוּ.

אִלּוּ עָשָׂה בָהֶם שְׁפָטִים, וְלֹא עָשָׂה בֵאלֹהֵיהֶם, דַּיֵּנוּ.

אִלּוּ עָשָׂה בֵאלֹהֵיהֶם, וְלֹא הָרַג אֶת בְּכוֹרֵיהֶם, דַּיֵּנוּ.

אִלּוּ הָרַג אֶת בְּכוֹרֵיהֶם וְלֹא נָתַן לָנוּ אֶת מָמוֹנָם, דַּיֵּנוּ.

אִלּוּ נָתַן לָנוּ אֶת מָמוֹנָם וְלֹא קָרַע לָנוּ אֶת הַיָּם, דַּיֵּנוּ.

אִלּוּ קָרַע לָנוּ אֶת הַיָּם וְלֹא הֶעֱבִירָנוּ בְתוֹכוֹ בֶּחָרָבָה, דַּיֵּנוּ.

דַּיֵּנוּ

Dayeinu

אִלּוּ קָרַע לָנוּ אֶת־הַיָּם וְלֹא הֶעֱבִירָנוּ בְתוֹכוֹ בֶּחָרָבָה, דַּיֵּנוּ

"Had He split the sea for us but not brought us through it dry . . ."

The Midrash offers two reasons why the waters split. It was in the merit of Avrohom. With regard to Krias Yam Suf, the posuk says, וַיִּבָּקְעוּ הַמָּיִם *"And the waters split"* (Shemos 14:21), and when Avrohom was taking Yitzchok to the Akeidah, the posuk says, וַיְבַקַּע עֲצֵי עֹלָה *"And he split wood for a burnt offering"* (Bereishis 22:3). Both incidents use the verb בָּקַע *"split."*

The second approach is that they were saved because of their emunah in Hashem.

The difference between the two opinions comes to the fore when considering whether the Yidden were permitted to see the Egyptians drowning.

When Lot was saved from Sodom, the angels warned him that he and his family were not permitted to turn around and see the destruction of Sodom because they had been saved in the merit of Avrohom. However, if they had been saved in their own merit, they would have been permitted to see the downfall of Sodom.

Similarly, if the Yidden were saved because of their faith, they would have been

How much good, layer upon layer, the Omnipresent has done for us:

Had He brought us out of Egypt without bringing judgment upon [our oppressors], that would have been enough for us.

Had He brought judgment upon them but not upon their gods, that would have been enough for us.

Had He brought judgment upon their gods without killing their firstborn sons, that would have been enough for us.

Had He killed their firstborn sons without giving us their wealth, that would have been enough for us.

Had He given us their wealth without splitting the sea for us, that would have been enough for us.

Had He split the sea for us but not brought us through it dry, that would have been enough for us.

permitted to witness the Egyptians drowning. However, if it was in the merit of Avrohom, they would not be permitted, just as Lot and his family were not permitted.

(Midrash Yehonatan Beshalach)

Chizkiyahu and the Yidden were saved from the hands of Sancheriv. The Talmud writes that it would have been appropriate for Chizkiyahu to sing a song of praise to Hashem. The reason he did not is because they were saved in the merit of Dovid.

The Talmud is of the opinion that we are entitled to sing a song of gratitude if we are the cause of our own salvation.

If the Yidden had been saved in the merit of Avrohom, they would not have been allowed to sing the song "Oz Yoshir." However, since they were saved due to their emunah, they were permitted to sing the "Oz Yoshir."

We will now appreciate the sequence of the posukim, *"Hashem saved the Yidden . . . The Yidden saw the Egyptians dying"* (Shemos 14:30–31). Since they were permitted to see them drown, this indicates they were saved in their own merit, and thus, *"Then Moshe and the Bnei Yisroel sang this song"* (Shemos 15:1). They were allowed to sing a song to Hashem. (Midrash Yehonatan Beshalach)

When Moshe was instructed, *"And you [Moshe] raise your staff and stretch out your hand over the sea and split it"* (Shemos 14:16), it was to save the mixed multitude, as they did not have the merit of the forefathers.

However, the Yidden were saved in the merit of Avrohom, Yitzchok, Yaakov, and Yoseph. As the Talmud writes, "The sea saw Yoseph's coffin and the waters split."

(Tiferet Yehonatan Beshalach)

There are four elements: fire, wind, water, and earth. The nature of fire and wind is to move in an upward direction. Earth descends. If we would remove the earth component in water, it would move in an upward direction.

When the Torah tells us that Moshe split the sea, it can be understood to mean that he separated the earth component from the water. As a result, the earth component gathered together and became dry land, and the waters naturally rose and miraculously formed walls on the right and the left.

(Tiferet Yehonatan Beshalach)

By the splitting of the sea, Hashem displayed simultaniously the attribute of mercy by saving the Yidden and the characteristic of strict judgment by drowning the Egyptians.

This is alluded to in the section of "Oz Yoshir" where the posuk says, יְהֹוָה יִמְלֹךְ לְעֹלָם וָעֶד "Hashem will reign for all eternity" (Shemos 15:18). The name Hashem represents the attribute of mercy while the word יִמְלֹךְ "will reign" signifies the attribute of strict justice. As the posuk says, *"A king establishes the country with justice"* (Mishlei 29:4).

How do we know that both attributes were functioning at the same time? Perhaps the Yidden had crossed the sea and were already on the banks of the other side when the Egyptians drowned?

The very next posuk reads, "When Pharaoh's horses came with his chariots and his horsemen in to the sea and Hashem brought the waters of the sea back upon them and the Beni Yisroel walked on dry land in the midst of the sea." Clearly, the waters came upon the Egyptians while the Yidden were walkimg on dry land.

Hashem implemets both traits at the same time: rachamim for the tzaddikim and din for the reshoim.

(Tiferet Yehonatan Beshalach)

The Egyptians realized they would perish in the raging waters and wanted to turn back. However, miraculously the horses did not obey their riders' instructions. Seeing this, they removed the wheels from the chariots, believing that this would stop the horses in their tracks. This did not occur, and they continued to drag the chariots forward.

The Egyptians understood that this was part of the Divine plan, and they screamed out, "*Hashem is fighting for them against the Egyptians,*" meaning "Hashem is in battle with the spiritual force of the Egyptians."

(Tiferet Yehonatan Beshalach)

Hashem would not punish a nation unless He had prior punished its ministering angel. This was not the case in Egypt. Hashem first punished the people, and then He punished their god. Hashem didn't want the Egyptians to say, "If our god were here, it would save us." Therefore, the Egyptian's ministering angel was punished *after* the Egyptians were punished.

This is alluded to in the words, "*Horse and rider.*" The horse represents the Egyptian people, and its rider symbolizes their god. Just as a rider steers his horse in the direction it wants it to go, likewise the Egyptian ministering angel leads the Egyptian in the path it wants them to go.

The posuk is understood to mean, "[First the] *Horse* [the Egyptian people and then] *its rider* [the Egyptian god were] *cast into the sea.*"

(Tiferet Yehonatan Beshalach)

The Egyptians didn't all drown at the same spot. Some drowned in the midst of the sea where the waters were at their deepest and some by the water's edge. This is alluded to in the posuk, "*Pharaoh's chariots and his army He cast into the sea and the elite of his officers sank in the Yam Suf*" (Shemos 15:4).

The words "*Cast into the sea*" refers to the Egyptians who drowned in the midst of the sea where the waters were at their deepest. The words "*sank in the Yam Suf*" refer to those Egyptians who drowned by the water's edge. As such, the chariots managed to make it to the middle of the sea while the horses drowned soon after entering the water.

Under normal conditions, we would imagine that the chariots, being heavy objects, together with their riders would drown immediately at the water's edge, while the horses and riders could have attempted to swim further into the sea. This

אִלּוּ הֶעֱבִירָנוּ בְתוֹכוֹ בֶּחָרָבָה וְלֹא שִׁקַּע צָרֵנוּ בְתוֹכוֹ, דַּיֵּנוּ.

אִלּוּ שִׁקַּע צָרֵנוּ בְתוֹכוֹ וְלֹא סִפֵּק צָרְכֵּנוּ בַּמִּדְבָּר אַרְבָּעִים שָׁנָה, דַּיֵּנוּ.

אִלּוּ סִפֵּק צָרְכֵּנוּ בַּמִּדְבָּר אַרְבָּעִים שָׁנָה וְלֹא הֶאֱכִילָנוּ אֶת הַמָּן, דַּיֵּנוּ.

did not occur; the exact opposite did. And this was simply one of the many miracles that occurred by the splitting of the sea.

(Tiferet Yehonatan Beshalach)

Some Egyptians among Pharaoh's inner circle believed in Hashem and wanted to let the Yidden leave. However, they were too frightened to challenge Pharaoh.

The death of those who drowned in the midst of the sea was far more painful than the death of those who perished at the water's edge.

Those who drowned in the midst of the sea were the most wicked, while those who perished by the edge were not as wicked. As such, when the posuk says, "*the elite of his officers sank in the Yam Suf,*" it does not necessarily refer to only the battle-hardened warriors but can also include those who believed in Hashem and wanted to let the Yidden leave.

(Tiferet Yehonatan Beshalach)

The Midrash writes that when Aaron's two sons, Nadav and Avihu, perished, the angels asked Hashem why He split the sea. Why did the passing of Nadav and Avihu prompt the question about Krias Yam Suf?

The Talmud discusses why Nadav and Avihu passed away, and it suggests because their father Aaron had made the golden calf.

The Talmud queries this suggestion and asks, "Wasn't Aaron coerced into making it? He had seen Chur murdered because he had refused to abide by the wishes of the people. As such, Aaron had no choice. Whey then were his sons punished?"

True, Chur had been killed. Nonetheless, Aaron should not have made the calf. It would seem that coercion cannot be a justification for a wrongful act.

The Midrash writes, "When the Yidden entered the sea, the angels asked why the Yidden are being saved while the Egyptian's are drowning, Both the Egyptians and the Yidden are idol worshippers."

Had He brought us through [the sea] dry without drowning our enemies in it, that would have been enough for us.

Had He drowned our enemies in it without providing for our needs for forty years in the desert, that would have been enough for us.

Had He provided for our needs for forty years in the desert, without feeding us with manna, that would have been enough for us.

Hashem explained that the Egyptians served the idols of their own will and desire, while the Yidden were forced into idol worship.

From Hashem's response, it is clear that there is a distinction between acting on one's own volition or being forced to do so. And since the Yidden were forced to serve idols, they were not held responsible for their actions. Therefore, the sea splitting for the Yidden and then causing the Egyptians to drown was appropriate.

Then, by extension, Aaron should not be responsible for making the golden calf; he had no choice in the matter as his life was at stake. It is, therefore, understood why Krias Yam Suf prompted the angels to ask why Nadav and Avihu perished.

Just as the Yidden were not held responsible for being forced to serve idols and the sea split, likewise Aaron should not have been held responsible for making the calf and his sons should not have perished.

(Divrei Yehonatan Acharei)

אִלוּ סִפֵּק צָרְכֵנוּ בַּמִּדְבָּר אַרְבָּעִים שָׁנָה וְלֹא הֶאֱכִילָנוּ אֶת הַמָּן דַּיֵּנוּ

"Had He provided for our needs for forty years in the desert, without feeding us with manna."

The Torah writes, *"Your clothing did not wear out upon you nor did your foot swell these forty years"* (Devorim 8:5).

During the forty years the Yidden were in the desert, they ate manna. The manna was unique in the sense that all of it was absorbed within the body; there was no waste. As such, there was no need for the Yidden to have to excrete anything.

If that was the case, why does the Torah instruct the Yidden, *"You shall keep a stake in addition to your weapons"* (Devorim 23:14), as the purpose of this equipment was to bury an excrement?

The Yidden were surrounded and protected by the clouds of glory. If a Yid sinned, he was spat out by these clouds. A Yid on the other side did not receive his daily portion of manna, and he would have to purchase food from travelers. Such food purchased was not fully absorbed into the body, and as such, there was need for a stake.

אִלּוּ הֶאֱכִילָנוּ אֶת הַמָּן וְלֹא נָתַן לָנוּ אֶת הַשַּׁבָּת, דַּיֵּנוּ.

אִלּוּ נָתַן לָנוּ אֶת הַשַּׁבָּת, וְלֹא קֵרְבָנוּ לִפְנֵי הַר סִינַי, דַּיֵּנוּ.

However, the clothes of those Yidden who were spat out miraculously remained fresh and clean.

(Tiferet Yehonatan Eikev)

The Yidden were sustained in the desert by the manna that fell from the heaven on a daily basis. Another miracle that occurred was that the Yidden's shoes and clothing always remained clean and fresh, and there was no need to wash or change them.

Just as their clothing miraculously lasted, why couldn't the manna last for an extended period of time? Why did it have to fall every single day?

If the manna had lasted, the Yidden would have been forced to transport their food, which would have been an extreme burden. To make the journey as pleasant as possible, Hashem performed a miracle on a daily basis. Conversely, the Yidden were already wearing their garments; the fact that they remained clean and fresh did not make the journey more difficult.

(Tiferet Yehonatan Eikev)

The cloud of glory ensured that the Yidden's clothing did not wear out. The cloud of glory functioned due to the merit of Aaron. Therefore, the Kohanim received the first shearing of wool from the sheep, as the posuk says, *"The first of the fleece of your sheep you shall give him"* (Devorim 18:4).

(Tiferet Yehonatan Shoftim)

אִלּוּ נָתַן לָנוּ אֶת הַשַּׁבָּת, וְלֹא קֵרְבָנוּ לִפְנֵי הַר סִינַי, דַּיֵּנוּ

"Had He given us Shabbos without drawing us close around Mount Sinai"

The Talmud (Shabbos 118a) writes, "Anyone who delights in the Shabbos, Hashem gives him a boundless portion." What is the boundless portion we will merit through our observance of the Shabbos?

Had He fed us with manna without giving us Shabbos, that would have been enough for us.

Had He given us Shabbos without drawing us close around Mount Sinai, that would have been enough for us.

The boundless portion refers to the Land of Israel. Why is it called a boundless portion?

The Talmud (Kesubos 112) quotes the posuk, *"And give you a pleasant land, the goodliest [tzvi] heritage"* (Yermiyahu 3:19). When describing Israel as a good land, the posuk refers to Israel as a *tzvi,* which means a "deer." The Talmud asks, "Why is Israel compared to a deer?"

It answers that a deer's skin cannot contain its meat once it has been skinned, so too, Eretz Yisroel, while a small country, can miraculously contain a vast number of people. And the more people who live there, the larger the land becomes. And this is the understanding of the blessing "a boundless portion."

That is why Eretz Yisroel is called "Yaakov's estate." When Yaakov slept by the future sight of the Beis Hamikdosh, Hashem promised him that the land he is lying on will be his inheritance. Hashem performed a miracle, and the Land of Israel rolled itself and was contained under him. This tiny portion of land would grow and be able to absorb all Yaakov's descendants.

If the nations of the world would have known this about the Land of Israel, they would have not despised it due to its small landmass. And they would have accepted the Torah.

Therefore, when Hashem offered them the Torah, He did not inform them of the reward for keeping Shabbos, as then they would have accepted the Torah, knowing that by keeping Shabbos the land would continue to grow larger and larger.

(Yaaros Dvash 2,10)

By observing Shabbos with joy, we are declaring that Hashem created the world; He created the world in six days and rested on the seventh.

Enosh and others believed that Hashem created the world with purpose and reason, and then Hashem handed the running of the world to the constellations.

How does the observance of the Shabbos with simcha refute the position of Enosh?

We have been instructed to rejoice on Shabbos, and many reasons have been given. One of them is that the planet Shabtai (Saturn) exerts influence on Shabbos,

אִלּוּ קֵרְבָנוּ לִפְנֵי הַר סִינַי, וְלֹא נָתַן לָנוּ אֶת הַתּוֹרָה, דַּיֵּנוּ.

conjuring feelings of melancholy and sadness. Therefore, we are commanded to rejoice and to be happy on the Shabbos to show that Shabtai does not run the world. Rather, Hashem constantly recreates and runs the world.

Hence, when we keep Shabbos with great simcha, we are declaring Hashem's constant involvement in the word's running.

(Yaaros Dvash 2,10)

While other religions have a day of rest, none have chosen Shabbos to be their day of rest. This is considered a gift from Hashem. Why so?

If other nations were to keep Shabbos, when Hashem wants to reward the Yidden for their observance of Shabbos, the prosecuting angels would highlight the other nations who were equally observing Shabbos. By ensuring no other nation keeps Shabbos, the angels would not be able to compare the Yidden to those nations.

As such, it is indeed a true gift from Hashem.

(Yaaros Dvash 3,2)

The Midrash shares an interesting conversation between Adam and Kayin after Kayin killed Hevel, his brother. Adam asks him about his judgment. Kayin responds that he has done teshuvah and an understanding had been reached. When Adam heard this, he proclaimed how great is the power of teshuvah and began to recite, "A song of praise for the day of Shabbos."

Undoubtedly, this Midrash needs further examination.

The posuk says, תָּשֵׁב אֱנוֹשׁ עַד דַּכָּא, *"You bring man to the crushing point"* (Tehillim 90:3). The word דַּכָּא is an anacronym for דָּם "blood-murder," כְּפִירָה "a denier-idol worship," and אִשָּׁה "women-illicit relationships." These are the three cardinal transgressions. As the three are on par one with the other, if teshuvah works by one of the three, then it will work by all three.

The Zohar writes that when Adam ate from the tree of knowledge, he transgressed the prohibition of idol worship as by his actions he had denied Hashem's existence. Adam was concerned whether he could be forgiven for one of

Had He drawn us close around Mount Sinai without giving us the Torah, that would have been enough for us.

the cardinal sins. When Kayin told him that he had been forgiven for murder, Adam knew that he could be forgiven for idol worship.

The question Adam faced was what path of teshuvah did he need to take. The Talmud (Shabbos 118b) writes, "If a person keeps the Shabbos, even if he is an idol worshipper similar to the generation of Enosh, he will be forgiven."

Adam understood that keeping Shabbos would atone for idol worship. Therefore, he immediately proclaimed, "A song of praise for the day of Shabbos."

(Midrash Yehonatan Bereishis)

אִלּוּ קֵרְבָנוּ לִפְנֵי הַר סִינַי, וְלֹא נָתַן לָנוּ אֶת הַתּוֹרָה, דַּיֵּנוּ

"Had He drawn us close around Har Sinai without giving us the Torah ..."

There are Yidden who feel they need to devote themselves to their own personal study, and once they have completed all their learning, they can then begin to teach others. This is a false approach, as a person can learn for a thousand years and will not have learned even a minute amount of Hashem's Torah. Rather, a person is obligated to impart the knowledge that Hashem has graced him with to others.

What is the basis for this?

Why was it necessary to bring the Yidden to Har Sinai to receive the Torah when Hashem's voice was heard throughout the world, as the posuk says, *"The voice of Hashem breaks the cedars"* (Tehillim 29:5)?

The posuk says, *"That they may learn to fear me ... and that they may teach their children"* (Devorim 4:11), and the next posuk states, *"And you approached and stood at the foot of the mountain."*

When the posuk says, *"They may teach their children,"* it is referring to a person's students. Just as Hashem brought us close to the mountain to receive the Torah, we to need to bring our students close and teach them the Torah.

(Tiferet Yehonatan Voeschanon)

The posuk states, *"And you approached and stood at the foot of the mountain"* (Devorim 4:12). The Talmud (Shabbos 80a) writes that Hashem placed the mountain above their heads and warned them that if they would not accept the Torah, the mountain would fall on them and they would perish.

Why would the demise of the Yidden need to be a result of the mountain crushing them?

Every time Hashem said one of the commandments, the spiritual revelation caused the souls of the Yidden to depart. Couldn't Hashem have taken a passive approach and not resurrected them after saying one of the commandments?

The significance of the mountain will become apparent based on the following:

The posuk says, "I lift up my eyes to the mountains, from where will my salvation come?" (Tehillim 121:1).

Why specifically the mountains?

The mountains refer to the influence of astrology. The Talmud (Nedorim 32a) relates that Hashem said to Avrom, "Emerge from your astrology because there is no constellation for the Jewish people." The Yidden are not subject to the influence of astrology.

The posuk can now be understood to mean, "I lift up my eyes to the mountains"—I say to the constellations, "We are not influenced by you. If so, from where will my salvation come?"

The answer is given in the posuk: "Help will come from Hashem, the One who created heaven and earth."

By placing the mountain on their heads, Hashem is saying to the Yidden, "If you will accept the Torah and mitzvos, then you will not be influenced by the constellations. However, if you don't, then you will be subject to the influences of astrology."

(Tiferet Yehonatan Voeschanon)

ᚼ

At the time of the Messianic era, the nations of the world will complain to Hashem and will argue, "If we had a mountain placed on our heads, we would have also accepted the Torah."

This challenge is without merit as the mountain hovering over the heads of the Yidden symbolized a shift from direct Divine influence to being influenced by the constellations. Hashem was warning the Yidden what would result if they refused to accept the Torah. This change can only occur by Yidden, as the nations of the world are always under the influence of astrology.

As such, placing the mountain above the nations would have made no difference.

(Tiferet Yehonatan Voeschanon)

ᚼ

The Talmud (Shabbos 88b) writes, "When the Yidden proclaimed, 'We will do and we will listen,' a heavenly voice proclaimed, 'Who revealed this secret that the ministering angels abide by, where they first do His will and then they listen to His words?'"

How do we understand this cryptic Talmudic statement?

There was an argument between the philosophers and the Rabbinic scholars. Aristotle and his compatriots felt that wisdom and intellectual pursuit were the key to spiritual connectivity. They also did not believe in prophecy. They assumed that since they were the wisest of all men and they did not experience prophecy, it must be that there is no such thing as communication between God and mankind.

The Torah scholars understood that the key to spiritual connectivity was through the performance of Hashem's mitzvos. When we build a sukkah for Hashem's sake and fulfill the mitzvah with great joy, then we can connect with Hashem on a far greater level then Aristotle could.

When the Yidden were in Egypt, they believed, as the philosophers did, that a person's intellect is the vehicle to harness spiritual growth. However, after witnessing Krias Yam Suf, they understood their error. And they came to the realization that, to access spirituality, we need to perform Hashem's mitzvos.

The Yidden proclaimed, "We will do," meaning, "We understand if we want to come close to Hashem, we need to perform the mitzvos"—and then "we will listen," meaning, "We will be able to listen to the Heavenly voice and receive Hashem's prophecy."

The statement, "Who revealed this secret that the ministering angels abide by?" means "How did the Yidden discover the secret that the path to spirituality and prophecy is through mitzvos?"

While the angels are intellectually superior creatures, they understand they first need to do Hashem's commands and then they will be in a position to be able to listen to His words.

(Yaaros Dvash 1:11)

🔥

The Talmud (Shabbos 88b) writes, "Each time Hashem said one of the Ten Commandments, the neshamos of the Yidden left them. Using the dew of the resurrection, Hashem brought the Yidden back to life."

Why couldn't Hashem ensure that the neshamos of the Yidden not leave them in the first place?

When the Yidden left Egypt, they were still filled with impurity and sin and their bodies were not pure enough to receive the Torah. Therefore, they needed their souls to depart. When their souls returned, they were reborn, and as such, they were now spiritually ready to receive the Torah.

This was similar to the Zohar's understanding of Moshe's experience by the

אִלּוּ נָתַן לָנוּ אֶת הַתּוֹרָה וְלֹא הִכְנִיסָנוּ לְאֶרֶץ יִשְׂרָאֵל, דַּיֵּנוּ.

burning bush. Hashem informed Moshe that he needed to remove his shoes. This is understood to mean that Moshe's body that had lived in Pharaoh's palace was not suitable to receive Hashem's prophecies. Therefore, in a sense, Moshe had to shed his old body and receive a new one.

So was it by Har Sinai and so will it unfold with the coming of Moshiach.

(Yaaros Dvash 1:10)

The Midrash writes that when Hashem gave the Torah to the Yidden, He first gave them the laws necessary to resolve monetary disputes and then He gave them the Torah.

Why was it necessary to first give the Yidden these laws prior to them receiving the rest of the Torah?

The Talmud (Shabbos 86b) writes, "When Hashem decided to give the Torah to the Yidden, the angels complained and said they were entitled to receive the Torah as they had the status of a *bar metzrah,* a neighbor. The law is that, if a person is selling his field, the neighbors whose field is next to the property to be sold have the first rights to the property. Hence, the angels claimed the that Torah was in heaven and since they were in heaven, the Torah should remain with them."

The halocho is that a person can sell his property to a non-neighbor if the purchaser is his business partner. The Talmud (Shabbos 10a) writes that when a judge rules correctly, he becomes a partner with Hashem in creation.

Therefore, Hashem gave the Yidden the laws relating to financial disputes. By adjudicating correctly, the Yidden would become Hashem's partner and, as such, were entitled to receive the Torah even though the Torah was in heaven and they were on earth.

(Pardes Reb Yehonatan)

Success in the study of Torah is not dependent on whether we are on the spiritual level of the generation that left Egypt and heard the voice of Hashem. Likewise,

Had He given us the Torah without bringing us to the land of Israel, that would have been enough for us.

it is irrelevant under which constellation we were born. Similarly, where we live, whether in Israel or in the diaspora, does not impact our ability to learn Torah.

(Tiferet Yehonatan Nitzovim)

אִלּוּ נָתַן לָנוּ אֶת־הַתּוֹרָה וְלֹא הִכְנִיסָנוּ לְאֶרֶץ יִשְׂרָאֵל, דַּיֵּנוּ.

"Had He given us the Torah without bringing us to the Land of Israel . . ."

What is the connection between giving of the Torah and entering the Land of Israel?

They both cause a person to become wise.

Concerning the Torah, the posuk says, *"The law of Hashem is perfect, restoring the soul; the testimony of Hashem is faithful, making the simple person wise"* (Tehillim 19:8).

As it relates to the Land of Israel, the Talmud (Bava Batra 158b) writes that the air of Israel makes a person wise.

(Midrash Yehonatan Haggadah)

In Pirkei Avos, it states, "Desire not the table of kings." What should we not desire about the table of kings?

A king generally spends an excessive amount of time indulging in worldly pleasures such as royal banquets and feasts. We are taught that there are more important things in life to devote our attention to such as the study of Torah.

(Ahavat Yehonatan Vayechi)

It is preferable to learn with other people in a Beis Midrash. Since when we learn alone, the learning may increase our haughtiness, as we may reflect on our achievements.

However, when we learn in a Beis Midrash, if other people are learning there and notice any bad quality traits such as an increase in arrogance, they will reprimand us, thus ensuring we remain humble.

(Yaaros Dvash 2:3)

אִלּוּ הִכְנִיסָנוּ לְאֶרֶץ יִשְׂרָאֵל וְלֹא בָנָה לָנוּ אֶת בֵּית הַבְּחִירָה, דַּיֵּנוּ.

אִלּוּ הִכְנִיסָנוּ לְאֶרֶץ יִשְׂרָאֵל וְלֹא בָנָה לָנוּ אֶת בֵּית הַבְּחִירָה, דַּיֵּנוּ

"Had He brought us to the Land of Israel without building for us the Beis Hamikdosh . . ."

Moshe did not merit to enter the Land of Israel. The Midrash records that Hashem said to Moshe, *"You killed an Egyptian and you still want to enter the Land of Israel?"* How are we to understand Hashem's question?

One of the reasons offered for why Moshe did not merit to lead the Jewish people into the Holy Land was because he was reluctant to fulfill Hashem's mission to go to Egypt and redeem the Jewish people.

One of the justifications given for Moshe's hesitancy was predicated on the following thought process. Moshe had the status of a Kohen and could not come in contact with a corpse, including the corpse of a non-Jew. We are told that there wasn't a home in Egypt where someone had not died during the plague of the slaying of the firstborn. Therefore, Moshe, as a Kohen, felt he could not venture into the land of Egypt.

What Moshe failed to consider is that the law is that a Kohen who takes the life of another human being can no longer serve in the Beis Hamikdosh. Hashem's question to Moshe, "You killed an Egyptian and you still want to enter the Land of Israel?" contains a number of subplots.

Hashem is asking, "Moshe, you are a Kohen, and therefore, you didn't want to go to Egypt to redeem the Jewish people. However, you killed a person, and as such, you cannot serve in the Beis Hamikdosh and the need to not come in contact with a corpse is no longer of any significance. So, you have no justification for your indecision and so you will not be allowed to enter the Land of Israel.

(Midrash Yehonatan)

The Land of Israel has always been central in the life of the Yid.

The Talmud writes that when we daven, we should focus that our tefillos are reaching heaven via the Land of Israel.

Likewise, when we perform one of the mitzvos, we should imagine that we are fulfilling it while standing on the holy earth of Israel.

(Tiferet Yehonatan)

Had He brought us to the land of Israel without building for us the House He chose that would have been enough for us.

A level higher would be, while performing the mitzvah, one needs to hope that they will merit to actually live in Israel and be performing the mitzvah in Israel.

(Yaaros Dvash)

"And did not build the Beis Hamikdosh, it would have sufficed."
The first Beis Hamikdosh was destroyed by Nebuchadnezzar the King of Babylon, while the second Beis Hamikdosh was destroyed by Titus of the Roman Empire. The Babylonian Empire neighbored the Land of Israel, while the Roman Empire was a fair distance away.

The Talmud writes, "The second Beis Hamikdosh was destroyed due to unwanted hatred amongst the Jewish people and the prevalence of lashon hara."

When we speak lashon hara about someone, that person could be living on the other side of the globe and your words could be as harmful and as devastating as if the person was living next door. Therefore, the second Beis Hamikdosh was destroyed by a nation that was not the next-door neighbor but rather a nation that lived a great distance away.

(Yaaros Dvash 1:16)

Why were the Yidden only obligated in building the Beis Hamikdosh after the seven years of conquest and the seven years of division?

It was not an easy task for a person to leave his home, family, and possessions and travel to the Beis Hamikdosh. Therefore, Hashem promised the Yidden, *"No man will desire your land"* (Shemos 34:24). The reason our property will be protected is based on the Talmudic ruling, when a person is traveling to fulfill a mitzvah, he will not encounter any harm.

The Talmud (Pesochim 8b) qualifies this ruling as not being applicable when the environment that the person is traveling in is dangerous. Therefore, during the first fourteen years when the Yidden were at war, there was no obligation to

כַּמָּה מַעֲלוֹת טוֹבוֹת לַמָּקוֹם עָלֵינוּ!

עַל אַחַת, כַּמָּה וְכַמָּה, טוֹבָה כְפוּלָה וּמְכֻפֶּלֶת לַמָּקוֹם עָלֵינוּ: שֶׁהוֹצִיאָנוּ מִמִּצְרַיִם, וְעָשָׂה בָהֶם שְׁפָטִים, וְעָשָׂה בֵאלֹהֵיהֶם, וְהָרַג אֶת בְּכוֹרֵיהֶם, וְנָתַן לָנוּ אֶת מָמוֹנָם, וְקָרַע לָנוּ אֶת הַיָּם, וְהֶעֱבִירָנוּ בְתוֹכוֹ בֶּחָרָבָה, וְשִׁקַּע צָרֵנוּ בְּתוֹכוֹ, וְסִפֵּק צָרְכֵּנוּ בַּמִּדְבָּר אַרְבָּעִים שָׁנָה, וְהֶאֱכִילָנוּ אֶת הַמָּן, וְנָתַן לָנוּ אֶת הַשַּׁבָּת, וְקֵרְבָנוּ לִפְנֵי הַר סִינַי, וְנָתַן לָנוּ אֶת הַתּוֹרָה, וְהִכְנִיסָנוּ לְאֶרֶץ יִשְׂרָאֵל, וּבָנָה לָנוּ אֶת בֵּית הַבְּחִירָה לְכַפֵּר עַל כָּל עֲוֹנוֹתֵינוּ.

רַבָּן גַּמְלִיאֵל הָיָה אוֹמֵר: כָּל שֶׁלֹּא אָמַר שְׁלֹשָׁה דְבָרִים אֵלּוּ בַּפֶּסַח, לֹא יָצָא יְדֵי חוֹבָתוֹ, וְאֵלּוּ הֵן:

פֶּסַח, מַצָּה, וּמָרוֹר

build the Beis Hamikdosh, as it would have been too dangerous to travel in the midst of a war.

This is alluded to in the sequence of the posukim, "He will give you rest from all your enemies surrounding you and you will dwell securely." Once that has been accomplished, the next posuk instructs the Yidden "And it will be that the place Hashem your God will choose in which to establish His name there" (Devorim 12:10,11).

Once there is peace, we need to build the Beis Hamikdosh.

(Tiferet Yehonatan Re'eh)

וְקָרַע לָנוּ אֶת הַיָּם

"He split the sea for us . . ."

The posuk says, "With this you shall be tested. By Pharaoh's life, you shall not leave this place unless your younger brother comes here" (Bereishis 42:15).

Yoseph informs his brothers that they will remain in Egypt until Binyamin comes.

The posuk can be understood to be a prophecy concerning the Exodus. The

How many and manifold then, the Omnipresent's kindnesses are to us—for He brought us out of Egypt and brought judgment upon [our oppressors] and upon their gods, and He killed their firstborn sons and gave us their wealth, and He split the sea for us and brought us through it on dry land and drowned our enemies there, and He provided for our needs for forty years in the desert and fed us manna, and He gave us Shabbos, and He drew us close around Mount Sinai and gave us the Torah, and He brought us to the Land of Israel and built for us the House He chose, So we could find atonement [there] for all our sins.

Rabban Gamliel would say: Anyone who does not say these three things on Pesach has not fulfilled his obligation, and these are they:

Pesach—the Pesach Offering

Matzah—the Unleavened Bread

Maror—the Bitter Herbs

Yidden will remain in exile until the tribe of Binyamin descends into the sea. The posuk writes, *"Benyamin the youngest rules over them"* (Tehillim 60:28). Rashi explains the phrase to mean, "the tribe of Benyamin crossed the sea at the head of the other tribes."

Yoseph is telling his brothers, "You will remain in exile until Benyamin enters the sea."

(Tiferet Yehonatan Vayigash)

The Midrash (Berishis Rabba 5:5) writes that during the six days of creation, Hashem ruled that, the moment the Yidden stepped into the Yam Suf, it must split. Why was it necessary for Hashem to make a condition at the time of creation? Why couldn't Hashem perform a miracle at the time of the Exodus?

The Talmud (Shabbos 32a) writes, "If a person experiences a miracle, the miracle will reduce the reward they will receive in the world to come." Hence, the Yidden didn't want to have a miracle performed on their behalf because it would reduce their merit and the Yidden knew that they could be saved without Hashem performing a miracle. Therefore, Hashem made a decree at the time of creation that the waters must split, and consequently, the Yidden did not have any of their merits removed.

(Tiferet Yehonatan Korach)

◊

The Midrash (Shemos Rabba 21:7) writes that when Satan appeared before Hashem and said, "Both nations are idol worshippers, and both should be destroyed," Hashem brought Iyov to the Satan. Why specifically was Iyov brought?

The Midrash writes that Hashem loves the persecuted more than the persecutor, the proof being that we offer on the altar only domesticated animals, not wild animals, as domesticated animals are persecuted, and wild animals are persecutors. Iyov was persecuted, and the Egyptians were persecutors.

In a figurative sense, by bringing Iyov to the Satan, Hashem is conveying why the Yidden were ultimately saved. The reason is that the Egyptians were the persecutors, and the Yidden were the persecuted. And Hashem loves the persecuted more than the persecutor.

(Pardes Reb Yehonatan)

Lomdus

The Midrash writes that when Moshe broke the luchos, the angels asked Hashem, "Why did you split the sea?"

What is the connection between breaking the luchos and splitting the sea that prompted the angels to question Hashem's actions?

Why did Moshe break the luchos?

The Talmud (Shabbos 87a) writes, "The Korban Pesach is only one of the six hundred and thirteen mitzvos and the Torah says, 'No stranger shall eat of it' (Shemos 12:43). The word stranger includes both a non-Jew and a Jew who is an apostate, meaning a Jew who is an apostate is not permitted to eat from the Korban Pesach. It stands to reason then that the Yidden should not receive the entire Torah, as they were idol worshippers. Hence Moshe broke them.

Tosfos posits, "Even though the apostate cannot partake of the Korban Pesach that should not preclude the Yidden from receiving the Torah. For when they receive it, they will be able to do teshuvah."

There is an opinion that teshuvah cannot eradicate the sin of idol worship. Moshe broke the luchos because he was of that opinion. The Talmud says that Hashem agreed with Moshe's actions. Seemingly then, Hashem is also of the opinion that teshuvah will not help with regard to idol worship.

The Midrash quotes a conversation that took place at the time of Krias Yam Suf. The angels asked Hashem, "Why are you splitting the sea to save the Yidden and at the same time you are drowning the Egyptians?" To which Hashem replied, "The Yidden did teshuvah, as the posuk says, *Draw forth or buy for yourselves sheep*" (Shemos 12:21). Rashi explains, at that time, the Yidden separated themselves from idol worship.

If teshuvah doesn't eradicate the sin of idol worship, the angels were justified in asking Hashem, "Why did you split the sea for the Yidden?"

(Pardes Reb Yehonatan)

◊

There is a tradition that a mamzer will perish by drowning.

Pharaoh declared that if they subjugated and enslaved the Jewish men, then most definitely, they could have their way with their wives. As such, the Jewish children would be illegitimate. To dispel such a claim, the Yidden were saved by Krias Yam Suf, for if they were illegitimate, they would have drowned in the waters.

This will also explain why Hashem performed the miracle of the splitting of the Jordan River to allow the Yidden to enter the Land of Israel. The Jordan River was not very wide, and the Yidden could have crossed it with boats. However, the nations accused the Yidden of leading immoral lives while living in the desert. Hashem performed a miracle to split the sea to demonstrate that the Yidden were not illegitimate; if they were, they would have drowned.

This will explain why Moshe was called by this name. The Torah writes that he was called Moshe because he was drawn from the water.

Moshe's parents were Amrom and Yocheved. Yocheved was Amrom's aunt. One of the Torah prohibitions is that an aunt cannot marry her nephew. As such, there may have been the suggestion that Moshe was illegitimate. If that was true, then he should have drowned when he was placed in the river. His name indicates that he was not a mamzer, as he was drawn from the river and did not drown.

(Tiferet Yehonatan Pinchas)

פֶּסַח שֶׁהָיוּ אֲבוֹתֵינוּ אוֹכְלִים בִּזְמַן שֶׁבֵּית הַמִּקְדָּשׁ הָיָה קַיָּם, עַל שׁוּם מָה? עַל שׁוּם שֶׁפָּסַח הַקָּדוֹשׁ בָּרוּךְ הוּא עַל בָּתֵּי אֲבוֹתֵינוּ בְּמִצְרַיִם, שֶׁנֶּאֱמַר: וַאֲמַרְתֶּם זֶבַח פֶּסַח הוּא לַיהֹוָה, אֲשֶׁר פָּסַח עַל בָּתֵּי בְנֵי יִשְׂרָאֵל בְּמִצְרַיִם בְּנָגְפּוֹ אֶת מִצְרַיִם, וְאֶת בָּתֵּינוּ הִצִּיל, וַיִּקֹּד הָעָם וַיִּשְׁתַּחֲווּ.

עַל שׁוּם שֶׁפָּסַח הַקָּדוֹשׁ בָּרוּךְ הוּא עַל בָּתֵּי אֲבוֹתֵינוּ בְּמִצְרַיִם

"It recalls the Holy One's passing over the houses of our fathers in Egypt."

When the Yidden entered the Land of Israel, they spent the next fourteen years conquering and settling the land. Certain mitzvos that could only be fulfilled in Israel became obligatory only after the fourteen years had transpired. Other mitzvos became mandatory immediately. One of those mitzvos was the mitzvah of bringing the Korban Pesach.

There is a sequence of posukim that discuss the mitzvah of bringing the Korban Pesach in the Land of Israel. The Torah writes, *"And it shall come to pass when you enter the land . . . you shall observe this service [of bringing the Korban Pesach] . . . And it will come to pass if your children say to you, what is this service to you? You shall say, it is a Passover sacrifice to Hashem"* (Shemos 12:26).

These posukim begin with a statement *"when you enter the land."* Then the children pose a question *"What is this service to you?"* This is followed by the response *"It is a Passover sacrifice to Hashem."*

The posukim are saying, when you enter Israel, your offspring will wonder about the mitzvah of bringing the Korban Pesach; you should tell them it is Hashem's commandment.

A deeper level of understanding is this:

The Talmud writes that whenever a mitzvah is introduced with the phrase, *when you enter the land,* the mitzvah begins after the years of conquest and settlement of the land had concluded.

The Pesach is what our fathers would eat while the Temple stood: and what does it recall?

It recalls the Holy One's passing over the houses of our fathers in Egypt, as it is said:

"You shall say: 'It is a Pesach offering for Hashem, for He passed over the houses of the Bnei Yisrael in Egypt while He struck the Egyptians but saved those in our homes'—and the people bowed and prostrated themselves."

The laws of bringing the Korban Pesach begin with the words *"when you enter the land."* Based on the Talmud, the mitzvah should be obligatory after the fourteen years have elapsed. However, the law is that the Yidden were immediately obligated to bring the Korban Pesach. The children know this and ask, *"What is this service to you?"* meaning, "Why is the obligation immediate and not after the fourteen years had elapsed?"

The child does not question the bringing per say; rather, he is confused about the timing of its introduction.

The father responds with the words *"to Hashem."* Hashem considered this mitzvah as an exception to the common rule of waiting fourteen years, and the obligation began on the first Pesach after entering the Holy Land.

(Divrei Yehonatan)

"For He passed over the houses of the children of Israel in Egypt."

Hashem did not enter the homes of the Yidden, for if He did, then the Yidden would have also perished, as they were also sinners. As the posuk says, *"Yet they deceived Him with their speech, lied to Him with their words* [when they were enslaved in Egypt]" (Tehillim 78:36).

(Pardes Reb Yehonatan)

מַצָּה זוֹ שֶׁאָנוּ אוֹכְלִים, עַל שׁוּם מַה? עַל שׁוּם שֶׁלֹּא הִסְפִּיק בְּצֵקָם שֶׁל אֲבוֹתֵינוּ לְהַחֲמִיץ עַד שֶׁנִּגְלָה עֲלֵיהֶם מֶלֶךְ מַלְכֵי הַמְּלָכִים, הַקָּדוֹשׁ בָּרוּךְ הוּא, וּגְאָלָם, שֶׁנֶּאֱמַר: וַיֹּאפוּ אֶת הַבָּצֵק אֲשֶׁר הוֹצִיאוּ מִמִּצְרַיִם עֻגֹת מַצּוֹת, כִּי לֹא חָמֵץ, כִּי גֹרְשׁוּ מִמִּצְרַיִם וְלֹא יָכְלוּ לְהִתְמַהְמֵהַּ, וְגַם צֵדָה לֹא עָשׂוּ לָהֶם.

מָרוֹר זֶה שֶׁאָנוּ אוֹכְלִים, עַל שׁוּם מַה? עַל שׁוּם שֶׁמֵּרְרוּ הַמִּצְרִים אֶת חַיֵּי אֲבוֹתֵינוּ בְּמִצְרָיִם, שֶׁנֶּאֱמַר: וַיְמָרְרוּ אֶת חַיֵּיהֶם בַּעֲבֹדָה קָשָׁה, בְּחֹמֶר וּבִלְבֵנִים וּבְכָל עֲבֹדָה בַּשָּׂדֶה אֵת כָּל עֲבֹדָתָם אֲשֶׁר עָבְדוּ בָהֶם בְּפָרֶךְ.

מַצָּה זוֹ שֶׁאָנוּ אוֹכְלִים, עַל שׁוּם מַה? עַל שׁוּם שֶׁלֹּא הִסְפִּיק בְּצֵקָם שֶׁל אֲבוֹתֵינוּ לְהַחֲמִיץ

"Why do we eat this matzah? Since the dough of our forefathers did not have time to rise."

Lomdus

What is the Haggadah trying to emphasize when it asks, "*this* matzah"?

The Talmud (Pesochim 35a) writes, "One cannot fulfill their obligation of eating matzah if it is made from rice or millet. The reason being, the posuk states, '*You shall eat no chametz with it; seven days you shall eat with it matzah, the bread of affliction*' (Devorim 16:3). This posuk indicates that only with substances that will come to a state of chametz, a person fulfills his obligation to eat matzah with them. This excludes rice and millet, even if flour is prepared from them and water is added to their flour; they do not come to a state of chametz but to a state of decay."

The Talmud (Pesochim 28b) derives from the same posuk, "*You shall eat no chametz with it; seven days you shall eat with it matzah*" (Devorim 16:3), that even after the destruction of the Beis Hamikdosh and there is no Korban Pesach, there is still a Torah obligation to eat matzah.

This Matzah that we eat: what does it recall? It recalls the dough of our fathers, which did not have time to rise before the King, King of kings, the Holy One, blessed be He, revealed Himself and redeemed them, as it is said: "They baked the dough that they had brought out of Egypt into unleavened cakes, for it had not risen, for they were cast out of Egypt and could not delay, and they made no provision for the way."

The bitter herbs are now lifted:

These Bitter Herbs that we eat: what do they recall? They recall the bitterness that the Egyptians imposed on the lives of our fathers in Egypt, as it is said: "They embittered their lives with hard labor, with clay and with bricks and with all field labors, with all the work with which they enslaved them was with hard labor."

How can we derive these two laws from the same posuk?

Rather, we must say that we learn one law from the posuk, and one law based on logic. We will learn that the matzah cannot be made from rice based on reasoning. The Torah tells us we eat matzah because when the Yidden left Egypt, the matzah did not have a chance to rise. As such, the matzah we eat at the Seder must be made from a food item that can rise, exempting rice that does not rise but decays. And we will be able to use the posuk to teach us that we are obligated to eat matzah even when there is no Beis Hamikdosh.

Based on this we can understand the opening words of this section as follows.

"This matzah" that we eat, how do we know that it must be made from wheat and not from rice? Initially, we would think that we derive it from the posuk *"You shall eat no chametz with it."*

If we use the posuk to teach us that we cannot use rice as matzah, then how will we learn the obligation of eating matzah even when there is no Korban Pesach?

Therefore, the Haggadah explains the reason we cannot use rice is not based on the posuk but rather because the matzah didn't rise. As such, we have the posuk available to teach us that we must eat matzah even when there is no Korban Pesach.

(Midrash Yehonatan Haggadah)

בְּכָל דּוֹר וָדוֹר חַיָּב אָדָם לִרְאוֹת אֶת עַצְמוֹ כְּאִלּוּ הוּא יָצָא מִמִּצְרַיִם,
שֶׁנֶּאֱמַר: וְהִגַּדְתָּ לְבִנְךָ בַּיּוֹם הַהוּא לֵאמֹר, בַּעֲבוּר זֶה עָשָׂה יְהוָה לִי
בְּצֵאתִי מִמִּצְרַיִם. לֹא אֶת אֲבוֹתֵינוּ בִּלְבַד גָּאַל הַקָּדוֹשׁ בָּרוּךְ הוּא, אֶלָּא
אַף אוֹתָנוּ גָּאַל עִמָּהֶם, שֶׁנֶּאֱמַר: וְאוֹתָנוּ הוֹצִיא מִשָּׁם, לְמַעַן הָבִיא אוֹתָנוּ,
לָתֶת לָנוּ אֶת הָאָרֶץ אֲשֶׁר נִשְׁבַּע לַאֲבֹתֵינוּ.

The matzos are covered, and the cup is raised.

לְפִיכָךְ אֲנַחְנוּ חַיָּבִים לְהוֹדוֹת, לְהַלֵּל, לְשַׁבֵּחַ, לְפָאֵר, לְרוֹמֵם, לְהַדֵּר,
לְבָרֵךְ, לְעַלֵּה, וּלְקַלֵּס לְמִי שֶׁעָשָׂה לַאֲבוֹתֵינוּ וְלָנוּ אֶת כָּל הַנִּסִּים הָאֵלּוּ:
הוֹצִיאָנוּ מֵעַבְדוּת לְחֵרוּת, מִיָּגוֹן לְשִׂמְחָה, וּמֵאֵבֶל לְיוֹם טוֹב, וּמֵאֲפֵלָה
לְאוֹר גָּדוֹל, וּמִשִּׁעְבּוּד לִגְאֻלָּה. וְנֹאמַר לְפָנָיו שִׁירָה חֲדָשָׁה: הַלְלוּיָהּ.

The cup is put down.

לֹא אֶת אֲבוֹתֵינוּ בִּלְבַד גָּאַל הַקָּדוֹשׁ בָּרוּךְ הוּא

"It was not only our fathers whom the Holy One redeemed."

When Moshe arrived to redeem the Yidden, many were hesitant and somewhat skeptical that the time of their redemption had arrived. What was the basis for their disbelief?

The posuk says, *"They did not hearken to Moshe because of [their] shortness of breath and because of [their] hard labor"* (Shemos 6:9).

The phrase *"shortness of breath"* can be understood to mean the Yidden lacked a spirit of purity, and the phrase *"hard labor"* can mean that they were immersed in idol worship.

The Yidden had a tradition that, prior to the coming of Moshiach, Hashem would imbue them with a spirit of holiness and remove *"their hearts of stone."*

Since they recognized their spiritual shortcomings, they felt that the time of the Messianic era had not yet arrived. *"They did not hearken to Moshe"* because of their spiritual shortcomings as alluded to by the words *"shortness of breath and [their] hard labor."*

(Tiferet Yehonatan)

In each generation each person must see himself as if he himself had come out of Egypt, as it is said: "And you shall tell your child on that day, 'Because of this Hashem acted for me when I came out of Egypt.'" It was not only our fathers whom the Holy One redeemed; He redeemed us too along with them, as it is said: "He took us out of there, to bring us to the land He promised our fathers and to give it to us."

The matzos are covered, and the cup is raised.

Therefore, it is our duty to thank, praise, laud, glorify, exalt, honor, bless, raise high, and acclaim the One who has performed all these miracles for our fathers and for us; who has brought us out from slavery to freedom, from sorrow to joy, from grief to celebration; from darkness to great light and from enslavement to redemption; and so we shall sing a new song before Him. Halleluya!

The cup is put down.

Moshe was a Levite, whose tribe was not enslaved. The Yidden who were experiencing *"shortness of breath"* and *"hard labor"* felt that their redeemer would be a man who had suffered equally as they have. In their eyes, Moshe was an outsider, a free man. And it made no sense to them that a person from the tribe of Levi would be given the task of redeeming an enslaved people.

The tribe of Levi did not endure enslavement. Why were they singled out for deferential treatment?

Pharaoh had been taught that the Jewish redeemer would be from among the Levites, and he falsely assumed that the redeemer must be a person who had personally experienced suffering. By freeing the tribe of the Levites, this would ensure they would not be redeemed.

(Tiferet Yehonatan)

הַלְלוּיָהּ הַלְלוּ עַבְדֵי יְהֹוָה, הַלְלוּ אֶת שֵׁם יְהֹוָה. יְהִי שֵׁם יְהֹוָה מְבֹרָךְ מֵעַתָּה וְעַד עוֹלָם. מִמִּזְרַח שֶׁמֶשׁ עַד מְבוֹאוֹ מְהֻלָּל שֵׁם יְהֹוָה. רָם עַל כָּל גּוֹיִם יְהֹוָה, עַל הַשָּׁמַיִם כְּבוֹדוֹ. מִי כַּיהֹוָה אֱלֹהֵינוּ הַמַּגְבִּיהִי לָשָׁבֶת. הַמַּשְׁפִּילִי לִרְאוֹת בַּשָּׁמַיִם וּבָאָרֶץ. מְקִימִי מֵעָפָר דָּל, מֵאַשְׁפֹּת יָרִים אֶבְיוֹן. לְהוֹשִׁיבִי עִם נְדִיבִים, עִם נְדִיבֵי עַמּוֹ. מוֹשִׁיבִי עֲקֶרֶת הַבַּיִת, אֵם הַבָּנִים שְׂמֵחָה, הַלְלוּיָהּ.

בְּצֵאת יִשְׂרָאֵל מִמִּצְרַיִם, בֵּית יַעֲקֹב מֵעַם לֹעֵז. הָיְתָה יְהוּדָה לְקָדְשׁוֹ,

מִמִּזְרַח שֶׁמֶשׁ עַד מְבוֹאוֹ מְהֻלָּל שֵׁם יְהֹוָה

"From the rising of the sun to its setting, may Hashem's name be praised."

Why are the constellations in a continuous orbit?

The Talmud (Bava Batra 25a) writes, "Rabbi Yehoshua ben Levi says: Come and let us be grateful to our ancestors who revealed to us the place of prayer, as it is written: *'And the hosts of heaven bow down to You'* (Nehemiah 9:6). Since the celestial bodies move from east to west, they bow in that direction, which indicates that the Divine Presence is in the west."

Hashem's presence is everywhere; however, in the west, Hashem's energy is more intensified. That is why the sun rises in the east and sets in the west. The setting of the sun is when it is bowing to Hashem, and it receives Hashem's blessings and bounty.

When the sun is in the west, it cannot remain there due to the intense spiritual energy, and it needs to move back. As such, the sun and the planets are in constant motion.

(Yaaros Dvash 4:1)

מְקִימִי מֵעָפָר דָּל

"He raises the poor from the dust."

Why does Hashem have to create a world where there are poor people and then He raises him from the dust? Why can't Hashem initially make them wealthy?

Halleluya! Servants of Hashem, give praise; praise the name of Hashem. Blessed be the name of Hashem now and for evermore. From the rising of the sun to its setting, may Hashem's name be praised. High is Hashem above all nations; His glory is above the heavens. Who is like Hashem our God, who sits enthroned so high, yet turns so low to see the heavens and the earth? He raises the poor from the dust and the needy from the refuse heap, giving them a place alongside princes, the princes of His people. He makes the woman in a childless house a happy mother of children. Halleluya!

When Israel came out of Egypt, the house of Yaakov from a people of foreign tongue, Judah became His sanctuary,

Hashem created the world in a manner that first it is lacking and then it becomes complete. With regard to creation, the Torah says, *"And the land was empty and desolate"* and then the Torah says, *"And Hashem said let there be light"* (Bereishis 1:2).

Likewise, with regard to the poor, he first needs to experience poverty in order to appreciate wealth. As the posuk says, *"He raises the poor from the dust, lifts up the needy from the dunghill, setting them with nobles, granting them seats of honor"* (Shmuel I 2:8). The person needs to first experience poverty and then he will be able to sit with the nobles.

(Ahavat Yehonatan Rosh Hashonoh)

בְּצֵאת יִשְׂרָאֵל מִמִּצְרַיִם

"When Israel came out of Egypt"

Moshe was unsure if he would be successful in convincing Pharaoh to let the Yidden leave. He said to Hashem, *"Behold, the children of Israel did not hearken to me. How then will Pharaoh hearken to me, seeing that I am of closed lips?"* (Shemos 6:12)

It would seem that Moshe's line of reasoning for why Pharaoh would not listen to him would seem to be flawed. The Torah had previously explained the reason why the Yidden did not listen to Moshe was "they did not hearken to Moshe because of [their] shortness of breath and because of [their] hard labor."

Pharaoh, on the other hand, did not experience hard labor. Why then should he not listen to Moshe?

Moshe knew that his position could be easily refuted. He was seeking any justification not to fulfill Hashem's instruction of confronting Pharaoh. Moshe was scared that perhaps Pharaoh would heed the call of Hashem, and this would be a slight on the Yidden since they had not listened to Moshe.

(Tiferet Yehonatan)

♨

When the posuk says, *"because of [their] hard labor,"* it means that the Yidden were idol worshippers. Moshe knew that Pharaoh considered himself to be an idol.

Moshe's rationale was therefore understandable. If the Yidden who were idol worshippers did not listen to Moshe, then Pharaoh, who believed he was an idol, would definitely not listen to him.

(Pardes Reb Yehonatan)

♨

Moshe was equally concerned that he would not be able to persuade the Yidden to want to leave. He said to Hashem, *"I am of closed lips."* Why did Moshe feel that since he was challenged when it came to his speech, it would impact the Yidden's belief in him and their resolve to follow his instructions?

The spiritual heights of the Novi are linked to the spiritual heights of the Jewish people. The more righteous the Yidden are, the greater will be the revelation emanating from the prophet.

Moshe feared that when the Yidden would see Moshe's difficulty in conveying Hashem's message, they would see it as a reflection of their own spiritual decline, and they would feel unworthy of being redeemed from Egypt.

(Tiferet Yehonatan Bo)

♨

A novi's level of holiness is linked to the spiritual level of the generation.

The Midrash writes that when the Yidden marched through the Yam Suf, the heavenly forces questioned the rationale for saving the Yidden and causing the Egyptians to drown, as they were both idol worshippers.

Moshe being of closed lips was a result of the spiritual decline of the Yidden. Therefore, Moshe declared, *"How then will Pharaoh hearken to me, seeing that I am of closed lips?"* In other words, "Pharaoh will understand that my speech impediment is a reflection of the Yidden's spiritual decline and as such will not want to let the Yidden go."

(Nefesh Yehonatan Shemos)

۵

The Midrash writes that Moshe was the mouthpiece of Hashem. As such, Moshe being of closed lips would seem to be irrelevant. Why then was Moshe worried that Pharaoh would not believe him due to his speech impediment?

Only when Moshe spoke lashon hakodesh was he able to speak freely. However, when speaking to Pharaoh, he would have to speak in Egyptian and the speech impediment would return.

Therefore, Moshe was concerned, *"How then will Pharaoh hearken to me, seeing that I am of closed lips?"*

(Tiferet Yehonatan Voera)

۵

It stands to reason that Hashem would send a redeemer who was perfect in all ways. Moshe thought if he presented before Pharaoh with a speech defect, Pharaoh would not believe that he was representing Hashem.

(Tiferet Yehonatan Voera)

۵

The spiritual level of a generation impacts the stature of a novi. When Moshe went to Egypt to redeem the Yidden, he stated that he was of closed lips. However, when the Yidden stood at Har Sinai to receive the Torah, the posuk says, *"And Moshe spoke"* (Shemos 19:19), meaning all the Yidden heard Moshe's voice as he no longer had a speech impediment. Moshe's ability to speak clearly was a result of the heightened spiritual level the Yidden reached at Har Sinai.

Similarly, when the Yidden reached the moment of their redemption, the Sifri writes, "When Moshe told the Yidden it was time to leave Egypt, his voice was heard throughout the land, as the Yidden had reached a high level of holiness."

That is why initially Moshe said to Hashem, "I have a speech impediment," as this surely indicated that the Yidden were not worthy of being redeemed.

(Ahavat Yehonatan Eikev)

יִשְׂרָאֵל מַמְשְׁלוֹתָיו. הַיָּם רָאָה וַיָּנֹס, הַיַּרְדֵּן יִסֹּב לְאָחוֹר. הֶהָרִים רָקְדוּ
כְאֵילִים, גְּבָעוֹת כִּבְנֵי צֹאן. מַה לְּךָ הַיָּם כִּי תָנוּס, הַיַּרְדֵּן – תִּסֹּב לְאָחוֹר.
הֶהָרִים – תִּרְקְדוּ כְאֵילִים, גְּבָעוֹת כִּבְנֵי צֹאן. מִלִּפְנֵי אָדוֹן חוּלִי אָרֶץ,
מִלִּפְנֵי אֱלוֹהַּ יַעֲקֹב. הַהֹפְכִי הַצּוּר אֲגַם מָיִם, חַלָּמִישׁ לְמַעְיְנוֹ מָיִם.

הַיָּם רָאָה וַיָּנֹס

"The sea saw and fled . . ."

The Midrash asks, "What did the sea see that cause it to flee?" It responded that it saw the braisa of Reb Yishmoel.

This Midrash is challenging to comprehend. The braisa of Reb Yishmoel is said every day in davening where it lists the thirteen principles of how to interpret the words of the Torah. Why would this cause the waters to flee?

When Hashem instructed the waters to split, the waters proclaimed, "Why should the Yidden be saved and the Egyptians should drown? The Yidden are also idol worshippers." Hashem responded that the Yidden had done teshuvah.

There is an argument whether teshuvah helps by a Ben Noach.

The Talmud (Yoma 37a) quotes the posuk, *"The names of the wicked should rot"* and learns from it that we should not name our children after the wicked. The question is posed, "How was a great rabbi given the name Yishmoel? Avrohom's son Yishmoel was wicked." The answer given is that Yishmoel had done teshuvah, and as such, this great rabbi could carry the name of Yishmoel, the son of Avrohom.

Yishmoel had the status of a Ben Noach and yet his teshuvah was accepted. Clearly this proves that when a Ben Noach does teshuvah, it is accepted. Likewise, the Yidden who, prior to receiving the Torah, had the status of a Ben Noach, their teshuvah was also accepted.

(Midrash Yehonatan Beshalach)

Why would seeing Yoseph's coffin cause the waters to divide?

When Hashem created the world, He established that when the Yidden left Egypt, the waters would split. When the waters saw the Yidden approaching, it was not sure if the appropriate time had arrived. However, once it saw Yoseph's coffin, it realized the time had arrived.

Israel His dominion. The sea saw and fled; the Jordan turned back.

The mountains skipped like rams, the hills like lambs. Why was it, sea, that you fled? Jordan, why did you turn back? Why, mountains, did you skip like rams, and you, hills, like lambs?

It was at the presence of Hashem, Creator of the earth, at the presence of the God of Jacob, who turned the rock into a pool of water, flint into a flowing spring.

Why were the waters convinced after seeing the coffin?

Yoseph's coffin had been placed at the bottom of the Nile River. Moshe approached the river and proclaimed that the time of the redemption had arrived, and the coffin should rise to the surface. If the correct time had not arrived, it would not have risen and Moshe would not have been able to take it.

Yoseph said, "*Hashem will surely remember you and you shall take up my bones out of here*" (Bereishis 50:25). This posuk can be understood as follows: "*You shall take up my bones out of here*" means that when my coffin miraculously rises from the bottom of the Nile to its surface then, "*Hashem will surely remember you,*" meaning, "You will know that the time for the redemption has arrived."

As such, when the waters saw the coffin, they knew the time of the Exodus had arrived. That is why Moshe took Yoseph's coffin to show the Yidden that the moment of the redemption was here.

(Tiferet Yehonatan Beshalach)

מַה לְּךָ הַיָּם כִּי תָנוּס הַיַּרְדֵּן תִּסֹּב לְאָחוֹר

"Why was it, sea, that you fled? Jordan, why did you turn back? Why, hills, did you skip like rams, and you, mountains, like lambs?"

The description of what occurred is very much out of the ordinary: "*Sea, that you fled? Jordan, why did you turn back?*" A large body of water such as the sea doesn't flee; it would normally turn back, while a river, which is a small body of water such as the Jordan, would flee rather than just turn back.

Similarly, hills are described as "*skipping like rams,*" while mountains are described as "*skipping like lambs.*" The hill being smaller than the mountain should skip like the lamb, which is more agile than the ram. And the mountain should be described as being only able to skip like the ram.

Why did Hashem do things in an extraordinary manner?

The next posuk offers us the answer. It states, "*It was at the presence of Hashem, Creator of the earth*" to teach us that most miracles occur beyond the

The cup is raised.
On Saturday night, the phrase in parentheses substitutes for the preceding phrase.

בָּרוּךְ אַתָּה יְהֹוָה אֱלֹהֵינוּ מֶלֶךְ הָעוֹלָם, אֲשֶׁר גְּאָלָנוּ וְגָאַל אֶת אֲבוֹתֵינוּ מִמִּצְרַיִם, וְהִגִּיעָנוּ הַלַּיְלָה הַזֶּה לֶאֱכָל בּוֹ מַצָּה וּמָרוֹר. כֵּן יְהֹוָה אֱלֹהֵינוּ וֵאלֹהֵי אֲבוֹתֵינוּ יַגִּיעֵנוּ לְמוֹעֲדִים וְלִרְגָלִים אֲחֵרִים הַבָּאִים לִקְרָאתֵנוּ לְשָׁלוֹם, שְׂמֵחִים בְּבִנְיַן עִירֶךָ וְשָׂשִׂים בַּעֲבוֹדָתֶךָ. וְנֹאכַל שָׁם מִן הַזְּבָחִים וּמִן הַפְּסָחִים [מִן הַפְּסָחִים וּמִן הַזְּבָחִים] אֲשֶׁר יַגִּיעַ דָּמָם עַל קִיר מִזְבַּחֲךָ לְרָצוֹן, וְנוֹדֶה לְךָ שִׁיר חָדָשׁ עַל גְּאֻלָּתֵנוּ וְעַל פְּדוּת נַפְשֵׁנוּ. בָּרוּךְ אַתָּה יְהֹוָה, גָּאַל יִשְׂרָאֵל.

בָּרוּךְ אַתָּה יְהֹוָה, אֱלֹהֵינוּ מֶלֶךְ הָעוֹלָם בּוֹרֵא פְּרִי הַגָּפֶן.

Drink while reclining to the left.

realm of nature and to impress upon mankind Hashem's strength and that He does whatever He desires.

This is further seen in the concluding posuk, *"Who turned the rock into a pool of water, flint into a flowing spring."*

A rock is not as hard as a flint, yet it only produced a pool of water, while a flint that is harder than a rock produced a flowing spring.

This understanding of the manner Hashem performs miracles is highlighted when Moshe hit the rock on two separate occasions. The first time the rock is called צוּר, and the posuk said, *"Water came from it"* (Shemos 17:6). The second time the rock is called סֶלַע, which is harder than a צוּר yet the posuk says, *"An abundance of water gushed forth"* (Bamidbar 20:11).

(Yaaros Dvash 1:16)

בָּרוּךְ אַתָּה יְהֹוָה גָּאַל יִשְׂרָאֵל.

"Blessed are You, Hashem, Redeemer of Israel."

The Zohar asks, "Where is the final redemption alluded to in the Torah?"

It answers, in the posuk *"The life you face shall be precarious; you shall be in terror, night and day, with no assurance of survival"* (Devorim 28:66).

The cup is raised.
On Saturday night, the phrase in parentheses substitutes for the preceding phrase.

Blessed are You, Hashem our God, King of the Universe, who has redeemed us and redeemed our fathers from Egypt, and brought us to this night to eat matzah and bitter herbs. So may Hashem our God bring us in peace to other seasons and festivals that are coming to us, happy in the building of Your city and rejoicing in Your service; and there we shall eat of sacrifices and Pesach offerings (of Pesach offerings and sacrifices), of which the blood will reach the side of Your altar to be accepted. And we shall thank You in a new song for our redemption and for our lives' salvation. Blessed are You, Hashem, Redeemer of Israel.

Blessed are You, Hashem our God, King of the Universe, who creates the fruit of the vine.

Drink while reclining to the left.

How does this posuk speak of the coming of Moshiach?

The following two sections of the Talmud shed light on the Zohar's answer:

The Talmud (Sanhedrin 98a) shares a fascinating conversation between Reb Shimon and Eliyahu HaNovi. Reb Shimon asked, "When is Moshiach coming?" To which Eliyahu responded, "Today." Reb Shimon then asked, "We see that he didn't come today." To which Eliyahu explained, "When I said today, I was quoting the first word of a posuk. The posuk reads in full, *'Today if you will listen to my voice'* (Tehillim 95:7). Moshiach will come when the Yidden do teshuvah and follow Hashem's mitzvos."

The Talmud (Kidushin 30a) describes what one should do when challenged by the yetzer hara. It says you should drag him to the Beis Hamidrash, and if that will not subdue him, then reflect on the day of your passing. As the posuk says, *"The life you face shall be precarious; you shall be in terror, night and day, with no assurance of survival."* When a person reflects on the day of his passing, he definitely will not sin.

Then if all the Yidden will think of their day of passing, no one will sin and, *"Today if you will listen to my voice"* will come to fruition.

(Divrei Yehonatan Ki Savo)

רָחְצָה

Since it is forbidden to interrupt unnecessarily between the washing of the hands and the eating of the Korech sandwich, the leader should relate to the participants the various rules of matzah consumption before washing his hands. He should remind everyone that they must eat a k'zayis of matzah within a time span of כְּדֵי אֲכִילַת פְּרָס (two minutes according to the most stringent opinion; four or even nine minutes according to more lenient opinions) and that the matzah and Korech must be eaten while reclining to the left. The hands are washed in preparation for the meal and the following blessing is said:

בָּרוּךְ אַתָּה יְהֹוָה, אֱלֹהֵינוּ מֶלֶךְ הָעוֹלָם, אֲשֶׁר קִדְּשָׁנוּ בְּמִצְוֹתָיו וְצִוָּנוּ עַל נְטִילַת יָדַיִם.

מוֹצִיא

The three matzos are held, and the following blessing is said:

בָּרוּךְ אַתָּה יְהֹוָה, אֱלֹהֵינוּ מֶלֶךְ הָעוֹלָם, הַמּוֹצִיא לֶחֶם מִן הָאָרֶץ.

מַצָּה

The bottom matzah is released. While the top two matzos are held, the following blessing is said:

בָּרוּךְ אַתָּה יְהֹוָה, אֱלֹהֵינוּ מֶלֶךְ הָעוֹלָם, אֲשֶׁר קִדְּשָׁנוּ בְּמִצְוֹתָיו וְצִוָּנוּ עַל אֲכִילַת מַצָּה.

A k'zayis of matzah is eaten, while reclining to the left.

מָרוֹר

A k'zayis of maror is dipped in Charoses. The Charoses should then be shaken off the maror (so as not to sweeten its bitter taste), and the following blessing is said:

בָּרוּךְ אַתָּה יְהֹוָה, אֱלֹהֵינוּ מֶלֶךְ הָעוֹלָם, אֲשֶׁר קִדְּשָׁנוּ בְּמִצְוֹתָיו וְצִוָּנוּ עַל אֲכִילַת מָרוֹר.

The k'zayis of maror is eaten (without reclining).

RACHTZAH

Since it is forbidden to interrupt unnecessarily between the washing of the hands and the eating of the Korech sandwich, the leader should relate to the participants the various rules of matzah consumption before washing his hands. He should remind everyone that they must eat a k'zayis of matzah within a time span of כְּדֵי אֲכִילַת פְּרָס (two minutes according to the most stringent opinion; four or even nine minutes according to more lenient opinions) and that the matzah and Korech must be eaten while reclining to the left. The hands are washed in preparation for the meal and the following blessing is said:

Blessed are You, Hashem our God, King of the Universe, who has made us holy through His commandments, and has commanded us about washing hands.

MOTZI

The three matzos are held, and the following blessing is said:

Blessed are You, Hashem our God, King of the Universe, who brings forth bread from the earth.

MATZAH

The bottom matzah is released. While the top two matzos are held, the following blessing is said:

Blessed are You, Hashem our God, King of the Universe, who has made us holy through His commandments, and has commanded us to eat matzah.

A k'zayis of matzah is eaten, while reclining to the left.

MAROR

A k'zayis of maror is dipped in Charoses. The Charoses should then be shaken off the maror (so as not to sweeten its bitter taste) and the following blessing is said:

Blessed are You, Hashem our God, King of the Universe, who has made us holy through His commandments, and has commanded us to eat bitter herbs.

The k'zayis of maror is eaten (without reclining).

<h1 style="text-align:center">כּוֹרֵךְ</h1>

*A k'zayis of the bottom matzah is taken together with a k'zayis of maror
(some people dip the maror in Charoses), and the following is said:*

זֵכֶר לַמִּקְדָּשׁ כְּהִלֵּל. כֵּן עָשָׂה הִלֵּל בִּזְמַן שֶׁבֵּית הַמִּקְדָּשׁ הָיָה קַיָּם: הָיָה כּוֹרֵךְ מַצָּה וּמָרוֹר וְאוֹכֵל בְּיַחַד, לְקַיֵּם מַה שֶּׁנֶּאֱמַר: עַל מַצּוֹת וּמְרוֹרִים יֹאכְלֻהוּ.

Eat while reclining to the left.

✦〰✦

זֵכֶר לַמִּקְדָּשׁ כְּהִלֵּל

"In memory of the Temple in the tradition of Hillel"

Lomdus

Why does the Haggadah need to inform us of what occurred when the Beis Hamikdosh was standing?

Further, everything Hillel did was to fulfill Hashem's mitzvos. Why then does the Haggadah need to state that Hillel ate the matzah and maror to fulfill what is said: "*You shall eat it with matzah and bitter herbs*"?

Why do we eat matzah and maror at the Seder?

One approach is that it is a *gezeras hakosuv*, an arbitrary distinction made in the Torah. This means that the Torah does not give a reason for the law. The other understanding is based on the Midrash's interpretation of the posuk "*He has filled me with bitterness. He has sated me with wormwood*" (Eicha 3:15).

The Midrash explains, "'*He has filled me with bitterness*' refers to the night of Pesach. '*He has sated me with wormwood*' refers to Tisha B'Av. The first day of Pesach and Tisha B'Av always fall on the same day of the week. Therefore, we are commanded to eat both matzah and maror, symbolizing freedom and slavery at the Seder.

The understanding of the Midrash is further enhanced by the reason given for why we eat the matzah before eating the maror. Matzah symbolizes freedom, and maror signifies slavery. The Yidden first experienced slavery and then freedom. Why then do we eat the matzah prior to eating the maror?

Maror is eaten last to inform us that we will experience other forms of servitude and slavery, including the destruction of the Beis Hamikdosh.

KORECH

A k'zayis of the bottom matzah is taken together with a k'zayis of maror
(some people dip the maror in Charoses), and the following is said:

In memory of the Temple, in the tradition of Hillel. This is what Hillel would do when the Temple still stood: he would wrap [the Pesach offering] up with matzah and bitter herbs and eat them together, to fulfill what is said: "You shall eat it with matzah and bitter herbs."

Eat while reclining to the left.

If maror is eaten to remind us of the destruction of the Beis Hamikdosh, why then did we eat maror when the Beis Hamikdosh was standing?

Hillel, who ate maror when the Beis Hamikdosh stood, must be of the opinion that we eat matzah and maror as it is a gezeras hakosuv; the Torah decreed it without offering an explanation. Consequently, there would be no difference if the Beis Hamikdosh was standing or not.

This also explains the concluding statement of the Haggadah, *"to fulfill that what it says, You shall eat it with matzah and bitter herbs."* We eat both because it is a gezeras hakosuv.

(Pardes Reb Yehonatan)

The Midrash explains the posuk הִשְׂבִּיעַנִי בַמְּרוֹרִים *"He has filled me with bitterness"* (Eicha 3:15) as referring to the night of Pesach.

The posuk can be understood to mean that the person feels full by eating the maror. According to halocho, a person is considered full if he has eaten food that is the size of an egg; the size of an egg is equal to two *k'zaysim*.

When the Beis Hamikdosh stood, the Yidden ate one k'zayis of maror together with the Korban Pesach. Since they only ate one k'zayis of maror, the maror itself was not enough for them to feel full.

However, after its destruction, the chachomim instituted that we eat two k'zaysim of maror. One together with matzah to remind us of the Korban Pesach and one k'zayis on its own.

Eating two k'zaysim of maror makes a person feel full.

The posuk is referring to the times of golus where we ate two k'zaysim, and as a result, we were satiated.

(Ahavat Yehonatan)

שֻׁלְחָן עוֹרֵךְ

It is customary to eat eggs at the beginning of the meal. Care should be taken to leave enough time in order to be able to eat the Afikomen before halachic midnight. One should also be sure to leave some appetite for the Afikomen.

צָפוּן

At the end of the meal, a k'zayis (according to some, two k'zaysim) of the matzah that had been hidden away is eaten as the Afikomen. The Afikomen should be eaten while reclining to the left. One may not eat anything after the Afikomen, nor may he drink anything (besides the third and fourth cups of wine) other than water.

בָּרֵךְ

The third cup of wine, over which the Grace is recited, is poured.

שִׁיר הַמַּעֲלוֹת, בְּשׁוּב יְהֹוָה אֶת שִׁיבַת צִיּוֹן הָיִינוּ כְּחֹלְמִים.
אָז יִמָּלֵא שְׂחוֹק פִּינוּ וּלְשׁוֹנֵנוּ רִנָּה, אָז יֹאמְרוּ בַגּוֹיִם,
הִגְדִּיל יְהֹוָה לַעֲשׂוֹת עִם אֵלֶּה. הִגְדִּיל יְהֹוָה לַעֲשׂוֹת עִמָּנוּ,

אָז יִמָּלֵא שְׂחוֹק פִּינוּ

"Then were our mouths filled with laughter."

There is a stark contrast between how the Yidden express their simcha and the nations of the world express their joy.

When the Yidden are rejoicing, they sing songs of praise to Hashem, as the posuk writes that when Moshiach comes *"They [the Yidden] will sing a new song to Hashem"* (Tehillim 96:1), praising Him for His abundance of kindness and compassion.

In contrast, when expressing their joy, the nations of the world too would sing and dance, yet they would not offer praise and thanks to Hashem. Since the nations recognize this distinction, they also understand why Hashem chose the Yidden to be His nation.

SHULCHAN ORECH

It is customary to eat eggs at the beginning of the meal. Care should be taken to leave enough time in order to be able to eat the Afikomen before halachic midnight. One should also be sure to leave some appetite for the Afikomen.

TZAFUN

At the end of the meal, a k'zayis (according to some, two k'zaysim) of the matzah that had been hidden away is eaten as the Afikomen. The Afikomen should be eaten while reclining to the left. One may not eat anything after the Afikomen, nor may he drink anything (besides the third and fourth cups of wine) other than water.

BARECH

The third cup of wine, over which the Grace is recited, is poured.

A song of ascents. When Hashem brought back the exiles of Zion, we were like people who dream. Then were our mouths filled with laughter, and our tongues with songs of joy. Then was it said among the nations, "Hashem has done great things for them." Hashem did do great things for us, and

This is alluded to in the concluding posukim in which the nations reflect on how they celebrate and how the Jewish nation rejoices. *"Then was it said among the nations, 'The LORD has done great things for them [for the Yidden] and they rejoiced by singing songs of praise to Hashem.'"* However, when we rejoice, we do not incorporate praising Hashem. As the posuk says, *"The LORD did do great things for us and we rejoiced."* However, the rejoicing was not directed toward Hashem.

(Yaaros Dvash 1:3)

וּלְשׁוֹנֵנוּ רִנָּה

"And our tongues with songs of joy."

The word רִנָּה refers to the Torah. As the posuk says, לִשְׁמֹעַ אֶל הָרִנָּה וְאֶל הַתְּפִלָּה, *"To listen to the song and to the prayer"* (Malochim I 8:28). The word רִנָּה is referring to the study of Torah.

הָיִינוּ שְׂמֵחִים. שׁוּבָה יְהֹוָה אֶת שְׁבִיתֵנוּ כַּאֲפִיקִים בַּנֶּגֶב. הַזֹּרְעִים בְּדִמְעָה, בְּרִנָּה יִקְצֹרוּ. הָלוֹךְ יֵלֵךְ וּבָכֹה נֹשֵׂא מֶשֶׁךְ הַזָּרַע, בֹּא יָבֹא בְרִנָּה נֹשֵׂא אֲלֻמֹּתָיו.

It is customary that the master of the house lead the Grace at the Seder.
The following invitation to say Grace is added when there are three adult males present.
When ten adult males are present, the words in parentheses are also added.

Leader רַבּוֹתַי נְבָרֵךְ

Others יְהִי שֵׁם יְהֹוָה מְבֹרָךְ מֵעַתָּה וְעַד־עוֹלָם

Leader יְהִי שֵׁם יְהֹוָה מְבֹרָךְ מֵעַתָּה וְעַד־עוֹלָם

בִּרְשׁוּת מָרָנָן וְרַבָּנָן וְרַבּוֹתַי, נְבָרֵךְ [אֱלֹהֵינוּ] שֶׁאָכַלְנוּ מִשֶּׁלּוֹ

Others בָּרוּךְ [אֱלֹהֵינוּ] שֶׁאָכַלְנוּ מִשֶּׁלּוֹ וּבְטוּבוֹ הָיִינוּ

Leader בָּרוּךְ [אֱלֹהֵינוּ] שֶׁאָכַלְנוּ מִשֶּׁלּוֹ וּבְטוּבוֹ הָיִינוּ

בָּרוּךְ אַתָּה יְהֹוָה, אֱלֹהֵינוּ מֶלֶךְ הָעוֹלָם, הַזָּן אֶת הָעוֹלָם כֻּלּוֹ

The posukim can be understood to mean, *"Then were our mouths filled with laughter, and our tongues with songs of joy."* The joy refers to Torah study.

(Ahavat Yehonatan)

הַזָּן אֶת הָעוֹלָם כֻּלּוֹ

"He gives food to all living things."

Lomdus

We are obligated in bentching, as the Torah says, וְאָכַלְתָּ וְשָׂבָעְתָּ וּבֵרַכְתָּ *"And you will eat and be sated, and you shall bless"* (Devorim 8:10).

The Talmud (Berochos 20b) writes, "The ministering angels said before Hashem: Master of the Universe, in Your Torah it is written: *'The great, mighty and awesome Hashem who favors no one and takes no bribe'* (Devorim 10:17), yet You, nevertheless, show favor to Israel, as it is written: *'The Lord shall show favor to you and give you peace'* (Bamidbar 6:26). He replied to them: 'And how can I not show favor to Israel, as I wrote for them in the Torah: *'And you shall eat and be satisfied, and bless the Lord your God'* (Devorim 8:10), meaning that there is no obligation to

we rejoiced. Bring back our exiles, Hashem, like streams in a dry land. May those who sowed in tears, reap in joy. May one who goes out weeping, carrying a bag of seed, come back with songs of joy, carrying his sheaves.

It is customary that the master of the house lead the Grace at the Seder.
The following invitation to say Grace is added when there are three adult males present.
When ten adult males are present, the words in parentheses are also added: The
following invitation to say Grace is added when there are three adult males present.
When ten adult males are present the words in parentheses are also added.

Leader: Gentlemen, let us say Grace.

Others: May the name of Hashem be blessed from now and forever.

Leader: May the name of Hashem be blessed from now and forever.

With the permission of my masters, teachers, and gentlemen, let us bless (*in a minyan:* our God) the One from whose food we have eaten.

Others: Blessed be (*in a minyan:* our God,) the One from whose food we have eaten, and by whose goodness we live.

Blessed are You, Hashem our God, King of the Universe, who in His

bless Hashem until one is satiated; yet they are exacting with themselves to bentch even if they have eaten as much as an olive-bulk or an egg-bulk. Since they go beyond the requirements of the law, they are worthy of favor."

There is another Talmudic section that records an interesting conversation that took place during a very dark period of Jewish history:

The Talmud (Berochos 48a) writes that King Yannai and the queen ate bread together. And since Yannai had executed the chachomim, there was no one to recite the bentching on their behalf. He said to his wife, "Who will provide us with a man to recite the blessing on our behalf?"

She said to him, "Swear to me that if I bring you such a man, you will not harass him."

He swore, and she brought her brother, Shimon ben Shataḥ. She sat her brother between the king's throne and hers.

The king said to him, "Do you see how much honor I am granting you?"

Shimon ben Shataḥ responded, "It is not you who honors me; rather, the Torah honors me, as it is written, '*Extol her and she will exalt you; she will bring you to honor when you embrace her*'" (Mishlei 4:8).

Yannai said to his wife, "You see that he does not accept authority."

בְּטוּבוֹ בְּחֵן בְּחֶסֶד וּבְרַחֲמִים, הוּא נוֹתֵן לֶחֶם לְכָל בָּשָׂר כִּי לְעוֹלָם חַסְדּוֹ. וּבְטוּבוֹ הַגָּדוֹל תָּמִיד לֹא חָסַר לָנוּ, וְאַל יֶחְסַר לָנוּ מָזוֹן לְעוֹלָם וָעֶד. בַּעֲבוּר שְׁמוֹ הַגָּדוֹל, כִּי הוּא אֵל זָן וּמְפַרְנֵס לַכֹּל וּמֵטִיב לַכֹּל, וּמֵכִין מָזוֹן לְכָל בְּרִיּוֹתָיו אֲשֶׁר בָּרָא. בָּרוּךְ אַתָּה יְהֹוָה, הַזָּן אֶת הַכֹּל.

נוֹדֶה לְךָ יְהֹוָה אֱלֹהֵינוּ עַל שֶׁהִנְחַלְתָּ לַאֲבוֹתֵינוּ אֶרֶץ חֶמְדָּה טוֹבָה וּרְחָבָה, וְעַל שֶׁהוֹצֵאתָנוּ יְהֹוָה אֱלֹהֵינוּ מֵאֶרֶץ מִצְרַיִם, וּפְדִיתָנוּ מִבֵּית עֲבָדִים, וְעַל בְּרִיתְךָ שֶׁחָתַמְתָּ בִּבְשָׂרֵנוּ, וְעַל תּוֹרָתְךָ שֶׁלִּמַּדְתָּנוּ, וְעַל חֻקֶּיךָ שֶׁהוֹדַעְתָּנוּ, וְעַל חַיִּים חֵן וָחֶסֶד שֶׁחוֹנַנְתָּנוּ, וְעַל אֲכִילַת מָזוֹן שָׁאַתָּה זָן וּמְפַרְנֵס אוֹתָנוּ תָּמִיד, בְּכָל יוֹם וּבְכָל עֵת וּבְכָל שָׁעָה:

They gave Shimon ben Shataḥ a cup of wine over which to bentch. He said, "How shall I recite the brocho? Shall I say, *Blessed is He from Whom Yannai and his companions have eaten?* I have not eaten anything."

He drank that cup of wine. They gave him another cup, and he recited the bentching. By drinking the first cup, he had joined the other diners and was therefore eligible to recite bentching on their behalf.

With regard to this story, when Shimon ben Shataḥ bentched on their behalf, he was following his own opinion, and not acting in accordance with the accepted halocho. The halocho is, if many people are obligated in bentching, they can elect one of the group to bentch, and everyone else will listen and it will be considered as if each person actually bentched. However, the person designated to lead the bentching must have eaten at least an olive-bulk of grain. And Shimon ben Shataḥ had not eaten an olive-bulk of grain.

The Behag rules-that a person who ate a k'zayis can exempt a person who also only ate a k'zayis. However, if a person ate more than a k'zayis, then the person who only ate a k'zayis cannot exempt him. This is because a person who only ate a k'zayis is obligated to bentch midrabbonon, a rabbinic obligation, while a person who ate a full meal is obligated to bentch min hatorah, a Torah obligation. And someone whose obligation is only of a rabbinic nature cannot exempt someone whose obligation is Torah based.

Rashi and Tosfos challenged the Behag's opinion based on the story of Shimon ben Shataḥ. The Talmud implies that if Shimon ben Shataḥ had eaten a k'zayis, he could have exempted the king and queen. It seems most unlikely that the king

goodness feeds the whole world with grace, kindness, and compassion. He gives food to all living things, for His kindness is forever. Because of His continual great goodness, we have never lacked food, nor may we ever lack it, for the sake of His great name. For He is God who feeds and sustains all, does good to all, and prepares food for all creatures He has created. Blessed are You, Hashem, who feeds all.

We thank You, Hashem our God, for having granted as a heritage to our fathers a desirable, good, and spacious land; for bringing us out, Hashem our God, from the land of Egypt, freeing us from the house of slavery; for Your covenant which You sealed in our flesh; for Your Torah which You taught us; for Your laws which You made known to us; for the life, grace, and kindness You have bestowed on us; and for the food by which You continually feed and sustain us, every day, every season, every hour.

and queen ate only a k'zayis; they must have eaten a full meal. Yet had Shimon ben Shatah eaten a k'zayis, he could have exempted the king and queen, who had eaten a full meal. This is contrary to the Behag's opinion that a person eating only a k'zayis cannot exempt someone who ate more than a k'zayis.

Rashi's and Tosfos's challenge can be refuted as follows: The Mordechai writes that Rashi and Tosfos are correct in their assumption that the king and queen ate a full meal. However, the full meal included only a k'zayis of bread, and such a meal only requires bentching as a rabbinic law. Only when one eats a full meal of bread is one obligated by the Torah to bentch. As such, if Shimon ben Shatach had also eaten a k'zayis, he could have exempted them, which is consistent with the opinion of the Behag.

(Gevuras Yehonatan 1)

וְעַל שֶׁהוֹצֵאתָנוּ יְהֹוָה אֱלֹהֵינוּ מֵאֶרֶץ מִצְרָיִם

"For bringing us out, Hashem our God, from the land of Egypt"

The posuk says, "*Hashem spoke to Moshe in the Sinai Desert in the Tent of Meeting on the first day of the second month from when they left Egypt . . . Take the sum of all the congregation of Bnei Yisroel*" (Bamidbar 1:1,2).

Why does the posuk link the Exodus from Egypt with the counting of the Yidden?

The question is posed "How could Hashem instruct Moshe to count the Yidden? The Talmud says that blessing is not found in something that is counted (Bava

וְעַל הַכֹּל יְהֹוָה אֱלֹהֵינוּ, אֲנַחְנוּ מוֹדִים לָךְ וּמְבָרְכִים אוֹתָךְ, יִתְבָּרַךְ שִׁמְךָ בְּפִי כָּל חַי תָּמִיד לְעוֹלָם וָעֶד. כַּכָּתוּב: וְאָכַלְתָּ וְשָׂבַעְתָּ וּבֵרַכְתָּ אֶת יְהֹוָה אֱלֹהֶיךָ עַל הָאָרֶץ הַטּוֹבָה אֲשֶׁר נָתַן לָךְ. בָּרוּךְ אַתָּה יְהֹוָה, עַל הָאָרֶץ וְעַל הַמָּזוֹן:

רַחֵם נָא יְהֹוָה אֱלֹהֵינוּ עַל יִשְׂרָאֵל עַמֶּךָ וְעַל יְרוּשָׁלַיִם עִירֶךָ וְעַל צִיּוֹן מִשְׁכַּן כְּבוֹדֶךָ וְעַל מַלְכוּת בֵּית דָּוִד מְשִׁיחֶךָ וְעַל הַבַּיִת הַגָּדוֹל וְהַקָּדוֹשׁ שֶׁנִּקְרָא שִׁמְךָ עָלָיו: אֱלֹהֵינוּ אָבִינוּ, רְעֵנוּ זוּנֵנוּ פַּרְנְסֵנוּ וְכַלְכְּלֵנוּ וְהַרְוִיחֵנוּ, וְהַרְוַח לָנוּ יְהֹוָה אֱלֹהֵינוּ מְהֵרָה מִכָּל צָרוֹתֵינוּ. וְנָא אַל תַּצְרִיכֵנוּ יְהֹוָה אֱלֹהֵינוּ, לֹא לִידֵי מַתְּנַת בָּשָׂר וָדָם וְלֹא לִידֵי הַלְוָאָתָם, כִּי אִם לְיָדְךָ הַמְּלֵאָה הַפְּתוּחָה הַקְּדוֹשָׁה וְהָרְחָבָה, שֶׁלֹּא נֵבוֹשׁ וְלֹא נִכָּלֵם לְעוֹלָם וָעֶד.

On Shabbos, say:

רְצֵה וְהַחֲלִיצֵנוּ יְהֹוָה אֱלֹהֵינוּ בְּמִצְוֹתֶיךָ וּבְמִצְוַת יוֹם הַשְּׁבִיעִי הַשַּׁבָּת הַגָּדוֹל וְהַקָּדוֹשׁ הַזֶּה. כִּי יוֹם זֶה גָּדוֹל וְקָדוֹשׁ הוּא לְפָנֶיךָ לִשְׁבָּת בּוֹ וְלָנוּחַ בּוֹ בְּאַהֲבָה כְּמִצְוַת רְצוֹנֶךָ. וּבִרְצוֹנְךָ הָנִיחַ לָנוּ יְהֹוָה אֱלֹהֵינוּ שֶׁלֹּא תְהֵא צָרָה וְיָגוֹן וַאֲנָחָה בְּיוֹם מְנוּחָתֵנוּ. וְהַרְאֵנוּ יְהֹוָה אֱלֹהֵינוּ בְּנֶחָמַת צִיּוֹן עִירֶךָ וּבְבִנְיַן יְרוּשָׁלַיִם עִיר קָדְשֶׁךָ כִּי אַתָּה הוּא בַּעַל הַיְשׁוּעוֹת וּבַעַל הַנֶּחָמוֹת.

Metzia 42a)." To this they answer, "If that which is being counted is holy, it will be able to receive blessing."

The question is also posed, "Why do we praise Hashem for redeeming the Yidden from Egypt? Hashem had promised Avrohom that he would redeem them." To this, the answer given is, "We praise Hashem in the manner that He redeemed

For all this, Hashem our God, we thank and bless You. May Your name be blessed continually

by the mouth of all that lives, forever and all time—for so it is written: "You will eat and be satisfied, then you shall bless Hashem your God for the good land He has given you."

Blessed are You, Hashem, for the land and for the food.

Have compassion, please, Hashem our God, on Israel Your people, on Jerusalem Your city, on Zion the dwelling place of Your glory, on the royal house of David Your anointed, and on the great and holy House that bears Your name. Our God, our Father, tend us, feed us, sustain us and support us, relieve us and send us relief, Hashem our God, swiftly from all our troubles. Please, Hashem our God, do not make us dependent on the gifts or loans of other people, but only on Your full, open, holy, and generous hand so that we may suffer neither shame nor humiliation forever and all time.

On Shabbos, say:

Favor and strengthen us, Hashem our God, through Your commandments, especially through the commandment of the seventh day, this great and holy Sabbath. For it is, for You, a great and holy day. On it we cease work and rest in love as ordained by Your will.

May it be Your will, Hashem our God, to grant us rest without distress, grief, or lament on our day of rest. May You show us the consolation of Zion Your city, and the rebuilding of Jerusalem Your holy city, for You are the Master of salvation and consolation.

us from Egypt. Hashem took us from the fiftieth gate of impurity to the fiftieth gate of holiness. As such the Yidden are called holy."

Based on the above, we will answer our original question. The reason the Yidden were able to be counted and still receive Hashem's blessing is because, when we were taken out of Egypt, we became a holy nation.

(Midrash Yehonatan Bamidbar)

אֱלֹהֵינוּ וֵאלֹהֵי אֲבוֹתֵינוּ, יַעֲלֶה וְיָבֹא וְיַגִּיעַ וְיֵרָאֶה וְיֵרָצֶה וְיִשָּׁמַע וְיִפָּקֵד
וְיִזָּכֵר זִכְרוֹנֵנוּ וּפִקְדוֹנֵנוּ, וְזִכְרוֹן אֲבוֹתֵינוּ, וְזִכְרוֹן מָשִׁיחַ בֶּן דָּוִד עַבְדֶּךָ,
וְזִכְרוֹן יְרוּשָׁלַיִם עִיר קָדְשֶׁךָ, וְזִכְרוֹן כָּל עַמְּךָ בֵּית יִשְׂרָאֵל לְפָנֶיךָ, לִפְלֵיטָה
לְטוֹבָה לְחֵן וּלְחֶסֶד וּלְרַחֲמִים, לְחַיִּים וּלְשָׁלוֹם בְּיוֹם חַג הַמַּצּוֹת הַזֶּה
זָכְרֵנוּ יְהֹוָה אֱלֹהֵינוּ בּוֹ לְטוֹבָה וּפָקְדֵנוּ בוֹ לִבְרָכָה וְהוֹשִׁיעֵנוּ בוֹ לְחַיִּים.
וּבִדְבַר יְשׁוּעָה וְרַחֲמִים חוּס וְחָנֵּנוּ וְרַחֵם עָלֵינוּ וְהוֹשִׁיעֵנוּ, כִּי אֵלֶיךָ
עֵינֵינוּ, כִּי אֵל מֶלֶךְ חַנּוּן וְרַחוּם אָתָּה.

וּבְנֵה יְרוּשָׁלַיִם עִיר הַקֹּדֶשׁ בִּמְהֵרָה בְיָמֵינוּ. בָּרוּךְ אַתָּה יְהֹוָה, בּוֹנֵה
בְרַחֲמָיו יְרוּשָׁלַיִם. אָמֵן.

בָּרוּךְ אַתָּה יְהֹוָה, אֱלֹהֵינוּ מֶלֶךְ הָעוֹלָם, הָאֵל אָבִינוּ מַלְכֵּנוּ אַדִּירֵנוּ
בּוֹרְאֵנוּ גּוֹאֲלֵנוּ יוֹצְרֵנוּ קְדוֹשֵׁנוּ קְדוֹשׁ יַעֲקֹב רוֹעֵנוּ רוֹעֵה יִשְׂרָאֵל הַמֶּלֶךְ
הַטּוֹב וְהַמֵּטִיב לַכֹּל שֶׁבְּכָל יוֹם וָיוֹם הוּא הֵטִיב, הוּא מֵטִיב, הוּא יֵיטִיב
לָנוּ. הוּא גְמָלָנוּ הוּא גוֹמְלֵנוּ הוּא יִגְמְלֵנוּ לָעַד, לְחֵן וּלְחֶסֶד וּלְרַחֲמִים
וּלְרֶוַח הַצָּלָה וְהַצְלָחָה, בְּרָכָה וִישׁוּעָה נֶחָמָה פַּרְנָסָה וְכַלְכָּלָה וְרַחֲמִים
וְחַיִּים וְשָׁלוֹם וְכָל טוֹב, וּמִכָּל טוּב לְעוֹלָם אַל יְחַסְּרֵנוּ.

הָרַחֲמָן הוּא יִמְלוֹךְ עָלֵינוּ לְעוֹלָם וָעֶד.

הָרַחֲמָן הוּא יִתְבָּרַךְ בַּשָּׁמַיִם וּבָאָרֶץ.

הָרַחֲמָן הוּא יִשְׁתַּבַּח לְדוֹר דּוֹרִים, וְיִתְפָּאַר בָּנוּ לָעַד וּלְנֵצַח נְצָחִים,
וְיִתְהַדַּר בָּנוּ לָעַד וּלְעוֹלְמֵי עוֹלָמִים.

הָרַחֲמָן הוּא יְפַרְנְסֵנוּ בְּכָבוֹד. הָרַחֲמָן הוּא יִשְׁבּוֹר עֻלֵנוּ מֵעַל צַוָּארֵנוּ,
וְהוּא יוֹלִיכֵנוּ קוֹמְמִיּוּת לְאַרְצֵנוּ.

Our God and God of our fathers, may there rise, come, reach, appear, be favored, heard, regarded and remembered before You, our recollection and remembrance, as well as the remembrance of our fathers, and of Moshiach son of David Your servant, and of Jerusalem Your holy city, and of all Your people the house of Israel—for deliverance and well-being, grace, kindness and compassion, life and peace, on this day of the festival of Matzos.

On it remember us, Hashem our God, for good; recollect us for blessing, and deliver us for life.

In accord with Your promise of salvation and compassion, spare us and be gracious to us; have compassion on us and deliver us, for our eyes are turned to You because You are God, gracious and compassionate.

And may Jerusalem the holy city be rebuilt soon, in our time. Blessed are You, Hashem, who in His compassion will rebuild Jerusalem. Amen

Blessed are You, Hashem our God, King of the Universe—God our Father, our King, our Sovereign, our Creator, our Redeemer, our Maker, our Holy One, the Holy One of Yaakov. He is our Shepherd, Israel's Shepherd, the good King who does good to all. Every day He has done, is doing, and will do good to us. He has acted, is acting, and will always act kindly toward us forever, granting us grace, kindness and compassion, relief and rescue, prosperity, blessing, redemption and comfort, sustenance and support, compassion, life, peace, and all good things, and of all good things may He never let us lack.

May the Compassionate One reign over us forever and all time.

May the Compassionate One be blessed in heaven and on earth.

May the Compassionate One be praised from generation to generation, be glorified by us to all eternity, and honored among us forever and all time.

May the Compassionate One break the yoke from our neck and lead us upright to our land.

הָרַחֲמָן הוּא יִשְׁלַח לָנוּ בְּרָכָה מְרֻבָּה בַּבַּיִת הַזֶּה, וְעַל שֻׁלְחָן זֶה שֶׁאָכַלְנוּ עָלָיו.

הָרַחֲמָן הוּא יִשְׁלַח לָנוּ אֶת אֵלִיָּהוּ הַנָּבִיא זָכוּר לַטּוֹב, וִיבַשֶּׂר לָנוּ בְּשׂוֹרוֹת טוֹבוֹת יְשׁוּעוֹת וְנֶחָמוֹת.

הָרַחֲמָן הוּא יְבָרֵךְ אֶת [אָבִי מוֹרִי] בַּעַל הַבַּיִת הַזֶּה. וְאֶת [אִמִּי מוֹרָתִי] בַּעֲלַת הַבַּיִת הַזֶּה, אוֹתָם וְאֶת בֵּיתָם וְאֶת זַרְעָם וְאֶת כָּל אֲשֶׁר לָהֶם. אוֹתָנוּ וְאֶת כָּל אֲשֶׁר לָנוּ, כְּמוֹ שֶׁנִּתְבָּרְכוּ אֲבוֹתֵינוּ אַבְרָהָם יִצְחָק וְיַעֲקֹב בַּכֹּל מִכֹּל כֹּל, כֵּן יְבָרֵךְ אוֹתָנוּ כֻּלָּנוּ יַחַד בִּבְרָכָה שְׁלֵמָה, וְנֹאמַר, אָמֵן.

בַּמָּרוֹם יְלַמְּדוּ עֲלֵיהֶם וְעָלֵינוּ זְכוּת שֶׁתְּהֵא לְמִשְׁמֶרֶת שָׁלוֹם. וְנִשָּׂא בְרָכָה מֵאֵת יְהוָה, וּצְדָקָה מֵאֱלֹהֵי יִשְׁעֵנוּ, וְנִמְצָא חֵן וְשֵׂכֶל טוֹב בְּעֵינֵי אֱלֹהִים וְאָדָם.

On Shabbos add:

הָרַחֲמָן הוּא יַנְחִילֵנוּ יוֹם שֶׁכֻּלּוֹ שַׁבָּת וּמְנוּחָה לְחַיֵּי הָעוֹלָמִים.

הָרַחֲמָן הוּא יַנְחִילֵנוּ יוֹם שֶׁכֻּלּוֹ טוֹב

הָרַחֲמָן הוּא יְזַכֵּנוּ לִימוֹת הַמָּשִׁיחַ וּלְחַיֵּי הָעוֹלָם הַבָּא.

מִגְדּוֹל יְשׁוּעוֹת מַלְכּוֹ וְעֹשֶׂה חֶסֶד לִמְשִׁיחוֹ לְדָוִד וּלְזַרְעוֹ עַד עוֹלָם. עֹשֶׂה שָׁלוֹם בִּמְרוֹמָיו, הוּא יַעֲשֶׂה שָׁלוֹם עָלֵינוּ וְעַל כָּל יִשְׂרָאֵל וְאִמְרוּ וְאָמְרוּ, אָמֵן.

May the Compassionate One send us many blessings to this house and this table at which we have eaten.

May the Compassionate One send us Elijah the prophet—may he be remembered for good—

to bring us good tidings of salvation and consolation.

May the Compassionate One bless—my father, my teacher [master of this house], and my mother, my teacher [lady of this house], them, their household, their children, and all that is theirs, together with us and all that is ours. Just as our forefathers Avraham, Yitzchok, and Yaakov were blessed in all, from all, with all, so may He bless all of us together with a complete blessing, and let us say: Amen.

On high, may grace be invoked for them and for us, as a safeguard of peace. May we receive a blessing from Hashem and a just reward from the God of our salvation, and may we find grace and good favor in the eyes of God and man.

On Shabbos add:

May the Compassionate One let us inherit the day that is all good. May the Compassionate One let us inherit the time that will be entirely Shabbos and rest for life everlasting.

May the Compassionate One make us worthy of the messianic age and life in the World to Come.

He is a tower of salvation to His king, showing kindness to His anointed, to David and his descendants forever. He who makes peace in His high places, may He make peace for us and all Israel, and let us say: Amen.

יְראוּ אֶת יְהוָה קְדֹשָׁיו, כִּי אֵין מַחְסוֹר לִירֵאָיו. כְּפִירִים רָשׁוּ וְרָעֵבוּ, וְדֹרְשֵׁי יְהוָה לֹא יַחְסְרוּ כָל טוֹב. הוֹדוּ לַיהוָה כִּי טוֹב כִּי לְעוֹלָם חַסְדּוֹ. פּוֹתֵחַ אֶת יָדֶךָ, וּמַשְׂבִּיעַ לְכָל חַי רָצוֹן. בָּרוּךְ הַגֶּבֶר אֲשֶׁר יִבְטַח בַּיהוָה, וְהָיָה יְהוָה מִבְטַחוֹ. נַעַר הָיִיתִי גַם זָקַנְתִּי, וְלֹא רָאִיתִי צַדִּיק נֶעֱזָב, וְזַרְעוֹ מְבַקֶּשׁ לָחֶם. יְהוָה עֹז לְעַמּוֹ יִתֵּן, יְהוָה יְבָרֵךְ אֶת עַמּוֹ בַשָּׁלוֹם.

עֹשֶׂה שָׁלוֹם בִּמְרוֹמָיו

"He who makes peace in His high places . . ."

The Midrash writes, "On earth, fire and water cannot coexist, while in heaven they live in peace and harmony."

According to Kabbalah, every form of matter is composed of four elements—fire, water, air, and earth. As such, why does the Midrash speak of harmony between fire and water only in the heavenly sphere when all matter is comprised of both fire and water?

There are two types of sholom. The first is when two people converse, are respectful of each other, and are constantly together but disagree on every facet of life. This scenario cannot be described as true peace. The other form of sholom is when two people may have had different ideologies and different attitudes and outlooks on life. However, due to the very strong bond between the two, each one desires what the other does. Each loves what the other loves. That is true sholom.

While fire and water coexist in this world, they are not at peace. Their natures are polar opposites. Fire gives warmth, and water brings coolness. Fire extends upward while water descends. However, in heaven, fire and water experience true peace. Each embraces the nature of the other.

The posuk writes, *"A river of fire was flowing and emerging from before Him. And the river of fire descends upon the heads of the wicked"* (Daniel 7:10). The nature of fire is to ascend, yet in heaven, it takes on the nature of water and descends. Likewise, the heavenly waters remain in its place, similar to the nature of fire. And the heavenly fire does not destroy, similar to water.

Fear Hashem, you His holy ones; those who fear Him lack nothing. Young lions may grow weak and hungry, but those who seek Hashem lack no good thing. Thank Hashem for He is good: His kindness is forever. You open Your hand and satisfy the desire of every living thing. Blessed is the person who trusts in Hashem, whose trust is in Hashem alone.

Once I was young, and now I am old, yet I have never watched a righteous man forsaken or his children begging for bread. Hashem will give His people strength.

Hashem will bless His people with peace.

This is the understanding of the phrase, "*He who makes peace above.*" True peace is when each accepts and embraces the nature of the other and become truly one.

(Yaaros Dvash 2,7)

יְהֹוָה עֹז לְעַמּוֹ יִתֵּן, יְהֹוָה יְבָרֵךְ אֶת עַמּוֹ בַשָּׁלוֹם

"Hashem will give His people strength. Hashem will bless His people with peace."

When Moshe ascended Har Sinai to receive the Torah, the angels requested that the Torah remain with them in heaven. Hashem responded, "The Torah speaks about things that are permitted and things that are prohibited. How can you then accept the Torah and fulfill it?"

The angels responded, "The Torah speaks about the duties and obligation of the Kohanim and the Leviim. How could they fulfill these laws?"

Hashem responded, "When the Beis Hamikdosh exists, they will be able to fulfill these laws."

This is alluded to in the posuk, *"Hashem will give His people strength."* Strength refers to the Torah. Hashem will give the Yidden the Torah. The angels ask how can the Kohanim and Leviim fulfill it? And Hashem responds, *"Hashem will bless His people with peace."* The Yidden will have peace when the Beis Hamikdosh is in existence.

(Midrash Yehonatan Yisro)

The third cup of wine is now drunk, while reclining to the left.

בָּרוּךְ אַתָּה יְהֹוָה, אֱלֹהֵינוּ מֶלֶךְ הָעוֹלָם, בּוֹרֵא פְּרִי הַגָּפֶן.

The "Cup of Eliyahu" is now filled. There are those who pour the fourth cup of
wine at this point as well. (Others pour it after the recitation of these verses.)
The door of the house is opened as the following verses are recited.
(Some have the custom to rise while reciting these passages.)

שְׁפֹךְ חֲמָתְךָ אֶל הַגּוֹיִם אֲשֶׁר לֹא יְדָעוּךָ וְעַל מַמְלָכוֹת אֲשֶׁר בְּשִׁמְךָ לֹא
קָרָאוּ. כִּי אָכַל אֶת יַעֲקֹב וְאֶת נָוֵהוּ הֵשַׁמּוּ. שְׁפָךְ עֲלֵיהֶם זַעְמֶךָ וַחֲרוֹן
אַפְּךָ יַשִּׂיגֵם. תִּרְדֹּף בְּאַף וְתַשְׁמִידֵם מִתַּחַת שְׁמֵי יְהֹוָה

The door is closed.

הַלֵּל

The fourth cup of wine is poured, and Hallel is completed.

לֹא לָנוּ, יְהֹוָה, לֹא לָנוּ, כִּי לְשִׁמְךָ תֵּן כָּבוֹד, עַל חַסְדְּךָ עַל אֲמִתֶּךָ. לָמָה
יֹאמְרוּ הַגּוֹיִם אַיֵּה נָא אֱלֹהֵיהֶם. וֵאלֹהֵינוּ בַשָּׁמַיִם, כֹּל אֲשֶׁר חָפֵץ עָשָׂה.
עֲצַבֵּיהֶם כֶּסֶף וְזָהָב מַעֲשֵׂה יְדֵי אָדָם. פֶּה לָהֶם וְלֹא יְדַבֵּרוּ, עֵינַיִם לָהֶם
וְלֹא יִרְאוּ. אָזְנַיִם לָהֶם וְלֹא יִשְׁמָעוּ, אַף לָהֶם וְלֹא יְרִיחוּן.

כִּי אָכַל אֶת יַעֲקֹב וְאֶת נָוֵהוּ הֵשַׁמּוּ

"For Yaakov is devoured; they have laid his places waste."

Yaakov endured three exiles. When he had to flee from Esov and live by Shem
and Ever, when he lived by his father-in-law, Lavan, and when he went down to live
in Egypt. As a result, he merited three crowns: the crown of Torah while learning

The third cup of wine is now drunk, while reclining to the left.

Blessed are You, Hashem our God, King of the Universe, who creates the fruit of the vine.

The "Cup of Eliyahu" is now filled. There are those who pour the fourth cup of wine at this point as well. (Others pour it after the recitation of these verses.) The door of the house is opened as the following verses are recited. (Some have the custom to rise while reciting these passages.)

Pour out Your rage upon the nations that do not know You, and on regimes that have not called upon Your name. For Yaakov is devoured; they have laid his places waste. Pour out Your great anger upon them, and let Your blazing fury overtake them. Pursue them in Your fury and destroy them from under the heavens of Hashem.

The door is closed.

HALLEL

The fourth cup of wine is poured, and Hallel is completed.

Not to us, Hashem, not to us, but to Your name give glory, for Your love, for Your faithfulness.

Why should the nations say, "Where now is their God?" Our God is in heaven; whatever He wills He does. Their idols are silver and gold, made by human hands. They have mouths but cannot speak; eyes but cannot see. They have ears but cannot hear; noses but cannot smell.

They have hands but cannot feel; feet but cannot walk. No sound comes from their throat.

in the Yeshiva of Shem and Ever; the crown of Kehuna while living by Lavan, as he became enriched with a vast amount of livestock that would be brought on the altar; and the crown of royalty while in Egypt. When we left Egypt, we became a free nation and so we celebrate by reclining in the manner that royalty do.

(Pardes Reb Yehonatan)

יְדֵיהֶם וְלֹא יְמִישׁוּן, רַגְלֵיהֶם וְלֹא יְהַלֵּכוּ, לֹא יֶהְגּוּ בִּגְרוֹנָם. כְּמוֹהֶם יִהְיוּ עֹשֵׂיהֶם, כֹּל אֲשֶׁר בֹּטֵחַ בָּהֶם. יִשְׂרָאֵל בְּטַח בַּיהוָה, עֶזְרָם וּמָגִנָּם הוּא. בֵּית אַהֲרֹן בִּטְחוּ בַיהוָה, עֶזְרָם וּמָגִנָּם הוּא. יִרְאֵי יְהוָה בִּטְחוּ בַיהוָה, עֶזְרָם וּמָגִנָּם הוּא.

יְהוָה זְכָרָנוּ יְבָרֵךְ, יְבָרֵךְ אֶת בֵּית יִשְׂרָאֵל, יְבָרֵךְ אֶת בֵּית אַהֲרֹן. יְבָרֵךְ יִרְאֵי יְהוָה, הַקְּטַנִּים עִם הַגְּדֹלִים. יֹסֵף יְהוָה עֲלֵיכֶם, עֲלֵיכֶם וְעַל בְּנֵיכֶם. בְּרוּכִים אַתֶּם לַיהוָה, עֹשֵׂה שָׁמַיִם וָאָרֶץ. הַשָּׁמַיִם שָׁמַיִם לַיהוָה וְהָאָרֶץ נָתַן לִבְנֵי אָדָם. לֹא הַמֵּתִים יְהַלְלוּ יָהּ וְלֹא כָּל יֹרְדֵי דוּמָה. וַאֲנַחְנוּ נְבָרֵךְ יָהּ מֵעַתָּה וְעַד עוֹלָם. הַלְלוּיָהּ.

אָהַבְתִּי כִּי יִשְׁמַע יְהוָה אֶת קוֹלִי תַּחֲנוּנָי. כִּי הִטָּה אָזְנוֹ לִי וּבְיָמַי אֶקְרָא. אֲפָפוּנִי חֶבְלֵי מָוֶת וּמְצָרֵי שְׁאוֹל מְצָאוּנִי, צָרָה וְיָגוֹן אֶמְצָא. וּבְשֵׁם יְהוָה אֶקְרָא, אָנָּא יְהוָה מַלְּטָה נַפְשִׁי. חַנּוּן יְהוָה וְצַדִּיק, וֵאלֹהֵינוּ מְרַחֵם. שֹׁמֵר פְּתָאִים יְהוָה דַּלּוֹתִי וְלִי יְהוֹשִׁיעַ. שׁוּבִי נַפְשִׁי לִמְנוּחָיְכִי, כִּי יְהוָה גָּמַל עָלָיְכִי. כִּי חִלַּצְתָּ נַפְשִׁי מִמָּוֶת, אֶת עֵינִי מִן דִּמְעָה, אֶת רַגְלִי מִדֶּחִי.

בֵּית אַהֲרֹן

"House of Aaron"

What was Aaron's role in the Exodus from Egypt?

The posuk says, *"Hashem spoke to Moshe and to Aaron, and He commanded them concerning the children of Israel and concerning Pharaoh, the king of Egypt, to let the children of Israel out of the land of Egypt"* (Shemos 6:13).

The posuk does not clarify if both brothers spoke to the Yidden and to Pharaoh. Or perhaps each spoke to only one group. If so, to whom did each one speak? The brothers didn't speak to each group together; rather, Moshe spoke to the Yidden and Aaron confronted Pharaoh.

There was an underlying reason why their duties were so divided. Hashem

Those who make them become like them; so will all who trust in them. Israel, trust in Hashem—He is their Help and their Shield. House of Aaron, trust in Hashem—He is their Help and their Shield. You who fear Hashem, trust in Hashem—He is their Help and their Shield.

Hashem remembers us and will bless us. He will bless the house of Israel. He will bless the house of Aaron. He will bless those who fear Hashem, small and great alike. May Hashem give you increase: you and your children. May you be blessed by Hashem, Maker of heaven and earth. The heavens are Hashem's, but the earth He has given over to mankind. It is not the dead who praise Hashem, nor those who go down to the silent grave. But we will bless Hashem, now and forever. Halleluya!

I love Hashem, for He hears my voice, my pleas. He turns His ear to me whenever I call.

The bonds of death encompassed me, the anguish of the grave came upon me, I was overcome by trouble and sorrow. Then I called on the name of Hashem: "Hashem, I pray, save my life."

Gracious is Hashem, and righteous; our God is full of compassion. Hashem protects the simple hearted. When I was brought low, He saved me. My soul, be at peace once more, for Hashem has been good to you. For You have rescued me from death, my eyes from weeping, my feet from stumbling.

was concerned that perhaps the Yidden would not listen to Moshe but Pharaoh would. This, of course, would cast the Yidden in a negative light, and He wanted to give them a defense for their behavior. He, therefore, instructed Moshe, who had a speech impediment, to speak to them. And their failure to follow Moshe's instructions could simply be explained as being a result of Moshe's inability to express himself clearly due to his speech impediment.

However, if Aaron was to address them and they would not listen, they would have no avenue in defending their behavior.

When it came time to meet Pharaoh, Aaron was given the task. Since Moshe had grown up in Pharaoh's palace, it would have been inappropriate for Moshe to challenge him and demand the release of the Yidden.

(Tiferet Yehonatan)

אֶתְהַלֵּךְ לִפְנֵי יְהֹוָה בְּאַרְצוֹת הַחַיִּים. הֶאֱמַנְתִּי כִּי אֲדַבֵּר, אֲנִי עָנִיתִי מְאֹד. אֲנִי אָמַרְתִּי בְחָפְזִי כָּל הָאָדָם כֹּזֵב.

מָה אָשִׁיב לַיהֹוָה כֹּל תַּגְמוּלוֹהִי עָלָי. כּוֹס יְשׁוּעוֹת אֶשָּׂא וּבְשֵׁם יְהֹוָה אֶקְרָא. נְדָרַי לַיהֹוָה אֲשַׁלֵּם נֶגְדָה נָּא לְכָל עַמּוֹ. יָקָר בְּעֵינֵי יְהֹוָה הַמָּוְתָה לַחֲסִידָיו. אָנָּה יְהֹוָה כִּי אֲנִי עַבְדֶּךָ, אֲנִי עַבְדְּךָ בֶּן אֲמָתֶךָ, פִּתַּחְתָּ לְמוֹסֵרָי. לְךָ אֶזְבַּח זֶבַח תּוֹדָה וּבְשֵׁם יְהֹוָה אֶקְרָא. נְדָרַי לַיהֹוָה אֲשַׁלֵּם נֶגְדָה נָּא לְכָל עַמּוֹ. בְּחַצְרוֹת בֵּית יְהֹוָה, בְּתוֹכֵכִי יְרוּשָׁלַיִם, הַלְלוּיָהּ.

אֶתְהַלֵּךְ לִפְנֵי יְהֹוָה בְּאַרְצוֹת הַחַיִּים

"I shall walk before Hashem in the land of the living."

Even though Hashem's Shechinah is found throughout the Land of Israel, there is a difference between the Land of Israel and the holy site of the Beis Hamikdosh. In Israel, a person walks before the Shechinah, as the posuk says, *"I walk before Hashem in the land of the living"* (Tehillim 116:9). However, in the Beis Hamikdosh, a Yid derives pleasure from the Shechinah itself.

(Yaaros Dvash 2, 12)

כּוֹס יְשׁוּעוֹת אֶשָּׂא

"I will lift up the cup of salvation."

The Talmud (Pesochim 117b) writes that Hashem blessed Avrohom: *"And I will make of you a great nation, and I will bless you, and I will make your name great, and you will be a blessing"* (Bereishis 12:2).

"And I will make of you a great nation" is fulfilled in the first brocho of the Shmonei Esrei, as Yidden say, "God of Avrohom."

I shall walk in the presence of Hashem in the land of the living. I had faith, even when I said, "I am greatly afflicted," even when I said rashly, "All men are liars."

How can I repay Hashem for all His goodness to me? I will lift the cup of salvation and call on the name of Hashem. I will fulfill my vows to Hashem in the presence of all His people.

Grievous in Hashem's sight is the death of His devoted ones. Truly, Hashem, I am Your servant; I am Your servant, the son of Your maidservant. You set me free from my chains. To You I shall bring a thanksgiving-offering and call on Hashem by name. I will fulfill my vows to Hashem in the presence of all His people, in the courts of the House of Hashem, in your midst, Jerusalem.

Halleluya!

"*And I will bless you*" is fulfilled when they say, "God of Yitzchok."

"*And I will make your name great*" is fulfilled when they say, "God of Yaakov."

To whom is the final phrase—"*and you will be a blessing*"—referring? It is referring to Dovid Hamelech.

The Zohar writes, "Avrohom, Yitzchok, and Yaakov are the three legs of a chair. The fourth leg is Dovid Hamelech."

Why is he the fourth leg?

The Talmud (Pesochim 119b) writes, "In the future, Hashem will prepare a feast . . . After they eat and drink, the celebrants will give Avrohom Avinu a cup of brocho, and Avrohom will say to them, 'I will not recite the brocho.' Yitzchok and many other great Jewish figures will also refuse until the cup is given to Dovid Hamelech. Dovid will say to them, 'I will recite the brocho, and it is fitting for me to recite the brocho, as it is stated, *I will lift up the cup of salvation* (Tehillim 117:2).'"

"*And you will be a blessing*" refers to Dovid, who will be reciting the brocho when Moshiach comes.

(Midrash Yehonatan 23)

הַלְלוּ אֶת יְהוָה כָּל גּוֹיִם, שַׁבְּחוּהוּ כָּל הָאֻמִּים. כִּי גָבַר עָלֵינוּ חַסְדּוֹ, וֶאֱמֶת יְהוָה לְעוֹלָם, הַלְלוּיָהּ.

הוֹדוּ לַיהוָה כִּי טוֹב כִּי לְעוֹלָם חַסְדּוֹ.

יֹאמַר נָא יִשְׂרָאֵל כִּי לְעוֹלָם חַסְדּוֹ.

יֹאמְרוּ נָא בֵית אַהֲרֹן כִּי לְעוֹלָם חַסְדּוֹ.

יֹאמְרוּ נָא יִרְאֵי יְהוָה כִּי לְעוֹלָם חַסְדּוֹ.

מִן הַמֵּצַר קָרָאתִי יָּהּ, עָנָנִי בַמֶּרְחָב יָהּ. יְהוָה לִי, לֹא אִירָא—מַה יַּעֲשֶׂה לִי אָדָם. יְהוָה לִי בְּעֹזְרָי וַאֲנִי אֶרְאֶה בְשֹׂנְאָי. טוֹב לַחֲסוֹת בַּיהוָה מִבְּטֹחַ בָּאָדָם. טוֹב לַחֲסוֹת בַּיהוָה מִבְּטֹחַ בִּנְדִיבִים. כָּל גּוֹיִם סְבָבוּנִי, בְּשֵׁם יְהוָה כִּי אֲמִילַם. סַבּוּנִי גַם סְבָבוּנִי, בְּשֵׁם יְהוָה כִּי אֲמִילַם.

בְּשֵׁם יְהוָה

"In Hashem's name"

Hashem is known by many names, each name reflecting a different trait.

The Talmud relates a fascinating conversation that took place between Moshe and Hashem. Moshe asked Hashem, "When I go to the Yidden, they will ask me, 'What is Your name?' What shall I tell them?"

Hashem responded, *"Ehyeh asher Ehyeh, I will be with them during this exile, and I will be with them during their future exiles"* (Shemos 3:13,14).

Moshe was concerned how the Yidden would react if they were told that they would experience further exiles in the future. He, therefore, cried out to Hashem and said, "It is sufficient that they are aware of this present exile."

Hashem agreed with Moshe's fear and instructed Moshe to say His name is simply *Ehyeh* and that Hashem will be with the Yidden during their present exile in Egypt and no mention should be made of any future exiles. The conversation continued, and Moshe raised the following fear: Perhaps the Yidden would not believe him if he tells them that Hashem's name implies that this is the only exile the Jewish people would ever experience.

Praise Hashem, all nations; acclaim Him, all you peoples; for His kindness to us is strong,

and Hashem' s faithfulness is everlasting. Halleluya!

Thank Hashem for He is good, His kindness is forever.

Let Yisroel say His kindness is forever.

Let the house of Aaron say His kindness is forever.

Let those who fear Hashem say His kindness is forever.

In my distress I called on Hashem. Hashem answered me and set me free. Hashem is with me; I will not be afraid. What can man do to me? Hashem is with me. He is my Helper. I will see the downfall of my enemies. It is better to take refuge in Hashem than to trust in man.

It is better to take refuge in Hashem than to trust in princes. The nations all surrounded me, but in Hashem's name I drove them off. They surrounded me on every side, but in Hashem's name I drove them off.

Second, regardless of what name of Hashem Moshe would convey to the Yidden, they were a holy nation. Why would Moshe question their faith and belief in their imminent redemption?

Prior to Yaakov's passing, he blessed his sons. He blessed Yehuda that Moshiach, the final redeemer of the Jewish people, would be his descendant. If the Exodus from Egypt was to be the final redemption, then the redeemer—that is, Moshiach—must be from the tribe of Yehuda. As such, this would preclude Moshe, who was from the tribe of Levi, from being the redeemer. If, however, the redemption from Egypt would not be the final redemption and the Yidden would experience further exiles until they merited the coming of Moshiach, then Moshe, being from the tribe of Levi, was not problematic since it was not the final redemption.

Therefore, if Moshe informed them that the name of Hashem was one that implies further exiles, then Moshe could be the redeemer and the Yidden would not question his credentials. However, if the Yidden were told that Hashem's name was one that implies this was the final redemption, then Moshe could not be the Moshiach, and that is why he told Hashem that the Yidden would not believe him.

The Yidden were a righteous nation and people of faith, and if they were told they were to be redeemed, they accepted it with complete faith. They were challenged and had difficulty reconciling Yaakov's final will and testament that Moshiach must be from the tribe of Yehuda, not from the tribe of Levi.

(Tiferet Yehonatan)

The posukim say, אֱלֹהִים *"Elokim spoke to Moshe and He said to Him, I am* יְהֹוָה *Hashem. I appeared to Avrohom to Yitzchak and Yaakov with the name* אֵל שַׁדָּי *El Shadai, but with my name* יְהֹוָה *Hashem, I did not become known to them"* (Shemos 6:3).

Why does the posuk begin with the name Elokim and then conclude with the name Hashem?

What does the posuk mean when it says, *"But with my name Hashem I did not become known"*?

Furthermore, Moshe asks Hashem, *"They will say to me, what is His name, what shall I tell them?"* (Shemos 3:13). Moshe and the Yidden definitely knew the name of Hashem. Moshe killed the Egyptian by using Hashem's name.

Hashem is called by different names. Each name reflects a different character trait of Hashem. When Hashem is sitting in judgment, He is called Elokim. When Hashem is being described as the Master of the world, He is called Adonai. When Hashem is changing the world's nature, he is referred to as Shaddai. And when Hashem is displaying mercy, He is referred to as Hashem YHVH. The name YHVH represents Hashem's essence.

At the time of the Exodus, the Yidden knew that if they were to be judged based on their merit, they were not worthy of being redeemed. However, if Hashem were to show compassion and mercy, then they could be redeemed even prior to the end of their exile.

As such, when Moshe asked Hashem, "When they ask what your name is, what shall I tell them?" he was asking, "What reason shall I give the Yidden for why they are being redeemed?"

Hashem responded, *"For my sake I will do"* (Yeshayahu 48:11) since *"I am with him in distress"* (Tehillim 91:15). And it is further written, *"I will go down with you to Egypt and I will also bring you up"* (Bereishis 46:4). Hashem told Moshe to inform the Yidden that they were being redeemed in "My sake."

If the Yidden had been redeemed with Hashem's complete mercy, then the redemption from Egypt would have been the final redemption. However, since they were redeemed for Hashem's sake, they still needed to endure further exiles. And that is why Hashem said, *"I will be with them in their future exiles."*

In truth, when the Yidden were redeemed from Egypt, they were redeemed with the name YHVH with mercy. However, there are two types of mercy. Sometimes Hashem's kindness is revealed, and at times, it is concealed. As the posuk says, "*To Him Who performs great wonders alone*" (Tehillim 136:4), meaning only Hashem knows that what the Yidden are experiencing is an act of kindness. In Egypt, Hashem's kindness was concealed as they experienced enslavement and hard labor.

In response to Moshe's question, "*What is your name?*" Hashem answers, "This is My name forever" (Shemos 3:15). The Hebrew word for *forever* is לְעוֹלָם, which is similar to the Hebrew word בְּהֶעָלֵם, which means *concealed*. This means that while we experience exile, Hashem's kindness is concealed. However, in the times of Moshiach, the novi says, "*With great mercy I will gather you*" (Yeshayahu 54:7). During the Messianic era, Hashem's mercy will be revealed.

This was Moshe's dilemma. On the one hand, the Yidden were not worthy of being redeemed. However, if Hashem was revealing Himself with the name YHVH with mercy, then the Yidden should not experience evil or justice. That is why Moshe says, "*Since I have come to Pharaoh to speak in Your name, he has harmed this people, and You have not saved Your people*" (Shemos 5:23). The Yidden should be experiencing Your mercy.

When Moshe appeared to Pharaoh, he did not say that he was coming in the name Adonai. Rather he said he was coming in the name YHVH. Pharaoh proclaimed, "*I do not know Hashem YHVH*" (Shemos 5:2). The reason Pharaoh did not recognize this name of Hashem was because Moshe, when sharing Hashem's name, he spelled it out Y-H-V-H. As such, Pharaoh didn't recognize it. Likewise, Pharaoh couldn't understand how punishment could come from the name YHVH.

That is why the posuk reads, "אֱלֹהִים *spoke to Moshe and He said to Him, I am* יְהֹוָה." Hashem was informing Moshe that justice emanating from the name Elokim is, in fact, an act of kindness when the wicked are punished; otherwise, the world would turn into a jungle.

This is one of Hashem's great strengths, usually a person who is by nature caring and kind cannot act in a strict and severe manner.

That is the understanding of the Posuk, "*I am Hashem*"—kindness is justice and justice is kindness. And if Hashem deals with a person with justice, this should be viewed as an act of kindness on Hashem's behalf, as it is an act of cleansing and refining the individual.

This idea is expressed by Dovid Hamelech, when he cries out, "*From the depths I call out to Hashem*" (Tehillim 130:1). Dovid's words can be understood to mean, "Even when I am in the depths of my pain and my struggles, I recognize that it is coming from the name of Hashem. The name of kindness as it is for my benefit."

Likewise, the Egyptian exile was an expression of Hashem's ultimate act of kindness.

(Tiferet Yehonatan Voera)

סַבּוּנִי כִדְבֹרִים, דֹּעֲכוּ כְּאֵשׁ קוֹצִים, בְּשֵׁם יְהֹוָה. כִּי אֲמִילַם. דָּחֹה דְּחִיתַנִי לִנְפֹּל, וַיהֹוָה עֲזָרָנִי. עָזִּי וְזִמְרָת יָהּ וַיְהִי לִי לִישׁוּעָה. קוֹל רִנָּה וִישׁוּעָה בְּאָהֳלֵי צַדִּיקִים, יְמִין יְהֹוָה עֹשָׂה חָיִל. יְמִין יְהֹוָה רוֹמֵמָה, יְמִין יְהֹוָה עֹשָׂה חָיִל. לֹא אָמוּת כִּי אֶחְיֶה, וַאֲסַפֵּר מַעֲשֵׂי יָהּ. יַסֹּר יִסְּרַנִי יָּהּ, וְלַמָּוֶת לֹא נְתָנָנִי. פִּתְחוּ לִי שַׁעֲרֵי צֶדֶק, אָבֹא בָם, אוֹדֶה יָהּ. זֶה הַשַּׁעַר לַיהֹוָה, צַדִּיקִים יָבֹאוּ בוֹ. אוֹדְךָ כִּי עֲנִיתָנִי וַתְּהִי לִי לִישׁוּעָה. אוֹדְךָ כִּי עֲנִיתָנִי וַתְּהִי לִי לִישׁוּעָה. אֶבֶן מָאֲסוּ הַבּוֹנִים הָיְתָה לְרֹאשׁ פִּנָּה. אֶבֶן מָאֲסוּ הַבּוֹנִים הָיְתָה לְרֹאשׁ פִּנָּה. מֵאֵת יְהֹוָה הָיְתָה זֹּאת הִיא נִפְלָאת בְּעֵינֵינוּ. מֵאֵת יְהֹוָה הָיְתָה זֹּאת הִיא נִפְלָאת בְּעֵינֵינוּ. זֶה הַיּוֹם עָשָׂה יְהֹוָה. זֶה הַיּוֹם עָשָׂה יְהֹוָה. נָגִילָה וְנִשְׂמְחָה בוֹ. זֶה הַיּוֹם עָשָׂה יְהֹוָה. נָגִילָה וְנִשְׂמְחָה בוֹ.

זֶה הַשַּׁעַר לַיהֹוָה צַדִּיקִים יָבֹאוּ בוֹ

"This is the gateway to Hashem, through it the tzaddikim will enter."

The Talmud (Berochos 8a) writes, "What is the meaning of the posuk *'Hashem loves the gates of Zion [Tziyyon] more than all the dwellings of Yaakov'* (Tehillim 87:2)?"

This means that Hashem loves the gates (places of study) that are distinguished in that they study halocho even more than the shuls that are a dwelling of Yaakov.

When the posuk states, *"This is the gateway to Hashem, through it the tzaddikim will enter"* (Tehillim 118:20), which gate is it referring to?

It is referring to the gates (places of study) where halocho is learned.

The posuk states, *"Her gates are sunk into the ground"* (Eicha 2:9), implying that the Yidden transgressed Torah prohibitions. Why did they transgress them?

The posuk continues, *"He has ruined and broken her bars."* *Her bars* refer to the boundaries and fences enacted by the chachomim to protect the Torah laws. Since the Yidden *ruined and broke* the Rabbinic laws, it resulted in the Yidden transgressed the Torah laws.

However, the tzaddik who is scrupulous in his observance of the Torah and the mitzvos does not need fences and boundaries to safeguard the Torah laws.

(Ahavat Yehonatan Eicha)

They surrounded me like bees, they attacked me as fire attacks brushwood, but in Hashem's name I drove them off. They thrust so hard against me, I nearly fell, but Hashem came to my help. Hashem is my strength and my song; He has become my salvation. Sounds of song and salvation resound in the tents of the righteous: "Hashem's right hand has done mighty deeds. Hashem's right hand is lifted high. Hashem's right hand has done mighty deeds." I will not die but live, and tell what Hashem has done. Hashem has chastened me severely, but He has not given me over to death. Open for me the gates of righteousness that I may enter them and thank Hashem. This is the gateway to Hashem; through it, the righteous shall enter.

I will thank You, for You answered me, and became my salvation. I will thank You, for You answered me, and became my salvation. The stone the builders rejected has become the main cornerstone. The stone the builders rejected has become the main cornerstone. This is Hashem's doing. It is wondrous in our eyes. This is Hashem's doing. It is wondrous in our eyes. This is the day Hashem has made. Let us rejoice and be glad in it. This is the day Hashem has made. Let us rejoice and be glad in it.

אֶבֶן מָאֲסוּ הַבּוֹנִים הָיְתָה לְרֹאשׁ פִּנָּה. מֵאֵת יְהֹוָה הָיְתָה זֹּאת הִיא נִפְלָאת
בְּעֵינֵינוּ

"The stone the builders rejected has become the main cornerstone.
This is Hashem's doing. It is wondrous in our eyes."

The Talmud (Megillah 15a) writes that there were four women of extraordinary beauty in the world: Sarah, Abigail, Rahab, and Esther. And according to the one who said that Esther was greenish in color and lacking natural beauty, only that a cord of divine grace was strung around her, remove Esther from the list and insert Vashti in her place, for she was indeed beautiful.

Tosfos asks, "Why didn't the Talmud mention Chava, as she was beautiful?"

Tosfos answers, "The Talmud only lists woman who were born to parents, while Chava was created by Hashem."

The word אֶבֶן refers to Chava, as she was the foundation of the world. The word הַבּוֹנִים refers to the chachomim. The posuk can be understood as follows: "Chava, who was the stone, was rejected by the chachomim, who were the builders, and was not included in the list of beautiful women." The question can be asked, "Why wasn't she, as she was *the main cornerstone?*"

אָנָּא יְהוָֹה, הוֹשִׁיעָה נָּא.

אָנָּא יְהוָֹה, הוֹשִׁיעָה נָּא.

אָנָּא יְהוָֹה, הַצְלִיחָה נָּא.

אָנָּא יְהוָֹה, הַצְלִיחָה נָּא.

בָּרוּךְ הַבָּא בְּשֵׁם יְהוָֹה, בֵּרַכְנוּכֶם מִבֵּית יְהוָֹה. בָּרוּךְ הַבָּא בְּשֵׁם יְהוָֹה, בֵּרַכְנוּכֶם מִבֵּית יְהוָֹה. אֵל יְהוָֹה וַיָּאֶר לָנוּ. אִסְרוּ חַג בַּעֲבֹתִים עַד קַרְנוֹת הַמִּזְבֵּחַ. אֵל יְהוָֹה וַיָּאֶר לָנוּ. אִסְרוּ חַג בַּעֲבֹתִים עַד קַרְנוֹת הַמִּזְבֵּחַ. אֵלִי אַתָּה וְאוֹדֶךָּ, אֱלֹהַי—אֲרוֹמְמֶךָּ. אֵלִי אַתָּה וְאוֹדֶךָּ, אֱלֹהַי—אֲרוֹמְמֶךָּ. הוֹדוּ לַיהוָֹה כִּי טוֹב, כִּי לְעוֹלָם חַסְדּוֹ. הוֹדוּ לַיהוָֹה כִּי טוֹב, כִּי לְעוֹלָם חַסְדּוֹ.

יְהַלְלוּךָ יְהוָֹה אֱלֹהֵינוּ כָּל מַעֲשֶׂיךָ, וַחֲסִידֶיךָ צַדִּיקִים עוֹשֵׂי רְצוֹנֶךָ, וְכָל עַמְּךָ בֵּית יִשְׂרָאֵל בְּרִנָּה יוֹדוּ וִיבָרְכוּ, וִישַׁבְּחוּ וִיפָאֲרוּ, וִירוֹמְמוּ וְיַעֲרִיצוּ, וְיַקְדִּישׁוּ וְיַמְלִיכוּ, אֶת שִׁמְךָ, מַלְכֵּנוּ. כִּי לְךָ טוֹב לְהוֹדוֹת וּלְשִׁמְךָ נָאֶה לְזַמֵּר, כִּי מֵעוֹלָם וְעַד עוֹלָם אַתָּה אֵל.

The answer is, as Tosfos writes, *"This is Hashem's doing."* She was created by Hashem and the list only includes those women born to a father and mother.

(Nefesh Yehonatan Vzos Habrocho)

"The stone" refers to the baal teshuvah, and *"the builders rejected"* refers to the angels who reject the baal teshuvah. Yet he *"has become the main cornerstone"*—he becomes the head, even greater than the tzaddik. How is this possible?

Hashem. please. save us.

Hashem, please, save us.

Hashem, please, grant us success.

Hashem, please, grant us success.

Blessed is one who comes in the name of Hashem; we bless you from the House of Hashem. Blessed is one who comes in the name of Hashem; we bless you from the House of Hashem. Hashem is God; He has given us light. Bind the festival offering with thick cords [and bring it] to the horns of the altar. Hashem is God; He has given us light. Bind the festival offering with thick cords [and bring it] to the horns of the altar. You are my God and I will thank You; You are my God, I will exalt You. You are my God and I will thank You; You are my God, I will exalt You. Thank Hashem for He is good, His kindness is forever. Thank Hashem for He is good, His kindness is forever.

All your works will praise you, Hashem our God, and Your devoted ones— the righteous who do Your will, together with all Your people the house of Israel—will joyously thank, bless, praise, glorify, exalt, revere, sanctify, and proclaim the sovereignty of Your name, our King. For it is good to thank You and fitting to sing psalms to Your name, for from eternity to eternity You are God.

"This is Hashem's doing. It is wondrous in our eyes." This is one of the wonders that Hashem has done with mankind to elevate the baal teshuvah to such a lofty level.

(Yaaros Dvash 1:15)

הוֹדוּ לַיהוָה כִּי טוֹב   כִּי לְעוֹלָם חַסְדּוֹ.

הוֹדוּ לֵאלֹהֵי הָאֱלֹהִים   כִּי לְעוֹלָם חַסְדּוֹ.

הוֹדוּ לַאֲדֹנֵי הָאֲדֹנִים   כִּי לְעוֹלָם חַסְדּוֹ.

לְעֹשֵׂה נִפְלָאוֹת גְּדֹלוֹת לְבַדּוֹ   כִּי לְעוֹלָם חַסְדּוֹ.

לְעֹשֵׂה הַשָּׁמַיִם בִּתְבוּנָה   כִּי לְעוֹלָם חַסְדּוֹ.

לְרוֹקַע הָאָרֶץ עַל הַמָּיִם   כִּי לְעוֹלָם חַסְדּוֹ.

לְעֹשֵׂה אוֹרִים גְּדֹלִים   כִּי לְעוֹלָם חַסְדּוֹ.

אֶת הַשֶּׁמֶשׁ לְמֶמְשֶׁלֶת בַּיּוֹם   כִּי לְעוֹלָם חַסְדּוֹ.

אֶת הַיָּרֵחַ וְכוֹכָבִים לְמֶמְשְׁלוֹת בַּלַּיְלָה   כִּי לְעוֹלָם חַסְדּוֹ.

לְמַכֵּה מִצְרַיִם בִּבְכוֹרֵיהֶם   כִּי לְעוֹלָם חַסְדּוֹ.

וַיּוֹצֵא יִשְׂרָאֵל מִתּוֹכָם   כִּי לְעוֹלָם חַסְדּוֹ.

בְּיָד חֲזָקָה וּבִזְרוֹעַ נְטוּיָה   כִּי לְעוֹלָם חַסְדּוֹ.

לְגֹזֵר יַם סוּף לִגְזָרִים   כִּי לְעוֹלָם חַסְדּוֹ.

וְהֶעֱבִיר יִשְׂרָאֵל בְּתוֹכוֹ   כִּי לְעוֹלָם חַסְדּוֹ.

וְנִעֵר פַּרְעֹה וְחֵילוֹ בְיַם סוּף   כִּי לְעוֹלָם חַסְדּוֹ.

וְנִעֵר פַּרְעֹה וְחֵילוֹ בְיַם־סוּף

"Casting Pharaoh and his army into the Yam Suf"

It would seem that the Egyptian riders wanted to cease the chase and tried to turn the horses around. However, the horses refused. The Egyptians removed the wheels, but this made no impact. The horses exerted more pressure and continued to drag the chariots.

The Egyptians immediately realized that it must be Hashem who was waging the battle and dragging their chariots. And their god called Egypt was being subdued.

Thank Hashem, for He is good, His kindness is forever.

Thank the God of gods, His kindness is forever.

Thank Hashem of Hashems, His kindness is forever.

To the One who alone works great wonders, His kindness is forever.

Who made the heavens with wisdom, His kindness is forever.

Who spread the earth upon the waters, His kindness is forever.

Who made the great lights, His kindness is forever.

The sun to rule by day, His kindness is forever.

The moon and the stars to rule by night, His kindness is forever.

Who struck Egypt through their firstborn, His kindness is forever.

And brought out Israel from their midst, His kindness is forever.

With a strong hand and outstretched arm, His kindness is forever.

Who split the Reed Sea into parts, His kindness is forever.

And made Israel pass through it, His kindness is forever.

Casting Pharaoh and his army into the Reed Sea, His kindness is forever.

The final phrase *"because the Lord is fighting for them against the Egyptians"* is to be understood as referring to the spiritual force of the Egyptians called Egypt.

(Tiferet Yehonatan Beshalach)

After the Yidden had crossed the sea, they were frightened that perhaps the Egyptians had also managed to reach dryland. Therefore, Hashem performed a miracle that the sea spat out the Egyptians, thereby allaying the Yidden's fears.

A person who drowns becomes disfigured, and the Yidden would still have been extremely anxious to know whether these corpses where, in fact, the Egyptians.

לְמוֹלִיךְ עַמּוֹ בַּמִּדְבָּר   כִּי לְעוֹלָם חַסְדּוֹ.

לְמַכֵּה מְלָכִים גְּדֹלִים   כִּי לְעוֹלָם חַסְדּוֹ.

וַיַּהֲרֹג מְלָכִים אַדִּירִים   כִּי לְעוֹלָם חַסְדּוֹ.

לְסִיחוֹן מֶלֶךְ הָאֱמֹרִי   כִּי לְעוֹלָם חַסְדּוֹ.

וּלְעוֹג מֶלֶךְ הַבָּשָׁן   כִּי לְעוֹלָם חַסְדּוֹ.

וְנָתַן אַרְצָם לְנַחֲלָה   כִּי לְעוֹלָם חַסְדּוֹ.

נַחֲלָה לְיִשְׂרָאֵל עַבְדּוֹ   כִּי לְעוֹלָם חַסְדּוֹ.

שֶׁבְּשִׁפְלֵנוּ זָכַר לָנוּ   כִּי לְעוֹלָם חַסְדּוֹ.

וַיִּפְרְקֵנוּ מִצָּרֵינוּ   כִּי לְעוֹלָם חַסְדּוֹ.

נֹתֵן לֶחֶם לְכָל בָּשָׂר   כִּי לְעוֹלָם חַסְדּוֹ.

הוֹדוּ לְאֵל הַשָּׁמָיִם   כִּי לְעוֹלָם חַסְדּוֹ.

נִשְׁמַת כָּל חַי תְּבָרֵךְ אֶת שִׁמְךָ, יְהֹוָה אֱלֹהֵינוּ, וְרוּחַ כָּל בָּשָׂר תְּפָאֵר וּתְרוֹמֵם זִכְרְךָ, מַלְכֵּנוּ, תָּמִיד. מִן הָעוֹלָם וְעַד הָעוֹלָם אַתָּה אֵל, וּמִבַּלְעָדֶיךָ אֵין לָנוּ מֶלֶךְ גּוֹאֵל וּמוֹשִׁיעַ, פּוֹדֶה וּמַצִּיל וּמְפַרְנֵס וּמְרַחֵם בְּכָל עֵת צָרָה וְצוּקָה. אֵין לָנוּ מֶלֶךְ אֶלָּא אַתָּה. אֱלֹהֵי הָרִאשׁוֹנִים וְהָאַחֲרוֹנִים, אֱלוֹהַּ כָּל בְּרִיּוֹת, אֲדוֹן כָּל תּוֹלָדוֹת, הַמְהֻלָּל בְּרֹב הַתִּשְׁבָּחוֹת, הַמְנַהֵג עוֹלָמוֹ בְּחֶסֶד וּבְרִיּוֹתָיו בְּרַחֲמִים. וַיהֹוָה לֹא יָנוּם וְלֹא יִישָׁן—הַמְעוֹרֵר יְשֵׁנִים וְהַמֵּקִיץ נִרְדָּמִים, וְהַמֵּשִׂיחַ אִלְּמִים וְהַמַּתִּיר אֲסוּרִים וְהַסּוֹמֵךְ נוֹפְלִים וְהַזּוֹקֵף כְּפוּפִים. לְךָ לְבַדְּךָ אֲנַחְנוּ מוֹדִים.

Therefore, the posuk says, *"They descended into the depths like a stone."* Just as a stone does not change its appearance due to being submerged in the sea, so to the Egyptians miraculously retained their appearance, thus dispelling the notion that perhaps these corpses were not the Egyptians.

(Tiferet Yehonatan Beshalach)

Who led His people through the wilderness, His kindness is forever.

Who struck down great kings, His kindness is forever.

And slew mighty kings, His kindness is forever.

Sihon, king of the Amorites, His kindness is forever.

And Og, king of Bashan, His kindness is forever.

And gave their land as a heritage, His kindness is forever.

A heritage for His servant Israel, His kindness is forever.

Who remembered us in our lowly state, His kindness is forever.

And rescued us from our tormentors, His kindness is forever.

Who gives food to all flesh, His kindness is forever.

Give thanks to the God of heaven. His kindness is forever.

The soul of all that lives shall bless Your name, Hashem our God, and the spirit of all flesh shall always glorify and exalt Your remembrance, our King. From eternity to eternity You are God. Without You, we have no King, Redeemer, or Savior, who liberates, rescues, sustains, and shows compassion in every time of trouble and distress. We have no King but You, God of the first and last, God of all creatures, Master of all ages, extolled by a multitude of praises, who guides His world with kindness and His creatures with compassion. Hashem neither slumbers nor sleeps. He rouses the sleepers and wakens the slumberers. He makes the dumb speak, sets the bound free, supports the fallen, and raises those bowed down. To You alone we give thanks.

The Zohar explains that Pharaoh thought that since Hashem was good and full of compassion no evil would emanate from Him. As such, he did not humble himself before Hashem.

(Tiferet Yehonatan Bo)

אִלּוּ פִינוּ מָלֵא שִׁירָה כַיָּם, וּלְשׁוֹנֵנוּ רִנָּה כַּהֲמוֹן גַּלָּיו, וְשִׂפְתוֹתֵינוּ שֶׁבַח
כְּמֶרְחֲבֵי רָקִיעַ, וְעֵינֵינוּ מְאִירוֹת כַּשֶּׁמֶשׁ וְכַיָּרֵחַ, וְיָדֵינוּ פְרוּשׂוֹת כְּנִשְׁרֵי
שָׁמַיִם, וְרַגְלֵינוּ קַלּוֹת כָּאַיָּלוֹת—אֵין אֲנַחְנוּ מַסְפִּיקִים לְהוֹדוֹת לְךָ,
יְהֹוָה אֱלֹהֵינוּ וֵאלֹהֵי אֲבוֹתֵינוּ, וּלְבָרֵךְ אֶת שְׁמֶךָ עַל אַחַת מֵאֶלֶף, אַלְפֵי
אֲלָפִים וְרִבֵּי רְבָבוֹת פְּעָמִים הַטּוֹבוֹת שֶׁעָשִׂיתָ עִם אֲבוֹתֵינוּ וְעִמָּנוּ.
מִמִּצְרַיִם גְּאַלְתָּנוּ, יְהֹוָה אֱלֹהֵינוּ, וּמִבֵּית עֲבָדִים פְּדִיתָנוּ, בְּרָעָב זַנְתָּנוּ
וּבְשָׂבָע כִּלְכַּלְתָּנוּ, מֵחֶרֶב הִצַּלְתָּנוּ וּמִדֶּבֶר מִלַּטְתָּנוּ, וּמֵחֳלָיִם רָעִים
וְנֶאֱמָנִים דִּלִּיתָנוּ. עַד הֵנָּה עֲזָרוּנוּ רַחֲמֶיךָ וְלֹא עֲזָבוּנוּ חֲסָדֶיךָ, וְאַל
תִּטְּשֵׁנוּ, יְהֹוָה אֱלֹהֵינוּ, לָנֶצַח. עַל כֵּן אֵבָרִים שֶׁפִּלַּגְתָּ בָּנוּ וְרוּחַ וּנְשָׁמָה
שֶׁנָּפַחְתָּ בְּאַפֵּינוּ וְלָשׁוֹן אֲשֶׁר שַׂמְתָּ בְּפִינוּ—הֵן הֵם יוֹדוּ וִיבָרְכוּ וִישַׁבְּחוּ
וִיפָאֲרוּ וִירוֹמְמוּ וְיַעֲרִיצוּ וְיַקְדִּישׁוּ וְיַמְלִיכוּ אֶת שִׁמְךָ מַלְכֵּנוּ. כִּי כָל
פֶּה לְךָ יוֹדֶה, וְכָל לָשׁוֹן לְךָ תִשָּׁבַע, וְכָל בֶּרֶךְ לְךָ תִכְרַע, וְכָל קוֹמָה
לְפָנֶיךָ תִשְׁתַּחֲוֶה, וְכָל לְבָבוֹת יִירָאוּךָ, וְכָל קֶרֶב וּכְלָיוֹת יְזַמְּרוּ לִשְׁמֶךָ.
כַּדָּבָר שֶׁכָּתוּב, כָּל עַצְמֹתַי תֹּאמַרְנָה, יְהֹוָה מִי כָמוֹךָ מַצִּיל עָנִי מֵחָזָק
מִמֶּנּוּ, וְעָנִי וְאֶבְיוֹן מִגֹּזְלוֹ. מִי יִדְמֶה לָּךְ וּמִי יִשְׁוֶה לָּךְ וּמִי יַעֲרָךְ לָךְ הָאֵל
הַגָּדוֹל, הַגִּבּוֹר וְהַנּוֹרָא, אֵל עֶלְיוֹן, קֹנֵה שָׁמַיִם וָאָרֶץ. נְהַלֶּלְךָ וּנְשַׁבֵּחֲךָ
וּנְפָאֶרְךָ וּנְבָרֵךְ אֶת שֵׁם קָדְשֶׁךָ, כָּאָמוּר: לְדָוִד, בָּרְכִי נַפְשִׁי אֶת יְהֹוָה
וְכָל קְרָבַי אֶת שֵׁם קָדְשׁוֹ.

הָאֵל בְּתַעֲצֻמוֹת עֻזֶּךָ, הַגָּדוֹל בִּכְבוֹד שְׁמֶךָ, הַגִּבּוֹר לָנֶצַח וְהַנּוֹרָא
בְּנוֹרְאוֹתֶיךָ, הַמֶּלֶךְ הַיּוֹשֵׁב עַל כִּסֵּא רָם וְנִשָּׂא.

שׁוֹכֵן עַד מָרוֹם וְקָדוֹשׁ שְׁמוֹ. וְכָתוּב: רַנְּנוּ צַדִּיקִים בַּיהֹוָה, לַיְשָׁרִים נָאוָה
תְהִלָּה. בְּפִי יְשָׁרִים תִּתְהַלָּל, וּבְדִבְרֵי צַדִּיקִים תִּתְבָּרַךְ, וּבִלְשׁוֹן חֲסִידִים
תִּתְרוֹמָם, וּבְקֶרֶב קְדוֹשִׁים תִּתְקַדָּשׁ.

וּבְמַקְהֲלוֹת רִבְבוֹת עַמְּךָ בֵּית יִשְׂרָאֵל בְּרִנָּה יִתְפָּאֵר שִׁמְךָ, מַלְכֵּנוּ, בְּכָל
דּוֹר וָדוֹר, שֶׁכֵּן חוֹבַת כָּל הַיְצוּרִים לְפָנֶיךָ, יְהֹוָה אֱלֹהֵינוּ וֵאלֹהֵי אֲבוֹתֵינוּ,
לְהוֹדוֹת לְהַלֵּל לְשַׁבֵּחַ, לְפָאֵר לְרוֹמֵם לְהַדֵּר לְבָרֵךְ, לְעַלֵּה וּלְקַלֵּס עַל כָּל
דִּבְרֵי שִׁירוֹת וְתִשְׁבָּחוֹת דָּוִד בֶּן יִשַׁי עַבְדְּךָ מְשִׁיחֶךָ.

If our mouths were as full of song as the sea, and our tongue with jubilation as its myriad waves, if our lips were full of praise like the spacious heavens, and our eyes shone like the sun and moon, if our hands were outstretched like eagles of the sky, and our feet as swift as hinds—still we could not thank You enough, Hashem our God and God of our fathers, or bless Your name for even one of the thousand thousands and myriad myriads of favors You did for our fathers and for us. You redeemed us from Egypt, Hashem our God, and freed us from the house of bondage. In famine You nourished us; in times of plenty You sustained us. You delivered us from the sword, saved us from the plague, and spared us from serious and lasting illness.

Until now Your mercies have helped us. Your love has not forsaken us. May You, Hashem our God, never abandon us. Therefore, the limbs You formed within us, the spirit and soul You breathed into our nostrils, and the tongue You placed in our mouth—they will thank and bless, praise and glorify, exalt and esteem, hallow and do homage to Your name, O our King. For every mouth shall give thanks to You, every tongue vow allegiance to You, every knee shall bend to You, every upright body shall bow to You, all hearts shall fear You, and our innermost being sing praises to Your name, as is written: "All my bones shall say: Hashem, who is like You? You save the poor from one stronger than him, the poor and needy from one who would rob him." Who is like You? Who is equal to You? Who can be compared to You? O great, mighty, and awesome God, God Most High, Maker of heaven and earth. We will laud, praise, and glorify You and bless Your holy name, as it is said: "Of David. Bless Hashem, O my soul, and all that is within me bless His holy name."

God—in Your absolute power; Great—in the glory of Your name; Mighty— forever; Awesome—in Your awe-inspiring deeds; The King—who sits on a throne, High and lofty.

He inhabits eternity; exalted and holy is His name. And it is written: Sing joyfully to Hashem, you righteous, for praise from the upright is seemly by the mouth of the upright You shall be praised. By the words of the righteous You shall be blessed. By the tongue of the devout You shall be extolled, and in the midst of the holy You shall be sanctified.

And in the assemblies of tens of thousands of Your people, the house of Israel, with joyous song shall Your name, our King, be glorified in every generation. For this is the duty of all creatures before You, Hashem our God and God of our fathers: to thank, praise, laud, glorify, exalt, honor, bless, raise high, and acclaim—even beyond all the words of song and praise of David, son of Yishai, Your servant, Your anointed.

יִשְׁתַּבַּח שִׁמְךָ לָעַד מַלְכֵּנוּ, הָאֵל הַמֶּלֶךְ הַגָּדוֹל וְהַקָּדוֹשׁ בַּשָּׁמַיִם וּבָאָרֶץ, כִּי לְךָ נָאֶה, יְהֹוָה אֱלֹהֵינוּ וֵאלֹהֵי אֲבוֹתֵינוּ, שִׁיר וּשְׁבָחָה, הַלֵּל וְזִמְרָה, עֹז וּמֶמְשָׁלָה, נֶצַח, גְּדֻלָּה וּגְבוּרָה, תְּהִלָּה וְתִפְאֶרֶת, קְדֻשָּׁה וּמַלְכוּת, בְּרָכוֹת וְהוֹדָאוֹת מֵעַתָּה וְעַד עוֹלָם. בָּרוּךְ אַתָּה יְהֹוָה, אֵל מֶלֶךְ גָּדוֹל בַּתִּשְׁבָּחוֹת, אֵל הַהוֹדָאוֹת, אֲדוֹן הַנִּפְלָאוֹת, הַבּוֹחֵר בְּשִׁירֵי זִמְרָה, מֶלֶךְ אֵל חֵי הָעוֹלָמִים.

The fourth cup of wine is now drunk, while reclining to the left.

בָּרוּךְ אַתָּה יְהֹוָה, אֱלֹהֵינוּ מֶלֶךְ הָעוֹלָם, בּוֹרֵא פְּרִי הַגָּפֶן.

After drinking the fourth cup, the following blessing is said
(on Shabbos the words in parentheses are added):

בָּרוּךְ אַתָּה יְהֹוָה, אֱלֹהֵינוּ מֶלֶךְ הָעוֹלָם, עַל הַגֶּפֶן וְעַל פְּרִי הַגָּפֶן, עַל תְּנוּבַת הַשָּׂדֶה וְעַל אֶרֶץ חֶמְדָּה טוֹבָה וּרְחָבָה שֶׁרָצִיתָ וְהִנְחַלְתָּ לַאֲבוֹתֵינוּ לֶאֱכוֹל מִפִּרְיָהּ וְלִשְׂבֹּעַ מִטּוּבָהּ. רַחֶם נָא יְהֹוָה אֱלֹהֵינוּ עַל יִשְׂרָאֵל עַמֶּךָ וְעַל יְרוּשָׁלַיִם עִירֶךָ וְעַל צִיּוֹן מִשְׁכַּן כְּבוֹדֶךָ וְעַל מִזְבְּחֶךָ וְעַל הֵיכָלֶךָ וּבְנֵה יְרוּשָׁלַיִם עִיר הַקֹּדֶשׁ בִּמְהֵרָה בְיָמֵינוּ וְהַעֲלֵנוּ לְתוֹכָהּ וְשַׂמְּחֵנוּ בְּבִנְיָנָהּ וְנֹאכַל מִפִּרְיָהּ וְנִשְׂבַּע מִטּוּבָהּ וּנְבָרֶכְךָ עָלֶיהָ בִּקְדֻשָּׁה וּבְטָהֳרָה [וּרְצֵה וְהַחֲלִיצֵנוּ בְּיוֹם הַשַּׁבָּת הַזֶּה] וְשַׂמְּחֵנוּ בְּיוֹם חַג הַמַּצּוֹת הַזֶּה, כִּי אַתָּה יְהֹוָה טוֹב וּמֵטִיב לַכֹּל, וְנוֹדֶה לְךָ עַל הָאָרֶץ וְעַל פְּרִי הַגָּפֶן.

נִרְצָה

חֲסַל סִדּוּר פֶּסַח כְּהִלְכָתוֹ, כְּכָל מִשְׁפָּטוֹ וְחֻקָּתוֹ. כַּאֲשֶׁר זָכִינוּ לְסַדֵּר אוֹתוֹ כֵּן נִזְכֶּה לַעֲשׂוֹתוֹ. זָךְ שׁוֹכֵן מְעוֹנָה, קוֹמֵם קְהַל עֲדַת מִי מָנָה. בְּקָרוֹב נַהֵל נִטְעֵי כַנָּה פְּדוּיִם לְצִיּוֹן בְּרִנָּה.

לְשָׁנָה הַבָּאָה בִּירוּשָׁלַיִם

May Your name be praised forever, our King, the great and holy God, King in heaven and on earth. For to You, Hashem our God and God of our fathers, it is right to offer song and praise, hymn and psalm, strength and dominion, eternity, greatness and power, song of praise and glory, holiness and kingship, blessings and thanks, from now and forever. Blessed are You, Hashem, God and King, exalted in praises, God of thanksgivings, Master of wonders, who delights in hymns of song, King, God, Giver of life to the worlds.

The fourth cup of wine is now drunk, while reclining to the left.

Blessed are You, Hashem our God, King of the Universe, who creates the fruit of the vine.

After drinking the fourth cup, the following blessing is said
(on Shabbos the words in parentheses are added):

Blessed are You, Hashem our God, King of the Universe, for the vine and the fruit of the vine, and for the produce of the field; for the desirable, good, and spacious land that You willingly gave as heritage to our fathers, that they might eat of its fruit and be satisfied with its goodness. Have compassion, Hashem our God, on Israel Your people, on Jerusalem, Your city, on Zion the home of Your glory, on Your altar and Your Temple. May You rebuild Jerusalem, the holy city swiftly in our time, and may You bring us back there, rejoicing in its rebuilding, eating from its fruit, satisfied by its goodness, and blessing You for it in holiness and purity.

(Be pleased to refresh us on this Sabbath Day.) Grant us joy on this festival of Matzos. For You, God, are good and do good to all and we thank You for the land and for the fruit of the vine.

NIRTZA

The Pesach service is finished, as it was meant to be performed, in accordance with all its rules and laws. Just as we have been privileged to lay out its order, so may we be privileged to perform it [in the Temple]. Pure One, dwelling in Your heaven, raise up this people, too abundant to be counted. Soon, lead the shoots of [Israel's] stock, redeemed, into Zion with great joy.

NEXT YEAR IN JERUSALEM

וּבְכֵן וַיְהִי בַּחֲצִי הַלַּיְלָה

אָז רוֹב נִסִּים הִפְלֵאתָ בַּלַּיְלָה

בְּרֹאשׁ אַשְׁמוֹרֶת זֶה הַלַּיְלָה

גֵּר צֶדֶק נִצַּחְתּוֹ כְּנֶחֱלַק לוֹ לַיְלָה

וַיְהִי בַּחֲצִי הַלַּיְלָה

דַּנְתָּ מֶלֶךְ גְּרָר בַּחֲלוֹם הַלַּיְלָה

וּבְכֵן וַיְהִי בַּחֲצִי הַלַּיְלָה

"And it happened at midnight"

Lomdus

The Midrash writes that when the Yidden left Egypt at midnight, the sun was shining. How does the Midrash know that it appeared as midday when the Yidden left at midnight?

The Midrash (Midrash Hagadol Bereshis 24) writes that Hashem does not attach his name to something that is considered to be a curse. This is seen by creation. The posuk reads, *"Hashem called the light day and the darkness night"* (Bereishis 1:5). It did not say, "Hashem called the light day and Hashem called the darkness night." Darkness represents negativity and therefore Hashem didn't want to attach his name to the creation of darkness.

When the Yidden left Egypt, the posuk says, *"It was at midnight and Hashem,"* how could Hashem attach His name to darkness, which is bad?

Therefore, the Midrash is of the opinion that while the posuk uses the word *midnight*, it cannot be understood to mean it was dark. Rather miraculously the sun was shining brightly.

(Midrash Yehonatan Bo 81)

"AND IT HAPPENED AT MIDNIGHT"

Many were the miracles You performed long ago, at night.

At the beginning of the watch, on this night,

You won [Avrohom's] battle, when [his men were] split, and the night

It happened at midnight.

You judged the king of Gerar in his dream at night.

דַנְתָּ מֶלֶךְ גְּרָר

"You judged the king of Gerar"

Hashem told Avrohom, "*Your children will be strangers in a land that is not theirs*" (Bereishis 15:13). The words "*not theirs*" are superfluous. By definition, children who are strangers in a land are living in a land that is not theirs.

The words *not theirs* is not referring to Avrohom's descendants rather it refers to the nation that will enslave them.

The posuk should read, "*Your children will be strangers in a land* (that is occupied by foreigners who are living) *in a land that is not theirs.*" As such, the Yidden were strangers in a land occupied by strangers.

The exile began with Yitzchak. For a period of time, he lived under the rulership of King Avimelech of Gerar. The word *gerar* means "to drag." The Midrash explains that the reason he was called Gerar was because he wasn't a native Philistine; he had conquered the land and self-appointed himself as king.

As such, Yitzchak experienced what his descendants did years later in Egypt.

(Tiferet Yehonatan Toldos)

הִפְחַדְתָּ אֲרַמִּי בְּאֶמֶשׁ לַיְלָה

וַיָּשַׂר יִשְׂרָאֵל לְמַלְאָךְ וַיּוּכַל לוֹ לַיְלָה

וַיְהִי בַּחֲצִי הַלַּיְלָה.

וַיָּשַׂר יִשְׂרָאֵל לְמַלְאָךְ וַיּוּכַל לוֹ לַיְלָה

"And Israel struggled with an angel and overcame him at night."

This refers to Yaakov Avinu who battled with Esov's angel throughout the night. As the posuk says, *"And a man wrestled with him till daybreak"* (Bereishis 32:25).

The Hebrew word for *wrestle* וַיֵּאָבֵק also means "dust." Rashi explains that their feet raised dust.

The word אָבָק is used in the phrase אֲבַק לְשׁוֹן הָרַע, the dust of lashon hara, meaning speech that incites the speaking of actual lashon hara.

In our context, Esov's angel wanted to attack Yaakov spiritually by finding fault in Yaakov's actions. However, he was only able to raise "dust," the dust of a sin, not an actual sin.

What "dust of a sin" did the angel find and why did it happen at night?

The novi Nehemiah writes, *"The day is designated for work and the night for guarding"* (4:16). When a posuk uses the word *guarding*, it refers to the negative mitzvos. As such, the night is connected to the negative mitzvos. The only behavior in which the angel felt that Yaakov could be viewed in a negative light was the prohibition of not being frightened of one's enemy—not that Yaakov was actually frightened of Esov; rather, it fell under the category of the dust of a sin.

Since it was a negative mitzvah, the spiritual battle had to take place at night.

(Tiferet Yehonatan Vayishlach)

Another reason the battle occurred at night was because that day was Yom Kippur and the forces of evil do not have permission to attack the Jewish people on Yom Kippur.

(Tiferet Yehonatan Vayishlach)

You put dread into [Laban] the Aramean's heart that night.

And Israel struggled with an angel and overcame him at night.

It happened at midnight.

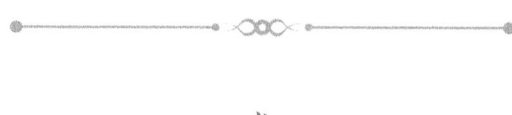

Yaakov's name was changed from Yaakov to Yisroel. The name Yaakov and Yisroel reflect on his life experiences. He was called Yaakov as he was born holding the heel of Esov. The pivotal moments in Yaakov's life had to be accomplished with a level of deceit and trickery, such as the purchase of the rights of the firstborn from his brother, Esov, ensuring that he received Yitzchak's brocho, not Esov, as well as dealing with his father-in-law, Lovon, in terms of the division of their assets.

However, this would no longer be the case with the change of name, as the word אֵל in the name יִשְׂרָאֵל means "strength" as written in the posuk, וְאֶת אֵילֵי הָאָרֶץ לָקַח "And the mighty of the land he took away" (Yechezkel 17:13).

(Tiferet Yehonatan Vayishlach)

"Your name shall no longer be called Yaakov, but Yisroel because you have commanding power with [an angel of] Hashem and with men and you have prevailed" (Bereishis 32:29).

Yaakov was not sure why the angel had confronted him. Was it to do battle or was it to bless him with a change of name?

Therefore, Yaakov wanted to know the name of the angel, as the name of an angel is dependent on its mission.

The angel responded, "Why do you want to know my name? As in truth I have been given two distinct missions giving me two different appearances, one of compassion and one of anger."

Therefore, Yaakov named the place 'פְּנִיאֵל', meaning "two faces." Yaakov continued, "*I saw an angel face to face*" (Bereishis 32:30), meaning I saw an angel with two faces—one of anger and one of compassion.

(Tiferet Yehonatan Vayishlach)

זֶרַע בְּכוֹרֵי פַתְרוֹס מָחַצְתָּ בַּחֲצִי הַלַּיְלָה

חֵילָם לֹא מָצְאוּ בְקוּמָם בַּלַּיְלָה

טִיסַת נְגִיד חֲרֹשֶׁת סִלִּיתָ בְּכוֹכְבֵי לַיְלָה

וַיְהִי בַּחֲצִי הַלָּיְלָה.

זֶרַע בְּכוֹרֵי פַתְרוֹס מָחַצְתָּ בַּחֲצִי הַלַּיְלָה

"You crushed the firstborns of Patros [Egypt] in the middle of the night."

The posuk reads, *"And it was about midnight"* (Shemos 12:29).

The Talmud (Berochos 4a) asks, "Since Moshe knew the precise moment of midnight, why did he say, *'about midnight'* instead of *'at midnight'"*?

While Moshe knew when midnight was, he was concerned that Pharaoh's astrologers would not. And when their midnight had passed and no disaster had occurred, then Moshe would be thought to be a liar.

This section of the Talmud needs further analysis. Why would we think that the astrologers would not be able to calculate the exact time? Couldn't they use an hourglass or water measurements to tell the time? Furthermore, by Moshe saying, *"about midnight,"* the astrologers could still think he was lying, as perhaps their calculations would be off by a considerable amount of time.

What is the significance of midnight?

The Talmud (Yevomos 72a) writes, "All the forty years that the Yidden were in the wilderness, the wholesome north wind would blow at midnight, as it is stated: *'And it came to pass at midnight, that Hashem killed all the firstborn in the land of Egypt'* (Shemos 12:29)." The Gemara asks, "How do we derive from this posuk that speaks of the Exodus from Egypt that a north wind blew at midnight during the forty years the Yidden wandered in the wilderness?"

The Gemara answers: "Since midnight had once been a time of divine favor at the beginning of the Exodus from Egypt, it continued to be a time of favor throughout the forty years that the Jewish people sojourned in the wilderness. As such the northerly wind blew at midnight."

The Zohar writes, "In heaven at midnight there is a spiritual awakening."

Since the world is round when it is midnight in France, it will not be midnight in

You crushed the firstborns of Patros [Egypt] in the middle of the night.

They could not find their strength, when they rose up [against Israel] at night.

You flung [Sisera] the commander of Haroshet off course with the stars of night.

It happened at midnight.

Spain. Every place on planet earth has a different moment when it turns midnight. The understanding of the Talmud is that in the twenty-four-hour period constituting a day and night, there is only one moment that is considered a spiritually auspicious moment.

When is that moment?

The spiritual manifestation of Hashem's mercy will be when it turns midnight in Israel.

The astrologers were able to calculate the exact time of midnight. What they did not know was that midnight in Egypt is irrelevant. Midnight Israeli time is what they would need to know. Therefore, Moshe said at "about midnight" since there would be a few minutes discrepancy between midnight in Egypt and midnight in Israel.

Moshe was not concerned that the astrologers would be off by many hours, as they had the apparatus to accurately tell time.

(Yaaros Dvash 1:14)

The astrologers believed that the source of evil emanates from the north. That is why they worshipped the sheep; that is the head of the zodiac of the north. This understanding is echoed by the novi: *"From the north evil will break forth"* (Yermiyahu 1:14).

Their error was in the understanding that if the north wind blew at midnight, it could not be a time of salvation for the Yidden. What they did not appreciate is that Hashem can join mercy and strict judgment together. At midnight, Hashem can display mercy and compassion to the Yidden *and punishment and death to the Egyptians.*

(Yaaros Dvash 1:14)

יַעַץ מְחָרֵף לְנוֹפֵף אִוּוּי, הוֹבַשְׁתָּ פְגָרָיו בַּלַּיְלָה

כָּרַע בֵּל וּמַצָּבוֹ בְּאִישׁוֹן לַיְלָה

לְאִישׁ חֲמוּדוֹת נִגְלָה רָז חֲזוֹת לַיְלָה

וַיְהִי בַּחֲצִי הַלַּיְלָה.

מִשְׁתַּכֵּר בִּכְלֵי קֹדֶשׁ נֶהֱרַג בּוֹ בַּלַּיְלָה

נוֹשַׁע מִבּוֹר אֲרָיוֹת פּוֹתֵר בְּעַתוּתֵי לַיְלָה

שִׂנְאָה נָטַר אֲגָגִי וְכָתַב סְפָרִים בַּלַּיְלָה

וַיְהִי בַּחֲצִי הַלַּיְלָה.

שִׂנְאָה נָטַר אֲגָגִי וְכָתַב סְפָרִים בַּלַּיְלָה

"[Haman] the Agagite bore his hatred and wrote his orders at night."

Lomdus

The Menos Halevi contrasts Haman's and Mordechais's actions:

Concerning Haman, the posuk says, *"On the thirteenth day of the first month, the king's scribes were summoned and a decree was issued, as Haman directed. . . . the orders were issued in the name of King Achashverosh and sealed with the king's signet"* (Esther 3:12). Due to his haughtiness, Haman instructed others to write the letters.

By Mordechai, it is written, *"So the king's scribes were summoned at that time, on the twenty-third day of the third month, that is, the month of Sivan; and letters were written, at Mordechai's dictation . . .* (Esther 8:9). The Menos Halevi stresses that Mordechai wrote, signed, and sent the letters himself.

The Megillah relates that the writing and sending of Mordechai's letters occurred on the twenty-third of Sivan. If Mordechai wrote the letters himself, we are presented with the following dilemma:

The Megillah writes, *"On the third day, Esther put on royal apparel and stood in the inner court of the king's palace"* (Esther 5:1). The events mentioned in the posuk occurred on the fifteenth of Nissan. The Talmud explains the phrase *"On the third day"* to either mean: on that day in Jewish history, three miracles took place—the Yidden left Egypt, Sancheriv was defeated, and Haman was hung; or that Esther stood by the inner court on a Tuesday, the third day of the week.

[Sancheriv] the blasphemer thought to raise his hand against the beloved [city]; but You dried up the bodies of his fallen in the night.

You overthrew Bel, idol and pedestal together, in the dead of night.

To [Daniel] the beloved man were revealed the secrets of that vision of the night.

It happened at midnight.

[Belshazzar], who drank himself merry from the holy vessels, was killed on that same night.

[Daniel] was brought out unharmed from the lions' den; he who had explained those terrors of the night.

[Haman] the Agagite bore his hatred and wrote his orders at night.

It happened at midnight.

The opinion that Esther stood by the king's palace on a Tuesday presents the following quandary: If the fifteenth of Nissan was a Tuesday, then the twenty-third of Sivan was a Shabbos. This conclusion is based on the following: If the fifteenth of Nissan was a Tuesday, then Rosh Chodesh Nissan was a Tuesday. As such, Rosh Chodesh Iyar was a Wednesday and Thursday, and Rosh Chodesh Sivan was on a Friday. Then the twenty-third of Sivan is a Shabbos. If the twenty-third of Sivan was on a Shabbos, how could Mordechai have written the letters himself?

As such *the third day* means the day that thee three miracles occurred, not that it was a Tuesday.

(Nefesh Yehonatan Pikudei)

🔥

The Midrash (Bereishis Rabbah 3:5) writes, "Hashem judges the nations of the world while they are sleeping." Haman's fate was sealed at night. Similarly, it was the night of Pesach that the Egyptians were struck with the plague of the slaying of the firstborn.

Likewise, Achashverosh was to be punished at night. However, due to Achashverosh's desire to reward Mordechai for saving his life, he woke in the middle of the night, and as a result, he was spared.

(Yaaros Dvash 2:15)

עוֹרַרְתָּ נִצְחֲךָ עָלָיו בְּנֶדֶד שְׁנַת לַיְלָה

פּוּרָה תִדְרוֹךְ לְשׁוֹמֵר מַה מִּלַּיְלָה

צָרַח כַּשּׁוֹמֵר וְשָׂח אָתָא בֹקֶר וְגַם לַיְלָה

וַיְהִי בַּחֲצִי הַלַּיְלָה.

קָרֵב יוֹם אֲשֶׁר הוּא לֹא יוֹם וְלֹא לַיְלָה

רָם הוֹדַע כִּי לְךָ הַיּוֹם אַף לְךָ הַלַּיְלָה

שׁוֹמְרִים הַפְקֵד לְעִירְךָ כָּל הַיּוֹם וְכָל הַלַּיְלָה

תָּאִיר כְּאוֹר יוֹם חֶשְׁכַּת לַיְלָה

וַיְהִי בַּחֲצִי הַלַּיְלָה.

עוֹרַרְתָּ נִצְחֲךָ עָלָיו בְּנֶדֶד שְׁנַת לַיְלָה

*"You awakened Your might against him, disturbing [King Achashverosh's]
sleep at night."*

The Talmud (Megillah 15a) quotes the posuk, וַיַּעֲבֹר מָרְדֳּכַי *"So Mordecai passed"*
(Esther 4:17). The word וַיַּעֲבֹר is similar to the word עֲבֵירָה, meaning sin. Mordechai
instituted that the Yidden must fast on the fourteenth, fifteenth, and sixteenth of
Nissan, thus transgressing the obligation to rejoice on Yom Tov.

Did the Yidden really not eat matzah on the night of Pesach?

The events recorded in Megillat Esther occurred in Bavel. At the same time, the
great Sanhedrin was functioning in Yerushalayim, and the majority of the men of
the Great Assembly and prophets were living in Israel.

They were the ones tasked to set the calendar. They would decide if a month
would be twenty-nine or thirty days, thereby decreeing when a new month would
begin. Initially, the Sanhedrin said that the month of Adar would be twenty-nine
days. However, they changed their minds, and they said that Adar would be a
thirty-day month.

The Yidden in Shushan were unaware of the calendar change; as a result, when
the Yidden in Israel marked the thirtieth of Adar, the Yidden in Shushan had
marked it as the first day of Nissan.

You awakened Your might against him, disturbing [King Achashverosh's] sleep at night.

You shall tread the winepress of [Se'ir], who asks anxiously, "What of the night?"

You will cry out like the watchman, calling, "Morning is come, and also night."

It happened at midnight.

Draw near the day that will be neither day nor night.

Highest One, make known that day is Yours and also night.

Appoint watchmen [to guard] Your city all day long and all night,

Light up like daylight the darkness of night.

It happened at midnight.

On the thirteenth of Nissan, Haman's decree was authorized by Achashverosh. Esther declared that all the Yidden and herself would fast on the thirteenth, the fourteenth, and the fifteenth of Nissan. Even though these three days of fasting would coincide with the Yom Tov of Pesach and they would not be able to fulfil the mitzvah of eating matzah, Esther felt that due to the seriousness of the situation, the need to fast outweighed the obligation of eating matzah.

On the fifteenth, the last day of fasting, Esther entered the king's private chambers. That night Achashverosh woke from his sleep. And at night on the fifteenth of Nissan, the Yidden were able to eat as the fast had concluded.

However, Hashem orchestrated things so that the Yidden would not miss out on eating matzah.

The Yidden in Shushan thought that the fast began on the thirteenth and concluded on the fifteenth. However, based on the Sanhedrin's ruling of adding an extra day to the month of Adar, the fast actually began on the twelfth and concluded on the fourteenth of Nissan. Hence, when the Yidden broke their fast and ate matzah, they fulfilled the mitzvah of eating matzah on the night of the fourteenth.

(Yaaros Dvash 9:2)

וּבְכֵן אֲמַרְתֶּם זֶבַח פֶּסַח.

אֹמֶץ גְּבוּרוֹתֶיךָ הִפְלֵאתָ בַּפֶּסַח

בְּרֹאשׁ כָּל מוֹעֲדוֹת נִשֵּׂאתָ פֶּסַח

גִּלִּיתָ לְאֶזְרָחִי חֲצוֹת לֵיל פֶּסַח

וַאֲמַרְתֶּם זֶבַח פֶּסַח.

דְּלָתָיו דָּפַקְתָּ כְּחֹם הַיּוֹם בַּפֶּסַח

הִסְעִיד נוֹצְצִים עֻגוֹת מַצּוֹת בַּפֶּסַח

וְאֶל הַבָּקָר רָץ זֵכֶר לְשׁוֹר עֵרֶךְ פֶּסַח

וַאֲמַרְתֶּם זֶבַח פֶּסַח.

וּבְכֵן אֲמַרְתֶּם זֶבַח פֶּסַח

"Tell [your children] 'This is Pesach.'"

Children were an integral part of the Exodus, as the posuk says, *"Moshe said, 'With our youth and with our elders we will go, with our sons and with our daughters, with our flocks and with our cattle we will go, for it is a festival of Hashem to us'"* (Shemos 10:9).

Moshe informed Pharaoh that even the very young children would be part of the Exodus. Why did Moshe insist that the babies accompany the elders?

Moshe explained to Pharaoh that they were going to celebrate "a festival of Hashem," meaning they would be proclaiming the oneness of Hashem and His Torah. As such, every single Jew needed to be present for such a declaration.

A similar experience took place during a year of Hakhel, where the king would address the people and focus on the theme of the oneness of Hashem. There, too, all the Jewish people, including the infants, would travel to the Beis Hamikdosh.

(Tiferet Yehonatan)

TELL [YOUR CHILDREN]: "THIS IS THE PESACH."

You showed Your immense power in wonders on Pesach;

to the head of all seasons You have raised up Pesach.

You revealed to [Abraham] the Ezrahi what would come at midnight on Pesach.

> Tell [your children]: "This is the Pesach."

You knocked at his doors in the heat of the day on Pesach;

he gave Your shining [messengers] unleavened cakes to eat on Pesach;

and he ran to the herd, hinting at the ox in the Torah reading of Pesach.

> Tell [your children]: "This is the Pesach."

דְּלָתָיו דְּפַקְתָּ כְּחֹם הַיּוֹם בַּפֶּסַח

"You knocked at his doors in the heat of the day on Pesach."

When Moshiach comes, Hashem will remove the cover of the sun, and its rays will heal the tzaddikim. Similarly, Hashem removed the cover of the sun after Avrohom's bris so that its rays would heal him.

(Tiferet Yehonatan Vayera)

Another reason the three angels who looked like Arabs came during the heat of the day is based on a Talmudic (Yevomos 122a) discussion concerning demons and angels. While a demon and an angel may have a shadow, they do not have a shadow of a shadow.

The "heat of the day" means at midday when the sun is directly above the person. When the sun is in that position, there is no shadow, and Avrohom would not be able to discern that the three individuals before him were angels.

(Tiferet Yehonatan Vayera)

זוֹעֲמוּ סְדוֹמִים וְלוֹהֲטוּ בָּאֵשׁ בַּפֶּסַח

חֻלַּץ לוֹט מֵהֶם וּמַצּוֹת אָפָה בְּקֵץ פֶּסַח

טִאטֵאתָ אַדְמַת מוֹף וְנוֹף בְּעָבְרְךָ בַּפֶּסַח

וַאֲמַרְתֶּם זֶבַח פֶּסַח.

יָהּ רֹאשׁ כָּל הוֹן מָחַצְתָּ בְּלֵיל שִׁמּוּר פֶּסַח

כַּבִּיר, עַל בֵּן בְּכוֹר פָּסַחְתָּ בְּדַם פֶּסַח

לְבִלְתִּי תֵּת מַשְׁחִית לָבֹא בִּפְתָחַי בַּפֶּסַח

וַאֲמַרְתֶּם זֶבַח פֶּסַח.

זוֹעֲמוּ סְדוֹמִים וְלוֹהֲטוּ בָּאֵשׁ בַּפֶּסַח

"The men of Sodom raged and burned in fire on Pesach."

After the angels left, Avrohom davened to Hashem to save the city of Sodom. He was unsuccessful. The posuk states, *"And Hashem departed when He finished speaking to Avrohom, and Avrohom returned to his place"* (Bereishis 18:8).

Why does the Torah need to inform us of where he went?

The Torah is teaching us that when there is danger and people's lives are in peril, we should not remain outside; rather, we should hide, and even a tzaddik such as Avrohom should go into hiding.

Even though it was the night of Pesach, which is *leil shimurim*, Avrohom was cautious and returned home even though the night was protected.

(Tiferet Yehonatan Vayera)

כַּבִּיר עַל בֵּן בְּכוֹר פָּסַחְתָּ בְּדַם פֶּסַח

"[But,] Mighty One, You passed over Your firstborn son when You saw the blood of the Pesach."

The Talmud (Rosh Hashonoh 11a) writes that Yitzchok was born on the night of Pesach. A tzaddik passes away on the day they are born. Yitzchok was a firstborn, and in the merit of the akeida, his firstborn descendants who were meant to perish on the night of Pesach along with the firstborn Egyptians where saved.

(Tiferet Yehonatan Vayera)

The men of Sodom raged and burned in fire on Pesach.

Lot was saved; he baked matzos at the end of Pesach.

You swept bare the land of Mof and Nof [Egypt] in Your great rage on Pesach.

Tell [your children]: "This is the Pesach."

The firstborns of [Egypt's] vigor You crushed, Hashem, on the night of guarding, on Pesach.

[But,] Mighty One, You passed over Your firstborn son when You saw the blood of the Pesach, allowing no destruction through my doors on Pesach.

Tell [your children]: "This is the Pesach."

Tosfos asks, "How does the Talmud know that Yitzchok was born on the first night of Pesach? Perhaps he was born on the last day of Pesach."

We can answer the question as follows:

Yitzchok instructed Esov to hunt and bring him meat, and then he would bless him. When did this happen?

Rivka overheard the conversation, and she immediately told Yaakov to bring her two goats. Rashi explains that one goat was for the Korban Pesach and the other was for the Korban Chagigah.

One animal was for the Korban Pesach, as it was Erev Pesach.

Prior to requesting that Esov appear before him, the posuk states, "And he [Yitzchok] said, *"Behold now I have grown old I do not know the day of my death"* (Bereishis 27:2).

If a tzaddik passes away on the day they are born, how could Yitzchok say he doesn't know when he will pass away? Rather Yitzchok was scared that he had limited time to bless Esov, as it was Erev Pesach, and he was born on the first day of Pesach.

According to Tosfos, who suggests that perhaps he was born on the last day of Pesach, then why was he frightened as he had another eight days to live?

(Tiferet Yehonatan Vayeitzei)

מִסְגֶּרֶת סֻגְּרָה בְּעִתּוֹתֵי פֶּסַח

נִשְׁמְדָה מִדְיָן בִּצְלִיל שְׂעוֹרֵי עֹמֶר פֶּסַח

שׂוֹרְפוּ מִשְׁמַנֵּי פּוּל וְלוּד בִּיקַד יְקוֹד פֶּסַח

וַאֲמַרְתֶּם זֶבַח פֶּסַח.

עוֹד הַיּוֹם בְּנֹב לַעֲמוֹד עַד גָּעָה עוֹנַת פֶּסַח

פַּס יַד כָּתְבָה לְקַעֲקֵעַ צוּל בַּפֶּסַח

צָפֹה הַצָּפִית עָרוֹךְ הַשֻּׁלְחָן בַּפֶּסַח

וַאֲמַרְתֶּם זֶבַח פֶּסַח.

קָהָל כִּנְּסָה הֲדַסָּה לְשַׁלֵּשׁ צוֹם בַּפֶּסַח

רֹאשׁ מִבֵּית רָשָׁע מָחַצְתָּ בְּעֵץ חֲמִשִּׁים בַּפֶּסַח

שְׁתֵּי אֵלֶּה רֶגַע תָּבִיא לְעוּצִית בַּפֶּסַח

תָּעֹז יָדְךָ תָּרוּם יְמִינְךָ כְּלֵיל הִתְקַדֶּשׁ חַג פֶּסַח

וַאֲמַרְתֶּם זֶבַח פֶּסַח.

קָהָל כִּנְּסָה הֲדַסָּה לְשַׁלֵּשׁ צוֹם בַּפֶּסַח

"Hadassah [Queen Esther] gathered the people to fast three days at Pesach."

When Esther instructed all Yidden to fast for three days, she cried out, *"My God, my God, why have you forsaken me?"* (Tehillim 22:2).

The Yalkut explains the reason Hashem's name is written twice is that one refers to Hashem by the sea and the other refers to Hashem at Mount Sinai.

Why did Queen Esther allude to the Exodus and the giving of the Torah at this moment of crisis?

What does it mean "Hashem by the sea" and "Hashem by the mountain"?

The Talmud (Chagigah 14a) writes that Hashem appeared like a mighty warrior when he split the sea and like an elder sitting and learning when he gave the Torah.

The walled city [of Jericho] was closed [for fear] when it was Pesach.

Midian was destroyed in the din, [after a dream of] Omer barley on Pesach.

The fat ones of [Assyria; of] Pul and Lud were burned away in fires on Pesach.

>Tell [your children]: "This is the Pesach."

This day [Sancheriv] halted at Nob [and laid siege] until the time of Pesach.

A hand wrote Babylonia's doom on the wall at Pesach:

the lamp was lit, the table was laid on Pesach.

>Tell [your children]: "This is the Pesach."

Hadassa gathered the people to fast three days at Pesach;

You crushed [Haman,] the head of that evil family, on a gallows fifty cubits high on Pesach.

[Loss and widowhood,] You will bring these two in a moment to [Edom, which rules us now,] on Pesach.

Strengthen Your hand, raise Your right hand, as on the night first sanctified as Pesach.

>Tell [your children]: "This is the Pesach."

The Arizal explains that Hashem's different appearances reflect on the nature of the miracle that the Yidden experienced. With regard to Krias Yam Suf, Hashem performed a miracle that was above nature. Therefore, Hashem appeared as a mighty warrior who conquers and destroys nature. However, when Hashem performed a miracle within nature, such as on Mount Sinai, Hashem appears as an elder who is sitting and learning.

Esther davened for Hashem to perform a miracle. She was unsure whether Hashem would perform a revealed miracle or a miracle clothed in nature. Therefore, Esther davened to Hashem, "*My God* [if the miracle will be beyond nature and You will appear as a mighty warrior], *My God* [if the miracle will be clothed in nature and You will appear as an elder learning], *why have You forsaken me?*"

(Yaaros Dvash 3:1)

כִּי לוֹ נָאֶה, כִּי לוֹ יָאֶה

אַדִּיר בִּמְלוּכָה, **בָּ**חוּר כַּהֲלָכָה, **גְּ**דוּדָיו יֹאמְרוּ לוֹ: לְךָ וּלְךָ, לְךָ כִּי לְךָ, לְךָ אַף לְךָ, לְךָ יְהֹוָה הַמַּמְלָכָה, כִּי לוֹ נָאֶה, כִּי לוֹ יָאֶה.

דָּגוּל בִּמְלוּכָה, **הָ**דוּר כַּהֲלָכָה, **וָ**תִיקָיו יֹאמְרוּ לוֹ: לְךָ וּלְךָ, לְךָ כִּי לְךָ, לְךָ אַף לְךָ, לְךָ יְהֹוָה הַמַּמְלָכָה, כִּי לוֹ נָאֶה, כִּי לוֹ יָאֶה.

זַכַּאי בִּמְלוּכָה, **חָ**סִין כַּהֲלָכָה **טַ**פְסְרָיו יֹאמְרוּ לוֹ: לְךָ וּלְךָ, לְךָ כִּי לְךָ, לְךָ אַף לְךָ, לְךָ יְהֹוָה הַמַּמְלָכָה, כִּי לוֹ נָאֶה, כִּי לוֹ יָאֶה.

יָחִיד בִּמְלוּכָה, **כַּ**בִּיר כַּהֲלָכָה לִמּוּדָיו יֹאמְרוּ לוֹ: לְךָ וּלְךָ, לְךָ כִּי לְךָ, לְךָ אַף לְךָ, לְךָ יְהֹוָה הַמַּמְלָכָה, כִּי לוֹ נָאֶה, כִּי לוֹ יָאֶה.

מוֹשֵׁל בִּמְלוּכָה, **נוֹ**רָא כַּהֲלָכָה **סְ**בִיבָיו יֹאמְרוּ לוֹ: לְךָ וּלְךָ, לְךָ כִּי לְךָ, לְךָ אַף לְךָ, לְךָ יְהֹוָה הַמַּמְלָכָה, כִּי לוֹ נָאֶה, כִּי לוֹ יָאֶה.

עָנָיו בִּמְלוּכָה, **פּוֹ**דֶה כַּהֲלָכָה, **צַ**דִּיקָיו יֹאמְרוּ לוֹ: לְךָ וּלְךָ, לְךָ כִּי לְךָ, לְךָ אַף לְךָ, לְךָ יְהֹוָה הַמַּמְלָכָה, כִּי לוֹ נָאֶה, כִּי לוֹ יָאֶה.

קָדוֹשׁ בִּמְלוּכָה, **רַ**חוּם כַּהֲלָכָה **שִׁ**נְאַנָּיו יֹאמְרוּ לוֹ: לְךָ וּלְךָ, לְךָ כִּי לְךָ, לְךָ אַף לְךָ, לְךָ יְהֹוָה הַמַּמְלָכָה, כִּי לוֹ נָאֶה, כִּי לוֹ יָאֶה.

תַּקִּיף בִּמְלוּכָה, **תּוֹ**מֵךְ כַּהֲלָכָה תְּמִימָיו יֹאמְרוּ לוֹ: לְךָ וּלְךָ, לְךָ כִּי לְךָ, לְךָ אַף לְךָ, לְךָ יְהֹוָה הַמַּמְלָכָה, כִּי לוֹ נָאֶה, כִּי לוֹ יָאֶה.

"FOR HIM IT IS FITTING"

Majestic in Kingship, truly chosen: His legions say to Him:
"Yours and Yours; Yours, for it is Yours; Yours, only Yours;
Yours, Hashem, is the Kingdom."
For Him it is fitting, for Him it is right.

Unmistakable in His Kingship, truly glorious: His venerable ones say to Him:
"Yours and Yours; Yours, for it is Yours; Yours, only Yours;
Yours, Hashem, is the Kingdom."
For Him it is fitting, for Him it is right.

Worthy of Kingship, truly mighty: His officers say to Him:
"Yours and Yours; Yours, for it is Yours; Yours, only Yours;
Yours, Hashem, is the Kingdom."
For Him it is fitting, for Him it is right.

One in Kingship, truly omnipotent: His learned ones say to Him:
"Yours and Yours; Yours, for it is Yours; Yours, only Yours;
Yours, Hashem, is the Kingdom."
For Him it is fitting, for Him it is right.

King in His Kingship, truly awesome: those surrounding Him say to Him:
"Yours and Yours; Yours, for it is Yours; Yours, only Yours;
Yours, Hashem, is the Kingdom."
For Him it is fitting, for Him it is right.

Humble in Kingship, truly the Redeemer, His righteous ones say to Him:
"Yours and Yours; Yours, for it is Yours; Yours, only Yours;
Yours, Hashem, is the Kingdom."
For Him it is fitting, for Him it is right.

Holy in Kingship, truly compassionate, His angels say to Him:
"Yours and Yours; Yours, for it is Yours; Yours, only Yours;
Yours, Hashem, is the Kingdom."
For Him it is fitting, for Him it is right.

Powerful in Kingship, truly our Support, His perfect ones say to Him:
"Yours and Yours; Yours, for it is Yours; Yours, only Yours;
Yours, Hashem, is the Kingdom."
For Him it is fitting, for Him it is right.

אַדִּיר הוּא יִבְנֶה בֵיתוֹ בְּקָרוֹב. בִּמְהֵרָה, בִּמְהֵרָה, בְּיָמֵינוּ בְּקָרוֹב. אֵל בְּנֵה, אֵל בְּנֵה, בְּנֵה בֵיתְךָ בְּקָרוֹב.

בָּחוּר הוּא, גָּדוֹל הוּא, דָּגוּל הוּא יִבְנֶה בֵיתוֹ בְּקָרוֹב. בִּמְהֵרָה, בִּמְהֵרָה, בְּיָמֵינוּ בְּקָרוֹב. אֵל בְּנֵה, אֵל בְּנֵה, בְּנֵה בֵיתְךָ בְּקָרוֹב.

הָדוּר הוּא, וָתִיק הוּא, זַכַּאי הוּא יִבְנֶה בֵיתוֹ בְּקָרוֹב. בִּמְהֵרָה, בִּמְהֵרָה, בְּיָמֵינוּ בְּקָרוֹב. אֵל בְּנֵה, אֵל בְּנֵה, בְּנֵה בֵיתְךָ בְּקָרוֹב.

חָסִיד הוּא, טָהוֹר הוּא, יָחִיד הוּא יִבְנֶה בֵיתוֹ בְּקָרוֹב. בִּמְהֵרָה, בִּמְהֵרָה, בְּיָמֵינוּ בְּקָרוֹב. אֵל בְּנֵה, אֵל בְּנֵה, בְּנֵה בֵיתְךָ בְּקָרוֹב.

כַּבִּיר הוּא, לָמוּד הוּא, מֶלֶךְ הוּא יִבְנֶה בֵיתוֹ בְּקָרוֹב. בִּמְהֵרָה, בִּמְהֵרָה, בְּיָמֵינוּ בְּקָרוֹב. אֵל בְּנֵה, אֵל בְּנֵה, בְּנֵה בֵיתְךָ בְּקָרוֹב.

נוֹרָא הוּא, סַגִּיב הוּא, עִזּוּז הוּא יִבְנֶה בֵיתוֹ בְּקָרוֹב. בִּמְהֵרָה, בִּמְהֵרָה, בְּיָמֵינוּ בְּקָרוֹב. אֵל בְּנֵה, אֵל בְּנֵה, בְּנֵה בֵיתְךָ בְּקָרוֹב.

פּוֹדֶה הוּא, צַדִּיק הוּא, קָדוֹשׁ הוּא יִבְנֶה בֵיתוֹ בְּקָרוֹב. בִּמְהֵרָה, בִּמְהֵרָה, בְּיָמֵינוּ בְּקָרוֹב. אֵל בְּנֵה, אֵל בְּנֵה, בְּנֵה בֵיתְךָ בְּקָרוֹב.

רַחוּם הוּא, שַׁדַּי הוּא, תַּקִּיף הוּא יִבְנֶה בֵיתוֹ בְּקָרוֹב. בִּמְהֵרָה, בִּמְהֵרָה, בְּיָמֵינוּ בְּקָרוֹב. אֵל בְּנֵה, אֵל בְּנֵה, בְּנֵה בֵיתְךָ בְּקָרוֹב.

He is majestic, may He build His house soon, soon, speedily in our days. Build, O God, build, O God, build Your house soon.

He is chosen, He is great, He is unmistakable, may He build His house soon, soon, speedily in our days. Build, O God, build, O God, build your house soon.

He is glorious, He is venerable, He is worthy, may He build His house soon, soon, speedily in our days. Build, O God, build, O God, build your house soon.

He is kind, He is pure, He is One, may He build His house soon, soon, speedily in our days. Build, O God, build, O God, build your house soon.

He is mighty, He is learned, He is King, may He build His house soon, soon, speedily in our days. Build, O God, build, O God, build your house soon.

He is awesome, He is elevated, He is strong, may He build His house soon, soon, speedily in our days. Build, O God, build, O God, build your house soon.

He is savior, He is righteous, He is holy, may He build His house soon, soon, speedily in our days. Build, O God, build, O God, build your house soon.

He is compassionate, He is Almighty, He is powerful, may He build His house soon, soon, speedily in our days. Build, O God, build, O God.

אֶחָד מִי יוֹדֵעַ? אֶחָד אֲנִי יוֹדֵעַ: אֶחָד אֱלֹהֵינוּ שֶׁבַּשָּׁמַיִם וּבָאָרֶץ.

שְׁנַיִם מִי יוֹדֵעַ? שְׁנַיִם אֲנִי יוֹדֵעַ: שְׁנֵי לֻחוֹת הַבְּרִית. אֶחָד אֱלֹהֵינוּ שֶׁבַּשָּׁמַיִם וּבָאָרֶץ.

שְׁלֹשָׁה מִי יוֹדֵעַ? שְׁלֹשָׁה אֲנִי יוֹדֵעַ: שְׁלֹשָׁה אָבוֹת, שְׁנֵי לֻחוֹת הַבְּרִית, אֶחָד אֱלֹהֵינוּ שֶׁבַּשָּׁמַיִם וּבָאָרֶץ.

אַרְבַּע מִי יוֹדֵעַ? אַרְבַּע אֲנִי יוֹדֵעַ: אַרְבַּע אִמָּהוֹת, שְׁלֹשָׁה אָבוֹת, שְׁנֵי לֻחוֹת הַבְּרִית, אֶחָד אֱלֹהֵינוּ שֶׁבַּשָּׁמַיִם וּבָאָרֶץ.

חֲמִשָּׁה מִי יוֹדֵעַ? חֲמִשָּׁה אֲנִי יוֹדֵעַ: חֲמִשָּׁה חוּמְשֵׁי תוֹרָה, אַרְבַּע אִמָּהוֹת, שְׁלֹשָׁה אָבוֹת, שְׁנֵי לֻחוֹת הַבְּרִית, אֶחָד אֱלֹהֵינוּ שֶׁבַּשָּׁמַיִם וּבָאָרֶץ.

שִׁשָּׁה מִי יוֹדֵעַ? שִׁשָּׁה אֲנִי יוֹדֵעַ: שִׁשָּׁה סִדְרֵי מִשְׁנָה, חֲמִשָּׁה חוּמְשֵׁי תוֹרָה, אַרְבַּע אִמָּהוֹת, שְׁלֹשָׁה אָבוֹת, שְׁנֵי לֻחוֹת הַבְּרִית, אֶחָד אֱלֹהֵינוּ שֶׁבַּשָּׁמַיִם וּבָאָרֶץ.

שִׁבְעָה מִי יוֹדֵעַ? שִׁבְעָה אֲנִי יוֹדֵעַ: שִׁבְעָה יְמֵי שַׁבַּתָּא, שִׁשָּׁה סִדְרֵי מִשְׁנָה, חֲמִשָּׁה חוּמְשֵׁי תוֹרָה, אַרְבַּע אִמָּהוֹת, שְׁלֹשָׁה אָבוֹת, שְׁנֵי לֻחוֹת הַבְּרִית, אֶחָד אֱלֹהֵינוּ שֶׁבַּשָּׁמַיִם וּבָאָרֶץ.

שְׁמוֹנָה מִי יוֹדֵעַ? שְׁמוֹנָה אֲנִי יוֹדֵעַ: שְׁמוֹנָה יְמֵי מִילָה, שִׁבְעָה יְמֵי שַׁבַּתָּא, שִׁשָּׁה סִדְרֵי מִשְׁנָה, חֲמִשָּׁה חוּמְשֵׁי תוֹרָה, אַרְבַּע אִמָּהוֹת, שְׁלֹשָׁה אָבוֹת, שְׁנֵי לֻחוֹת הַבְּרִית, אֶחָד אֱלֹהֵינוּ שֶׁבַּשָּׁמַיִם וּבָאָרֶץ.

Who knows one?

אֶחָד מִי יוֹדֵעַ? אֶחָד אֲנִי יוֹדֵעַ: אֶחָד אֱלֹהֵינוּ שֶׁבַּשָּׁמַיִם וּבָאָרֶץ

"Who knows one? I know one: our God is One, in heaven and on earth."

The posuk says, *"It was evening, it was morning, יוֹם אֶחָד one day"* (Bereishis 1:5). Rashi asks why the Torah didn't say יוֹם רִאשׁוֹן, the first day? He answers, "To impress upon us that on day one, Hashem was the Sole Being in His Universe, since the angels were not created until the second day."

Who knows one? I know one: our God is One, in heaven and on earth.

Who knows two? I know two: two Tablets of the Covenant; but our God is One, in heaven and on earth.

Who knows three? I know three: three fathers, two Tablets of the Covenant; but our God is One, in heaven and on earth.

Who knows four? I know four: four mothers, three fathers, two Tablets of the Covenant; but our God is One, in heaven and on earth.

Who knows five? I know five: five books of the Torah, four mothers, three fathers, two Tablets of the Covenant; but our God is One, in heaven and on earth.

Who knows six? I know six: six divisions of the Mishna, five books of the Torah, four mothers, three fathers, two Tablets of the Covenant; but our God is One, in heaven and on earth.

Who knows seven? I know seven: seven days from Shabbos to Shabbos, six divisions of the Mishna, five books of the Torah, four mothers, three fathers, two Tablets of the Covenant; but our God is One, in heaven and on earth.

Who knows eight? I know eight: eight days to a *brit*, seven days from Shabbos to Shabbos, six divisions of the Mishna, five books of the Torah, four mothers, three fathers, two Tablets of the Covenant; but our God is One, in heaven and on earth.

This is what the Haggadah is asking when it possess the question "Who knows one?" Who knows why on the first day of creation the Torah uses the word *echod* and not *rishon*? To which the Haggadah answers, "to impress upon us that on day one there was only Hashem in heaven and on earth as the angels were only created on the second day."

(Midrash Yehonatan Haggadah)

תִּשְׁעָה מִי יוֹדֵעַ? תִּשְׁעָה אֲנִי יוֹדֵעַ: תִּשְׁעָה יַרְחֵי לֵדָה, שְׁמוֹנָה יְמֵי מִילָה, שִׁבְעָה יְמֵי שַׁבַּתָּא, שִׁשָּׁה סִדְרֵי מִשְׁנָה, חֲמִשָּׁה חוּמְשֵׁי תוֹרָה, אַרְבַּע אִמָּהוֹת, שְׁלֹשָׁה אָבוֹת, שְׁנֵי לֻחוֹת הַבְּרִית, אֶחָד אֱלֹהֵינוּ שֶׁבַּשָּׁמַיִם וּבָאָרֶץ.

עֲשָׂרָה מִי יוֹדֵעַ? עֲשָׂרָה אֲנִי יוֹדֵעַ: עֲשָׂרָה דִבְּרַיָּא, תִּשְׁעָה יַרְחֵי לֵדָה, שְׁמוֹנָה יְמֵי מִילָה, שִׁבְעָה יְמֵי שַׁבַּתָּא, שִׁשָּׁה סִדְרֵי מִשְׁנָה, חֲמִשָּׁה חוּמְשֵׁי תוֹרָה, אַרְבַּע אִמָּהוֹת, שְׁלֹשָׁה אָבוֹת, שְׁנֵי לֻחוֹת הַבְּרִית, אֶחָד אֱלֹהֵינוּ שֶׁבַּשָּׁמַיִם וּבָאָרֶץ.

אַחַד עָשָׂר מִי יוֹדֵעַ? אַחַד עָשָׂר אֲנִי יוֹדֵעַ: אַחַד עָשָׂר כּוֹכְבַיָּא, עֲשָׂרָה דִבְּרַיָּא, תִּשְׁעָה יַרְחֵי לֵדָה, שְׁמוֹנָה יְמֵי מִילָה, שִׁבְעָה יְמֵי שַׁבַּתָּא, שִׁשָּׁה סִדְרֵי מִשְׁנָה, חֲמִשָּׁה חוּמְשֵׁי תוֹרָה, אַרְבַּע אִמָּהוֹת, שְׁלֹשָׁה אָבוֹת, שְׁנֵי לֻחוֹת הַבְּרִית, אֶחָד אֱלֹהֵינוּ שֶׁבַּשָּׁמַיִם וּבָאָרֶץ.

שְׁנֵים עָשָׂר מִי יוֹדֵעַ? שְׁנֵים עָשָׂר אֲנִי יוֹדֵעַ: שְׁנֵים עָשָׂר שִׁבְטַיָּא, אַחַד עָשָׂר כּוֹכְבַיָּא, עֲשָׂרָה דִבְּרַיָּא, תִּשְׁעָה יַרְחֵי לֵדָה, שְׁמוֹנָה יְמֵי מִילָה, שִׁבְעָה יְמֵי שַׁבַּתָּא, שִׁשָּׁה סִדְרֵי מִשְׁנָה, חֲמִשָּׁה חוּמְשֵׁי תוֹרָה, אַרְבַּע אִמָּהוֹת, שְׁלֹשָׁה אָבוֹת, שְׁנֵי לֻחוֹת הַבְּרִית, אֶחָד אֱלֹהֵינוּ שֶׁבַּשָּׁמַיִם וּבָאָרֶץ.

שְׁלֹשָׁה עָשָׂר מִי יוֹדֵעַ? שְׁלֹשָׁה עָשָׂר אֲנִי יוֹדֵעַ: שְׁלֹשָׁה עָשָׂר מִדַּיָּא. שְׁנֵים עָשָׂר שִׁבְטַיָּא, אַחַד עָשָׂר כּוֹכְבַיָּא, עֲשָׂרָה דִבְּרַיָּא, תִּשְׁעָה יַרְחֵי לֵדָה, שְׁמוֹנָה יְמֵי מִילָה, שִׁבְעָה יְמֵי שַׁבַּתָּא, שִׁשָּׁה סִדְרֵי מִשְׁנָה, חֲמִשָּׁה חוּמְשֵׁי תוֹרָה, אַרְבַּע אִמָּהוֹת, שְׁלֹשָׁה אָבוֹת, שְׁנֵי לֻחוֹת הַבְּרִית, אֶחָד אֱלֹהֵינוּ שֶׁבַּשָּׁמַיִם וּבָאָרֶץ.

Who knows nine? I know nine: nine months until birth, eight days to a *brit,* seven days from Shabbos to Shabbos, six divisions of the Mishna, five books of the Torah, four mothers, three fathers, two Tablets of the Covenant; but our God is One, in heaven and on earth.

Who knows ten? I know ten: Ten Commandments, nine months until birth, eight days to a *brit,* seven days from Shabbos to Shabbos, six divisions of the Mishna, five books of the Torah, four mothers, three fathers, two Tablets of the Covenant; but our God is One, in heaven and on earth.

Who knows eleven? I know eleven: eleven stars [in Yosef's dream], Ten Commandments, nine months until birth, eight days to a *brit,* seven days from Shabbos to Shabbos, six divisions of the Mishna, five books of the Torah, four mothers, three fathers, two Tablets of the Covenant; but our God is One, in heaven and on earth.

Who knows twelve? I know twelve: twelve tribes, eleven stars, Ten Commandments, nine months until birth, eight days to a *brit,* seven days from Shabbos to Shabbos, six divisions of the Mishna, five books of the Torah, four mothers, three fathers, two Tablets of the Covenant; but our God is One, in heaven and on earth.

Who knows thirteen? I know thirteen: thirteen attributes [of God's compassion], twelve tribes, eleven stars, Ten Commandments, nine months until birth, eight days to a *brit,* seven days from Shabbos to Shabbos, six divisions of the Mishna, five books of the Torah, four mothers, three fathers, two Tablets of the Covenant; but our God is one, in heaven and on earth.

חַד גַּדְיָא, חַד גַּדְיָא דְּזַבִּין אַבָּא בִּתְרֵי זוּזֵי, חַד גַּדְיָא, חַד גַּדְיָא.

וְאָתָא שׁוּנְרָא וְאָכְלָה לְגַּדְיָא, דְּזַבִּין אַבָּא בִּתְרֵי זוּזֵי. חַד גַּדְיָא, חַד גַּדְיָא.

וְאָתָא כַלְבָּא וְנָשַׁךְ לְשׁוּנְרָא, דְּאָכְלָה לְגַּדְיָא, דְּזַבִּין אַבָּא בִּתְרֵי זוּזֵי. חַד גַּדְיָא, חַד גַּדְיָא.

וְאָתָא חוּטְרָא וְהִכָּה לְכַלְבָּא, דְּנָשַׁךְ לְשׁוּנְרָא, דְּאָכְלָה לְגַּדְיָא, דְּזַבִּין אַבָּא בִּתְרֵי זוּזֵי. חַד גַּדְיָא, חַד גַּדְיָא.

וְאָתָא נוּרָא וְשָׂרַף לְחוּטְרָא, דְּהִכָּה לְכַלְבָּא, דְּנָשַׁךְ לְשׁוּנְרָא, דְּאָכְלָה לְגַּדְיָא, דְּזַבִּין אַבָּא בִּתְרֵי זוּזֵי. חַד גַּדְיָא, חַד גַּדְיָא.

וְאָתָא מַיָּא וְכָבָה לְנוּרָא, דְּשָׂרַף לְחוּטְרָא, דְּהִכָּה לְכַלְבָּא, דְּנָשַׁךְ לְשׁוּנְרָא, דְּאָכְלָה לְגַּדְיָא, דְּזַבִּין אַבָּא בִּתְרֵי זוּזֵי. חַד גַּדְיָא, חַד גַּדְיָא.

Chad Gadya

חַד גַּדְיָא

Chad Gadya (One Kid)

Note: *Reb Yehonatan wrote extensively on this song. It was printed in Maamar Yehonatan. His writings primarily focus on the kabalistic interpretation. These small snippets offer insight into the complex and the deep analysis Reb Yehonatan presents on what is seemingly a simple song.*

"Gadya"

The word *gadya* is spelled גדיא. The letters ג,ד,י spell the Hebrew word גְּדִי, which translates to "a goat with the letter א attached to it."

The word גְּדִי refers to the nations of the world. The root word of גְּדִי is גַּד, meaning "mazal" or "a spiritual flow of energy."

The nations receive their sustenance via the mazalot, as the Midrash writes (Bereishis Rabbah 10:6), "There is not a single blade of grass that does not have a constellation in the firmament, a heavenly force or an angel that strikes it and says to it: 'Grow.'"

One Little Goat, One little goat my father bought for two zuzim; one little goat, one little goat.

Along came a cat and ate the goat my father bought for two zuzim; one little goat, one little goat.

Then came a dog and bit the cat who ate the goat my father bought for two zuzim; one little goat, one little goat.

Then came a stick and hit the dog who bit the cat who ate the goat my father bought for two zuzim; one little goat, one little goat.

Then came a fire and burned the stick that hit the dog who bit the cat who ate the goat my father bought for two zuzim; one little goat, one little goat.

Then came water and put out the fire that burned the stick that hit the dog who bit the cat who ate the goat my father bought for two zuzim; one little goat, one little goat.

The Yidden are called גַּדְיָא. They have the letter א added to their name. The letter aleph symbolizes unity. The author of the Haggadah had good cause to add the letter aleph, as no matter which way you place the aleph, upright or upside down, it still remains an aleph. This indicates that the Yidden will remain eternal no matter what they encounter.

Similarly, the numerical value of the word *gadya* is nine.[1] The number nine represents eternity since when you times any number by nine and you add together the result, you always have nine.

The letter aleph is composed of two יׅ and a וׅ.[2] Their sum is twenty-six, which is the same numerical value of Hashem's name י-ה-ו-ה[3].

The letter aleph, when spelled in full, is written אָלֶךְ. The first two letters—aleph and lamed—is the name of Hashem אֵל. The name אֵל represents Hashem's chesed,

---

1. א-1, י-1(10), ד-4, ג-3 The letter yud's numerical value is ten. However, by removing the zero from the number ten, we have the number one. Such counting is known as mispar katan, a letter's small number. Ten is one, twenty is two, etc.

2. י-10 ו-6

3. י-10 ה-5 ו-6 ה-5

וְאָתָא תוֹרָא וְשָׁתָה לְמַיָּא, דְּכָבָה לְנוּרָא, דְּשָׂרַף לְחוּטְרָא, דְּהִכָּה לְכַלְבָּא, דְּנָשַׁךְ לְשׁוּנְרָא, דְּאָכְלָה לְגַדְיָא, דְּזַבִּין אַבָּא בִּתְרֵי זוּזֵי. חַד גַּדְיָא, חַד גַּדְיָא.

וְאָתָא הַשּׁוֹחֵט וְשָׁחַט לְתוֹרָא, דְּשָׁתָה לְמַיָּא, דְּכָבָה לְנוּרָא, דְּשָׂרַף לְחוּטְרָא, דְּהִכָּה לְכַלְבָּא, דְּנָשַׁךְ לְשׁוּנְרָא, דְּאָכְלָה לְגַדְיָא, דְּזַבִּין אַבָּא בִּתְרֵי זוּזֵי. חַד גַּדְיָא, חַד גַּדְיָא.

וְאָתָא מַלְאַךְ הַמָּוֶת וְשָׁחַט לְשׁוֹחֵט, דְּשָׁחַט לְתוֹרָא, דְּשָׁתָה לְמַיָּא, דְּכָבָה לְנוּרָא, דְּשָׂרַף לְחוּטְרָא, דְּהִכָּה לְכַלְבָּא, דְּנָשַׁךְ לְשׁוּנְרָא, דְּאָכְלָה לְגַדְיָא, דְּזַבִּין אַבָּא בִּתְרֵי זוּזֵי. חַד גַּדְיָא, חַד גַּדְיָא.

וְאָתָא הַקָּדוֹשׁ בָּרוּךְ הוּא וְשָׁחַט לְמַלְאַךְ הַמָּוֶת, דְּשָׁחַט לְשׁוֹחֵט, דְּשָׁחַט לְתוֹרָא, דְּשָׁתָה לְמַיָּא, דְּכָבָה לְנוּרָא, דְּשָׂרַף לְחוּטְרָא, דְּהִכָּה לְכַלְבָּא, דְּנָשַׁךְ לְשׁוּנְרָא, דְּאָכְלָה לְגַדְיָא, דְּזַבִּין אַבָּא בִּתְרֵי זוּזֵי. חַד גַּדְיָא, חַד גַּדְיָא.

meaning that only kindness and compassion emanate from Hashem. As the posuk says, "*From the One above evil and good do not come*" as only good comes from Hashem (Eichah 3:38).

"My father"

Hashem's name אֵל represents kindness. "*My father*" refers to Avrohom. Avrohom excelled in the attribute of chesed. As the posuk says, "*And he [Avrohom] planted a tree in Beer Sheba and he called there in the name of the Lord the E-L of the world*" (Bereishis 21:33). Avrohom refers to Hashem by His attribute of kindness.

"Bought for two zuzim."

Prior to the birth of Avrohom, the world was under the dominion of the seventy *Sarim*. And when Nimrod, with his power of black magic, saw that Avrohom would transcend the laws of nature, he had him thrown into the furnace. However, Avrohom was unharmed because he was unaffected by the laws of nature.

Hashem appeared to Avrohom by the Bris Ben Habsorim and informed him that his children would be strangers in a foreign land. He was also told that they would be governed by the rules of nature, as the posuk says, "*Now the sun was ready to set, and a deep sleep fell upon Avram, and behold, a fright, a great darkness*

Then came an ox and drank the water that put out the fire that burned the stick that hit the dog who bit the cat who ate the goat my father bought for two zuzim; one little goat, one little goat.

Then came a slaughterer and slew the ox who drank the water that put out the fire that burned the stick that hit the dog who bit the cat who ate the goat my father bought for two zuzim; one little goat, one little goat.

Then came the angel of death and slew the slaughterer who slew the ox who drank the water that put out the fire that burned the stick that hit the dog who bit the cat who ate the goat my father bought for two zuzim; one little goat, one little goat.

Then came the Holy One and slew the angel of death, who slew the slaughterer who slew the ox who drank the water that put out the fire that burned the stick that hit the dog who bit the cat who ate the goat my father bought for two zuzim; one little goat, one little goat.

was falling upon him" (Bereishis 15:12). The phrase *"Now the sun was ready to set"* alludes to the Yidden being influenced by the zodiac.

However, Hashem informed him that He would redeem the Yidden and He would not send an angel.

Hashem then promised Avrohom that he would be blessed with a son, Yitzchok, indicating that he and his children would live beyond the realm of nature.

Avrohom traveled to Gerar and Egypt, and in each place, he elevated the hidden sparks of holiness. Thus, his children merited to be called גּוֹיָא, with an aleph, indicating that they are above nature.

The word zuz can translate to mean "travel." We speak of two zuzim, as Avrohom traveled on two occasions. And that is why we repeat the words chad gadya, chad gadya.

"Along came the cat."

The cat represents the impurity of Egypt. The Talmud writes that a cat doesn't recognize its master (Horiyos 13a). Similarly, the posuk says, *"Who is Hashem that I [Pharaoh] should listen to his voice? I do not know Hashem"* (Shemos 5:2).

Pharaoh likewise did not recall the Master of the universe.

The Talmud writes that if we eat the leftover food of a rat, it will cause forgetfulness (Horiyos 13a). By extension, eating the actual rat will cause forgetfulness. Cats eat rats and mice. As such, the cat symbolizes forgetfulness.

The cat represents both Pharaoh and the Egyptians, as they both had forgotten Yoseph. The posuk says, *"The butler did not remember Yoseph, and he forgot him"* (Bereishis 40:23).

Furthermore, the posuk says, *"And [Pharaoh] did not know Yoseph"* (Shemos 1:8), even though Yoseph had sustained all of Egypt and saved the country from starvation.

"Then came the dog."

The dog symbolizes Amalek. Amalek is called the "evil dog." Unlike the cat, a dog knows who his owner is. Amalek knew Hashem, yet he rebelled against Him. And that is the kabbalistic understanding of the posuk *"Amalek was the first of the nations and his fate shall be everlasting destruction"* (Bamidbar 24:20).

Amalek was the first nation that attacked Bnei Yisroel after they left Egypt. This is alluded to in the Talmud where it writes, "At the beginning of the second part of the night, the dogs begin to bark," meaning Amalek attacked the Yidden at the beginning of the second part of the night, after the exile and Exodus from Egypt, which was during the first part of the night (Berochos 3a).

The battle with Amalek, in a sense, was worse than the years of enslavement in Egypt, since the war with Amalek was the beginning of all the future exiles.

And that is the meaning of "the dog biting the cat." The exile of the dog (Amalek) was far worse than the exile of the cat (Egypt), as we see that the dog bites the cat, as it is stronger than the cat.

In Megillat Esther (8:16) we read, *"And the Yidden had light, simcha and joy."* The Talmud (Megillah 16b) explains that "joy" refers to the mitzvah of bris milah that protects us against Amalek.

That is why Moshe did not go to battle against Amalek. as he was born circumcised; he sent Yehoshua in his place. Likewise, Dovid Hamelech did not go to war against Edom, descendants of Amalek, as he too was born circumcised; he sent his general Yoav in his place.

Amalek is the evil dog. The counterbalance to that is Calev. The name Calev is spelled כלב, the same way you write dog in Hebrew. Calev spied out the land together with Yehoshua.

Yehoshua and Calev caused the impurity of Bilam and Balak to be subservient. The Hebrew spelling of Bilam בִּלְעָם and Balak בָּלָק gives us the words Bavel Amalek בְּבֶל עֲמָלֵק.

Amalek is alluded to in the beginning of Bereishis. The posuk says, *"And darkness was on the face of the deep"* (Bereishis 1:2).

The Hebrew word for darkness חֹשֶׁךְ is an acronym for חֲמוֹר donkey, שׁוֹר ox, and כֶּלֶב dog. And the dog is the symbol of Amalek. And if you rearrange the letters of the Hebrew word for depth תְּהוֹם you get the word הַמָּוֶת death.

"Then came a stick."

That is the understanding of the posuk *"And you shall take the stick in your hand and with it perform the signs"* (Shemos 2:17).

The stick weakened the strength of Amalek, as the posuk says, *"When Moshe raised his hands it weakened Amalek's strength"* (Shemos 17:11).

Moshe's staff was a branch from the Tree of Knowledge, good and evil. That is why at times it was a staff and at times it became a snake.

Moshe rectified Adam's sin. Concerning Moshe Rabbeinu, the Torah tells us, *"The skin of Moshe became radiant"* (Shemos 34:35).

After Adam sinned, the posuk says, *"And Hashem made garments of skins for Adam and his wife, and clothed them"* (Bereishis 3:21).

With regard to Moshe and Adam, the Torah uses the word *skin* עוֹר, as one was to be an atonement for the other. Moshe's skin becoming radiant was to rectify the sin of Adam.

Adam sinned by eating from the Tree of Knowledge, good and evil. The Hebrew word for *and evil* וָרָע has the same letters as the Hebrew word for *skin* עוֹר, indicating the connection between the sin and the need for Adam to clothe himself with clothing made from skins.

Amalek's power stemmed from the snake that convinced Adam and Chava to sin. Esov had a snake tattooed on his thigh.

When the Yidden were in Egypt, they were being subjugated by the impurities of the donkey and the cat. As such, the impurities of the dog could not dominate. As the Talmud (Berochos 48b) writes, "One evil sovereignty cannot intrude on another." Therefore, immediately after the Yidden left Egypt, Amalek attacked them as a reminder of the hatred that the primordial snake had for the Yidden.

"Then came a fire."

This refers to the destruction of the Beis Hamikdosh. The Mishkan, which preceded the Beis Hamikdosh, had forty-eight beams. Each beam was ten amos, a total of four hundred eighty amos. Similarly, there are four hundred eighty words in the Torah's description of creation. Likewise, in Yerushalayim, there were four hundred eighty shuls.

The Hebrew letters ת and פ have a numerical value of four hundred eighty. When Miriam led the women in song after crossing the Yam Suf, it says they took tambourines. The Hebrew word for *tambourine* is תֹף spelled with the letters ת and

פ. And when Avrohom fed the three angels, the posuk says he gave them bread פַּת, spelled with the letters פ and ת.

The sin of the Tree of Knowledge is connected with the destruction of the Beis Hamikdosh. The Hebrew word for *knowledge* [2]הַדַּעַת has a numerical value of four hundred seventy-nine and by adding one for the word itself, we have four hundred eighty.

When Shlomo built the first Beis Hamikdosh, he merited to receive a spark of the Neshomo of Moshe. By rearranging the Hebrew letters שְׁלֹמָה, you have the Hebrew word לְמֹשֶׁה "to Moshe."

The first Beis Hamikdosh stood for four hundred ten years. Add the seventy years of exile in Bavel, and you have four hundred eighty.

"Then came water."

This refers to the decrees of Haman and Achashverosh. As the Talmud (Megillah 15a) explains the posuk in Megillat Esther "So Mordecai passed" (4:17), it means that he crossed over a stream on Pesach to inform the Yidden that they need to fast as Achashverosh had decreed a terrible decree against the Yidden.

"The water came and extinguished the fire."

This means that the suffering the Yidden experienced in the times of Haman far outweighed the burning of the Beis Hamikdosh.

🔥

Water represents the Torah, as the posuk says, *"All who are thirsty come for water"* (Yeshayahu 55:1). The first Beis Hamikdosh was destroyed because the Yidden became idol worshippers; they no longer believed that Hashem created the world or that Hashem had bestowed prophecy on mankind. This all stemmed from their lack of Torah study. As the Novi says, *"And Hashem said because you have forsaken my Torah"* (Yermiyahu 9:12).

However, during the exile in Bavel, between the first and second Beis Hamikdosh, Anshei Knesset HaGedolah led by Ezra established many decrees to fortify and strengthen the study of Torah. They enacted that every city should have teachers and there should always be ten people studying Torah. Moreover, they ensured that the Torah was written accurately.

When Hashem saw that the Yidden were strengthening their commitment to the Torah, He awakened within King Koresh of Persia to give permission to Nehemiah to rebuild the Beis Hamikdosh.

"The water came and extinguished the fire" means that the Torah came and extinguished the fires of Nebuchadnetzer who had destroyed the Beis Hamikdosh.

---

2. 400-ת 70-ע 4-ד 5 5-ה

"The ox came"

The ox represents the Greek exile, as the Midrash (Bereishis Rabbah 2:5) writes that the Greeks issued decrees that darkened the eyes of the Yidden, one of them being that they were instructed to write on the horn of a bull "you have no portion in the God of Israel." This was a punishment for the sale of Yoseph, which the Torah describes as "to his firstborn ox" (Devorim 33:17).

Antiochus brought a pig as a sacrifice in the Beis Hamikdosh. The Hebrew name for a pig [3] חֲזִיר has a numerical value of two hundred twenty-five, the same numerical value of the Hebrew word for impurity [4] קְלִיפָה.

The posuk says, "They [the brothers] saw him [Yoseph] from the distance" (Bereishis 37:19). The brothers saw that Yerovom, who would descend from Yoseph, would cause the Yidden to sin. The Hebrew spelling of Yerovom [5] יְרָבְעָם has a numerical value of three hundred thirty-two, the same numerical value as the Hebrew words for evil dog [6] כֶּלֶב רָע and impure chariot [7] מֶרְכָּבָה טְמֵאָה. Antiochus [8] אַנְטִיוֹכּס has the numerical value of one hundred fifty-six, the same numerical value as Yoseph [9] יוֹסֵף and the same numerical value as the words king of the Greeks [10] מֶלֶךְ יָוָן. This was all as a result of Yerovom's sin of placing two oxen idols by the tribe of Dan and in Bet El.

The Mishna says that there are four primary categories of damages—the ox, pit, teeth of an animal, and fire. The ox refers to the golden calf and the calves erected by Yerovom. The pit refers to Yoseph being thrown into the pit and then sold into slavery. The *teeth* refers to Adam eating from the tree of knowledge. And fire represents the sin of the spies that led to the burning of the Beis Hamikdosh.

"The ox came and drank the water."

The Greek exile weakened the holiness of the Yidden until the era of the Maccabees.

"Then came the shochet"

The shochet refers to Herod. Herod slaughtered all the great rabbis, leaving only Bava ben Buta alive. The *shochet* cannot be referring to a non-Jewish nation since a non-Jew cannot be a shochet. It is referring to Herod, who was a slave and made himself a free man. Bava ben Buta encouraged Herod to rebuild the second Beis Hamikdosh.

---

3. ח-8 י-7 ר-10 200.

4. ק-100 ל-30 י-10 פ-80 ה-5.

5. י-10 ר-200 ב-2 ע-70 מ-40.

6. כ-20 ל-30 ב-2 ר-200 ע-70.

7. מ-40 ר-200 כ-20 ב-2 ה-5 ט-9 מ-40 א-1 ה-5.

8. א-1 נ-50 ט-9 י-10 ו-6 כ-20 ס-60.

9. י-10 ו-6 ס-60 ף-80.

10. מ-40 ל-30 ך-20 י-10 ו-6 ן-50.

"The shochet came and slaughtered the ox."

This means that the suffering the Yidden endured during the reign of Herod was far worse than the suffering caused by Antiochus.

"Then came the angel of death."

This refers to Titus.

"Then came Hashem."

As the posuk says, *"On that day Hashem shall visit with His hard and great and strong sword. And He will subjugate"* (Yeshayahu 27:1). This refers to the klipa of Yishmoel. The klipa is referred to as a donkey, as the posuk says, *"[Avrohom instructs Yishmoel] 'Stay here with the donkey'"* (Bereishis 22:5). The posuk also says, *"[Moshiach will be a] Poor man riding on a donkey"* (Zecharya 9:9).

Then Hashem will cause the downfall of the klipa of Esov and Amalek, symbolized by the pig and the dog.

We are told that Amalek will fall by the hands of a descendant from the tribe of Yoseph. There will be Moshiach, the descendant of Dovid Hamelech and Moshiach, the descendant of Yoseph.

The posuk says, *"The scepter will not depart from Yehuda"* (Bereishis 49:10). This refers to Moshiach ben Dovid. *"Nor the student of the law from between his feet"* refers to Moshiach ben Yoseph. *"Until Shiloh comes"* refers to Moshe. The numerical value of the Hebrew name Shiloh [11]שִׁילֹה and Moshe [12]מֹשֶׁה are both forty.

Dovid's and Yoseph's descendants merited to be the redeemers of the Yidden as the two spies who didn't sin when the spies searched the Land of Israel were from the tribes of Yehuda and Ephraim.

In summary:

one little goat: Bnei Yisroel

Along came a cat: Egypt

Then came a dog: Amalek

Then came a stick: The staff of Moshe

Then came the fire: Burning of the Beis Hamikdosh

Then came the water: Haman and Achashverosh

Then came the ox: Antiochus Greek exile

Then came the shochet: Herod

Then came the angel of death: Titus, Roman exile

Then came Hashem: Moshiach ben Dovid and Moshiach ben Yoseph

---

11. ש-300 י-10 ל-30 ה-5.   12. מ-40 ש-300 ה-5.

Pesach Torah Readings

Haftorah First Day Pesach

בָּעֵת הַהִיא אָמַר יְהֹוָה אֶל יְהוֹשֻׁעַ עֲשֵׂה לְךָ חַרְבוֹת צֻרִים וְשׁוּב מֹל אֶת בְּנֵי יִשְׂרָאֵל שֵׁנִית

"At that time Hashem said to Yehoshua, make for yourself sharp knives and circumcise again the Bnei Yisroel the second time" (Yehoshua 5:2).

Note: Reb Yehonatan shares a thought from his illustrious father, Reb Nossan Nota. He asks, "What is the significance of the Novi stating, *'At that time'*?"

After Shechem raped Dinah, he wanted to marry her. Shimon and Levi declared, "If you and your people will have a bris, we will allow our sister to marry you." Shimon and Levi had no intention of allowing their sister to marry Shechem. Rather the third day after a bris, a person is extremely weak, and Shimon and Levi would be able to defeat them in battle. As the posuk says, "*On the third day, when they were in pain, Shimon and Levi, two of Yaakov's sons, brothers of Dinah, took each his sword, came upon the city unmolested, and slew all the males"* (Bereishis 34:25).

Having a bris weakens a person: therefore, a soldier would not want to be circumcised prior to entering a battle, as that would weaken him. As such, the Yidden who entered Israel together with Yehoshua may have been hesitant to have a bris because that would affect their ability in waging war. Yet the Novi instructs the Yidden, *"At that time"* to have a bris.

The Novi further states, *"Nor the strong man boast of his strength."* He is teaching us that everything comes from Hashem. Whether we are weak or strong will not decide the outcome of the war; it is dependent on Hashem's wishes. Therefore, having a bris, *"At that time"* may weaken us, but since we are fulfilling His wishes, we will be victorious."

(Ahavat Yehonatan)

🔥

Yehoshua instructed the Yidden to have a bris on the tenth of Nissan.

The Talmud (Rosh Hashonoh 9a) records an argument regarding whether the world was created in the month of Tishrei or Nissan.

We follow the opinion that the world was created in Tishrei, meaning that Adam was created on the first day of Tishrei, which was the sixth day of creation. As such, the first day of creation was on the twenty-fifth day of Elul. On the day Adam was created, he sinned by eating from the Tree of Knowledge. The sixth day of creation was a Friday. The following day, Shabbos, Adam was not punished. On the Sunday, the third day of Tishrei, Adam was reprimanded for seven days. As the posuk says,

"Hashem replied to Moshe, If her [Miriam's] father were to spit in her face would she not be humiliated for seven days?"

Just as Miriam was chastised for seven days so was Adam.

The eighth day being the tenth of Tishrei, Adam did teshuvah. Hence, the tenth of Tishrei became known as Yom Kippur, a day designated for teshuvah for all time.

If the world had been created in Nissan, then the tenth of Nissan would also have been designated as a day of teshuvah. At the same time that Adam sinned by eating from the tree, he also performed a procedure to be no longer circumcised.

Therefore, in the times of Yehoshua, on the tenth of Nissan (a day conducive to teshuvah) the Yidden had to rectify this aspect of Adam's sin by having everyone perform the mitzvah of bris milah.

Hence, "At that time" alludes to the day designated for teshuvah, and the Yidden underwent a bris as an atonement for Adam's sin of bris milah. (Ahavat Yehonatan)

٨

After the Yidden left Egypt, they were attacked by Amalek. Moshe instructed Yehoshua to gather the men and lead them in battle, as the posuk says, "And Moshe said to Yehoshua choose for us men and go and do battle with Amalek" (Shemos 17:9).

Why didn't Moshe lead the army into battle?

Yitzchok had told Esov, "You will live by your sword" (Bereishis 27:40). Esov's mazel will be madim, blood. To counter that the Yidden were given the mitzvah of circumcision, the knife of bris milah would be more powerful than the sword of Esov. The Midrash writes that Moshe was born circumcised; as such, he did not have the protection of the blade of bris milah.

Therefore, Moshe sent Yehoshua, who had a bris, to do battle with Amalek, who was a descendent of Esov. Likewise, Dovid sent his general Yoav to wage war against Edom. He did not lead the army, as he was born circumcised, and Edom were the offspring of Esov.

There are twenty-eight days in a lunar month. The month has seven mazals, each extending over a four-day period. The first four days is Shabtai, the second being Tzedek, and the third Madim. The third phase starts on the ninth and lasts four days. As such, the tenth of Nissan falls during the mazal of blood, which is the energy of Esov, to counter that the Yidden were instructed to ensure that they were all circumcised.

Therefore, the posuk says, "At that time." Being it was the tenth of Nissan, it was imperative that the Yidden would be circumcised to counter Esov's mazal of blood.

(Ahavat Yehonatan)

Dovid writes, "*You save both man and beast*" (Tehillim 36:7).

The posuk can be understood to be referring to man's two souls—our animal soul and our intellectual soul. When we sin, we have to atone for both. The Korban Pesach atoned for the animal soul and bris milah for the intellectual soul.

Likewise, "*At that time*"—as they were entering Israel, the Yidden needed both modes of forgiveness: a korban and a bris.

(Ahavat Yehonatan)

וַיֹּאמֶר יְהֹוָה אֶל יְהוֹשֻׁעַ הַיּוֹם גַּלּוֹתִי אֶת חֶרְפַּת מִצְרַיִם מֵעֲלֵיכֶם וַיִּקְרָא שֵׁם הַמָּקוֹם הַהוּא גִּלְגָּל עַד הַיּוֹם הַזֶּה

"This day I have removed the criticism of Egypt from you" (Yehoshua 5:9).

The Talmud (Shabbos 156a) writes, "One who was born under the influence of Madim [Mars] will be one who spills blood." Rav Ashi said: "He will be either a blood letter, or a thief, or a shochet, or a mohel."

Esov was born under the influence of Madim, as the posuk says concerning Esov, "*You will live by your sword.*" However, the mitzvah of shechita or bris milah will defeat the sword of Esov.

While the Yidden were in the desert, they did not give their sons a bris, and they ate meat without it being ritually slaughtered. Therefore, they were not in a position to defeat Esov and his offspring. Pharaoh saw this, and as a result, he thought that the Yidden would fall in the hands of Esov. However, when Yehoshua instructed the Yidden to have a bris, this gave them the spiritual strength to defeat the enemy.

This is the meaning of the posuk, "*This day I have removed the criticism of Egypt from you.*" This day being the day Yehoshua instructed the Yidden to have a bris; Pharoah could no longer speak of the downfall of the Yidden.

(Yaaros Dvash 2:11)

The Talmud (Shabbos 156a) writes, "*ein mazal l'Yisroel.*" There is no constellation that influences the Jewish people; The Jewish people are not subject to the influence of astrology.

This is true after a Yid has had a bris; however, prior to having a bris, a yid is subject to the influence of astrology similar to a non-Jew.

Pharaoh declared, "*See that evil [ra'ah] is before your faces*" (Shemos 10:10). Rashi explains that there is a star named Ra'ah. Pharaoh said to Moshe and Aaron, "*With my astrology I see that star ascending toward you in the desert, and that is a sign of blood and slaughter."* Pharaoh was referring to the Yidden sinning with the golden calf and Hashem sought to kill the Yidden. Moshe said in his prayer, "Why should the Egyptians say, 'With Ra'ah He took them out...'?"

As a response, Hashem turned the bloodshed symbolized by this star into the blood of the circumcision, for Yehoshua circumcised them.

This is the meaning of the posuk: *"This day I have removed the criticism of Egypt from you,"* for the Egyptians were saying to you, *"We see blood over you in the desert."* And Hashem swapped the bloodshed of the golden calf to the bloodshed of bris milah.

(Ahavat Yehonatan)

❧

When Yoseph was appointed by Pharaoh to govern the Egyptians during the years of plenty and famine, he insisted that the Egyptians circumcise themselves. The Egyptians, therefore, challenged the Yidden's claim of spirituality by stating that they had also been circumcised.

Hashem, therefore, instructed Yehoshua that the Yidden should undergo an additional aspect of the milah process. As such, *"Hashem has removed the criticism of Egypt from you."* The Egyptians had claimed that they too where circumcised. However, they had not performed this additional step when they were circumcised in the times of Yoseph.

(Ahavat Yehonatan)

וַיַּחֲנוּ בְנֵי יִשְׂרָאֵל בַּגִּלְגָּל וַיַּעֲשׂוּ אֶת הַפֶּסַח בְּאַרְבָּעָה עָשָׂר יוֹם לַחֹדֶשׁ
בָּעֶרֶב עַרְבוֹת יְרִיחוֹ

"They made the Pesach sacrifice on the fourteenth day of the month at evening" (Yehoshua 5:10).

The Talmud (Zevachim 118) asks why it was necessary for the posuk to tell us that they brought the korban on the fourteenth.

Moshe passed away on the seventh of Adar. The Rosh asks, "Was the seventh of Adar on Friday or Shabbos?"

If it was on Friday, then Rosh Chodesh Adar was on Shabbos. As such, Rosh Chodesh Nissan was on Sunday and Erev Pesach was on Shabbos.

Therefore, the posuk is teaching us that the korban can be brought on Shabbos.

(Brocho Meshuleshes no 57)

Tosfos (Kiddushin 37a) quotes the Yerushalmi that, when the Yidden entered Eretz Yisroel, they did not eat matzah due to the prohibition of Chodosh.

The question is posed, "If they didn't eat matzah, perhaps they did not bring the Korban Pesach?" The posuk says, "On this night they shall eat the meat [of the Korban Pesach] roasted over the fire and matzah with bitter herbs they shall eat it" (Shemos 12:8), implying that if a person doesn't have matzah, he cannot eat the korban.

Therefore, the posuk informs us that when the Yidden entered Eretz Yisroel, they still brought the korban on the fourteenth of Nissan, even though they didn't have matzah.

(Brocho Meshuleshes no 57)

וַיֹּאכְלוּ מֵעֲבוּר הָאָרֶץ מִמָּחֳרַת הַפֶּסַח מַצּוֹת וְקָלוּי בְּעֶצֶם הַיּוֹם הַזֶּה

"And they ate of the grain of the land on the day after [sacrificing] the Pesach matzah and parched on this very day" (Yehoshua 5:11).

When we make kiddush and say, "You have commanded us with your mitzvos," this is an atonement for Adam's sin of eating from the Tree of Knowledge.

What was the fruit that he ate?

The Talmud (Berochos 40a) quotes two opinions: either wheat or grapes.

There is an argument regarding the preferred way of making kiddush. One opinion says it should be said over wine, while the other says over challah. What is the basis for this disagreement?

The opinion that kiddush is to be recited with wine says that Adam ate grapes, and we need to atone for Adam's sin of eating grapes. The opinion that kiddush is to be said with challah says that Adam ate wheat, and by eating challah, we atone for Adam's sin of eating wheat.

(Ahavat Yehonatan)

The Tree of Knowledge was both good and evil. We, therefore, break the matzah in two, reflecting on the fact that the Tree of Knowledge contained two parts, good and evil.

On the Yom Tov of Shavuos, we offer as a korban two complete loaves of bread. This is to indicate that in the period between Pesach and Shavuos, we have rectified Adam's sin, and there is no longer a component of evil, as the evil has been turned into good.

(Ahavat Yehonatan)

The Talmud (Eiruvin 65a) writes that wine was created to comfort the mourners. When the world was created, there was no concept of death; as such, there would be no mourners. Why then was there a need to create wine?

Death was a result of Adam's sin. Prior to that, if Adam wished to drink wine, he did not need to squeeze grapes; rather, eating the grapes would taste like wine. It was only after the sin did the grape no longer taste like wine, and it first needed to be crushed and processed for the liquid to taste like wine. As the Talmud (Sanhedrin 70a) writes, "After Adam sinned, Chava squeezed grapes to make wine to comfort him."

The Talmudic statement that wine was created to comfort the mourner refers to what Chava did to comfort Adam. This explains why, when we drink wine, the brocho is "Blessed is Hashem . . . the creator of the fruit of the grapes." Why don't we say, "the creator of wine"? This is because Hashem didn't initially create wine; He created grapes that tasted like wine.

(Ahavat Yehonatan)

⁂

When discussing the consequences of Adam's actions, the Torah says, *"And it will cause thorns and thistles to grow for you . . . And I shall place hatred between you [the snake] and between the woman"* (Bereishis 3:15).

Hashem, therefore, placed the snake in the desert far removed from humanity, as the posuk says, *"[Hashem] who led you through that great and awesome desert [in which were] snakes"* (Devorim 8:15). To rectify the consequences of Adam's sin, we received the Torah in the desert and Hashem appeared to Moshe at the burning bush, as the bush symbolized the "thorns and the thistles."

(Ahavat Yehonatan)

וַיְהִי בִּהְיוֹת יְהוֹשֻׁעַ בִּירִיחוֹ וַיִּשָּׂא עֵינָיו וַיַּרְא וְהִנֵּה אִישׁ עֹמֵד לְנֶגְדּוֹ
וְחַרְבּוֹ שְׁלוּפָה בְּיָדוֹ וַיֵּלֶךְ יְהוֹשֻׁעַ אֵלָיו וַיֹּאמֶר לוֹ הֲלָנוּ אַתָּה אִם לְצָרֵינוּ

"When Yehoshua was in Jericho that he lifted up his eyes and saw and behold a man was standing opposite him with his sword drawn in his hand and Yehoshua went to him and said to him, 'Are you for us or for our enemy?'" (Yehoshua 5:13).

The Talmud (Megillah 3a) records the discussion that took place between the man (an angel) and Yehoshua. The Talmud explains that the angel said to Yehoshua, "Yesterday, during the afternoon, you neglected the afternoon daily offering due to the impending battle, and now, at night, you have neglected Torah study, and I have come to rebuke you." Yehoshua said to him, "For which of these sins have you come?" The angel said to him, "I have come now," indicating that neglecting Torah study is more severe than neglecting to sacrifice the daily offering.

Tosfos asks how this discussion is alluded to in the words *"Are you for us or for our enemy?"*

Tosfos answers the question. However, another explanation is that Torah study protects Yidden and the smoke of the korbonos protect the nations of the world. As such Yehoshua's question is, *"Are you for us,"* meaning for neglecting the study of Torah that is *"only for* us?" Or *"for our enemy,"* meaning for not bringing the korban that is beneficial for our enemies?

(Ahavat Yehonatan)

&

The posuk says, *"And he [Moshe] said to Him, If Your presence does not go [with us] do not take us up from here"* (Shemos 33:14,16).

After the Yidden sinned with the golden calf, Hashem said that He would no longer lead the Yidden; rather, He would send an angel in His place.

When Yehoshua saw an angel standing before him, he recalled Hashem's words after they had sinned. He became extremely scared, realizing that the presence of an angel could only mean that he had sinned, and he, therefore, asked the angel what sin they had committed.

(Tiferet Yehonatan)

וַיֹּאמֶר לֹא כִּי אֲנִי שַׂר צְבָא יְהֹוָה עַתָּה בָאתִי וַיִּפֹּל יְהוֹשֻׁעַ אֶל פָּנָיו אַרְצָה
וַיִּשְׁתָּחוּ וַיֹּאמֶר לוֹ מָה אֲדֹנִי מְדַבֵּר אֶל עַבְדּוֹ

"And he said, 'No, but I am the captain of the host of Hashem. I have now come.' And Yehoshua fell on his face to the earth and prostrated himself and said to him, 'What does Hashem say to his servant?' And the captain of the Lord's host said to Yehoshua, 'Remove your shoe from your foot for the place upon which you stand is holy'" (Yehoshua 5:14).

What is the significance of the angel informing Yehoshua to remove his shoes?

With the Exodus, Hashem redeemed the Bnei Yisroel, and He did not send an angel. The reason for this is that Egypt was saturated with impurity, and an angel would have become contaminated.

Yericho was also steeped in idolatry. Its very name indicates that the inhabitants worshipped the moon as their god. The Hebrew word for *moon* is Yoreach יָרֵחַ, which is similar sounding to the name of the city *Yericho* יְרִיחוֹ.

As such, an angel would be forbidden to enter the city. To allay Yehoshua's concern, the angel tells him to remove his shoes as the land he is treading on is holy. Therefore, unlike the land of Egypt, an angel would be permitted to enter it.

(Ahavat Yehonatan)

🔥

The Midrash (Vayikra Raba 32:5) writes that the Yidden were redeemed in the merit that they did not change their names or their language. They also did not marry Egyptian women, and they did not speak lashon hara.

The Midrash writes that Yoseph shared with his father that the brothers were interested in non-Jewish women, that they called the sons of the midwives slaves, and that they ate *eiver min hachai,* meat taken from a living animal.

Of Yoseph's three claims, two of them can be substantiated. There are numerous opinions that the brothers married wives from the tribe of Canaan. Likewise, the brothers were of the opinion that the children of slaves were also considered slaves.

However, how could Yoseph suspect that the brothers ate eiver min hachai when it is prohibited as one of the seven Noahite laws?

The brothers only ate meat that had been *shechted.* However, they told Yoseph that the meat came from a living animal. They were testing whether he would believe that they were sinners and inform their father.

And even if Yoseph knew that the brothers had not eaten non-kosher meat, the very fact that they had uttered a lie and declared that they were sinners was a sin in itself. Yoseph and the brothers were very careful with their speech as the Talmud (Moed Katan 18a) writes that a covenant is made with the lips.

The posuk says, *"And Yoseph brought evil tales about them to their father"* (Bereishis 37:2). The posuk can be understood to mean that it was the evil tales, the utterances of falsehoods itself that was the sin.

The Midrash writes concerning Yoseph, "Since you spoke ill about your brothers, you will be punished with the incident of the Potiphar's wife." What is the connection between the two?

Further, the story is difficult to comprehend. How could Potiphar's wife make such an outrageous accusation that Yoseph wanted to be with her and that she had grabbed his clothing?

On a daily basis. Yoseph would be hounded and harassed by Potiphar's wife to be with her. Wanting to avoid any confrontation, Yoseph would tell her that the house was full of people and when the house was empty. he would agree to her request. On the day that the house was empty, she approached Yoseph and demanded that he stand by his word.

As such, there was validity to her claim when she said, *"He [Yoseph] came to me to lie with me"* (Bereishis 39:14).

Yoseph was placed in this predicament due to the words he had spoken to Potiphar's wife as a punishment for the words that he had spoken to his father.

(Yaaros Dvash 1:15)

Torah Reading Seventh Day

וַיְהִי בְּשַׁלַּח פַּרְעֹה אֶת הָעָם וְלֹא נָחָם אֱלֹהִים דֶּרֶךְ אֶרֶץ פְּלִשְׁתִּים כִּי קָרוֹב הוּא

"It came to pass when Pharaoh let the people go" (Shemos 13:17).

The Talmud writes that whenever the phrase וַיְהִי *"it came to pass"* is used to introduce an occurrence, it is to indicate that what is about to unfold is considered undesirable. Pharaoh is finally sending the Yidden to their freedom. How could this be viewed in a negative manner?

The Zohar writes that when the Torah refers to the Yidden as הָעָם *"the people,"* the posuk is referring to the mixed multitude, which included people from all different lands.

The Yidden leaving Egypt was considered a sanctification of Hashem's name, as no servant had ever escaped the land of Egypt. However, our posuk relates that Pharaoh released other people as well, and this would certainly diminish the sanctification of Hashem's name as it would seem that other spiritual forces have the same ability to let their people leave Egypt as well. Therefore, what unfolded was to be viewed negatively.

(Tiferet Yehonatan)

🔥

The Zohar writes whenever the Torah refers to the Jewish people with the term הָעָם *"the people,"* it is not referring to the Jewish people, the descendants of Avrohom and Sarah; rather, it is referring to the *erev rav*, the mixed multitude of nations who escaped from Egypt together with the Jewish people.

The following two posukim state:

וַיְהִי בְּשַׁלַּח פַּרְעֹה אֶת הָעָם וְלֹא נָחָם אֱלֹהִים דֶּרֶךְ אֶרֶץ פְּלִשְׁתִּים כִּי קָרוֹב הוּא כִּי אָמַר אֱלֹהִים פֶּן יִנָּחֵם הָעָם בִּרְאֹתָם מִלְחָמָה וְשָׁבוּ מִצְרָיְמָה

"It came to pass when Pharaoh let the people go, that Hashem did not lead them [by] way of the land of the Philistines for it was near, because Hashem said, Lest the people reconsider when they see war and return to Egypt."

וַיַּסֵּב אֱלֹהִים אֶת הָעָם דֶּרֶךְ הַמִּדְבָּר יַם סוּף וַחֲמֻשִׁים עָלוּ בְנֵי יִשְׂרָאֵל
מֵאֶרֶץ מִצְרָיִם

"So Hashem led the people around [by] way of the desert [to] the Reed Sea, and the children of Israel were armed when they went up out of Egypt" (13:17,18).

Twice in the first posuk, it refers to the Jewish nation as *people,* implying that the posuk is specifically speaking about the mixed multitude. Hashem was concerned that the mixed multitude would want to return to Egypt.

The second posuk informs us that the *"children of Israel,"* meaning the descendants of Avrohom and Sarah, were leaving Egypt with weapons.

What were the weapons the Jewish people had when they left Egypt?

The posuk prior reads, וְהָיָה לְאוֹת עַל יָדְכָה וּלְטוֹטָפֹת בֵּין עֵינֶיךָ כִּי בְּחֹזֶק יָד הוֹצִיאָנוּ יְהֹוָה מִמִּצְרָיִם *"And it shall be for a sign upon your hand and for ornaments between your eyes, for with a mighty hand did the Lord take us out of Egypt"* (Shemos 13:16), where it discusses the obligation of wearing tefillin.

When discussing the mitzvah of wearing tefillin, the Talmud quotes the posuk, *"Then all the peoples of the earth will see that the name of the Lord is called upon you, and they will fear you"* (Devorim 28:10).

It explains that when the nations of the world see a Yid wearing tefillin shel rosh, the tefillin placed on the person's head, it instills fear and trepidation in their hearts.

The weapons the Yidden were carrying were not spears or bows and arrows; rather, they were the Yidden's secret weapon, the wearing of the tefillin. Only the Yidden wore tefillin; the mixed multitude did not. Since the mixed multitude did not wear tefillin, the nations would not fear them and would attack them. Therefore, Hashem was concerned that they would want to return to Egypt.

The Yidden, on the other hand, did wear tefillin; this would cause the nations to fear them and not want to wage war against them. Hence, there would be no reason for the Yidden to want to return to Egypt.

If, however, the weapons referred to at the Exodus were conventional weapons of war, then both the Yidden and the mixed multitude would have been armed, and neither group would have had a need to worry.

(Divrei Yehonatan)

וְלֹא נָחָם אֱלֹהִים דֶּרֶךְ אֶרֶץ פְּלִשְׁתִּים כִּי קָרוֹב הוּא

"Hashem did not lead them [by] way of the land of the Philistines for it was near."

The simple reading of the text is, "Hashem was worried that the Yidden's escape route would keep them close to Egypt, and upon encountering an enemy, they might think it would be safer to return to Egypt than clash with the enemy. Distancing them from Egypt would ensure that they would not want to return."

The posuk can be understood to mean that Hashem wanted the mixed multitude to return to Egypt. He, therefore, did not take them on a direct route to Israel; rather, he took them in a roundabout manner.

Why would taking the mixed multitude in a roundabout manner encourage them to return to Egypt?

When the mixed multitude fled Egypt, they knew that conquering a country entailed taking up arms, and they were prepared to join the Yidden in battle to settle the Holy land. By taking them on a direct route, the only confrontation they would encounter would be the war for the Land of Israel.

Leading them in a circular route ensured that the mixed multitude would have to face many battles. Besides Pharaoh chasing after the Yidden at the Yam Suf and the war waged against the Amalekites, the Yidden must have encountered clashes with other nations and tribes during their forty years in the desert.

Being forced to go to war on numerous occasions would encourage them to return.

(Tiferet Yehonatan)

‽

The Yidden were meant to be in exile for four hundred years, and since they left after two hundred ten years, they would have to endure further exiles to complete the missing years.

Hashem wanted the Yidden to be aware of this at the time of their redemption. Moshe felt that the Yidden should be made to believe that they were experiencing the final redemption. Hashem agreed to Moshe's request.

When Yehoshua conquered the Land of Israel, they still had to complete the missing years of exile.

If the Yidden had gone on a direct route to the Holy Land and had to take up arms, they would have realized that the persecution of the Yidden had not concluded. They would have immediately wanted to return to Egypt and conclude the preordained years of exile and then experience the ultimate redemption. They knew what to expect in Egypt and were used to it; perhaps a different exile would be far worse. Therefore, they were taken on a longer route.

(Tiferet Yehonatan)

וַיִּקַּח מֹשֶׁה אֶת עַצְמוֹת יוֹסֵף עִמּוֹ כִּי הַשְׁבֵּעַ הִשְׁבִּיעַ אֶת בְּנֵי יִשְׂרָאֵל לֵאמֹר
פָּקֹד יִפְקֹד אֱלֹהִים אֶתְכֶם וְהַעֲלִיתֶם אֶת עַצְמֹתַי מִזֶּה אִתְּכֶם

"Moshe took Yoseph's bones with him for he [Yoseph] had adjured the sons of Israel, saying, Hashem will surely remember you, and you shall bring up my bones from here with you." (Shemos 13:19).

The sale of Yoseph to Egypt led to the Yidden's exile there. Shimon and Levi played a central role in the sale. Therefore, Moshe, who was a descendant of Levi, felt an added responsibility to ensure that Yoseph's bones be taken with the Yidden at the time of their redemption.

(Tiferet Yehonatan)

The Midrash quotes the posuk, *"The wise hearted takes mitzvos"* (Mishlei 10:8) as referring to Moshe, who took the bones of Yoseph at the time of the Exodus, while the rest of the Yidden were busy taking the Egyptian's wealth. The posuk refers to Moshe as taking mitzvos, meaning that he fulfilled more than one mitzvah. Besides taking the bones, what other mitzvah did Moshe accomplish?

Moshe was from the tribe of the Levites. Since they were not enslaved in Egypt, they did not have a mitzvah to take from the spoils of the Egyptians. Hence, if Moshe would not have taken the bones of Yoseph, he would not have been busy taking their spoils.

Therefore, aside from a Levite, everyone else who would have taken the bones would have had to forgo the mitzvah of taking any of the Egyptian's wealth.

By Moshe taking Yoseph's bones, he fulfilled two mitzvos—the first, taking Yoseph's bones, and the second, giving the Yidden the ability to fulfill the mitzvah of taking the Egyptian's wealth.

(Tiferet Yehonatan)

The Midrash writes that the Egyptians had placed Yoseph's body in a metal coffin and let it sink in the Nile River.

Why is Moshe praised for gathering Yoseph's bones? One could argue that he had no choice because no one else had the ability to cause the coffin to rise from the riverbed to the surface.

The Midrash writes that Elisha, a disciple of Eliyahu HaNovi, caused sunken metal to rise.

It would stand to reason that the Yidden, who were students of Moshe, would equally have had the capacity to cause metal to rise. As such, Moshe is indeed praised; he was not the only person capable of taking Yoseph's coffin out of Egypt.

(Tiferet Yehonatan)

Moshe is praised for taking Yoseph's coffin, and his actions ensured a greater level of protection for the Yidden.

Why did his actions impact the Yidden?

Prior to Yoseph's passing, he made the Yidden take an oath that they would make their offspring take an oath that when the Yidden were redeemed, they would take his coffin with them.

From the age of three months, Moshe was raised in Pharaoh's palace. As a young man, he had to flee Egypt and retuned at the age of eighty to redeem the Jewish people. When he returned, his father, Amrom, had already passed. Amrom never had the opportunity to instruct his son, Moshe, to take an oath to ensure that Yoseph's remains would be taken from Egypt at the time of the Exodus.

Yet it was Moshe who fulfilled Yoseph's final request. Therefore, his act was considered a great merit and added protection for the Yidden.

(Tiferet Yehonatan)

"Hashem will surely remember you, and you shall bring up my bones from here with you."

Prior to his passing, Yoseph wanted to ensure that the Yidden would know when their true redeemer had arrived. He, therefore, told them that when the time for the Exodus arrived, his coffin would miraculously float to the surface.

The posuk can be understood to reflect this by reading it backward, *"and you shall bring up my bones from here with you,"* meaning if you are in a position to take my bones because they have risen to the surface, then the first part of the posuk is true and *"Hashem will surely remember you."*

(Tiferet Yehonatan)

With regard to Krias Yam Suf, the posuk says, *"The sea saw and it fled [it split]"* (Tehillim 114:3) .The Midrash asks what the sea saw that became the impetus to split? And answers that it saw Yoseph's coffin.

The sea saw Moshe and the Yidden coming toward it; however, it was not sure whether the time of the Exodus had arrived. Once it saw the coffin, its fears were allayed since it knew that the coffin would not have risen to the surface if the designated time had not yet arrived.

(Tiferet Yehonatan)

◊

Another beautiful way of interpreting the phrase *"the sea saw and it fled [it split]"* is as follows:

In the times of the Beis Hamikdosh, there were four death penalties, one being strangulation. The Midrash writes that after its destruction, a person who was guilty of a crime that would have carried with it the death penalty would have died of unnatural causes. If a person's punishment would have been strangulation, he would perish by drowning.

The Egyptians chased the Yidden into the sea. They thought that the married Jewish women were guilty of being unfaithful with the Egyptian men, and their punishment would be to drown in the Yam Suf.

When Yoseph was serving in the house of Potiphar, Potiphar's wife falsely accused him of being immoral. If this had been true, his punishment would have been death by drowning—not to eventually become the viceroy of Egypt.

When the sea saw Yoseph's coffin, it was reminded that Yoseph did not succumb to the temptation of being with Potiphar's wife. And since Moshe was proudly carrying his coffin, Moshe was declaring that the Jewish women had remained faithful to their husbands.

The posuk now reads, *"The sea saw Yoseph's coffin, and it was reminded of his moral standing; it therefore fled [it split] as it no longer suspected the Jewish women of being adulterous."*

(Tiferet Yehonatan)

◊

Why did the women feel it necessary to sing a song of praise to Hashem besides the song they had sung collectively with the men?

They were concerned that the sea would falsely suspect them of leading an immoral life in Egypt and their punishment would be to drown in the Yam Suf. Therefore, when they reached dry land, they felt an added sense of joy and gratitude. They, therefore, expressed it by singing a song independent of the men.

(Tiferet Yehonatan)

וַיהוָה הֹלֵךְ לִפְנֵיהֶם יוֹמָם בְּעַמּוּד עָנָן לַנְחֹתָם הַדֶּרֶךְ וְלַיְלָה בְּעַמּוּד אֵשׁ לְהָאִיר לָהֶם לָלֶכֶת יוֹמָם וָלָיְלָה

"And the Lord went before them by day in a pillar of cloud to cause it to lead them on the way and at night in a pillar of fire to give them light, [they thus could] travel day and night" (Shemos 13:21).

The Egyptians were planning to use black magic to enable the sun, the moon, and the stars to attack the Yidden. Hashem, therefore, used the pillar of cloud to conceal the heavens, and as a result, the celestial bodies would not be able to harm the Jewish people.

Since the moon was concealed by the clouds, Tosfos draws the conclusion that the Yidden could not calculate the beginning of the month based on the appearance of the moon. They had to rely on a calendar to calculate the months.

(Tiferet Yehonatan)

וַיִּקַּח שֵׁשׁ מֵאוֹת רֶכֶב בָּחוּר וְכֹל רֶכֶב מִצְרָיִם וְשָׁלִשִׁם עַל כֻּלּוֹ

"He took six hundred select chariots and all the chariots of Egypt, with officers over them all" (Shemos 14:7).

Pharaoh chased the Yidden with six hundred choice riders. Why specifically six hundred?

The Torah writes that, in the future, due to their sins, the Yidden may be attacked and defeated by an enemy army of a ratio of one to a thousand. Pharaoh was an exponent of black magic and mistakenly believed that the fulfillment of the prophecy would occur during his reign. He, therefore, took six hundred soldiers to defeat the six hundred thousand Jewish soldiers.

(Tiferet Yehonatan)

וּבְנֵי יִשְׂרָאֵל יֹצְאִים בְּיָד רָמָה

"And the children of Israel were marching out triumphantly" (Shemos 14:8).

The literal translation of בְּיָד רָמָה is *"[and the Yidden left] with an outstretched hand."*

The nature of a tzaddik is to raise his hands when he is beseeching Hashem, as the posuk says, *"Lift up your hands, sanctify them, and bless Hashem"* (Tehillim 135:2).

Since the Yidden leaving Egypt were all righteous, they left with their hands in an outstretched manner.

(Tiferet Yehonatan)

וַיִּרְדְּפוּ מִצְרַיִם אַחֲרֵיהֶם וַיַּשִּׂיגוּ אוֹתָם חֹנִים עַל הַיָּם

"The Egyptians chased after them and overtook them encamped by the sea"
(Shemos 14:9).

It would seem that the Egyptians were justified in chasing after the Yidden. The Yidden had taken their possessions and had promised that they were leaving for only three days.

When the Egyptians reached the Yidden, they had begun to backtrack and were encamped facing Egypt. The impression was that they were indeed planning to return to Egypt. Therefore, the Egyptians were not justified in attacking them. By attacking them, the Egyptians sealed their own fate.

(Tiferet Yehonatan)

וּפַרְעֹה הִקְרִיב

"Pharaoh drew near" (Shemos 14:10).

The word הִקְרִיב can mean "a sacrifice" or "draw near."

The simple explanation of the posuk is that Pharaoh came *close* toward the Yidden.

Another explanation is that Pharaoh brought *sacrifices* to the idols of Baal Tzafon. This led to the ministering angel of the Egyptians to come to their aid.

When the posuk relates that the Yidden became frightened when they saw the Egyptians, it is not referring to the Egyptian army; rather, it is referring to the Egyptian's ministering angel.

(Tiferet Yehonatan)

וַיִּצְעֲקוּ בְנֵי יִשְׂרָאֵל אֶל יְהוָֹה

"And the Yidden cried out to Hashem" (Shemos 14:10).

The Midrash writes that the Yidden were redeemed in the merit of their faith that Hashem would redeem them. The Talmud writes, "If someone davens in a loud voice and others hear the prayers, he lacks faith."

Our posuk writes that the Yidden cried out seemingly in a loud voice. Praying aloud demonstrates a lack of faith. How then can we say the Yidden were redeemed due to their faith?

We must say that when the Yidden cried out to Hashem, they did so in a low voice.

(Tiferet Yehonatan)

וַיֹּאמְרוּ אֶל מֹשֶׁה הֲמִבְּלִי אֵין קְבָרִים בְּמִצְרַיִם לְקַחְתָּנוּ לָמוּת בַּמִּדְבָּר

"They said to Moshe, is it because there are no graves in Egypt that you have taken us to die in the desert?" (Shemos 14:11).

When the Yidden were taken in a more circuitous manner they didn't ask why, as they understood Hashem didn't want them to encounter warrying nations and want to return to Egypt.

However, when they were confronted by Pharaoh, they saw that they hadn't gained anything by not taking the direct route. They therefore complained to Moshe.

The only understanding they could muster why they had gone on a longer route was that the designated time of entering the Land of Israel had not yet arrived. And they would have to wander in the desert till that time.

They therefore said to Moshe why should we wander in the desert we would have preferred to remain in Egypt in servitude till the correct time of our redemption has arrived.

They then said to Moshe, if you think it is preferable to be buried in the desert because it is closer to Israel then to be buried in Egypt that is an impure land. We are happy to be buried in Egypt and have the same fate as all the other Yidden buried there.

And that is a deeper understanding of the question they posed, is it because there are no graves in Egypt?

(Tiferet Yehonatan)

The Talmud writes that prior to the coming of Moshiach, there will be many deaths.

The Yidden, therefore, asked Moshe why they still needed to pass away in the desert, *"Are there not enough graves in Egypt?"* meaning haven't enough Yidden perished in Egypt to warrant Moshiach's arrival?

(Tiferet Yehonatan)

יְהוָֹה יִלָּחֵם לָכֶם וְאַתֶּם תַּחֲרִשׁוּן

"Hashem will fight for you, but you shall remain silent" (Shemos 14:14).

Why were the Yidden instructed to remain silent?

The Talmud writes that Hashem desires the tefillos of the tzaddikim. Moshe informs the Yidden that they are not tzaddikim and Hashem is not seeking to hear their tefillos. Therefore, Moshe tells them *"remain silent"* and Hashem will save them even before they begin to daven.

(Tiferet Yehonatan)

A person who has experienced a miracle can only sing songs of praise to Hashem if the person was deserving of the miracle in his own right, not in the merit of someone else. At this time, the Yidden were lacking in faith, and Hashem saved them nonetheless. Therefore, Moshe told them to remain silent and not offer any songs of praise.

However, after the Yidden had crossed the Yam Suf, the posuk says, *"and they [the Yidden] believed in Hashem."* They were no longer lacking faith and thus were permitted to sing a song of praise.

The first understanding is that they should remain silent and not pray for salvation. The second interpretation is for the Yidden to remain silent in offering words of praise while they still lacked faith.

(Tiferet Yehonatan)

וַיֹּאמֶר יְהֹוָה אֶל מֹשֶׁה מַה תִּצְעַק אֵלָי דַּבֵּר אֶל בְּנֵי יִשְׂרָאֵל וְיִסָּעוּ

"Hashem said to Moshe, why do you cry out to Me? Speak to the children of Israel and let them travel" (Shemos 14:15).

Hashem told Moshe that there is no need to daven: "Simply by walking toward the sea, the Yidden will be showing their faith in Me, and in that merit, they will be saved."

(Tiferet Yehonatan)

In times of crisis, Yidden daven to Hashem. Why then does Hashem tell Moshe that they should stop davening and instruct them to travel onward?

Why was Moshe afraid of Pharoah and his army, when Hashem had promised him, *"I will be with your mouth"* (Shemos 4:15), meaning "I will protect you"?

Moshe was concerned that perhaps the Yidden were sinners and were no longer worthy of Hashem's protection.

The Rambam (Yesodei Hatorah 10:4) writes, "If Hashem makes a promise to a novi, even if Hashem made the commitment dependent on something that does not eventuate, Hashem will still fulfill His promise because if the novi's words are not fulfilled, the Yidden will suspect that he is a false prophet."

Therefore, Hashem says to Moshe, "Speak to the Yidden. Tell them to enter the water, and they will have to be saved, as once Moshe has spoken it must happen."

(Midrash Yehonatan Beshalach)

וְאַתָּה הָרֵם אֶת מַטְּךָ וּנְטֵה אֶת יָדְךָ עַל הַיָּם וּבְקָעֵהוּ

"And you raise your staff and stretch out your hand over the sea and split it" (Shemos 14:16).

While the Yidden showed their faith by walking toward the sea, the mixed multitude did not have such merit. As such, Moshe was directed by Hashem to split the sea with his staff.

(Tiferet Yehonatan)

וְיָדְעוּ מִצְרַיִם, כִּי־אֲנִי יְהוָה, בְּהִכָּבְדִי בְּפַרְעֹה, בְּרִכְבּוֹ וּבְפָרָשָׁיו

"And the Egyptians shall know that I am Hashem, when I will be glorified through Pharaoh, through his chariots, and through his horsemen" (Shemos 14:18).

There are many different names to identify God. The two primary names are Hashem and Elokim. The name Elokim signifies strict justice, while the name Hashem symbolizes compassion and kindness.

The posuk refers to God with the name Hashem. It is stating that the Egyptians will come to recognize that God is kind and compassionate.

(Tiferet Yehonatan)

וַיַּאֲמִינוּ בַּיהוָה וּבְמֹשֶׁה עַבְדּוֹ

"And they believed in Hashem and His servant Moshe" (Shemos 14:31).

The Talmud (Sotah 12b) writes that on the twenty-first of Nissan, Yocheved placed her son Moshe in the river. And it was on the twenty-first of Nissan that the Yidden entered the Yam Suf. There is a discussion whether the sea split in the merit of Moshe or in the merit of the Yidden.

When the posuk says, *"And they believed in Moshe,"* this phrase can be understood to mean the Yidden believed that it was in the merit of Moshe that the waters split.

(Pardes Reb Yehonatan)

אָז יָשִׁיר מֹשֶׁה וּבְנֵי יִשְׂרָאֵל אֶת הַשִּׁירָה הַזֹּאת לַיהוָה וַיֹּאמְרוּ לֵאמֹר

"Then Moshe and the Yidden sang this song to Hashem. They said, saying" (Shemos 15:1).

The Talmud (Sotah 30b) explains the expression *"They said saying"* in the following manner. Moshe said, אָשִׁירָה לַיהוָה "I will sing unto Hashem" and the Yidden said after Moshe, אָשִׁירָה לַיהוָה "I will sing unto Hashem."

The Talmud (Chullin 91b) writes, "The Yidden are dearer to Hashem than the angels. One of the proofs for this is the Yidden mention the name of Hashem after two words, as it is stated: *"Hear, Israel: Hashem our God, Hashem is one."* But the angels mention the name of Hashem only after three words, as it is written: *"And one called unto another, and said: 'Kadosh, kadosh, kadosh is Hashem of hosts; the whole earth is full of His glory.'"*

The Arizal writes that each group of angels do not say the words *kadosh* three times; rather, there are three groups of angels and each group say the word *kadosh* once. Since each group heard the other two groups saying the word *kadosh*, we apply the Talmudic rule that hearing something will have the same status as actually saying it. As such, each group will be considered as if they had said the word *kadosh* three times.

How could the Yidden say, אָשִׁירָה לַיהֹוָה, as they would be saying Hashem's name after only mentioning one word?

Since Moshe said אָשִׁירָה and the Yidden heard him say it, we consider it as if the Yidden had also said the word אָשִׁירָה. As such, when the Yidden said Hashem's name, they had preceded it by saying the word אָשִׁירָה twice.

(Tiferet Yehonatan)

When the Yidden were by the sea, they merited to be imbued with Hashem's Shechinah, and when they sang, it was as if Hashem was singing. The mixed multitude did not merit this level of spiritual revelation.

Hence, the posuk is understood to mean, *"Then Moshe sang a song* [with Ruach Hakodesh] *and the Yidden sang this song* [in the same manner that Moshe did with Ruach Hakodesh] *to Hashem.* [They the Yidden] *said* [to the mix multitude] *saying* [they should repeat what they had just heard]."

(Tiferet Yehonatan)

אָשִׁירָה לַיהֹוָה כִּי גָאֹה גָּאָה סוּס וְרֹכְבוֹ רָמָה בַיָּם

"I will sing to the Lord, for very exalted is He; a horse and its rider He cast into the sea" *(Shemos 15:1).*

The Talmud (Megillah 31a) writes, "Wherever you find a reference in the Torah to Hashem's greatness, you also find a reference to His humility adjacent to it."

This is true when the person is also displaying humility. If the person is haughty, then Hashem will deal with him with the attribute of haughtiness. Pharaoh was extremely arrogant; therefore, the posuk says, "Hashem was very exalted."

(Tiferet Yehonatan)

עָזִּי וְזִמְרָת יָהּ וַיְהִי לִי לִישׁוּעָה

"The Eternal's strength and His vengeance were my salvation" (Shemos 15:2).

The word עָזִּי refers to the Torah the Yidden were to receive on Mount Sinai. As the posuk says, *"Hashem gave strength to His people."* The Talmud (Berachos 6b) explains the posuk to mean that Hashem gave the Yidden the Torah.

The word וְזִמְרָת means *to sever.* By cutting off the foreskin, the Yidden would be attached to Hashem's name יָהּ. As the Hebrew word for *hand* is יָד, we remove the foreskin with the hand. The foreskin is a small piece of skin; we can give it the numerical value of one. Hence together with the יָד, we have יָה, the name of Hashem. Similarly, the word מִילָה is comprised of two words מָל יָה.

The posuk reads, *"In the merit of the* עָזִּי *Torah and* זִמְרָת *bris milah we are connected to Hashem's name* יָהּ *then* לִי לִישׁוּעָה *we will be redeemed."*

(Tiferet Yehonatan)

זֶה אֵלִי וְאַנְוֵהוּ אֱלֹהֵי אָבִי וַאֲרֹמְמֶנְהוּ

"This is my God, and I will make Him a habitation, the God of my father, and I will ascribe to Him exaltation" (Shemos 15:2).

By the sea, the Yidden saw Hashem and they declared, *"This is my God"* וְאַנְוֵהוּ [I will make Him a habitation.] Hashem's name rested in the Mishkan. As the posuk says, *"The house on which the name of Hashem is called"* (Yermiyahu 7:10).

However, the name of Hashem שַׁדַּי is concealed above, as the posuk says יֹשֵׁב בְּסֵתֶר עֶלְיוֹן בְּצֵל שַׁדַּי יִתְלוֹנָן *"He who dwells in the covert of the Most High will lodge in the shadow of the Almighty"* (Tehillim 91:1).

When the posuk says, אֱלֹהֵי אָבִי *"the God of my father,"* it is referring to the name of Hashem שַׁדַּי, as the posuk says, וָאֵרָא אֶל אַבְרָהָם אֶל יִצְחָק וְאֶל יַעֲקֹב בְּאֵל שַׁדַּי *"I appeared to Avrohom, to Yitzchok, and to Yaakov with [the name] Almighty God* וַאֲרֹמְמֶנְהוּ *[and I will ascribe to Him exaltation]. This name of Hashem remains in the heavens and does not rest in the Mishkan."*

(Tiferet Yehonatan)

יְהֹוָה אִישׁ מִלְחָמָה יְהֹוָה שְׁמוֹ

"Hashem is a Master of war; Hashem is His Name" (Shemos 15:3).

The name Hashem, which symbolizes compassion, is mentioned twice in the posuk to teach us that even though Hashem was at war, it was done with compassion.

(Tiferet Yehonatan)

The Midrash (Bamidbar Rabba 10:5) writes, "Of the wicked, the posuk will first mention his name and then write, 'this is his name.' For example, נָבָל שְׁמוֹ 'Naval was his name' גָּלְיָת שְׁמוֹ 'Goliath was his name.' Of tzaddikim, the posuk will first write, 'And his name was' and then write the name. For example, וּשְׁמוֹ יִשַׁי 'And his name was Yishai.' וּשְׁמוֹ מָרְדְּכַי 'And his name was Mordechai.'"

Why then does our posuk first mention Hashem's name and then say, *"This is His name"*?

The posuk says, *"The mention of a righteous man is a blessing but the name of the wicked shall rot"* (Mishlei 10:7). Therefore, of a tzaddik we write, "his name" first as "his name" symbolizes blessing. And we begin with blessing. Of a rosho, we write "his name" last as "his name" symbolizes a curse. And the curse should come at the end. However, with Hashem, there is no concept of tzaddik or rosho; therefore, the posuk says, יְהֹוָה שְׁמוֹ *"Hashem is His name."*

(Tiferet Yehonatan)

The name of a tzaddik represents mercy, and therefore, we begin with the words *his name* as it symbolizes mercy. However, the name of the wicked is strict justice, and therefore, we mention the words *his name* at the end. Therefore, when Hashem is relating to the world with the attribute of strict justice *"He is a man of war,"* then Hashem is *"His name."* The phrase *"His name"* is written at the end.

(Tiferet Yehonatan)

An angel's name is dependent on the mission he is being tasked. At times, he is sent for rain; as such, his name will reflect that. Likewise, if he were sent for the purpose of war.

However, this is not the case by Hashem. Therefore, the posuk says, *"Hashem is a Master of war"* yet *"Hashem is His Name"* does not change.

(Tiferet Yehonatan)

תְּהֹמֹת יְכַסְיֻמוּ יָרְדוּ בִמְצוֹלֹת כְּמוֹ אָבֶן

"The depths covered them; they descended into the depths like a stone"
(Shemos 15:5).

Hashem had pity on the Egyptians by causing their bodies to descend to the depths; as such, they were not eaten by the large fish.

(Tiferet Yehonatan)

יְמִינְךָ יְהוָה נֶאְדָּרִי בַּכֹּחַ יְמִינְךָ יְהוָה תִּרְעַץ אוֹיֵב

"Your right hand, Hashem, is most powerful; Your right hand, Hashem, crushes the foe" (Shemos 15:6).

The Zohar explains that the Yidden were not worthy of being redeemed; however, Hashem showed His mercy and saved the Yidden. Why is this not considered showing favoritism to the Yidden?

Hashem demonstrated mercy to both the Yidden and the Egyptians.

The term "right hand" represents mercy. As such, this is the understanding of the posuk: *"Your right hand, Hashem, is most powerful."* Hashem saved the Yidden with His right hand, meaning Hashem saved the Yidden with mercy. The second half of the posuk reads, *"Your right hand, Hashem, crushes the foe."* Hashem dealt with the Egyptians with His right hand, meaning Hashem acted toward the Egyptians with mercy. However, due to their sins, the Egyptians were guilty and drowned in the sea.

(Tiferet Yehonatan)

Whenever Hashem changes the order of the world, the Torah describes Hashem as acting with strength. After the Yidden had sinned, Moshe davened to Hashem that He should have pity on them. The posuk says, *"Now let the strength of Hashem be increased"* (Bamidbar 14:17). Moshe uses the word *strength* because he wanted Hashem to forgive the Yidden's sins.

In our posuk, *"Your right hand, Hashem, is most strong; Your right hand, Hashem, crushes the foe."* Why does Moshe use the word *strong*?

Even though Hashem's right hand does not punish the enemy, the posuk says, *"Your right hand, Hashem, crushes the foe."* Hashem destroyed the enemy with His right hand. Therefore, Moshe uses the word *strength*.

(Tiferet Yehonatan)

When a Yid transgresses, Hashem distances him with His left hand and draws him near with His right hand. However, by a non-Jew, Hashem punishes him with His right hand.

This is the understanding of the posuk, *"Your right hand, Hashem, is most powerful."* Hashem's right hand draws Yidden near and His left hand pushes away. However, with the non-Jew, *"Your right hand, Hashem, crushes the foe."* Hashem's right hand punishes them.

(Tiferet Yehonatan)

וּבְרֹב גְּאוֹנְךָ תַּהֲרֹס קָמֶיךָ תְּשַׁלַּח חֲרֹנְךָ יֹאכְלֵמוֹ כַּקַּשׁ

"And with Your great pride You tear down those who rise up against You; You send forth Your burning wrath; it devours them like straw" (Shemos 15:7).

"And with Your great pride You tear down those who rise up against You" is to be understood to mean that Hashem acted in a merciful manner with the Egyptians. Even though they all deserved to die, Hashem only caused the Egyptians by the sea to perish. The people who remained in Egypt did not perish.

Because if *"You send forth Your burning wrath"*—that is, if Hashem had judged the Egyptians with the attribute of strict justice—then *"it devours them like straw,"* which means that even the Egyptians in Egypt would have perished.

(Tiferet Yehonatan)

"And with Your great pride You tear down those who rise up against You" refers to the Egyptian's ministering angels. *"And You send forth Your burning wrath; it devours them like straw"* refers to the Egyptian people.

(Tiferet Yehonatan)

וּבְרוּחַ אַפֶּיךָ נֶעֶרְמוּ מַיִם נִצְּבוּ כְמוֹ נֵד נֹזְלִים קָפְאוּ תְהֹמֹת בְּלֶב יָם

"And with the breath of Your nostrils the waters were heaped up; the running water stood erect like a wall; the depths congealed in the heart of the sea" (Shemos 15:8).

"The depths congealed in the heart of the sea" refers to the still waters of the Yam Suf. Waters that are stagnant become smelly and foul. Therefore, if the waters of the sea had stood erect, they would have become putrid and not pleasant to

the eye. Therefore, the waters of the sea were absorbed in the depths, as the word נֶעֶרְמוּ also means "to mix," meaning the waters of the sea became mixed within the seabed.

"The running water stood erect like a wall" refers to the rivers that flow into the sea miraculously standing erect, while the sea became part of the dry land, thus allowing the Yidden to cross the sea in an easier manner.

(Tiferet Yehonatan)

⟁

The Egyptians claimed that Krias Yam Suf was not a miracle as waters ebb and flow. Therefore, *"the waters congealed in the heart of the sea."* That is truly miraculous.

(Tiferet Yehonatan)

אָמַר אוֹיֵב אֶרְדֹּף אַשִּׂיג אֲחַלֵּק שָׁלָל תִּמְלָאֵמוֹ נַפְשִׁי אָרִיק חַרְבִּי תּוֹרִישֵׁמוֹ יָדִי

"[Because] the enemy said, I will pursue, I will overtake, I will share the booty; my desire will be filled from them; I will draw my sword, my hand will impoverish them" (Shemos 15:9).

"I will share the booty" refers to Pharaoh saying that when they defeated the Yidden, they would divide the spoil equally amongst themselves. However, not every Egyptian incurred the same loss. Why then was the booty to be divided equally?

Therefore, the posuk says, *"my desire will be filled from them."* Pharaoh promised that he would compensate them from his own treasury.

Pharaoh then stated, *"I will draw my sword,"* meaning "I will only draw my sword, but I will not kill the Yidden. Because what will I gain by killing them?" Rather, *"my hand will impoverish them,"* meaning "I will once again enslave them."

(Tiferet Yehonatan)

⟁

Pharaoh did not want any of the spoil. He promised to give it all to his soldiers. Rather, *"My desire will be filled from them,"* meaning when the Yidden left Egypt, they took with them all the sparks of holiness. Pharaoh wanted to recapture them and take back the sparks of holiness.

(Tiferet Yehonatan)

נָשַׁפְתָּ בְרוּחֲךָ כִּסָּמוֹ יָם צָלְלוּ כַּעוֹפֶרֶת בְּמַיִם אַדִּירִים

"You blew with Your wind, the sea covered them; they sank like lead in the powerful waters" (Shemos 15:10).

This posuk is linked to the previous posuk. Since Pharaoh said that he intends to only draw his sword and not kill the Yidden, Hashem rewarded them: *"They sank like lead in the powerful waters."*

When waters are raging, objects do not sink to the bottom, as recorded in the Talmud.

The Talmud (Bava Basra 73b) writes, "And a Divine Voice emerged and said to us: Do not go down here, as the ax of a carpenter fell into it seven years ago and it has still not reached the bottom. And this is not because the water is so large and deep. Rather, it is because the water is turbulent."

The miracle was that their bodies were not being thrown about in the sea, and they sank and rested on the riverbed.

(Tiferet Yehonatan)

מִי כָמֹכָה בָּאֵלִם יְהֹוָה מִי כָּמֹכָה נֶאְדָּר בַּקֹּדֶשׁ נוֹרָא תְהִלֹּת עֹשֵׂה פֶלֶא

"Who is like You among the powerful, Hashem? Who is like You, powerful in the holy place? Too awesome for praises, performing wonders!" (Shemos 15:11).

"Who is like You, powerful in the holy place?" refers to the Yidden whose holiness is all powerful as they are able to perform miracles that change the laws of nature. Moshe split the sea. Eliyahu revived the dead. And tzaddikim, at times, perform miracles similar to Hashem.

(Tiferet Yehonatan)

נָטִיתָ יְמִינְךָ תִּבְלָעֵמוֹ אָרֶץ

"You inclined Your right hand; the earth swallowed them up" (Shemos 15:12).

The word יָמִין can also mean "an oath." Hashem had made an oath that He would not bring another flood to destroy humanity. If the Egyptians had drowned and their bodies had not been buried, it would have been as if they had died by a flood.

Hence, the posuk can be understood to mean *"You made a promise"* not to destroy mankind through drowning; therefore, *"the earth swallowed them up."* You, therefore, decreed that the ministering angel of water should cause the bodies to rest on the shore, and then they could be buried.

(Tiferet Yehonatan)

נָחִיתָ בְחַסְדְּךָ עַם זוּ גָּאָלְתָּ נֵהַלְתָּ בְעָזְּךָ אֶל נְוֵה קָדְשֶׁךָ

"With Your loving kindness You led the people You redeemed; You led [them]
with Your might to Your holy abode" (Shemos 15:13).

The Yidden merited to reach the level of prophecy by Krias Yam Suf. The
question posed, prophecy can only be experienced in the Land of Israel how then
did the Yidden experience prophecy by the sea?

Hashem performed a miracle and they were able to see from where they were
to Israel and from there their prayers went up to heaven. As the Talmud (Berochos
30a) writes, One who was standing in prayer in the Diaspora should focus his heart
toward Eretz Yisroel, as it is stated: *"And they shall pray to You by way of their land*
which You have given to their fathers" (Divrei Hayomim II 6:38).

This is the understanding of the posuk, *"You led [them] with Your might to Your*
holy abode', meaning the Yidden were miraculously able to see the Beis Hamikdosh
while at the Yam Suf.

(Tiferet Yehonatan)

שָׁמְעוּ עַמִּים יִרְגָּזוּן חִיל אָחַז יֹשְׁבֵי פְּלָשֶׁת

"Peoples heard, they trembled; a shudder seized the inhabitants of Philistia"
(Shemos 15:14).

Hashem becomes angry when the nations of the world serve idols. As the
Talmud (Berochos 7a) writes, "When the sun rises and the kings of the East and
the West place their crowns on their heads and bow down to the sun, Hashem,
immediately grows angry."

This is the understanding of the posuk *"Peoples heard."* When the nations
heard of the miracle of Krias Yam Suf, they offered sacrifices to their idols. *"They*
trembled," as this caused Hashem to become angry.

"A shudder seized the inhabitants of Philistia." The Pelishtim were gripped
with fear. Initially they thought the reason the Yidden were not traveling through
their land was because they were more powerful than the Yidden. However,
after the miracle of Krias Yam Suf, they realized Hashem wanted the world to
know how powerful His people were. As such, *"A shudder seized the inhabitants*
of Philistia."

(Tiferet Yehonatan)

אָז נִבְהֲלוּ אַלּוּפֵי אֱדוֹם נָמֹגוּ כֹּל יֹשְׁבֵי כְנָעַן

**"Then the chieftains of Edom were startled; all the inhabitants
of Canaan melted" (15:15).**

Edom thought that the blessings Yaakov received from Hashem and those that
he received from Yitzchak had not been fulfilled because the Yidden had been
persecuted and were wandering in the desert. However, after seeing the miracle of
Krias Yam Suf, they realized that the blessings had become a reality.

Why did Krias Yam Suf cause them to have a change of heart?

Hashem blessed Yaakov וּפָרַצְתָּ יָמָּה *"and you shall gain strength westward"*
(Bereishis 28:14). The word יָמָּה can also mean "the sea." When the waters of the
sea split and the dry land appeared, this was the fulfilment of the brocho *"and you
shall gain strength by the waters."*

Esov's strength was in the sea as the Talmud (Shabbos 56b) writes, "When
Shlomo Hamelech married Pharaoh's daughter, the angel Gabriel descended from
heaven and implanted a reed into the sea, and a sandbar grew around it, growing
larger each year, and upon it the great city of Rome was built, which became
Hashem's instrument to punish Israel."

Since the Yidden showed their strength to overcome the challenges of the sea,
they would be able to defeat Edom, whose strength was in the sea. As such, Edom
became extremely fearful.

(Tiferet Yehonatan)

אֵילֵי מוֹאָב יֹאחֲזֵמוֹ רָעַד

**"[As for] the powerful men of Moav, trembling seized them"
(Shemos 15:15).**

Moav believed that the Yidden were not the children of Avrohom but had
descended from Avimelech. As such, they would receive Avrohom's blessings.

The generation of the flood were steeped in immoral behavior and their
punishment was drowning. Similarly, it is known that a mamzer will perish by
drowning. Pharaoh believed that the Jewish children born in Egypt were mamzerim
because the Jewish men were enslaved, and the Egyptian men could do what they
wanted with the Jewish women, who were also enslaved. That is why he instructed
the Jewish boys to be cast into the sea.

So when Moav heard that the Yidden did not drown in the sea, they realized
that they were the children of Avrohom, and his blessings were given to the Yidden.
Therefore, *"the powerful men of Moav, trembled."*

(Tiferet Yehonatan)

"All the inhabitants of Canaan melted" (Shemos 15:15).

The Canaanites knew that the Yidden were going to conquer their land. When the Yidden left Egypt and traveled in a roundabout route, the Canaanites believed that the Yidden were not going toward Canaan.

However, once they heard of the miracle of Krias Yam Suf, they realized the reason for traveling in the roundabout manner was so that Hashem could perform the miracle of Krias Yam Suf. As such, the Yidden were traveling toward the land of Canaan. For this reason, *"All the inhabitants of Canaan melted."*

(Tiferet Yehonatan)

תִּפֹּל עֲלֵיהֶם אֵימָתָה וָפַחַד בִּגְדֹל זְרוֹעֲךָ יִדְּמוּ כָּאָבֶן

"May dread and fright fall upon them; with the arm of Your greatness may they become as still as a stone" (Shemos 15:16).

"May dread and fright fall upon them" is a continuation of the previous posuk in which we are told *"All the inhabitants of Canaan melted."*

The Talmud (Yerushalmi Shviis 6:1) writes that when Yehoshua went to the land of Canaan, he offered his hand in peace to the Canaanites. It would stand to reason that the Canaanites, who were gripped with fear, would want to make peace with the Yidden. However, the posuk continues, "With the arm of Your greatness." Hashem demonstrated His greatness by causing the hearts of the Canaanites to "Become as still as a stone" so they would be unwilling to make peace with the Yidden, resulting in the Yidden's ability to conquer and inhabit the Land of Israel.

(Tiferet Yehonatan)

תְּבִאֵמוֹ וְתִטָּעֵמוֹ בְּהַר נַחֲלָתְךָ מָכוֹן לְשִׁבְתְּךָ פָּעַלְתָּ יְהוָֹה מִקְּדָשׁ אֲדֹנָי כּוֹנְנוּ יָדֶיךָ׃

"You shall bring them and plant them on the mount of Your heritage, directed toward Your habitation, which You made, Hashem; the sanctuary Hashem, [which] Your hands founded" (Shemos 15:17).

Hashem could have easily established a homeland for the Yidden in the desert. Why was there a need to bring them to the Land of Israel?

The posuk says, *"You shall bring them and plant them on the mount of Your heritage, directed toward Your habitation."* Hashem wanted to bring them to the site of the Beis Hamikdosh. And the site of the Beis Hamikdosh is directly opposite the Beis Hamikdosh in heaven *"[which] Your hands founded."*

(Tiferet Yehonatan)

יְהוָֹה יִמְלֹךְ לְעֹלָם וָעֶד כִּי בָא סוּס פַּרְעֹה בְּרִכְבּוֹ וּבְפָרָשָׁיו בַּיָּם

"Hashem will reign forever. When Pharaoh's horses came with his chariots and his horsemen into the sea" (Shemos 15:18,19).

The Midrash writes, "See what is written after [the posuk, *Hashem will reign to all eternity*]. It is written, '*When Pharaoh's horses came.*'"

What is the Midrash conveying?

Dovid Hamelech writes, "Hashem will reign forever" (Tehillim 146:10).

In our posuk, Hashem's name is written first and then it says, "He will reign" יְהוָֹה יִמְלֹךְ. However, Dovid Hamelech first mentions the kingship and then Hashem's name יִמְלֹךְ יְהוָֹה.

Why the change?

In Tehillim, the previous posuk reads, "He perverts the ways of the wicked."

The Talmud writes that Hashem distances His name from punishment. In Tehillim, the previous posuk speaks of punishment. The posuk first says יִמְלֹךְ and then it writes Hashem's name.

In our posuk, it speaks of punishment after the phrase, "' Hashem will reign to all eternity." To distance Hashem's name from punishment, we first write Hashem's name and then about His reign.

This is the understanding of the Midrash. It quotes the posuk יְהוָֹה יִמְלֹךְ [it is troubled why Dovid Hamelech says יִמְלֹךְ יְהוָֹה]. The Midrash answers, "Look at the continuation of the posuk [it speaks of punishment]. 'When Pharaoh's horses came with his chariots.' [And we have a rule that we distance the name Hashem from punishment]."

(Tiferet Yehonatan)

וַתִּקַּח מִרְיָם הַנְּבִיאָה אֲחוֹת אַהֲרֹן אֶת הַתֹּף בְּיָדָהּ וַתֵּצֶאןָ כָל הַנָּשִׁים אַחֲרֶיהָ בְּתֻפִּים וּבִמְחֹלֹת

"Miriam, the prophetess, Aaron's sister, took a timbrel in her hand, and all the women came out after her with timbrels and with dances" (Shemos 15:20).

After the miracle of the splitting of the Yam Suf, Miriam led the women in joyous song. The women accompanied their singing with timbrels. Why didn't the men also play musical instruments when they sang "Oz Yoshir"?

A prerequisite for a person to achieve Ruach Hakodesh was to be b'simcha. By playing musical instruments, this would help a person attain simcha.

The Jewish men at the time were on a very exalted level, and they were able to have divine inspiration even without the accompaniment of musical instruments.

However, the women were not on such a high level, and they needed the musical instruments to enhance their simcha.

(Tiferet Yehonatan)

🔥

The Talmud (Berochos 24a) writes that, when a woman sings, it is considered an act of immodesty. Using musical instruments drowned out the voices of Miriam and the other women.

Why did they specifically use timbrels?

The timbrel reminded Hashem of the sins of the Egyptians.

The posuk says, *"And toward morning the sea returned to its strength"* (Shemos 14:27). This was at midday when the sun is the hottest. The Egyptians served the sun. Even though the sun was at its hottest, it could not save the Egyptians.

Furthermore, the Ibn Ezra writes that each of the ten musical instruments mentioned in Tehillim correspond to one of ten constellations. And the timbrel corresponds to the sun. They, therefore, took the timbrel to demonstrate that the sun could not help them.

(Tiferet Yehonatan)

וַתַּעַן לָהֶם מִרְיָם שִׁירוּ לַיהוָה

"And Miriam called out to them, Sing to Hashem" (15:21).

There is a distinct contrast between the manner in which the men sang to Hashem and the way the woman did. With regard to Moshe, the posuk says, *"I will sing"* in the singular, meaning only Moshe sang. While by the women, it says, *"to them,"* meaning that all the women sang.

When King Chizkiyahu was saved from Sancheriv, he did not sing a song of praise to Hashem, as he was not saved in his own merit. As the posuk says, "I will protect this city to save it for My sake and for the sake of My servant Dovid" (Malochim II 19:34).

While the Yidden were in Egypt, they were lacking faith, as the Talmud (Sotah 12a) writes, "We are laboring for nothing by bringing children into the world to be killed. Therefore, he [Amram] arose and divorced his wife. All others who saw this followed his example and arose and divorced their wives."

Miriam convinced her father that he had erred, as the Talmud writes, "His daughter, Miriam, said to him: 'Father, your decree is harsher for the Jewish people than that of Pharaoh.'"

Amram accepted his daughter's words and arose and remarried, his wife, and all others who saw this followed his example and arose and brought back their wives.

The women never were in doubt of Hashem's promise to redeem them from captivity. As the Talmud writes, "It was in the merit of the righteous women we were redeemed from Egypt." As such, the miracle of the Exodus occurred in the merit of the women; therefore, all the women were entitled to sing a song of praise to Hashem.

However, lacking Emunah, the men did not have the right to sing to Hashem; hence, it was Moshe who sang the song of thanksgiving.

(Tiferet Yehonatan)

כִּי גָאֹה גָּאָה סוּס וְרֹכְבוֹ רָמָה בַיָּם

"For very exalted is He; a horse and its rider He cast into the sea"
(Shemos 15:21).

When Miriam and the women sang a song of praise to Hashem, they paid tribute to Hashem for drowning the Egyptians; however, they did not thank Hashem for saving their lives as the men did. Why was this so?

The Talmud writes that the Jewish people were redeemed from Egypt in the merit of the righteous women. As such, the men needed to thank Hashem for their miraculous redemption because they were not worthy of being saved.

The women, on the other hand, were deserving of redemption. It was the drowning of the Egyptians that was the true miracle. Therefore, the women only praised Hashem for the demise of the enemy.

(Yaaros Dvash 2,15)

🔥

The Talmud (Avoda Zarah 22b) writes, "The animal of a Jew is more appealing to gentiles than their own wives." If this is correct, then undoubtedly, they would find the Jewish women more appealing. As such, the Egyptians would not have harmed the Jewish women. Hence, the women had no need to thank Hashem for saving their lives; their lives were not at risk.

(Tiferet Yehonatan)

GLOSSARY

Aaron: Brother of Moses

Abigail: King David's third wife

Adar: Eleventh month in the Jewish Calendar

Akeida: Binding of Isaac

Akiva, Reb: He taught and led the Jewish people during the tumultuous years of the destruction of the Second Holy Temple and was ultimately executed by the Romans for the "crime" of teaching Torah.

Amalek: Leader of the Amalakites

Amalekites: Nation that attacked the Jewish people when they left Egypt

Amrom: Father of Moses

Anshei Knesset Hagedolah: Men of the Great Assembly. Founded by Ezra in approximately 520 B.C.E., this institution of Torah Sages led the Jewish People at the beginning of the Second Temple Era

Antiochus: King of Syria from 175–164 BCE

Avimelech: King during the life of Abraham who had taken Sarah captive

Avinu: Our father

Avoda Zarah: Idol worship

Avos: Forefathers

Avrohom Avinu: Avrohom our father

Avrohom: First of our forefathers

B'simcha: With joy

Baal Haturim: Rabbi Jacob Ben Asher (The Tur) 1269–1340; a legal scholar and biblical commentator

Bamidbar: Numbers, second book of the Bible

Bava Basra: Literal translation "last gate"; one of the sixty-three tractates of the Talmud that comprise the oral tradition

Bava ben Buta, Rabbi: A Jewish sage who lived at the time of Herod

Bava Kama: Literal translation "first gate"; one of the sixty-three tractates of the Talmud that comprise the oral tradition

Bava Metziah: Literal translation "middle gate"; one of the sixty-three tractates of the Talmud that comprise the oral tradition

Bavel, Tower of: Tower built in Babylonia after the flood; recording in the Book of Genesis chapter 11

Behag, the: Hebrew acronym for "Ba'al Halachot Gedolot" (author of the Great Laws); Its authorship and date of composition are subject to debate, but the predominant opinion is that Simeon Kayyara authored the book in the early eighth century in Babylon. Others date the work as late as the tenth century.

Beis Din: Jewish court of law

Beis Hamidrash: House of study

Beis Hamikdosh: The Temple. There were two Temples—the first built by King Solomon stood from 833–423 BCE, and the second built by Ezra and Nehemiya stood from 349 BCE–19 CE.

Ben Noach: Literal translation "sons of Noah"; a reference to all of mankind

Ben Zoma: Rabbi of the first and second century CE

Bereishis: Genesis, first book of the Bible

Bnei Brak: Town in Israel

Bnei Yisroel: Jewish People

Brayso: Elaboration of the Mishna

Bris Bein Habsorim: Literal translation "Covenant of the Parts"; covenant established between God and Avraham

Bris Milah: Circumcision of an eight-day old boy

Brocho Meshuleshes: Threefold blessing

Brochos: Literal translation "blessing"; the first of the sixty-three tractates of the Talmud that comprise the oral tradition

Bubba: Grandmother

Chachomim: Sages

Chagigah: One of the sixty-three tractates of the Talmud that comprise the oral tradition

Challah: Two loaves of bread eaten at the shabbat meal

Chametz: Foods with leavening agents

Chava: Eve

Chizkiyahu: King Hezekiah of Judea, reigned from 562–533 BCE

Chochom: Wise person

Chosid: Disciple of a Rebbe

Chulin: Profane foods

Colel Chabad: The oldest continuously operating charity in Israel, founded in 1788 by the first Chabad-Lubavitch Rebbe, R' Schneur Zalman of Liadi

Dayeinu: Literal translation "it would have sufficed"; a section of the Haggadah

Devorim: Deuteronomy, fifth book of the Bible

Dovid Hamelech: King David, second King of Israel from 1010–970 BCE

Ehyeh asher Ehyeh: "I Am that I Am"

Eicha: Lamentation

Einklech: Grandchildren

Eiruvin: A name of one of the sixty-three tractates of the Talmud that comprise the oral tradition

Elazar ben Azaria, Rabbi Circa 70 CE-circa 135 CE) A Mishnaic sage (circa 70–135 CE); at age eighteen, he was appointed as head of the academy in Yavneh, replacing Rabban Gamaliel II as Prince.

Elazar ben Azaria: First-century rabbi mentioned in the Mishna

Eliezer, Reb: First-century rabbi mentioned in the Mishna

Elisha, the Prophet: Student of Elijah the Prophet

Eliyahu HaNovi: Elijah the Prophet

Emunah: Faith

Enosh: Son of Sheis

Eretz Yisroel: Land of Israel

Erev: Eve

Esov: Esau, son of Isaac

Esther: a young Jewish woman who lived in the Persian diaspora and found favor with the king, became queen, and risked her life to save the Jewish people from destruction, as recorded in the Book of Esther

Ever: founded a Yeshiva together with his great grandfather where Jacob studied

Frierdiker Rebbe: Literal translation, "the previous rebbe"; Reb Yoseph Yitzchok Schneersohn (1880–1950), the sixth Chabad Rebbe

Gehenom: Hell

Gemara: Talmud

Gezeras hakosuv: a method of interpreting the Torah through comparison

Golus: Exile

Goshen: Area in Egypt where the Jews lived

Hadassah: Another name of Queen Esther

Halocho: Jewish law

Haman: An official who sought to annihilate the Jews in the story of Purim

Har Sinai: Mount Sinai

Hashem: Literal translation "the Name," referencing God

Hevel: Abel, son of Adam

Hillel: Rabbi of the Mishnaic era who lived during the end of the first century BCE and the beginning of the first century CE.

Huna, Rav: Rabbi of the Talmudic era

Hurdos: Herod (circa 72–4 BCE), a Roman Jewish client king of the Herodian kingdom of Judea

Ibn Ezra: Avrohom ben Meir (1089–1167), a biblical commentator

K'zayis (pl. K'zaysim): Literal translation "like an olive"; a measurement of volume

Kabbalah: Jewish mysticism

Kabolas Hatorah: Receiving of the Torah on Mount Sinai

Kares: Premature death

Kesubos: One of the sixty-three tractates of the Talmud that comprise the oral tradition

Kevaterin: The couple who brings the baby boy to his bris

Kiddush: Prayer said on wine to usher in the Sabbath

Kiddushin: One of the sixty-three tractates of the Talmud that comprise the oral tradition

Klipa: Literal translation "peel"; impurity

Kodshim: Sacred foods

Kohen: Priest

Korban Chagigah: Sacrifice brought on a festival

Korban Omer: Sacrifice of barley brought on the second day of Pesach

Korban Pesach: Sacrifice of a lamb brought on the eve of Pesach

Korban: Sacrifice

Korbonos: Sacrifices

Krias Yam Suf: Splitting of the Reed Sea

Kuzari: famous work written by Reb Yehuda Halevi (circa 1075–1141)

Lashon Hakodesh: Literal translation "holy tongue"; the Hebrew language

Lashon Hara: Literal translation "evil tongue"; speaking ill of another person

Lavan: Father-in-law of Jacob

Leil Shimurim: Literal translation "the night that is guarded," referring to the night of Passover

Levi: Third son of Jacob

Leviim: Levites

Lomdus: Analytical analysis of the Talmud

Lot: Nephew of Abraham

Luchos: Two tablets

Madim: Red

Maharsho: Rabbi Shmuel Eidels (1555–1631), wrote commentary on the Talmud

Mamzer: Child born from a prohibited relationship

Manna: Food that fell from heaven during the forty years the Jews wandered in the desert

Maror: Bitter herbs

Matzah ashira: Matzah made with juice

Matzah: Unleavened bread eaten on Passover

Mazal: Flow of spiritual energy

Meforshim: Commentators

Megillah: One of the sixty-three tractates of the Talmud that comprise the oral tradition

Megllat Esther: The Book of Esther, one of the five megillot (scrolls), part of the section of the Hebrew Bible called Writings

Melochim: Angels

Menos Halevi: A commentary on the Book of Esther, written by the kabbalist Rabbi Shlomo HaLevi Alkabetz

Midrabbonon: Rabbinic law

Midrash: A section of the oral

tradition, Mode of interpretation of the written tradition

Min Hatorah: From the Torah

Miriam: Sister of Moses

Mishkan: Tabernacle

Mishlei: Proverbs

Mishna: The first major written collection of the Oral Torah; the Mishnah was redacted by Rabbi Yehuda the Prince at the beginning of the third century CE.

Mispar katan: Literal translation "small number"; the number's value is after the zero has been removed—for example, the value of 10 is 1.

Mitzvah (pl. Mitzvos): Commandment

Moed Koton: One of the sixty-three tractates of the Talmud that comprise the oral tradition

Mordechai: Leader of the Jews in the Purim story

Moreh Nevuchim: Guide to the perplexed written by Maimonides

Moshe: Moses, redeemer of the Jewish people from Egypt

Moshiach ben Dovid: Messiah the son of Dovid

Moshiach ben Yoseph: Messiah the son of Yoseph

Moshiach: Messiah

Nadav: Lived during the period of the exodus from Egypt

Nebuchadnetzer: Babylonian king who destroyed Jerusalem in 526 BCE

Nechemiah: Rebuilt the Second Temple in Jerusalem together with Ezra

Neshomo: The soul

Niddah: A women during her menstrual period and a period after

Nimrod: A mighty warrior in the times of Abraham

Nissan: First month of the Jewish calendar

Novi: Prophet

Olam ha'emet: Literal translation "world of truth"; the afterlife

Oz Yoshir: The song the Jewish people sang after crossing the Reed Sea

Parshat: Torah portion

Pesach seder: Literal translation "the order of Pesach"

Pesach: Passover

Pesocim: One of the sixty-three tractates of the Talmud that comprise the oral tradition

Philishtim: Philistine

Pirkei Avos: Ethics of the Fathers, a section of the oral tradition, which presents a series of ethical principles articulated by the rabbis whose legal opinions appear elsewhere in the Mishnah

Posuk (pl. Posukim): Verse

Potiphar: an Egyptian in whose house Joseph worked

Rabbeinu: Our teacher

Rahab: a non-Jew who lived in Jericho when Joshua conquered the Land of Israel

Rambam: Rabbi Moshe ben Maimon (1138–1204), a Talmudist, Halachist, physician, philosopher, and communal leader

Ramban: Rabbi Moshe Ben Naimon (1195–1270), wrote many scholarly works that are studied today

Rashab, Rebbe: Rabbi Sholom Dov Ber Schneerson, the fifth Lubavitcher Rebbe

Rashi: Rabbi Shlomo Yitzchaki (1040–1105), a French rabbi who authored commentary on Tanach and the Talmud

Rebbeshe Einikel: Descendant of a Chasidic master

Reuven: Reuben, eldest son of Jacob

Rosh Chodesh: First day of the month

Rosh Hashanah: Jewish New Year

Rosho: Wicked person

Ruach Hakodesh: Holy spirit

Sancheriv: King of Assyria (circa 548 BCE) who conquered all the areas surrounding Judea who then threatened to conquer Judea and asked for its surrender while blaspheming God.

Sanhedrin: One of the sixty-three tractates of the Talmud that comprise the oral tradition; also Jewish judicial court

Sarah: First of our matriarchs

Shabbos: Literal translation "rest"; the seventh day of the week, Saturday. A day of spirituality and holiness. Also one of the sixty-three tractates of the Talmud that comprise the oral tradition

Shaddchan: Matchmaker

Shavuos: Feast of weeks, one of the biblically ordained Three Pilgrimage Festivals, marking the day God gave the Torah to the Jewish people

Shechinah: Literal translation "dwelling," referring to the presence of God in the world

Shechted: Ritually slaughtered meat

Shem: Son of Noah

Shema: Text from the Torah that is recited twice a day during the morning and evening service. One of the most important prayers, it incorporates the themes of the Oneness of God and love of God.

Shemos: Exodus

Shevat: Tenth month of the Jewish calendar

Shidduch: Matchmaking

Shimon, Reb: Reb Shimon bar Yochai, a rabbi of the Mishnaic era and author of the Zohar

Shimon: Jacob's second son

Shir Hashirim: Song of Songs written by King Solomon

Shira: Song

Shlomo Hamelech: King Solomon, third King of Israel (970–931 BCE)

Shmonei Esreh: Literal translation "18 Benedictions"; a prayer recited three times a day

Shoah: Holocaust

Shushan: Capital of Persia in the times of Mordechai

Sifri: Midrash on Numbers and Deutoronony

Sivan: Third month of the Jewish calendar

Sotah: One of the sixty-three tractates of the Talmud that comprise the oral tradition

Taamuz: Fourth month in the Jewish calendar

Talmidei Chachomim: Torah scholars

Talmud: Literal translation "study"; the work that comments and expands upon the Mishnah (oral tradition); central text of Rabbinic Judaism

Talmud Bavli: Central text of Rabbinic Judaism compiled in Babylonia

Talmud Yerushalmi: Central text of Rabbinic Judaism compiled in Israel

Tarfon, Rabbi: A rabbi who lived at the time of the destruction of the second Temple

Tashbetz: Simeon ben Zemah Duran, also Tzemach Duran (1361–1444), a medieval scholar

Tefillin: Phylacteries, worn by males over the age of thirteen during the morning service. Comprised of two small black boxes with leather straps. One box is worn above the forehead and the other on the bicep opposite the heart. Each box contains four different sections of the Torah.

Tehillim: Psalms

Teshuvah: Repentance

Tevel: Produce prior to the removal of tithe

Tisha B'Av: Ninth day of the month of Av, marking the day of the destruction of the first and second Temples

Tishrei: Seventh month in the Jewish calendar

Tomei: Impurity

Torah: Compilation of the first five books of the Hebrew Bible, namely the books of Genesis, Exodus, Leviticus, Numbers, and Deuteronomy

Tosfos: Commentary on the Talmud

Tzaddik: Righteous individual

Tzoraas: Skin affliction due to a person's spiritual decline

Yaakov: Jacob, third of our forefathers

Yalkut: Midrash

Yam Suf: Reed Sea

Yannai, King: a Hasmonean king who ascended the throne at age twenty-three and ruled from 103–76 BCE

Yechezkel: Prophet, Ezekiel is the seventh book of the Prophets, speaking from Babylonian exile during the first Temple's destruction

Yehoshua ben Levi, Rabbi: First generation of Amoraim (rabbis of the Talmudic era)

Yehudah HaNasi, Rebbi: Rabbi Judah the Prince, a second-century rabbi and chief redactor and editor of the Mishnah

Yehudah: Judah, fourth son of Yaacov. The kings of Israel descended from the tribe of Yehudah.

Yemach Shemom v'zichrom: "May their name and memory be erased"

Yericho: Jericho

Yermiyahu: Jeremiah the Prophet, witnessed the destruction of Jerusalem and the holy Temple

Yerovom: Jeroboam king of the ten tribes of Israel, reigned from 797–776 BCE

Yerushalayim: Jerusalem

Yeshayahu: Isaiah the Prophet

Yetzer Hara: Evil inclination

Yetzer Tov: Good inclination

Yevomos: One of the sixty-three tractates of the Talmud that comprise the oral tradition

Yid (pl. Yidden): Jew

Yishmoel, Reb: Rabbi Ishmael ben Elisha; he lived some fifty years after the destruction of the second Temple at the time of Rabbi Akiva. Along with Rabbi Akiva, he was one of the Ten Martyrs who were cruelly put to death by the Roman governor.

Yishmoel: Ishmael, son of Isaac

Yisroel: Israel

Yitzchok: Isaac, second of our forefathers

Yocheved: Mother of Moses

Yom Kippur: Day of Atonement

Yom Tov: Festival

Yoma: One of the sixty-three tractates of the Talmud that comprise the oral tradition

Yoreach: Moon

Yoseph: Joseph, son of Jacob

Yosi Hagelili, Rabbi: A third-generation rabbi of the Mishnaic era and one of the Sages of Yavneh

Yud: Tenth letter of the Hebrew alphabet

Zaida: Grandfather

Zecharya: Zechariah ben Iddo (circa fourth century BCE), a contemporary of Haggai and Malachi, the last prophets, prophesied during the construction of the second Temple

Zevachim: One of the sixty-three tractates of the Talmud that comprise the oral tradition

Zichoron: In memory of

Zoche: Merit

Zohar: A foundational work in the literature of Jewish mystical thought known as Kabbalah, written by Rabbi Shimon bar Yochai in approximately the second century

Acknowledgments

This is the fourth book I have written based on the teachings of Rabbi Yehonatan Eybeshitz. The fifth book in the series, *Generations of Wisdom* is now being edited.

The blessing I give to all writers is may you be blessed in having such gracious and passionate partners as Richie and Julie Gerber. They have been the driving force behind the Rabbi Yehonatan Eybeshitz Wisdom series. Richie and Julie, may the Almighty bless you and your loved ones with long life and good health and may all your dreams become a reality. I feel extremely fortunate to be part of the journey of bringing your dream into a reality.

As mentioned in the previous books in the series, Julie is a direct descendant of Rabbi Yehonatan Eybeshitz. Julie and Richie's dream is to bring the wisdom of Reb Yehonatan to the English-speaking audience. They can pride themselves that the books have been purchased in such far-flung places as Germany, Japan, Israel, Canada, France, and others. What began as a one-book project has blossomed into a five-book series. The Gerbers are constantly looking for more projects that will enhance the Wisdom series, and even before one work has been completed, they are already throwing out ideas for the next book. Knowing them, I have no doubt this series will continue to grow beyond these five books.

My relationship with the Gerbers is a shidduch. A shidduch very often will have a shadchan. This shidduch is no different; our shadchan was my dear son-in-law Rabbi Ephraim Duchman. He is an integral part of the team at Colel Chabad. I am in awe of the work Colel Chabad does, especially during these very trying times for our brothers and sisters in Israel. The Gerbers are to be commended that part of the sale of all the books in this series goes to support Colel Chabad and its life-saving work in Israel. (Thank you, Ephraim.)

As the saying goes, when you are on a good thing, stick to it. From day one, Carol Killman Rosenberg understood and appreciated what we are trying to accomplish. Reb Yehonatan's ideas are, at times, esoteric of a Kabbalistic nature or deep Talmudic and halachic writings that even a seasoned Torah scholar would find challenging. However, this did not phase her in the slightest. Carol, thank you for your guidance; your editorial skills have greatly enhanced the book.

There is another saying, "Never judge a book by its cover." Anyone in the publishing industry knows how far from the truth this statement is. Therefore, a debt of gratitude to Gary Rosenberg, who has created covers that are both strikingly appealing and capture the essence of each of the books. How the text is presented is equally important, and Gary once again has surpassed all expectations. To The Book Couple, my greatest compliment is that you are the go-to team for all the books in the Wisdom series.

I would like to dedicate this book to my wonderful children and grandchildren. They all continue to be a great source of nachas for myself and their late mother, Rivkie in olam ha'emet. The greatest nachas Rivkie a"h and I have is seeing how they have established their own homes and the way they are raising their children in the manner they saw in their home and the homes of their grandparents. My blessing to them is one that my late father, Reb Meir A"H, would always say after hearing of the birth of another grandchild or great grandchild, *kein yirbu*. May our family continue to grow and be blessed with good health, nachas, and joy.

I would also like to dedicate this Haggadah in memory of my beloved family members who have passed away. While they are no longer present in this physical world, their memory and their shining example live on in their children, grandchildren, and great grandchildren.

My late wife, Rivkie, passed away on the 19th of Adar 2 5774 (2014). Rivkie was a respected Rebbetzin and a devoted teacher. Her warmth and friendliness, humor and vibrancy, authenticity and compassion touched the lives of all who crossed her path.

Pesach was Rivkie's Yom Tov. She ensured that our Sedorim were truly magical. We had people join us from all walks of life, young and old. The special Pesach food she prepared was something our family looked forward to. Being the true Rebbetzin, Rivkie would share Divrei Torah, stories, and anecdotes that inspired everyone. The Seder would not conclude until we had sung the songs she had sung growing up in the home of her parents.

My late father, Reb Meir Barber, passed away on the 18th of Elul 5779 (2019). He was one of the pillars of the Sydney *frum* community. My father was a Holocaust survivor; he spent most of the war years with his family in Siberia. He was a child when the war broke out, never really having the opportunity to study in a yeshivah. However, after the war, he ended up in Bergen-Belsen. He attended a yeshivah that had been established in what was once an infamous concentration camp. Prior to coming to Australia, his family received a brocho from a great tzaddik Reb Itzikel of Pshevorsk, who eventually reestablished his chassidus in Antwerp. He said that the family would have *dor yeshurum um'vorach* (blessed offspring) who would continue in the righteous path of our tradition. This brocho was given over seventy years ago, and the brocho is clearly evident now in its fourth generation. May this blessing remain with his descendants for generations to come.

My father eventually made his way to Sydney, Australia, and in his small suitcase, he brought with him one of our family's great treasures. He brought his Gemorah. On the first page, it says his name and the name of the yeshivah, *Sheirit Hapleito* (The Survivng Remnant) Bergen-Belsen. Once a concentration camp, it had then become the home of Jewish learning and Jewish revival. Perhaps this encapsulates the secret of Jewish survival. The recognition of the inseparable bond between the Torah and the Jewish people. It speaks of the strength of the Jewish people that, even in our darkest hours, we continue to learn and teach Hashem's Torah. That Gemorah continues to inspire his children, grandchildren, and great grandchildren.

Only a few short months ago, our family was given a treasure, one that we never knew existed. Buried in a box in someone's basement for over seventy years was another sefer my father must have brought with him on his journey to a country of refuge. Besides the obvious joy of discovering a sefer that my father had studied from way back in 1946, it was the name of the sefer that caused such joy and introspection. It was the *Shagaas Aryeh*.[1] The sefer is extremely challenging and is Torah study at a very high level. To imagine after living through *gehenom* (hell) in this world, my father enters a yeshivah that is studying Torah at the highest level. As a side note, the Shagaas Aryeh succeeded Reb Yehonatan as rabbi in Metz.

My late father-in-law, Rabbi Asher Halevi Heber, passed away on the 8th of Nisan 5780 (2020); he merited that the Lubavitcher Rebbe and Rebbetzin were the *kevaterin* at his bris in prewar Paris. For over forty years, he was a beloved teacher in Manhattan Jewish Day School. It was astounding to hear and read the accolades his students shared with the family on the occasion

---

1. Reb Arye Leib (1695–1785), famed Talmudic scholar

of his untimely passing. Many had been in his class more than thirty years before, and they were still able to recall so much of what he had taught them and how he had inspired them to lead Torah-observant lives coupled with a great thirst for the study of Torah.

He taught fourth grade; many of his former students (now parents themselves) shared with us that every Pesach they take out their Pesach booklets from Rabbi Heber's class and share the ideas and drawings with their own children.

My beloved uncle Reb Shabsi passed away on the 2nd of Adar 5772 (2012). He came from an illustrious family of Radomsk Chasidim. He was an everlasting link of the Chasidic world of prewar Poland and the Jewish world I grew up in in Australia. His stories of Chasidic life in Sosnowiec and his heroic self-sacrifice for Torah and mitzvos during the Holocaust inspire me to this very day.

My uncle would share the following every year at the Seder: He spent close to five years in the camps, and throughout those five years, he never ate bread on Pesach. I don't believe our minds can grasp what it means for a teenager to have such unwavering strength of spirit. He did share that when he was forced on the death march to Buchenwald, where he was *bafreit*, liberated, he had no choice but to eat bread. As a zichoron for one of the kedoshim, he would share that there was a *Rebbeshe einikel*, Reb Avrohom, who would not eat bread and everyone would support and help him, knowing full well if a Yid fell to the ground, he would be killed. May my uncle's story inspire the reader, as it has inspired me.

My beloved aunt Rebbeca Kornwasser, wife to my uncle Reb Shabsi, passed away on the 21st of Shat 5779 (2019). Auntie Becca, as she was affectionately called, was beloved by everyone. She was imbued with great *simchat hachayim* (love of life), which she shared with all who knew her. One could say she lived to give. She had a heart of gold and only saw the good in people.

To my dear mother, Esther Barber, and my dear *shviger*, Nechama Heber. May you both find a level of solace in seeing the beautiful generations you are both the proud matriarchs of. May Hashem bless you both with many years of good health and be *zoche* to greet *Moshiach Tzidkeiynu b'karov mamosh*.

Rabbi Yacov Barber

19 Kislev 5785 – December 2024

Publisher's Dedication

To our son, Isaac Pablo; our daughter-in-law,
Christine; and our incredible grandson, Toby Simon.
May they continue to grow and prosper.

And to Julie's mother, Ana Ejbszyc, and her father, Isaac Meler.

We also remember Julie's maternal grandparents José and
Josefina Ejbszyc, the patriarch and matriarch of the family,
as well as the other Ejbszyc siblings—Dr. Enrique Eiber,
Bertha Fuchs, and Julio Ejbszyc. And also Julie's paternal
grandparents, Leon and Rosa Meler, and Aunt Bertha Rivas.

May their memories be for a blessing.

We also remember those in Richie's family who have passed:
Sam and Pearl Gerber, Richie's father and mother; Aunt Molly
and Uncle Aron Furman; Uncle Hymie and Aunt Tillie; Uncle
Max and Aunt Ruth; Uncle Dave and Aunt Lila; and Uncle Dave
and Aunt Henrietta; Richie's brother Edwin and Cousin Shirley.

May Hashem bless them all.

In loving memory of James Oppenheimer

Publisher's Acknowledgments

Overseeing the translation of Rabbi Yehonatan Eybeshitz's prolific writings from Hebrew into English has become our life's mission. As Julie is a direct descent of the great tzaddik, we have a mutual passion to share her ancestor's extraordinarily profound thoughts, and we acknowledge the efforts of those who have helped make this undertaking a reality.

We therefore express our deepest gratitude to Rabbi Yacov Barber for making the books in the Wisdom of Rabbi Yehonatan Eybeshitz Series possible. Without him, this series would still be a dream. He unites his singular skills as a rabbi, scholar, and writer to create these thought-provoking, insightful books. In *The Haggadah of Wisdom*, he expertly weaves Rabbi Yehonatan's deep commentary into the traditional Haggadah text, offering a renewed look at the Passover Seder.

We connected with Rabbi Barber through his incredible son-in-law, Rabbi Efraim Duchman, Director of Colel Chabad, which is dedicated to helping those in need in Israel. Many years back, because of our long relationship with Rabbi Efraim, we asked him if he knew someone who could translate some of Rabbi Yehonatan's works. He told us he might have the guy. And, indeed, he did have the perfect person for the job: his father-in-law, Rabbi Yacov Barber.

This book, as well as the previous three in the Wisdom of Rabbi Yehonatan Eybeshitz, has relied on the talents of the amazing Book Couple. Carol Killman Rosenberg displays her superb editing prowess with each project, while Gary Rosenberg creates marvelous covers along with masterful interior book designs.

Appreciations to Sinai Publishers, Tel Aviv, for once again granting us permission to use the image of Rabbi Yehonatan Eybeshitz on the front cover of this book.

Many thanks to our friend, Maine humorist, artist, musician, and television personality Tim Sample for creating the logo for Gerber's Miracle Publishers, which adorns all the books in The Wisdom of Rabbi Yehonatan Eybeshitz Series.

About Rabbi Barber

RABBI YACOV BARBER was born to Holocaust survivors. He is the father of six children and a proud grandfather. He has lived and studied in Israel, Canada, and Melbourne. He is currently living in New York. Having received both Rabbinic Ordination and Judiciary Ordination, he has also completed courses in palliative care, mediation, family violence, and arbitration.

Rabbi Barber is an internationally acclaimed motivational speaker and a much sought-after communicator on ethics as well as spiritual and personal growth. He has lectured across the United States, Europe, Australia, and Canada.

He is the author of *Generation to Generation: Insights into the Haggadah*; *Wit & Wisdom: Sermons on the Weekly Torah Reading*; *Pearls of Wisdom,* a translation of insights of Reb Yehonatan Eybeshitz on the weekly portion and the festivals; *Sparks of Wisdom,* Reb Yehonatan Eybeshitz insights on a wide range of topics including modern-day applications; and *Gates of Wisdom,* stories that display Eybeshitz's brilliant mind from a very young age, including how he created "Am Yisrael Chai."

For more information, visit RabbiBarber.com.